*Mother*

## GREEK TRAGEDY

*Happy Birthday
Barbara
xxx*

FRONTISPIECE. Tragedy, personified as a maenad, with a thyrsus and leveret; detail of an Athenian red-figure vase now in Compiègne, c. 440–430 BCE.

# GREEK TRAGEDY

*Suffering under the Sun*

EDITH HALL

UNIVERSITY PRESS

# OXFORD
## UNIVERSITY PRESS

Great Clarendon Street, Oxford OX2 6DP

Oxford University Press is a department of the University of Oxford.
It furthers the University's objective of excellence in research, scholarship,
and education by publishing worldwide in

Oxford New York

Auckland Cape Town Dar es Salaam Hong Kong Karachi Kuala Lumpur
Madrid Melbourne Mexico City Nairobi New Delhi Shanghai Taipei Toronto

With offices in

Argentina Austria Brazil Chile Czech Republic France Greece
Guatemala Hungary Italy Japan South Korea Poland Portugal
Singapore Switzerland Thailand Turkey Ukraine Vietnam

Oxford is a registered trade mark of Oxford University Press
in the UK and in certain other countries

Published in the United States
by Oxford University Press Inc., New York

© Edith Hall 2010

The moral rights of the author have been asserted
Database right Oxford University Press (maker)

First published 2010

All rights reserved. No part of this publication may be reproduced,
stored in a retrieval system, or transmitted, in any form or by any means,
without the prior permission in writing of Oxford University Press,
or as expressly permitted by law, or under terms agreed with the appropriate
reprographics rights organization. Enquiries concerning reproduction
outside the scope of the above should be sent to the Rights Department,
Oxford University Press, at the address above

You must not circulate this book in any other binding or cover
and you must impose this same condition on any acquirer

British Library Cataloguing in Publication Data
Data available

Library of Congress Control Number: 2009935896

Typeset by SPI Publisher Services, Pondicherry, India
Printed in Great Britain
on acid-free paper by the
MPG Books Group, Bodmin and King's Lynn

ISBN 978–0–19–923251–2

5 7 9 10 8 6

*Then I saw again all the oppressed who are suffering under the sun, and beheld the tears of the oppressed, and they had no comforter, and with their oppressors there was violence, and they had no comforter; and I esteemed the dead happy who have died long ago, more than the living who are still alive; and happier than both, him who hath not been born.*
*(Ecclesiastes* 4: 1–2)

# CONTENTS

*Acknowledgements* ix
*List of Illustrations* x
*Note on Abbreviations and Translations* xiv

Introduction: What is Greek Tragedy? 1

1  Play Makers 12
2  Community Identities 59
3  Confrontations 104
4  Minds 156
5  Aeschylean Drama 198
6  Euripidean Drama 231
7  Sophoclean Drama 299
8  Greek Tragedy and Tragic Fragments Today 328

*Notes* 347
*Further Reading* 359
*Index* 398

# ACKNOWLEDGEMENTS

So many people have helped me enjoy Greek tragedy over the last forty years that it is almost churlish to single out individuals. Nevertheless, I cannot fail to record that I have been inspired by the teaching at Nottingham Girls' High School of Sheila Harris and Kathleen Reddish and at Oxford of the late Tom Stinton and Ruth Padel; by the examples of Pat Easterling, Helene Foley, Margot Heinemann, and Froma Zeitlin; by the writings of Lewis Campbell, Allardyce Nicoll, and R. P. Winnington-Ingram; and by the enthusiasm of the hundreds of students and members of the general public I have been lucky enough to harangue. I have enjoyed watching scores of productions, and have been truly overwhelmed by the impact of several, especially Ninagawa's *Medea*, Peter Sellars's *Ajax*, Northern Broadsides' *Oedipus*, Katie Mitchell's *Iphigenia in Aulis*, Tony Harrison's feature film *Prometheus*, and Yael Farber's *Molora*. Theatre writers and directors who have been kind enough to talk to me about their work include Claudia Bosse, Marina Carr, Tony Harrison, Frank McGuinness, Ellen McLaughlin, Blake Morrison, Barrie Rutter, Colin Teevan, Jatinder Verma, and Yana Zarifi. Conversations with Fiona Macintosh (the most astute theatre critic alive) and with my other colleagues at the Archive of Performances of Greek and Roman Drama—Peter Brown, Felix Budelmann, Stephen Harrison, Stephe Harrop, Pantelis Michelakis, Scott Scullion, Rosie Wyles, and especially Oliver Taplin—underlie every page of this book. So do discussions of the continuing impact of ancient politics and philosophy with Ahuvia Kahane and Richard Alston at the Centre for the Reception of Greece and Rome, Royal Holloway. Everyone at OUP has been as kind and efficient as usual, especially Hilary O'Shea, Dorothy McCarthy, Jenny Wagstaffe, Kathleen Fearn, my excellent copy-editor, Tom Chandler, and Sarah Newton who read the proofs. I also thank my family for refusing to see life tragically, especially my remarkable husband Richard Poynder, to whom the book is dedicated.

E.H.

# LIST OF ILLUSTRATIONS

*Frontispiece*: Tragedy, personified as a maenad, with a thyrsus and leveret; detail of an Athenian red-figure vase now in Compiègne, *c*.440–430 BCE.

1.1 Prize-winning actor dedicating his mask; a Herculaneum wall-painting, now in the Naples Archaeological Museum, probably copied from a Greek original of *c*.300 BCE. 18

1.2 Colin Blakeley as Philoctetes at the Old Vic, London (1964). Photo reproduced courtesy of the APGRD. 31

1.3 The blinded Polymestor on an Apulian vase of the later 4th century BCE, reproduced courtesy of the Trustees of the British Museum. 42

1.4 Theatro Technis' *Persians*, directed by Karolos Koun (1965), reproduced courtesy of the APGRD. 44

1.5 Tragedy attends Dionysus' drinking party on an Athenian red-figure vase now in Compiègne, *c*.440–430 BCE. Photo reproduced courtesy of the Musée Antoine Vivenel. 51

1.6 Marble mask of Dionysus, crowned with ivy berries (1st–2nd century CE), reproduced courtesy of the Trustees of the British Museum. 56

2.1 George Romney's illustration of the ghost scene in *Persians* (1778–9). Photo reproduced courtesy of the Walker Art Gallery, Liverpool. 70

2.2 The scholar Jane Ellen Harrison as Alcestis in an Oxford production (1887), reproduced courtesy of the APGRD. 72

2.3 *The Death of Hippolytus* by Lawrence Alma-Tadema (1860). 73

2.4 Sybil Thorndike as Hecuba in *Trojan Women*, *c*.1919, reproduced courtesy of the APGRD. 78

LIST OF ILLUSTRATIONS xi

2.5 Edouard Toudouze, *Farewell of Oedipus to the Corpses of His Wife and Sons* (1871). École Nationale Supérieure des Beaux-Arts, Paris. 84

2.6 Benjamin West, *Aegisthus, Raising the Veil, Discovers the Body of Clytemnestra* (1780), reproduced courtesy of the Trustees of the British Museum. 85

3.1 Phaedra listens with horror to Hippolytus and the Nurse. Victorian book illustration, unknown origin, reproduced courtesy of the APGRD. 125

3.2 Barrie Ingham as Dionysus in *The Bacchae* at the Mermaid Theatre (1964), reproduced courtesy of the APGRD. 127

3.3 The entrance of Clytemnestra in *Electra* at Girton College, Cambridge (1883), reproduced courtesy of the APGRD. 136

3.4 Cadmus and Tiresias in *The Bacchae* at the Mermaid Theatre, London (1964), reproduced courtesy of the APGRD. 138

3.5 Sybil Thorndike as Medea outside Christ Church Library, Oxford, reproduced courtesy of the APGRD. 152

4.1 A transvestite Mercury/Hermes in a Victorian burlesque of *Prometheus Bound* (1865), reproduced courtesy of the APGRD. 157

4.2 Athena arrives to arbitrate in *Eumenides*; drawing of a 4th-century South Italian vase, now in the British Museum. 162

4.3 The libation scene in *Persians* in a performance at Bradfield School, England, reproduced courtesy of the APGRD. 168

4.4 *Philoctetes on the Island of Lemnos*, engraving (1785) by Francesco Rosaspina after a painting by James Barry, reproduced courtesy of the Trustees of the British Museum. 175

4.5 George Romney, *Medea Contemplating the Murder of her Children* (mid-1770s), reproduced courtesy of the Trustees of the British Museum. 190

5.1 Fragmentary 4th-century Lucanian vase in Basel, probably depicting Agamemnon and Clytemnestra, reproduced courtesy of the Herbert Cahn Collection, Basel. 213

5.2 George Romney's illustration of the ghost scene in *Eumenides* (mid-1770s), reproduced courtesy of the Trustees of the British Museum. 221

xii    LIST OF ILLUSTRATIONS

5.3  Io in a Greek production of the *Prometheus Bound* of the 1950s, reproduced courtesy of the APGRD.    228
6.1  Athenian chorusmen dress for a satyr play on an Apulian vase, 400–380 BCE, reproduced courtesy of the Nicholson Museum, Sydney.    238
6.2  The programme for Ted Hughes' *Alcestis* performed by Northern Broadsides (2000), reproduced courtesy of the APGRD.    239
6.3  Eileen Herlie as Medea at the Edinburgh Festival (1948), reproduced courtesy of the APGRD.    243
6.4  Hecuba in Euripides' play on an Apulian vase of the later 4th century BCE, reproduced courtesy of the Trustees of the British Museum.    258
6.5  Margot dan der Burgh as Hecuba in *The Trojan Women*, The Theatre Royal, London (1964), reproduced courtesy of the APGRD.    270
6.6  Benjamin West, *Pylades and Orestes brought as Victims before Iphigenia* (1766), reproduced courtesy of the Trustees of the British Museum.    274
6.7  Drawing of a sarcophagus relief in Rome showing Pentheus being torn apart by maenads, reproduced courtesy of the Trustees of the British Muscum.    292
7.1  The programme for Andrzej Wajda's production of *Antigone* in Krakow (1984), reproduced courtesy of the APGRD.    309
7.2  Zoe Wanamaker as Electra at the Chichester Festival Theatre (1997), reproduced courtesy of the APGRD.    310
7.3  The suicide of Ajax, on an Etrurian red-figure wine-bowl (400–350 BCE), reproduced courtesy of the Trustees of the British Museum.    315
7.4  The blind Oedipus being led through the wilderness by his daughter Antigone. Mezzotint by Johann Gerhard Huck (1802), after a painting by Charles Thévenin, reproduced courtesy of the Trustees of the British Museum.    326
8.1  Frontispiece to a volume commemorating the Cambridge Greek play (1887), reproduced courtesy of the APGRD.    329

8.2 The Queen's Dream, from the programme to the Braunschweig production of *Persians* (2008), reproduced courtesy of the APGRD. 336

8.3 The programme for *Cock o' the North*, inspired by Euripides' fragmentary *Alcmaeon in Corinth* (2004), reproduced courtesy of the APGRD. 342

8.4 Helios driving his chariot, on an Athenian red-figure wine-bowl of the 5th century BCE, reproduced courtesy of the Trustees of the British Museum. 345

# NOTE ON ABBREVIATIONS AND TRANSLATIONS

| | |
|---|---|
| APGRD | Archive of Performances of Greek and Roman Drama |
| Csapo & Slater | Eric Csapo and and W. J. Slater, *The Context of Ancient Drama* (Ann Arbor, Mich., 1994) |
| DK | Hermann Diels and Walther Kranz (1966), *Die Fragmente der Vorsokratiker*. 3 vols. (Dublin and Zurich, 1966) |
| Hall (1989) | Edith Hall, *Inventing the Barbarian* (Oxford, 1989) |
| Hall (2006) | Edith Hall, *The Theatrical Cast of Athens* (Oxford, 2006) |
| PCG | R. Kassel and C. Austin (eds.), *Poetae Comici Graeci* (Berlin, 1983– ). |
| PMG | D. L. Page, *Poetae Melici Graeci* (Oxford, 1962) |
| TrGF | Bruno Snell and Richard Kannicht (eds.), *Tragicorum Graecorum Fragmenta* (Göttingen, 1971–2004) |

Translations from the Greek are my own unless otherwise indicated

# Introduction: What is Greek Tragedy?

> The sun looks upon the suffering of both of us,
> Neither of whom has done anything against the gods
> To deserve your death.
>
> (Admetus to his dying wife in Euripides' *Alcestis*, 246–7)

Two and a half thousand years ago three Athenian Greek men—Aeschylus, Euripides, and Sophocles—between them composed between two and three hundred tragic dramas. But only thirty-three plays, perhaps ten per cent of their total output, survived to be performed in theatres and read today. My book has just one purpose, which is to make the texts of these thirty-three plays more interesting and accessible. The texts, after all, consist merely of rows of printed words—usually all that survives of the dazzling multi-medial open-air shows that enthralled the ancient Greeks for centuries.

It is worth thinking about why their tragedies matter in the first place. Greek tragedy (which in practice always means 'Athenian tragedy') only matters if you believe that tragedy, more widely defined, has itself played a significant role in your own culture. The word 'tragedy' was the word that was given by the ancient Greeks to their more serious theatrical performances, performed in the open air under the unforgiving Mediterranean sun. It was a term that probably once meant 'goat-song', a reminder that tragedy had an ancient and intimate relationship with religion and especially with rituals involving praise of the gods and animal sacrifice to them. But by the fifth century BCE, 'tragedy' meant a specific kind of solemn drama performed in particular public contexts; it has subsequently come to name not only a whole genre but an emotional register and an aesthetic and indeed ethical category. When we see the word 'tragedy' in a news headline, we know that the article will contain an account of terrible suffering. But how do we define what was so distinctive about these ancient Greek plays that they became the foundational examples of a medium that would exert such a lasting cultural influence?

There have been as many definitions of Greek tragedy as there are surviving plays, but most definitions centre on a handful of specific features. With the solitary exception of the earliest tragedy, Aeschylus' *Persians* (472 BCE), which is a 'history play' set only eight years before it was first performed, all the Greek tragedies were set in what even their original audience felt was the distant past. The heroes and heroines they portray—Agamemnon, Antigone, Heracles—were believed by the Athenians of the fifth century BCE really to have existed, but several centuries earlier. Greek tragedy therefore involved a form of communal ghost-raising—bringing famous but long-dead figures back to life. This dimension is brought into focus when a ghost appears within the tragedy itself: Clytemnestra in Aeschylus' *Eumenides*, for example, whose physical corpse the audience has seen only minutes previously, or Polydorus in Euripides' *Hecuba*, who can find no peace because he has received no burial rites. Nietzsche had a point when he identified the uncanny moment when Heracles leads the veiled Alcestis back from the Underworld to her living husband, at the climax of Euripides' *Alcestis*, as the scene that epitomizes every spectator's experience of tragic actors.[1]

Tragedy's focus on death is expressed in other ways than in breathing new life into the stories of the long deceased. Greek tragic audiences repeatedly heard characters who were about to die deliver their last words.[2] In such significant speeches and songs, one of the main poetic images for denoting the boundary dividing life from death is sunlight. When Antigone sings her own funeral lament, she takes one last, lingering look at the 'bright Sun', before leaving the stage to die (879–80). Just before he impales himself on Hector's sword, Ajax says farewell to the Sun forever, asking him to take the news across the Aegean Sea to his parents in distant Salamis, on which he also shone (845–51):

> And you, O Sun, as you drive your chariot across the steep sky,
> When you catch sight of my fatherland,
> Hold tight your golden rein
> And report my ruin and my doom

> To my ageing father and to her who nursed me.
> The poor woman! When she hears this news,
> The whole city will resound with her loud lamentation.

All these tragic heroes or heroines uttered their laments under the sun which beat down upon them and whose light they were about to leave forever; the audiences who watched and listened shared that sunlight with them. The same sun that watched their miseries still shines down on our troubled planet today.

Whether the heroic figures in tragedy die or not during their plays, they live in unusually close communion with the dead. The deceased whose absence troubles the living are almost always close relations: spouses, parents, children, siblings. The living who perform rituals, lament inconsolably, or are harassed by spectres and Erinyes (Furies), are suffering because they are bereaved of their kin, or because they have killed them. This feature distinguishes the ancient Greeks' tragedy fundamentally from their other serious genre, Homeric epic. Kin-killing hardly features in the main frame narratives of the *Iliad* and the *Odyssey*, where people stick by their kin while slaughtering enemies from rival households and kingdoms. But in tragedy the murder of another member of the same household is a recurring plot-type. Clytemnestra kills her husband, Orestes kills his mother, Oedipus kills his father, Medea kills her children, Agave kills her son, Creon sentences his niece Antigone to death.

The first person to analyse systematically the differences between tragedy and other kinds of poetry was a northern Greek called Aristotle. He studied with the Athenian philosopher Plato a few decades after most of the extant tragedies were composed, and while living in Athens no doubt attended theatrical productions as well as reading the plays. Eventually he began to lecture on literature himself, and his *Poetics* contains the gist of what he argued to his students was essential to tragedy. He said that tragedy's effectiveness was partly a result of the emotions aroused 'where the suffering involves people closely connected, for instance where brother kills brother, son father, mother son, or son mother' (ch. 14, 1453b 19–22). Here a key word is added to the fundamental tragic constituents of death and familial ties, and that key word is *suffering*. Tragedy is a representation of a serious event that involves suffering, which made audience members feel pity for the sufferer and fear that the same thing could happen to them. Centuries later, when the concept has divested itself of many of its other, specifically Greek, characteristics, this constituent—suffering—remains central to the definition of all 'tragic' events in the theatre, fiction, or newspapers.[3] The representation of specific instances of suffering is one of the very few things that will always be central to the historically mutable medium of tragic drama. The suffering can take many forms, and the sufferers react to it in diverse ways. But suffer they do, or the play they are in would not be a tragedy.

Many of the other elements that have sometimes been deemed necessary and definitive constituents of the genre (for example, the high social class of the sufferer, or tragedy's ability to *ennoble* suffering) prove not, on consideration of significant twentieth-century examples such as Arthur Miller's *Death of a Salesman* (1949), to be necessary to tragedy at all. It is suffering that unites Sophocles' Oedipus, Shakespeare's Hamlet, and Miller's Willy Loman, who dies after suffering, with precious little dignity, as a way of life: his son Biff says that the result of the career path Willy chose is 'To suffer fifty weeks a year for the sake of a two-week vacation'.[4] That in Loman's life the proportion of suffering to non-suffering is as high as 50:2 is, moreover, in itself suggestive of the *concentration* on suffering implied by tragedy. As Aldous Huxley put it in a brilliant essay that discussed the difference between tragedy and other 'serious' genres, tragedy omits all the everyday parts of life that dilute its effect. Tragedy does not tell the 'whole truth' about life—that even at times when you are terribly bereaved, domestic tasks must be done.[5] Moreover, in order to build up its effect, tragedy takes a certain period of time—what Aristotle called its *mēkos* or extension (*Poetics* ch. 7, 1451a 5): a joke can make someone laugh in a matter of seconds, but it is almost impossible to imagine what might constitute an effective one-minute tragedy.

A tragedy that did not represent suffering in some concentration and with some sustained build-up could not be tragic, by any criterion—ancient Greek, Renaissance, or contemporary. There is always *agony* inherent in it—whether psychological or physical, whether bereavement, boredom, or bodily mutilation. Yet 'the dramatic representation of suffering', although necessary to the definition of tragedy, is in itself insufficient. The process of staging agony as spectacle must in a sense be abusive. We must have a good reason for wanting to watch another human suffering terribly, even in the theatre, if we are not to become sensation-addicted voyeurs. There remains, however, an obvious difference between the way that suffering is represented in tragedy and the way that it was represented in ancient Roman gladiatorial displays (which often were staged quasi-dramatically as combat between mythical heroes) and its manifestation in contemporary hardcore pornographic films. Tragedies, gladiatorial shows, and pornographic movies share dramatic form, enacted narrative, and agony, but neither the sole nor central goal of tragedy is the arousal of excitement or desire.

Many tragic poets have written scenes that play on this difficult borderline between arousing desire and arousing a more contemplative reaction: in Euripides' *Hecuba*, the reported death of the half-naked Trojan princess Polyxena, in front of an internal audience of thousands of Greek soldiers, is a graphic example. It invites the external spectators to take sexualized pleasure in the description of the young woman, who has torn her gown 'from her shoulders to her waist beside the navel, revealing her breasts and her torso, most beautiful, like those of a statue' (558–61). Yet the account simultaneously insists that the spectators raise to consciousness their own suspect reaction; moreover, and most importantly, the pornographic element in this scene is inseparable from the overriding *ethical* question it asks, which is why the Greeks had seen fit to sacrifice the young woman in the first place.

Greek literature elsewhere gives thought to the processes by which shocking or repulsive sights can simultaneously fascinate. In Plato's *Republic* these conflicting impulses illustrate the way that discrete elements in the soul combat one another, and this process is illuminated by the example of an individual named Leontius. On walking past the dead bodies lying near the place of Athenian public execution, he 'felt at the same time a desire to see them and a repugnance and aversion'. In the end he gazed his fill, but felt angry with himself for so doing (4.439e 7–440a 3). It may have been thinking about this issue that led Aristotle to his remarkable insight in the *Poetics* into the aesthetic process by which repulsive sights are alchemically transformed through art into something not only bearable, but actually enjoyable, legitimate and instructive to contemplate. In arguing that the desire to imitate is innate in humans, he introduces the analogy of learning from works of visual art: 'We feel pleasure in looking at the most exact portrayals of things that give us pain to look at in real life, the lowest animals, for instance, or corpses' (ch. 4, 1448b 10–12). This statement articulates the process by which the painful constituents of material reality, even the decay-prone physical remains of the dead, is aestheticized by art. This sentence partly explains why the art galleries of the West are crammed with pictures of individuals undergoing death, combat, assault, rape, and torture. It also suggests how tragedy can be understood. The misery undergone in tragedy is not something we would elect to see another individual suffer in reality, but in the theatre we can 'feel pleasure in looking' at it as well as learn from it.

One working definition of tragedy, therefore, could be that it constitutes the dramatic expression of an *enquiry* into suffering, an aesthetic question mark performed in enacted pain. For tragedy, while representing an instance of suffering in dramatic form, always asks *why* it has occurred. It is not a matter of whether the suffering is of a particular type or quality: neither the Greek audiences nor Shakespearean ones are likely to have drawn much distinction between pitiful and 'tragic' agony. Philoctetes' abscessed foot is as fit for arousing tragic fellow-feeling as Iphigenia's death sentence, Lear's isolation, or Hamlet's alienation. The philosophical interest is in the *causes* of the suffering rather than its neuropathology.

Suffering and enquiry into it are in turn closely linked with the two emotions that Aristotle, in his lectures, associated with the tragic audience. The function of tragedy, he said was to arouse pity and fear (*Poetics* ch. 6, 1449b 27). Spectators feel pity for the sufferer who is being impersonated—Oedipus or Orestes, for example. If the tragedy works properly, they will also feel fear, since they will realize that something similar could perfectly well happen to them; the fear is born of a recognition of the uncontrollability of the forces in human life that have brought the suffering on its victims. The cause of the suffering could be mistaken identity, uncontainable emotion, divine wrath, a family curse, the conventions of ancient warfare, or simple bad luck; but the tragedy will explore the causes of agony and bring home to spectators the extent to which they were or were not avoidable. This means that what is essential to tragedy's function is to elicit a response that is both emotional and intellectual.

This is not to say that Greek tragedy always presents suffering as ineluctable, which some critics of tragedy have argued is the philosophical position that defines tragedy. Far from it. There are plenty of scenes in Greek tragedy where a character is shown actually taking the decision that precipitates the suffering, and even considering alternative courses of action. Orestes, sword in hand, wavers before killing his mother in *Libation-Bearers* (899). Medea changes her mind repeatedly before making the final decision to kill her children. In Terry Eagleton's recent study of tragedy, *Sweet Violence*, he uses *Iphigenia in Aulis* to show how a play can actually tantalize the audience with the possibility that the disaster can be averted, and in possessing this quality groups it with *Othello* and two of Ibsen's late plays: *The Wild Duck* (1884), and *When We Dead Awaken* (1899).[6] The characters in *Iphigenia in Aulis* may be stranded in an ethical vacuum, but this does not mean that they need to *choose* to perform and suffer an inhumane atrocity.

In the face of confusing or non-existent signs from the gods, the humans in Greek tragedy are often bewildered. They are baffled by suffering, and often extremely angry about it. Like many philosophers in more modern times, their ability to believe in the benevolence and even the existence of the gods is stretched to the limit by the presence of suffering in human life. This bafflement was no doubt compounded by the physical inclusion of gods within the original spaces where tragedy was performed, indeed the physical inclusion of gods who seemed to enjoy describing precisely how and why they intended to cause human suffering, often regardless of the victim's guilt or innocence. The dramatic universe was organized vertically: but although a ghost like the dead king Darius could be summoned from the Underworld, and indeed in Aristotle's *Poetics* (ch. 18) we hear of spectacular tragedies that were indeed 'set in Hades', in the surviving plays there were only two *visible* planes of existence within the stage world: the dancing space (*orchēstra*) and the actors' platform where mortal life was represented, and the higher level inhabited by the gods. By the time of Euripides and Sophocles, gods could make appearances aloft in the machine (*mēchanē*), suspended from a crane on the special level reserved for superhuman beings.[7] In ancient vase-paintings inspired by tragic performances, the gods inhabit the upper level of the vase, looking down on the suffering mortals as if from windows in the upper storeys of a building.[8]

There was another group within the theatre, and that was the audience. The faculty of hearing implied in the word *audience* was just as important as the faculty of sight; Oedipus wishes that he could block off the stream of sound by which he apprehends his destroyed world, as well as blinding himself (Sophocles, *Oedipus Tyrannus* 1386–8). But the ancient audience is more accurately termed the ancient 'spectators', since the word *theatre* meant 'a place for viewing'. The spectators who witnessed the enacted enquiry into suffering sat in tiered seats—originally of wood, later of stone—which rose from approximately the level of the stage to a point that was elevated far above it, like the gods in the machine. Tragic audiences shared their humanity—their vulnerability to suffering and their inevitable mortality—with the heroic characters the wrecking of whose lives they were witnessing. But as elevated spectators they had more in common with the 'internal audience' of gods who caused that suffering.

When the Greeks included the gods and the gods' immortal perspective within tragedy's visual fields, the sense of struggling to understand the factors that ultimately determined human lives was incorporated forever in the medium. The tragic spectator knows much more than the characters—is almost as omniscient as the gods—yet has absolutely no power to intervene. Watching a tragedy is like sitting in the seat of a god, but bound in shackles. The spectator is a moral witness but not a moral agent. The tragedians exploited this by writing many scenes in which suffering individuals scream from the stage or from backstage for assistance that the spectator is completely incapable of giving. We can only respond to the terrible scenes that we witness—we can never prevent Medea from murdering her children or Agamemnon from authorizing the sacrifice of Iphigenia. But we can hope to have a better idea *why* these catastrophes happened towards the end of their plays rather than at the beginning.

One small comfort that this extra-terrestrial perspective can bring is a profound sense of the passing of time. As spectators, the original audiences were watching events they believed had occurred

INTRODUCTION: WHAT IS GREEK TRAGEDY? 9

many generations ago, and this knowledge brings with it a certain emotional distancing, a little immunity from the pain. The world moves on, and although this can mean the end of things that are good, there is nothing—either good or evil—in human life that lasts forever. More than two millennia before Shelley composed his 'Ozymandias' (1818) on the theme of time's erasure of all human institutions, Oedipus predicts to Theseus that one day the Greek political map will change drastically (607–13):

> Dearest son of Aegeus, only gods
> Never suffer old age and death.
> Everything else is ruined by overmastering Time.
> A country's power fails her, as the strength of the body fails,
> Trust dies, and distrust is born,
> And the same feelings are never maintained constantly
> Either between individual friends or city-states.

The solemn beauty of this tragic vision evokes a response that is of course not only emotional and intellectual: it is always aesthetic as well. As Aristotle saw, the instructive element of tragedy was inseparable from the pleasure it offered. All three tragedians were exceptionally gifted poets, and the recent resurgence of verse translations used in performance, rather than the plain, pared-down, 'naturalist' prose idiom so popular in the post-war period, shows that the poetry of Greek tragedy has arrived back on the agenda.[9] We can once again appreciate that Euripides' teenager Iphigenia not only suffers wholly without deserving it, but that she also delivers one the greatest poetic monologues of all time, when she pleads with her father to spare her (*Iphigenia in Aulis* 1021–51). This how she begins:

> If I had the eloquence of Orpheus, father,
> And could by intoning spells
> Persuade rocks to follow me,
> Or by speaking enchant anyone I wanted,
> Then that's what I would have done.
> But as it is, I offer you my expertise in tears,
> For this is something even I am able to do.

Tragedy was beautiful; like all poetry it could bring delight. Yet, as the nurse in *Medea* complains, the lovely arts of music and poetry, so prominent in the genre in which she is herself participating, can never *cure* human suffering. Poets are fools since they have never discovered anything that can do so (195–9):

> Nobody has ever invented a way
> To put a stop to human bitterness and hurt
> By music or songs accompanied by the strings of the lyre.
> Yet hurt causes deaths, and the terrible events that wreck families.
> Finding a cure would bring benefits.

Tragedy consisted aurally of variegated theatrical verse, composed in heightened poetic language, and performed by highly trained vocalists.

There is a story told in a comedy by the tragedians' contemporary playwright Aristophanes that shows how spellbinding the Athenians found the experience of hearing an actor deliver a fine tragic speech. One source of relief from the boredom of jury service is offered when an actor finds himself in the dock: then you can make him recite the famous soliloquy from a tragedy about Niobe (*Wasps* 579–80). We do not have this tragedy, but since Niobe caused the death of all her children by offending the gods, it must have been affecting. Both a passage in Aristophanes as well as a number of vase-paintings suggest that the tragic audiences also remembered the visual power of the silent, veiled figure of Niobe and of the corpses of her seven sons and seven daughters, killed by the archer siblings Artemis and Apollo.[10] Besides its aural beauty, tragedy's masks and costumes were designed to appeal to the eye, and a strong sense of the visual pleasure on offer at a tragic performance emanates from the many vase-paintings related to tragedy we are fortunate enough to be able to study.[11]

The Greeks' vision of human suffering was just one constituent of a wider cultural sensibility shared by the several ethnic and linguistic groups inhabiting the complicated and interactive world of the eastern Mediterranean two and a half thousand years ago. There are many links that relate the tone and content of Greek tragic poetry to the literature of Mesopotamia (above all the *Epic of Gilgamesh*) or to the Old Testament. The author of the passage from *Ecclesiastes* quoted at the beginning of this book has been contemplating all the suffering and violence he sees under the sun,

INTRODUCTION: WHAT IS GREEK TRAGEDY?   11

and come to the conclusion that the happiest man is the one who has never been born. This thinker was Jewish, and was writing at about the same time as the authors of Greek tragedy.[12] His ruminations are strikingly similar to those of the chorus of *Oedipus at Colonus* (1224–35):

> On any account, it is best not to be born at all.
> But once you are born, the next best thing
> Is to return to where you came from as soon as possible.
> When you are young, light-headed and unthinking,
> What agonizing blows, what hardships do not afflict you?
> Bloodshed, strife, quarrels, battles, and resentful envy.

The quality which makes this poetry different from the Sumerian narrative poem or the Hebrew scripture is less its content and melancholy world-view than the medium in which it was enjoyed. Its defining characteristic is that it was performed, partly to music, by men in masks and costumes, who danced as they impersonated imaginary long-dead people.

However grave the actions portrayed in Greek tragedies, and however weighty their philosophical content, the audiences who packed the ancient theatres seem to have been completely stage-struck. When the tragedians' near contemporaries discuss tragic theatre—even philosophers like Plato, who is harshly critical of its moral content—they always and emphatically acknowledge its allure. All Greek tragedies are serious and substantial artworks that explore the relationship between the living and the dead; portray mortal bafflement at the workings of the universe; enquire philosophically into the causes, effects, and nature of suffering; and yet provide considerable aesthetic pleasure—that is, *entertainment*. But every play and indeed many episodes within each play are remarkably different in tone and total effect, while belonging very much to the same social and economic system which produced them all. It is therefore time to stop generalizing and begin to work in detail through the tragedies' characteristics, in the context of the world in which they were first composed, performed, and enjoyed.

# 1
# Play Makers

PERSONNEL

The creative achievement of the Greek tragedians in turning myths into theatre takes the breath away. As we read through the plays and imagine them being enacted, scene after scene shocks and terrifies us; as Aristotle said, the plot of a well-made tragedy could make us shudder even if we only heard it reported (*Poetics* ch. 14, 1453b 3–7). Everyone has their favourites. One of mine is the stunning moment in the Aeschylean *Prometheus* when Io, who is half-way to being fully transformed into a heifer, leaps wildly into the view of the Titan fettered on his Caucasian crag (561). Another is the final entrance of Creon in Sophocles' *Antigone*, carrying the corpse of his fully grown son, two millennia before Lear first carried in Cordelia and howled. The imaginative efforts of Euripides achieved so many memorable effects that it is hard to choose amongst them. For sheer excitement the prize must go to the earthquake in *Bacchae*, when the theatre-god Dionysus himself breaks free from gaol; but the all-time greatest scene for pathos is Hecuba's lament over the tiny cadaver of her grandson Astyanax as she composes his limbs on Hector's shield in *Trojan Women*.

Then there is the poetry. Even the centuries that have passed between us and the Greek tragedians, and the linguistic betrayal involved in translation, do not hide the intellectual force and beauty of the disgraced Ajax's meditation on the effects of the passage of time (Sophocles, *Ajax* 646–9):

> Time, so long, so immeasurably long,
> Reveals everything that has been obscure, and
> Conceals what has been apparent. Nothing is
> Impossible. Even the sternest oath
> Can be broken, and the strongest will.

Communities can be broken over time as well, and some of the best lyrics in Greek tragedy are suffused with a nostalgic longing for a society's better days in the past. One example is the sensual memory of an idyllic sanctuary of Zeus at sunrise, on which the chorus of Euripides' *Trojan Women* linger just before they are forcibly deported (1060–70):

> So, O Zeus, you have betrayed to the Achaeans
> Your shrine in Ilium, your fragrant altar,
> The flaming sacrificial juices, rising skyward
> In smoke infused with myrrh; you have betrayed
> Sacred Pergamum, and Ida—the ivy-meshed vales of Ida,
> Where streams of melting snow pour down,
> The hallowed recipient of the first sunbeam,
> Bathed in light at the edge of the world.

It is scenes and poetry like this, components of a profound intellectual enquiry into suffering encoded in exquisite art, that have ensured that Greek tragedy is today once again a living cultural presence. It is taught in schools, performed in both professional and amateur theatres, broadcast on radio, and appears in various guises in novels by major contemporary writers of fiction.[1] People who have never read any Greek tragedy in a modern-language translation, let alone studied it in ancient Greek, often know something about the heroes of Sophocles' *Oedipus* or Euripides' *Medea*—the king who killed his father and slept with his mother, or the woman who killed her own children. The climate of our times, with the rise and partial victory, at least in some arenas, of feminism, the Civil Rights movement, anti-colonialism, anti-militarism and gay rights, has made the confrontational ancient Greek tragedies seem powerfully relevant and immediate.

Yet Greek tragedy can be deceptive. For many people today a Greek play will be the first text from antiquity that they encounter. It is often the first to which they feel they can relate, precisely because it can seem so fresh and accessible. Audiences still gasp when Medea complains about the unfair status of women not only in society and in the economy but in the bedroom (see below, pp. 152–3). When Oedipus, the brilliant, elected leader of Thebes in *Oedipus Tyrannus*, throws his weight about and loses his temper with people who are trying to help him, he seems to foreshadow all those politicians, to be seen daily on our televised news programmes, whose power has gone to their heads. But for every passage in the surviving plays that seems immediate and easy to understand, there is another that seems obscure or irrelevant. It is the purpose of this book to attempt, at least, to make *all* of Greek tragedy enjoyable. Part of this task involves thinking about each play individually, which is the function of Chapters 5 to 7. But the project also requires putting together what information we can about the people who created the plays, and the context in which they were originally performed.

The pagan, patriarchal, slave-holding Mediterranean society for whom the tragedies were composed and first performed can indeed seem remote and inscrutable. But a vital principle to grasp is that the 'audience' of Greek tragedy was, socially speaking, inseparable from its creative personnel. Theatre was less a public institution than a process, a public *activity*; in linguistic terms, it was more of a verb than a noun. The men—and they *were* all men—involved in making Greek tragedies between 472 and 401 BCE, the seven decades from which (with one exception[2]) thirty-two of the thirty-three plays discussed in this book certainly date, were almost all members of the Athenian public. More importantly, many of the spectators would have performed in a tragic chorus at some stage of their lives, probably when they were young men; numerous others would be proudly watching one of their brothers, sons, nephews, grandsons, or neighbours performing. Greek tragedy seems less daunting if we remember that it was community theatre, and a significant proportion of the men involved in the productions were what we would call amateurs.

Yet they were also different men, from varied backgrounds. Athens' total territory, the ancient name of which was Attica, encompassed many miles of coastline, along with some islands, three vast plains divided by mountain ranges, extensive forests, and the long river Cephisus, which flows from the Parnes mountain range in the North to the Saronic Gulf in the West. While some citizens lived inside the walls of the city itself (their numbers swelled in wartime), and could have walked to the theatre from their homes in half an hour, others lived at distances of twenty or more miles, and would have required a day or two to travel up to town. Attica was in fact made up of a hundred and thirty-nine separate communities—villages or districts—called 'demes', and when two Athenian citizens were talking to one another, they identified one another by the name of their father and their deme. The demes were divided into three groups—coastal, inland, and city—and no doubt that type of regional identity was an important factor in domestic relations as well.

Village identity remained strong during the fifth century, long after the unification of Attica traditionally attributed to Theseus. This becomes clear from the historian Thucydides' report of the social dislocation caused when the rural Athenians had to move into the city centre after the outbreak of the Peloponnesian War (2.16):

In ancient and more recent times, up until the present war, the majority of the Athenians still lived in the countryside with their families, and were unwilling to move now… They were extremely upset and uneasy at the prospect of leaving behind their homes and what (according to the old political order) were their ancestral sanctuaries, of changing their habits of daily life, and of abandoning what every person regarded as his own city-state.

The demes held their own political assemblies, and some of them also had their own theatres, in which touring productions of the famous plays that had premiered at festivals in the city could be enjoyed, at least by the later years of the fifth century. Those who were fellow demesmen of the famous playwrights Aeschylus, Euripides, and Sophocles will have known them well; they will have supported them when they won accolades in the theatre, and will have encountered them in other public arenas, such as the Assembly where they voted alongside the other citizens, or the nearby agora (market-place) where much business was conducted.

The three great Greek tragedians were all citizens of Athens and residents of Attica, and indeed the distance between the demes from which they hailed illustrates the range of communities that comprised the city-state. Aeschylus, who was born in 525 BCE, nearly two decades before the revolution that lead to the instalment of the democracy in 507, came from Eleusis, a settlement in the far west of Attica renowned for its ancient cult of Demeter and the mysteries conducted in her honour there. Euripides' family owned property on the island of Salamis, where he is said to have been born at least three decades after Aeschylus; tradition had it that he had composed some of his tragedies in a cave on the island. Certainly there is plenty of imagery connected with the sea and seafaring in his plays. But his deme was actually Phlya, well inland beyond the Mountain of Hymettus east of the city, and this upbringing may be connected with the character type of morally upright peasant farmer who features in his *Electra* and is mentioned in his *Orestes* (917–22). Euripides' near-coeval Sophocles, on the other hand, was born in Colonus Hippios, a suburban deme only about a mile to the north-west of the centre, although it was rural in character (it is still named Kolonos but is now a densely populated urban district). His last surviving play, *Oedipus at Colonus*, is actually set in the sacred grove of goddesses called the 'Semnai' or 'Eumenides' ('Holy' or 'Kindly' ones) which he must have visited himself on many occasions.

From the time of the earliest available records, it seems clear that particular families were collectively involved in theatrical activity, producing both playwrights and actors.[3] Such families were either in the tragedy business or the comedy business: the two were regarded as distinct skills. Aeschylus' sons included Euphorion, a tragic poet and successful theatrical producer, and also Euaion, an actor famous for his virtuosic dancing. Over a century later, Aeschylus' great-grandson or (possibly great nephew) Astydamas was a distinguished tragic playwright. There is an ancient tradition that Sophocles had started out as an actor himself, and played roles in his own tragedies, but the relative feebleness of his voice had led him to retire from the stage and devote himself to playwriting;[4] there is no reason to doubt that this was true, since in an acting family the younger members would almost inevitably have been encouraged to attempt roles. Sophocles' son Iophon and grandson Sophocles were actively involved in tragic theatre, as was Euripides' son (also called Euripides), who staged his father's plays posthumously, including *Iphigenia in Aulis* and *Bacchae*.

The three great tragedians all came from well-established, elite families that must have been sufficiently financially independent to allow them to work on theatrical productions more or less full-time.

Although the financial arrangements that underlay such productions as early as the fifth century are obscure, there is no talk of large cash prizes. The point seems to have been to win acclaim and popularity, which in Athens meant accruing influence, powerful alliances and friendships, and unlimited dinner invitations. There were other theatrical families in Athens that produced poets and actors and competed for these advantages. Both Aeschylus and Euripides, however, wrote plays not only for the Athenians but for statesmen far away, in Sicily and Macedon, work for which they will have been handsomely remunerated.

It was to an inland deme called Icaria, often associated with the theatre-god Dionysus, that the traditional inventor of tragedy, Thespis, belonged. The story went that he was a singer of dithyrambs (hymns to Dionysus), or a mummer who travelled around the villages with a special wagon, staging masked entertainments as he went.[5] He was believed to have won the first ever competition in tragedy, held at Athens in 534 BCE, nine years before Aeschylus was born. This was during the reign of the tyrant Pisistratus, and nearly three decades before the democracy was founded in 507 BCE.

Some scholars think that Thespis' itinerant 'theatrical' performances were actually the ancestors of classical comedy rather than tragedy. Yet the issue is clouded because, even centuries before theatre had come into existence, many of its aspects had been anticipated in Greek life. The performance of epic, a practice which stretched back hundreds of years into the Mycenaean past and beyond, had included extended passages of direct speech where the bard recited the actual words of Achilles, or Hecuba, or Odysseus. There had been mimetic elements in rituals which involved mythological stories—noises imitating thunder and chariot wheels, for example, had been simulated in enactments of the appearance of gods from the Underworld. Choruses of the 'archaic' period (i.e. before the fifth century BCE), such as the choruses of young women who participated in the cult of Apollo on Delos, had always played with alternative identities and incorporated mimetic gestures into their performances. But there is a big difference between singing in the persona of a nymph while retaining your own physical appearance, and pretending to be someone else altogether.

FIG. 1.1. Prize-winning actor dedicating his mask; a Herculaneum wall-painting, now in the Naples Archaeological Museum, probably copied from a Greek original of *c*.300 BCE.

What made tragic theatre distinctively *theatrical* when it was invented in the sixth century was the uncanny phenomenon of an actor assuming a role by masking his identity and speaking in the voice of a long-dead character such as Pentheus or Tiresias. Throughout antiquity, tragedy and the actor's mask were conceptually wholly inseparable, and actors are represented with, or contemplating, their masks (see Fig. 1.1). Theatre happened on the cusp between the world that the Athenians could see around them—the reality of the south slope of the Acropolis—and the imaginary world of the play, heroic Thebes or Troy. Crossing this boundary happened at the moment the actor brought to life his fictive identity. Costumes and masks are not just decorative accessories of the actor; in an important sense they are what makes a performer an *actor* rather than any other kind of performer.

The earliest theatre must have made an overwhelming impression. From the perspective of the early twenty-first century, the actor's assumption of another identity is so much a part of our cultural environment that it can be difficult to recreate the enormity of its original impact, just as the soaking of our own third-millennial culture in celluloid, videotape, and digital images means that we will never experience the excitement felt by the earliest cinema audiences. The Greek tragic actor or chorus-man superimposed upon his own features a mask depicting another individual, and impersonated that individual's speech and movement. In numerous roles this entailed shedding a masculine identity and substituting a female one. The actors' physical assumption of the personae of women was a practice that probably sent shockwaves through early Athenian audiences.

The introduction of the first female role was traditionally attributed to a tragedian called Phrynichus, who was working in the years between Thespis and Aeschylus. Indeed, despite much speculation surrounding the appearance of maenads in the vase-painting of the period in the sixth century when the tyrant Pisistratus introduced tragic competitions to Athens, there is little reason to suppose that the preponderance of female characters and choruses in the extant tragedies was ever a traditional and aboriginal feature of the genre. The titles attributed to Thespis, the only tragedian certainly known to have been working before Phrynichus, are *Funeral Games of Pelias*, *Priests*, and *Pentheus*, none of which requires us to imagine a female character or even chorus, since violent encounters with maenads do not have to be enacted visibly: they could be reported (as they are in Euripides' *Bacchae*) and lamented by men. Tragedy, then, far from being a genre preoccupied with the feminine from the beginning, may have evolved into this, even as late as Phrynichus' heyday in the first third of the fifth century. Watching actors impersonate females, with the concomitant phenomenon of the sculpted female mask, may still have been very recent developments in Aeschylus' early manhood.

Who were these Athenians whose city created the surviving Greek tragedies? Current scholarship estimates that the total population of Attica during this period was about a quarter of a million, but that the large proportion of resident foreigners ('metics') and slaves meant that only perhaps thirty thousand inhabitants were adult male citizens. The major theatrical contests, which seem to have been extremely popular, may have accommodated just over fifty per cent of this citizen body; it is unlikely that the theatre of Dionysus could have seated significantly more. The evidence does not allow us to be absolutely certain, but on balance it is unlikely that women were present at the City Dionysia premieres of tragedy, except perhaps for one or two important and mature priestesses. The first audiences of the plays therefore seem to have been dominantly (some scholars argue almost exclusively) free, Athenian or allied to Athens, and male.[6] Yet when considering the impact that these plays had on their audiences, it is crucial to remember that the more popular and successful were revived, in places other than Athens, as early as the 460s, and by the last decade of the fifth century with increasing frequency. The venues included not only smaller neighbourhood theatres in some of the demes, but cities as far afield as Sicily, southern Italy, and Macedon. Scholars have also stressed the likely diversity of the audiences of theatrical performances in deme theatres and far beyond the borders of Attica; in such venues it becomes hazardous to make assumptions about the sex, status, or ethnicity of the spectators.[7]

The festivals of the wine-god Dionysus, during the course of which drama competitions were held at Athens, fell respectively in the month called the Lenaea (approximately equivalent to January) and the month called Elaphebolion (approximately equivalent to April). The festival held in Lenaea was itself called 'the Lenaea', and was a smaller affair, attended only by residents of Athens; the three great tragedians do not seem to have produced their plays much at this venue. We know far more about the much bigger festival, the 'City Dionysia' or 'Great Dionysia'. This was held after the start of each year's sailing season, thus allowing spectators to attend from all over the Greek world, making it truly 'Panhellenic' as well as giving the Athenians a chance to display their artistic gifts to their allies and associates everywhere.

Tragic authors submitted proposals for plays to the senior city magistrate called the *archōn eponymos*. He was otherwise in charge of administering secular and political affairs rather than religious ones, which underlines how tragedy, although performed at a religious festival, fused social, political, and spiritual concerns. There was a symbiotic relationship between the practices of the democratic city-state and its dramas, which were enacted at one of the two most important festivals in the religious calendar. Tragedy sat on a cusp between the sacred and the secular, and it is this that allowed it to *crystallize*, by transmuting into memorable mythical storylines, the anxieties, aspirations, tensions, and contradictions that underlay Athenian society and thought.

The plays were submitted for the archon's consideration by a date between a year and few months or so before the next festival. Each tragedian had to propose a group of four plays (a 'tetralogy'), three tragedies and a satyr drama, to be performed consecutively on a single day of the festival. In 458 BCE, for example, Aeschylus submitted his tetralogy the *Oresteia*, consisting of *Agamemnon*, *Libation-Bearers*, *Eumenides*, and a satyr drama called *Proteus*. We know nothing of how much actual text he was required to submit, and little about the means by which the archon—probably in consultation with other officials—arrived at his decision as to which three tragedians were to compete at the next festival. It is likely that a poet whose production in a previous competition had proved disastrous could be excluded, and we hear of complaints when Sophocles, as a favourite poet, was not selected.[8]

The three selected tragedians were allocated their principal actors, their chorus, and also their *chorēgos*. This was a wealthy man who sponsored the production by funding the maintenance, costuming, and training of the chorus of citizens that would be made available to each of the tragedians. Some of the rich grumbled about the expense, and went to considerable lengths to avoid being selected; a character in a comedy complains that if a man is chosen to be *chorēgos*, he ends up in rags himself while dressing his chorus-men in gold.[9] But the more enterprising rich men realized that this kind of tax offered a massive opportunity for enhancing their reputations, and therefore careers. The selection of the *chorēgoi* took place nearly a whole year before the actual festival. Making this contribution to a festival was an extremely costly business, and since there was pressure to win, the spending by the three tragic *chorēgoi* no doubt became competitive in itself. The economic basis of theatrical activity was therefore related to the political life of the city.

The drama competitions at the City Dionysia were inaugurated at an event called the *Proagōn* (which means 'preliminary to the competition' or 'before the competition'). After about 440 BCE this was held in a roofed building called the 'Song Hall' (*Ōideion*) next to the theatre. All the dramatists who were about to compete ascended a rostrum, along with their actors and chorus-men (wearing garlands but neither masks nor costumes), and 'announced' or 'talked about' their compositions.[10] Tradition had it that when Sophocles heard that his great rival Euripides had died, he reduced the people to tears by appearing at the *Proagōn* to the festival in 406 BCE dressed in black, with the heads of his troupe bare of the customary festive garlands.[11] It would be fascinating to know more about the *Proagōn*, especially the degree to which the details of the plot and special effects were made public, and how far the actual masked performances at the festival assumed knowledge of the personnel that had been gained when they appeared without their masks.

It was probably on the day following the *Proagōn* that the religious rituals themselves began, with the procession called the 'Introduction' (*Eisagōgē*), which annually reproduced the introduction of Dionysus to his theatre in the city sanctuary. According to myth, this commemorated his original journey from Eleutherae, on the border with Boeotia, into Attica.[12] Instead of recreating the entire journey, the icon of Dionysus, which consisted of a wooden pole with a mask at one end, was adorned with a costume and ivy. It was carried from his city sanctuary to an olive-grove outside the city called the Academy, which was on the road that headed out towards Eleutherae. The Academy was sacred to Athena. A day or two later, after hymns and sacrifices, Dionysus was brought by torchlight in a great procession back to the theatre in his sanctuary from which he had been taken.[13]

Once Dionysus had been installed, the festival opened officially the next morning with the *Pompē*, which simply means 'procession'.

All the city was now in a state of high excitement: the Assembly could not be held, nor legal proceedings initiated, and it seems that even prisoners could be released temporarily on bail.[14] The procession, which probably led from the city walls, would stop at each of several shrines on its way to the sanctuary of Dionysus in order to sing and dance for different gods. At the same time, it defined, by symbolical enactment, the relationships between the different social groups that made up Athenian society. It was led by a virginal young woman from an aristocratic family, who carried the ceremonial golden basket that would contain the choicest pieces of meat from the sacrifice. The *chorēgoi* who had funded the productions wore expensive costumes, sometimes made of gold. Provision had to be made for the public feast, and the many thousands of people attending the festival would have needed a great deal to eat: the bull specially chosen to be the principal sacrificial animal, as 'worthy of the god', was accompanied by younger citizens in military training (*ephebes*). There were, in addition, hundreds of lesser sacrifices; the sanctuary of Dionysus must have resembled a massive sunlit abattoir attached to a barbecue. It resounded with the bellowing and bleating of frightened animals, was awash with their blood, and smelled powerfully of carcasses and roasting meat.

To accompany the meal, enormous loaves of bread on spits and wine in leather skins was carried in procession by citizens, while the metics carried the bowls for mixing the wine with water, which was borne in pitchers by their daughters. More groups of men brought up the rear, carrying the ritual phalluses of Dionysus and singing hymns. The City Dionysia in the period from which our tragedies date, i.e. after the Persian Wars, therefore still bore traces of the raucous processions that were such an important part of festivals of Dionysus in the country neighbourhoods. They included the carrying of a phallus pole to the accompaniment of obscene songs, and worshippers dressed in 'ithyphallic' costumes (i.e. with inbuilt or attached erect artificial phalluses). It is probable that the separate competitions in choral singing by fifty-strong choruses of citizens took place soon after the procession, and before the drama competitions.[15]

The theatre itself was prepared for the culmination of the festival, the performance of the plays, by various ceremonial activities.

These began with a purification rite that may have involved yet another sacrifice, this time of very young piglets. The ten *stratēgoi* ('generals'), the most senior elected officers of state, then poured out libations of wine to the gods. A public herald made a series of announcements, naming recent benefactors of the city. When the theatre was full, there was a display of rows of golden money bars ('talents'), the revenue Athens had accrued that year from the states allied with her, who in practice were her imperial subjects and thus required to pay tribute. The imperial flavour was heightened by the public presentation of a suit of armour to all those sons of Athenian war dead who had achieved military age, before they were invited to take prominent seats near the front of the theatre.

A herald, probably with the aid of a trumpet, announced each of the dramatic productions. Although the programme of the festival was altered over the fifth century, especially in terms of the performances of the comedies, the programme for tragedy remained constant: each of the three competing poets had his tetralogy performed in one go on a single day, probably starting early in the morning. The order in which the tetralogies were performed was decided by lot. At the end of the competition, the results were decided by the judges, who were ordinary citizens selected at the last minute from a cross-section of all the tribes, rather than elected, in order to try to avoid corruption. The judges were under a great deal of pressure, however, to vote in accordance with public opinion, which would be quite clear from the applause generated during and after the performances. The victorious tragedian was crowned with ivy, and led in a procession, like a victorious athlete returning from the Olympic games, to a wealthy friend's house for a private party. The general atmosphere of such a party, with drinking competitions, a sexual undercurrent, pipe-girls, and carousing outside in the streets into the small hours, is well conveyed by the post-performance party dramatized in Plato's *Symposium*.

The dramatic performances were framed by civic ceremonies that involved a large and diverse personnel. All this information is interesting in its own right, especially to anthropologists of theatre. But it also casts light on the content of the plays. The many rituals performed in tragedy will have taken on particular meanings in the minds of an audience who had just participated in large-scale animal sacrifice and public libation. All the processions will have provided a point of reference for the processions within the plays, for example Aeschylus' *Eumenides*, which concludes with a procession of Athenian women. The 'psychic geography' internalized by all those who had participated in the *Eisagōgē*, the route from the periphery to the centre via shrines of significant local gods, will have provided a mental framework onto which to graft their experiences of the Bronze Age public spaces conjured up in the theatre. The prominent role given to a young woman in the great civic procession to the theatre, which also included metics' daughters carrying water jugs, may have been remembered by spectators watching the many scenes in tragedy where women perform rituals, for example Ismene's libation to atone for her father's pollution of the grove of the Eumenides in *Oedipus at Colonus*, or appear as priestesses, such as Iphigenia in *Iphigenia among the Taurians*.

The ceremonies set a political tone as well. The presence in the theatre of Greeks from many allied states, as well as the resident aliens of Athens in the procession, provided a suitable context for the exploration of confrontation between different ethnic groups that is such a feature of the tragedies. The imperial tone set by the display of tribute could surely provide a source of irony when plays questioned the conduct of cities in war. The award of arms to fatherless youths provided a telling psychological reference point for the scenes, such as Ajax's encounter with his little son in Sophocles' *Ajax*, where armour or the death of a warrior-father provides the dramatic focus. And the trumpets of the past resounded once again during tragedies where large groups of people needed to be assembled or herded around, for example in Aeschylus' *Eumenides* (567–8).

There must have been a good deal of excitement and gossip about the actors who would be starring in the plays, yet we know little of individual actors in Aeschylus' day. Their expertise needs to be inferred from the texts, and we can be sure that they were already required to memorize hundreds of lines to be delivered in quite different personas across a whole tetralogy. By the second half of the fifth century, superstar actors began to appear, like Andron, a prizewinner at the Dionysia, and the superb Tlepolemos. He was Sophocles' favourite actor for several years, and therefore may have been the first person to realize some of the most famous roles in world theatre. Oiagros was a moving Niobe (*Wasps* 579–80).[16] These actors could squeeze huge emotion just from their posture, or silence, or the contrast between their controlled speech and their laments. The most important actor in the later fifth century was probably a man named Nikostratos. Nikostratos was still winning at the Dionysia in 399 BCE. What spectators remembered was the way he could reduce them to tears simply by a particular way he recited a certain kind of verse (tetrameters) to pipe accompaniment, and above all his superb delivery of messenger speeches.[17] Callipides, however, was the most lively and emotive of tragic actors, and his innovative style went to extremes. He was outstandingly popular in the later fifth century at Athens, as an exceptional mimic, who enjoyed imitating the gestures of all social types, including the movements of 'low-grade' women. Callipides was only doing what many in the tragic audience by then wanted.[18] The same mimic element could be seen in the voice many tragic actors used, in their quest to affect exact pitch and rhythm. Actors now risked derision if they clung to the old-fashioned exaggerated type of vocal delivery, which aimed at volume and depth, rather than subtle affective modulation (see below, pp. 42–3).

The physical demands made on actors were considerable. Their vocal training was arduous, and they needed to be able to sing solo as well as deliver rapid-fire dialogue and extended orations. They had to switch mask and role under pressure, quickly, and often. They needed to take care not to turn their back on the audience for very long,[19] which is a challenge in the ancient Greek theatrical space with spectators sitting in a semi-circle. Some roles required a strong presence even through extended passages when they remained silent, such as Cassandra in Aeschylus' *Agamemnon*. Others required conveying a character's qualities through gait. Actors also needed to be physically fit. Some roles require outstanding physical qualities, for example that of Io in *Prometheus*, who needs to leap across the stage as if incessantly goaded by a gadfly, or Philoctetes, who must convey what it feels like to live in unremitting pain. Some spend time prostrate or on their knees, such as Hecuba in *Trojan Women*. Others had to climb onto palace roofs, appear through trapdoors, and fly in the theatrical crane.

Some sources imply that these energetic, creative, and expressive ancient Greek actors had a reputation for effeminacy;[20] they could certainly be temperamental. The brilliant fourth-century actor Theodorus insisted on having plays rewritten so that he always performed the first speech (Aristotle, *Politics* 7.1336b 27–31). Another tragic actor, when playing a queen, demanded that the *chorēgos* supply him with a retinue of richly dressed attendants; when this was refused, the actor sulked and refused to appear at all (Plutarch, *Phocion* 19.2–3). But it is important to keep the idea of real, known individuals with specific skills in mind when we think about individual plays, since the playwrights were almost certainly responding to the talents available to them when they created particular roles. Euripides must have had access to an expert in impersonating powerful women when he wrote *Medea*, old women when he wrote *Hecuba* and *Trojan Women*, and one who could sing elaborate arias at a high pitch when he wrote *Orestes*, since it contains two.

We must not be so awe-struck by the professional actors of tragedy that we neglect the core element of the chorus (see below), and indeed the numerous 'backstage' operatives and technicians whose names and labours have vanished almost without trace. We know the words for the trainer (as opposed to the funder) of the chorus, the *chorodidaskalos*. We know the word used for the man in charge of the crane in which gods could appear; he was the *mēchanopoios* or 'machine-operator'. In Plato's *Republic*, when Socrates is criticizing theatre on the ground that it portrays things which are false and do not exist, his list of culpable performance personnel, 'many of them occupied with figures and colours and many with music', includes 'the poets and their assistants... actors, chorus-dancers, contractors, and the manufacturers of equipment, especially those that have to do with the adornment of women' (2.373b5–c1). Elsewhere we hear of the scenery painter (Aristotle, *Poetics* ch. 4, 1449a 18). The productions were probably much more sophisticated in terms of their special effects and visual design than we have the evidence to demonstrate. One of the few types of theatre personnel that the ancient tragedians emphatically did *not* require to help their plays come to life in performance was the lighting designer or technician. The suffering in Greek tragedy took place by the light of the sun.

## WRITING ROLES

The Greek tragedians, from the moment they began writing, knew that they needed to think in terms not of a complete and unified text but an ensemble work designed to be performed in 'parts' as a number of separate roles. Whatever the form taken by the document that the tragedian submitted for approval to the magistrates, once it had been chosen for the competition, he would certainly have had to produce a workable script so that the actors and chorus-men could begin to learn their parts. We have one visual image of a tragedian with his papyrus rolls, dating from around the end of the fifth century: his name is Demetrios, and he is a strangely depressed looking character, depicted sitting in a scene where his victorious company of actors and chorus-men celebrate in costume.[21] It is very likely that each of the actors had their own rehearsal scripts, or individual 'parts' from which to learn their lines: one such rehearsal part—that of Admetus in Euripides' *Alcestis*—has survived on paper, albeit from the days of the Roman Empire.[22]

Yet it was only novice tragedians, according to Aristotle, who began with their characters (*who* was in the play?), rather than its plot (what *happened* in the play?, *Poetics* ch. 6, 1450a 16–26). So how did a tragedian set about turning a story concerning mythical heroes, often derived from a very long epic narrative, into a tight, psychologically powerful plot? The mental effort involved must never be underestimated. Aeschylus may have called his plays 'slices from the banquet of Homer' (Athenaeus, *Deipnosophistae* 8.347e), but tragedies were entirely different poems, even long before they left the mind of the tragedian to be enacted by actors and a chorus, since tragic poetry has an utterly different relationship with time from the epic poetry of Homer. In almost all our surviving examples the action does indeed take place, as Aristotle saw, 'within a single revolution of the sun' (*Poetics* ch. 5, 1449b 13). If a tragedian wanted to compose a play about Oedipus, or Agamemnon, or Medea, he had to pick the one day in which the action and its causes and antecedents, as well as its likely consequences, could all be explored, indeed articulated verbally by one of the characters or in the plural voice of the chorus. The tragedians developed numerous strategies for looking into the future within their plays (prophets and gods in machines were especially useful here), and others for recalling the past: even the most ordinary mortals represented in choruses can have long memories. But it was not ever thus. In the same passage Aristotle also records that in the earliest tragedies the practice was the same as in epic, which 'is unlimited in point of time'. If this is true, then the 'unity of time' which gives our surviving tragedies so much of their intensity and ability to confer aesthetic satisfaction came about by trial and error.

In his *Agamemnon*, for example, Aeschylus decided to cover the entire trans-generational history of the house of Atreus until Clytemnestra and Aegisthus took up the reins of power. He could have chosen to set the play on the day Thyestes slept with Atreus' wife, or Atreus cooked Thyestes' children, or Agamemnon sacrificed Iphigenia. The action of *Agamemnon*—Clytemnestra's murder of her husband and his lover Cassandra and her ascent of the throne—could have been prophesied, just as they are by Polymestor in the closing scene of Euripides' *Hecuba* (1275–81). But the sun that revolves in *Agamemnon* has already witnessed many deaths in this household, and the ghosts of dead children haunt the poetry as they haunt the building that Aeschylus had physically represented in the theatrical space. It was his dazzling skill with a medium as yet less than a century old that led him to choose the day he did. The long historical view on the events unfolding is achieved primarily through the perspectives of the chorus, Cassandra, and Aegisthus—perspectives formed verbally into the carefully planned 'parts', or rows of lines, that Aeschylus composed for the actors who played them.

If the unity of time entailed a choice about *action*, then the physical 'unity' of most of the plays was a decision that primarily was linked with the identity of the chorus. The choral performers were Athenian men, and most scholars think it is likely that they were young men in their late teens and early twenties, for whom choral training was bound up with the formal passage from boyhood to manhood and military induction. But these youths could be asked to impersonate beings of either sex, and any age or ethnicity. A key factor in the choice of choral identity is the relationship between the group and the imagined space it occupies—the setting of the play. Tragic choruses are always either space defenders or space invaders.

The physical setting of the tragedy is closely related to the group of people that might be expected to be found there and to their perspective on the events that are taking place. In the majority of the plays, the chorus 'belongs' to the space where the action occurs: they are inhabitants of the town where the tragic family resides. Thus in *Agamemnon* the chorus consists of citizens of Argos, and in *Medea* of local women of Corinth. Often the house is the royal palace, and the chorus' relationship to the principal characters is that of social inferiors—subjects in *Oedipus Tyrannus* or slaves in *Libation-Bearers*. Such choruses, as members of the local community, have a major stake in maintaining the peace and upholding the law, and their involvement is informed by this agenda.

Other choruses, however, are not attached to the place where the play is set, and bring a different perspective. In Euripides' *Bacchae*, for example, the chorus are not the local women of Thebes, but an alien retinue of maenads from Asia who pose a real threat to order in the city. In Sophocles' *Philoctetes* the chorus-men had to play members of the Greek navy who must set foot, nervously, on the desert island (see Fig. 1.2). It has only one human inhabitant, and he is likely to be hostile. In Aeschylus' *Eumenides* the chorus impersonate snaky-haired supernatural females ('Erinyes'), whose presence is felt to defile both spaces portrayed in the action (the oracle of Apollo in Delphi and the hill of the Areopagus in Athens). The tension between the group perspective of the chorus and locality is thus a crucial element in tragedy.

In a few plays, a second chorus appears, but not for more than a scene and a single song. At the end of *Eumenides*, a procession of Athenian women arrives to escort the chorus of Erinyes to their new home. In Euripides' *Hippolytus*, the hero sings his hymn to Artemis in company with a group of fellow huntsmen (61–71), who leave with him before the primary chorus of Troezenian women arrive; some scholars think the male chorus reappeared to share the final song of the play antiphonally with the women at the end (1101–52). In his *Suppliant Women*, the main chorus consists of the suppliant mothers of the Argive warriors slain in Polynices' campaign against Thebes. At the beginning of the play, they sit bearing the olive branches that mark them as suppliants at an altar before the temple

FIG. 1.2. Colin Blakeley as Philoctetes at the Old Vic, London (1964). Photo reproduced courtesy of the APGRD.

of Demeter and Persephone in Eleusis. But there seems to be, additionally, a group of their grandchildren, the sons of the same warriors chiefs, whom Adrastus eventually leads to the funeral pyre so that they can collect the ashes (948), and who sing with their grandmothers near the end of the play (1113–64).

One of the factors involved in deciding when and what the chorus would sing was a simple dramaturgical one—the requirement to allow the actors enough time to change mask and costume when necessary. In Sophocles' *Oedipus Tyrannus*, for example, one of the most important role changes occurs after Jocasta has realized that Oedipus is her son, and leaves the stage in ominous silence. Soon afterwards the actor playing her has to exchange the identity of a royal female for that of her own slave, the old male herdsman to whom she entrusted the baby Oedipus long ago. Sophocles carefully inserts a resonant ode, in which the chorus address Cithaeron, the towering limestone mountain range, sacred to Dionysus, that lies between Thebes and Attica. This is where Oedipus was supposed to have been exposed. It is from that very mountain that the herdsman, played by the same actor as Jocasta, soon arrives.

After deciding on the basic action of the play, the playwright had to organize the material into 'parts' that could be performed by his actors and chorus. Greek tragedies, although highly variable in form, quickly built up a common 'pool' of conventional types of scene and speech from which the dramatist could draw: denunciation, persuasion, debate, supplication. All these are of course composed in verse rather than prose. When Euripides' Phaedra describes her battle with her obsession for her stepson, she begins with philosophical ruminations, in elegant language, chiselled into rhythmical phrases (*Hippolytus* 373–81):

> Women of Troezen, you who live here, at the outward-facing edge of
>     Pelops' land,
> There have been many times, in the long watches of the night,
> When I have wondered why life is catastrophic.
> I do not believe that it is poor judgement that makes people fail,
> Since many of them possess intelligence. The matter
> Needs to be looked at in this way instead: we know and understand
> The right thing to do, but don't carry it through to completion.

Even in this stolid translation, the heightened nature of the poetic communication can still be discerned. Rather than opening with her specific, personal quandary, she asks a universal question about the nature of life, lending the speech its philosophical and interrogative tone. Rather than saying, as if giving directions to a traveller, 'this coastal region of the Peloponnese', she talks of the 'outward-facing edge of Pelops' land'. Rather than put the question to the chorus direct, she paints a picture of herself, sleepless in the lonely darkness, which complements the theme of her sexual deprivation. Moreover, this great monologue, like most of the speeches and dialogue delivered by the speaking actors in Greek tragedy, is in a poetic metre. It is composed in an iambic line not dissimilar to the Shakespearean iambic pentameter (into which ancient Greek tragedy is often translated in English), although the underlying effect is a triple pulse ($\times - \smile - | \times - \smile - | \times - \smile -$), rather than a quintuple one. The Greeks regarded the iambic metre as creating verse that sounded much more akin than other metres to the flow of normal speech.

How did the playwright begin to compose the actual verses? It is of course possible that he began with the prologue or opening chorus, and worked through to the end. In a competition, the opening few moments of any performance are crucial in determining spectator response, and there are discernible differences between the three great playwrights in their techniques for opening a play. Two of Aeschylus' plays begin with grand, spectacular barbarian choruses (*Persians* and *Suppliants*), both of which have an important reason for arriving at the public space where the play is set, an ancient council hall and a sanctuary respectively. When Aeschylean tragedies are opened by individual characters, they are always doing something significant. Eteocles has called his citizens together in *Seven against Thebes* to arm for the collective defence of their country; the watchman of *Agamemnon* is on the palace roof, scanning the horizon for fire signals; Orestes in *Libation-Bearers* is praying to Hermes after arriving at his father's tomb to place a lock of hair there. Sophocles preferred to open his action during an intense moment of dialogue, such as the laying of the revenge plot in *Electra*, the urgent quarrel about the illegal plan to bury Polynices between the two bereaved sisters in *Antigone*, or the discussion between Antigone and her blind old father when they arrive at the sanctuary in *Oedipus at Colonus*.

A prominent feature of Euripidean tragedy, however, is the spoken 'programmatic' prologue with which most of his plays open. Euripides' contemporaries already laughed at this idiosyncrasy (even though there is a similar prologue in Sophocles' *Women of Trachis*); in Aristophanes' *Frogs* it is characterized as predictable in both metrical form and in 'scene-setting' function (1182–247). But this is a rather reductive response to a feature that probably developed to answer the need for democratic audiences (not all of whom were trained in the less familiar myths in the repertoire) to grasp the exotic settings and antecedents of what in Euripides were often innovative tragedies. Euripidean prologues are, moreover, far from mere descriptions of the setting and what has already happened.

They typically establish expectations, themes, and images which will subsequently become central to the drama. Euripides varied the impact by his choice of speaker: he opens *Iphigenia among the Taurians* with its reflective heroine, thus allowing her to charm the audience with her personal story. He alienates the audience of *Bacchae* from Pentheus partly by letting his deadly enemy, Dionysus, have the first word. The chanted opening of *Iphigenia in Aulis*, moreover, suggests that Euripides was capable of experimenting with opening scenes in which the speakers are locked in agitated, restless dialogue.

An important genre of communication in tragedy is the 'messenger speech', often the longest speech in the play, which provides the extended spoken narrative relating the off-stage crisis, often involving physical violence. In tragedy, the eyewitness account not only usually signals the moment that the tragic action becomes irrevocable, but was for the ancient audiences a highlight of the performance. We can infer this from the numerous messengers painted on vases, together with images illustrating the actions they narrated, which had remained unseen by the audience. In *Persians* the messenger's grim speeches recount the destruction of the Persian navy and heavy infantry at the battle of Salamis; in *Oedipus Tyrannus*, the messenger describes the suicide of Jocasta and the self-blinding of Oedipus in heart-rending detail. Messenger speeches are often rich in description, enamelled with adjectives describing colour and spectacle, and enlivened with passages in direct speech that allow the actor delivering them to impersonate one of the agents in the offstage scenes he is describing.

There are many other types of speech in tragedy, reflecting the nature of the classical city-state as a community engaged in incessant verbal interaction. Aristotle divided public rhetoric into three different kinds. The first is display oratory, which exhorts or praises people or institutions and addresses matters in the immediate present; the second is deliberative oratory, which considers the best course of action and therefore looks, even if only slightly, to the future; and the third is legal oratory, which tries to discover the truth of what has happened in the past and who is to be held accountable (*Rhetoric* 1.1357a 36–b 29). Although these categories often merge in Greek tragedy, where a scene or dialogue contains elements from more than one, they collectively illuminate the whole. An outstanding example of display oratory is Eteocles' opening exhortation of the Thebans in *Seven against Thebes*, a pre-battle speech addressing present dangers, praising the fatherland and the city, and encouraging its men to fight in the name of patriotism and duty (1–3, 10–16):

> Citizens of Cadmus, the man in charge of the city's
> State affairs, who steers the helm of government,
> Must keep awake so as to speak exactly when required...
> It is everyone's duty now to defend our city—
> Youths still not quite grown to manhood,
> Older men past their peak, and every man
> In the prime of life whose physical strength flourishes.
> Defend the altars of the gods who guard our land,
> And thus ensure the eternal preservation of the honours
> Due to our children, and to mother Earth, who nursed us.

Eteocles' rousing harangue sets the whole tone for this military drama. But when Medea debates within herself about whether or not to kill her children, the dominant idiom is deliberative (*Medea* 1021–80). So is Haemon's speech in *Antigone* when he attempts to persuade his father to be more flexible (683–723). When Hecuba 'prosecutes' Polymestor for the murder of Polydorus in Euripides' *Hecuba*, on the other hand, the speeches strongly resemble surviving legal speeches, and the stage is virtually turned into a court of law.

The most elaborately rhetorical speeches draw on all three styles of public oratory. They are usually to be found in the scene that constituted the fundamental confrontation of the play. When Agamemnon returns to Argos, the superficial issue (whether Clytemnestra can persuade Agamemnon to walk up the red carpet) symbolically expresses the real issue (which one of them can actually overpower the other). In *Antigone*, the crucial 'face-off' is between Creon and Antigone, a contest between two different definitions of lawful action. In *Ajax*, Teucer battles in debate against both Menelaus and Agamemnon. In this he is a strictly fifth-century version of an archaic Greek hero. To meet the increasing need for polished public speaking and its assessment under the widened franchise, the study of the science of persuasion, or the art of rhetoric, developed rapidly in the second half of the fifth century.

Teachers of rhetoric, often called 'sophists', began to ply their trade in Athens. This phenomenon is reflected in tragedy's increased use of the structured debate scene (*agōn*) and the type of technique and content that the sophists taught—formal rhetorical figures, tropes, 'common topics' such as pragmatism and expediency, and hypothetical arguments from probability.

The *agōn* was similar to one form of exercise available to the trainee orator, the 'double argument'—the construction or study of twin speeches for and against a particular proposition, or for the defence and prosecution in a hypothetical trial. As a character in Euripides' lost *Antiope* said, 'If someone were clever at speaking, he could have a competition between two arguments in every single case' (fr. 189 *TrGF*). The Athenians enjoyed competitive rhetorical performances as much as those in athletics or poetry. The statesman Cleon (himself a notoriously effective speaker) is said by Thucydides to have upbraided the Athenian citizenry for turning the Assembly into a showcase for competitive displays of rhetoric (Thucydides 3.38): '"You are simply victims of your own pleasure in listening," he said, "and are more like an audience sitting at the feet of a professional lecturer than a parliament discussing matters of state."' There seems to have been some truth in these words; in practice, the power and prestige which excellence in oratory now promised to the aspiring politician certainly led at times to the medium superseding the message. Tragic victims (e.g. Hecuba in her name-play at 1185–94) understandably complain about this tendency in relation to tragedy's masters of persuasion (especially the incomparable spin-doctor Odysseus). It was not unknown for politicians to prosecute one another simply in order to compete publicly at speaking in court.

Modern readers and actors are undoubtedly struck by the formality of some of the debates in Euripides, and the Roman rhetorician Quintilian (10.1.67) was probably correct when he judged Euripides to be of more use to the trainee orator than Sophocles. Euripides was strongly influenced by the most famous teacher of rhetoric, the Sicilian Gorgias, whose prose speeches took a course as near to poetry as was conceivably possible, being laden with rhetorical patterning, especially rhyme, alliteration, antithesis, and 'isocolon'—a technique whereby clauses of equal or similar length rhythmically balance one another. He specialized in the sophistic art of defending the indefensible, and for a fee (in private houses or at venues such as the Olympic games) he would offer an exhibition piece in which to display his brilliance. Audiences of tragedies by the late fifth century might have felt short-changed if they had not been treated to at least one oratorical performance of comparable skill internal to each tragedy.

One of the most rhetorically flamboyant orations in tragedy, Helen's self-defence speech in Euripides' *Trojan Women*, was influenced not only by Gorgias' techniques, but by a particular showcase speech he had written. This is *Encomium of Helen*, a display oration defending, in a hypothetical trial, the 'indefensible' mythical Helen, who was held by most other authors to have been solely responsible for the carnage at Troy. It was not perversity that led the sophists to practise writing defence speeches by choosing 'indefensible' defendants, but a desire to create a systematic method that could be applied in a court of law. In this passage, Gorgias, as Helen's advocate, uses the rhetorical defence technique of preemptively putting the blame on someone else's shoulders, a technique labelled '*antikatēgoria*' (section 7):

But if it was forcefully that she was abducted and lawlessly that she was constrained and wrongfully that she was violated, it is clear that on the one hand the abductor acted wrongfully when he violated her, and that she, on the other hand, as the abductee, being violated, suffered misfortune. The perpetrator, then, a barbarian who perpetrated something barbaric in speech and law and actuality, deserves to suffer blame through speech, dishonour under the law, and actual punishment. But she who was violated and deprived of her fatherland and isolated from her friends, how could she not be pitied rather than disparaged? For while he did terrible things, it was she who suffered them.

It turns out to have been all Paris' fault, after all. But in *Trojan Women*, Euripides makes Helen deliver her own Gorgianic defence through preemptive prosecution. She assigns the blame for the war on (amongst others) Hecuba for bearing Paris, Priam for not destroying the ill-omened baby, and on Aphrodite. As if there were not enough culprits already, she now turns to her first husband to accuse him, as well as her second spouse, of responsibility for her abduction (937–43):

> But you will say that I have as yet omitted to address
> The real issue before us, which is how
> I secretly left your house in the first place.
> It was with the aid of no minor goddess that he came,
> My punisher, regardless of whether
> You want to call him Alexander or Paris.
> It was him, you reprobate, that *you* left in your home
> When you sailed off from Sparta to Cretan soil.

It is, however, not Menelaus but Hecuba who answers Helen point by point (969–1032).

The 'double arguments' in tragedy often take the form of speeches of the same, or almost exactly the same, number of iambic lines, thus replicating in poetry the experience of listening to prosecution and defence speeches in actual trials, which were strictly allotted the same amount of time by means of a water-clock. When Medea accuses Jason of perfidy and he responds in a speech of almost identical length (*Medea* 465–18, 522–75), Euripides squeezes into a formal *agōn* the entire history of a relationship and the mutual favours it had entailed as well as an exploration, in a more abstract sense, of the rights and responsibilities that come with marriage. A similar general/specific oscillation, this time between the details of the case and more general consideration of international law, is apparent in the 'war crimes' trial of Hecuba *versus* Polymestor in *Hecuba*. Lycus and Amphitryon's quarrel about the reputation of Heracles in *Heracles* is also a debate on the sociopolitics of hoplite warfare; the *agōn* of Eteocles and Polynices concerning their rival claims to rule Thebes in *Phoenician Women* is also a discussion of forms of statecraft; Tyndareus' 'prosecution' of Orestes for killing Clytemnestra in *Orestes* is a rhetorical compression of the rival claims of the state and the family to jurisdiction in blood crimes that been staged fifty years earlier in Aeschylus' *Eumenides*.

Conflict can be expressed in other ways than the formal debate, and its pace and style can be varied with rapid-fire one-line dialogue (stichmomythia) and dialogue interchanges with slightly longer speeches of two, three, or rather more lines as well. Some of the most exciting moments in tragedy come in sequences of rapid-fire exchange, when one character puts another under pressure, sometimes with a third individual, or the chorus, interjecting. These scenes often feature less formal language and also physical contact, whether aggressive or affectionate. Rapid dialogue is a feature, for example, of scenes where information is extracted, such as the confrontation of Oedipus with the Theban shepherd in *Oedipus Tyrannus* (with the Corinthian shepherd also participating), discussed below, pp. 119–21. Such dialogue is also a pronounced feature of the recognition scene (*anagnōrisis*), where a brother and sister, husband and wife, or parent and child embrace one another after an accelerating series of questions and answers.

There are far more verse forms and metres in the plays, however, than the iambic trimeter. Greek tragedies bore little aural relation to the five-act tragedies in uniform blank verse that dominated the European neoclassical stage. Dionysus is a god of newness, arrival, transformation, surprise, experiment, and elaborate variety; this is reflected in the complicated, constantly shifting, verse forms of his dramas. The total effect might be compared to listening to Shakespearean blank-verse dialogue alternating with madrigals, sonnets, ballads, psalms, dances, and military marching songs. People who do not know Greek, especially if they are not musically trained, tend to get completely put off at the mention of metre, and even those who *do* know Greek often find it a topic of deadly difficulty and dullness. But that is because they are not encouraged to think of it in terms of the experience of a *performance*.

We have lost almost completely the melodies to which the lyrics of tragedy were sung to the invariable accompaniment of the same, plangent instrument (the double, reeded, oboe-like pipes called *auloi*), although a handful of papyrus scraps allow us to hear just a little of the choruses of *Orestes* and *Iphigenia in Aulis*.[23] But it is possible partially to decipher what John Gould called 'strategies of poetic sensibility'[24] within the formal, conventional media open to the tragedian: besides the choral passages, which were danced and sung, the tragedian had several modes of delivery to choose from for his individual actors. In addition to speeches and spoken dialogue, they included solo song (*monody*), duet, sung interchange with the chorus (*kommos*), and an intermediate mode of delivery, probably chanting to pipe accompaniment, signalled by the anapaestic rhythm. Here units of ⏑ ⏑ –, – ⏑ ⏑ and – –, probably each equivalent to a pace, interchanged with one another in long sequences which are particularly associated with the chorus marching or processing around the theatre space.

Tragedy was multi-medial, and the metres can tell us whether a particular passage was spoken, sung solo, sung and danced by the chorus, or provided the rhythmic background to marching movements as either actor or chorus entered or left the stage. Within the sung passages, different metres could create different psychological and ritual effects, being associated with funerals, for example, or weddings or madness. This may sound complicated, but for a modern person, the most important thing is simply to be able to see from a translation whether the passage was intended to be sung or spoken, since this can affect its meaning and impact. Most recent translations, for example those published by Oxford World's Classics, do include this information.

Sequential variety of poetry, song, and dance is at the heart of the experience of Greek tragedy. In this it represented a completely new type of performance even for its original audiences. There is a massive difference between tragedy and what we know about all the types of poetic performance that preceded it, in the archaic period. Homeric epic was performed by a single bard in an identical six-foot rhythm (the hexameter) that is repeated over and over again for thousands of lines until the performance is over, and was accompanied by a special kind of lyre. The choral songs sung to honour athletes at the Olympic games were in more fluid lyric metres than epic, but nevertheless repeated identical metrical patterns in groups of stanzas of the same shape. Songs to be sung at the symposium had their own distinct metres, including the elegiac, a two-line pattern repeated over and over again to the music of pipes. But tragedy incorporates all these metres and introduces new ones, in a dazzling display of different rhythmic patterns, as one would expect in modern musical theatre. This composite, inclusive, and variegated form is one of tragedy's most important cultural contributions.

Thinking about the reasons why individual characters sing matters because it mattered in antiquity. The musicologist Aristoxenus said that speech begins to sound like song when we are emotional (*Elements of Harmony* 1.9–10). It is thus fascinating that in *Persians*, Xerxes is never heard speaking at all. In the *Oresteia*, the first great scene by a singing actor is Cassandra's extraordinary prophetic frenzy (1072–177). In *Oedipus Tyrannus,* the protagonist does not sing until his 'blind' entrance; Pentheus never sings in *Bacchae,* a sign, perhaps, of his emotional repression, while his mother Agave moves from song in her madness to speech as she recovers sanity; for much of *Iphigenia in Aulis* male spoken rhetoric contrasts sharply with the songs of the female chorus and Iphigenia's own funeral lament, performed before her weeping mother.[25]

The music that accompanied tragedy developed over the fifth century, especially during its second half. One of the few qualitative differences between Aeschylean tragedy and later Euripidean tragedy of which we can be sure concerns the type of music the audiences would have heard. Songs in Aeschylus feature refrains and each verse (called a 'strophe', or 'turn', perhaps reflecting choral dance manoeuvres at the beginning and end of stanzas) sounds rhythmically like its partner. Performers and audience alike always knew what position had been arrived at in the overall metrical scheme. But Euripides came under the influence of an avant-garde composer named Timotheus, who composed 'stream of consciousness' solo songs which were flamboyantly performed, but without a mask, to the accompaniment of a stringed instrument called the cithara. Euripides began to insert elaborate songs of this kind—although accompanied by the *auloi* and performed by a masked actor—into his tragedies. They are asymmetrical, rhythmically 'freeform' songs of technical arduousness which demanded specialist singing actors: astrophic ('stanza-less') song severely challenges the performer's memory and expressivity, which explains why in tragedy it is usually associated with soloists rather than with the songs of the amateur chorus-men ([Aristotle], *Problemata* 19.15). See, for example, Polymestor's 'blinded' entrance aria (Euripides, *Hecuba* 1056–106, see Fig. 1.3):

> Aahh! Poor me! Where can I go,
> Where can I stay still, where can I turn?
> Crawling on my hands, following their tracks
> Like a four-footed mountain beast?
> What direction shall I turn in—this one? or that one?—
> I'm desperate to get hold of the murderous she-Trojans
> Who have annihilated me.
> Curses on you, accursed daughters of Phrygia!

FIG. 1.3. The blinded Polymestor on an Apulian vase of the later 4th century BCE, reproduced courtesy of the Trustees of the British Museum.

> What nook or cranny are you cowering in to escape me?
> O Sun-god, how I wish you could cure, cure my bleeding
>   eye-sockets,
> Take away my blindness, give me back the daylight!

Here the psychological torment and physical pain the blinded Polymestor is undergoing are expressed formally in the metrical disjointedness of his song as well as in the emotional register and alternating questions and exclamations.[26]

Polymestor is not Greek but a 'barbarian' (see below, pp. 110–16). Astrophic monodies are not the medium usually chosen for Greek men, to whom the tragedians usually allocated the 'rational' mode of communication represented by speech. Monodies are usually sung by either disturbed barbarians or self-absorbed women at moments of emotion or interiority. They involve much repetition of individual words (e.g. *Iphigenia in Aulis* 1289–90), and the distinctive feature of 'melism', where one syllable is extended over more than one note; in the parody of recent Euripidean lyric in *Frogs* (1309–64), Aristophanes had certainly identified its key idiosyncrasies. The New Music really did sound new; its practitioners were lambasted by traditionalists. Even the physical production of the voice was different. The actors had to use a much more relaxed sound; Timotheus distinguished his own beguiling vocal timbre from the out-of-date singers who 'mauled' their songs, straining and yelling with the far-ringing voices of heralds (*PMG* 791.218–20).

The voices that were heard singing the most, however, were those of each tragedy's chorus-men. We know little for certain about their selection and training, but they were amateurs who must nevertheless have developed a high level of skill in group singing and movement; in the assessment of choral singing, individual voices that stood out from the rest, however beautiful, were censured. Tragic choruses use both the singular pronoun 'I' and the plural 'we' as they shift between moods and in and out of a marked group identity. But there is no certain evidence that they ever sang in any way but collectively and in unison, despite passages where fragmentation into smaller groups or even individual voices might seem appropriate, such as their frantic self-questioning while Clytemnestra is murdering her husband in *Agamemnon* (1343–71). Nor is there any way of proving that the chorus had a recognizable leader, whose individual speaking or singing voice was ever heard in the theatre during the original productions.

The chorus in Greek tragedy is both its most distinctive feature and its greatest strength. Yet since the revival of Greek tragedy in the Renaissance, it has often been regarded as an obstacle that makes it more difficult to understand and relate to the plays. The poet Goethe, who dropped the chorus of *Iphigenia among the Taurians* altogether when he adapted it into German, said that he found the convention to be a 'burdensome tradition, useless and discordant'.[27] In our fragmented society, which places so much emphasis on individual experience and private fulfilment, the community's response to an individual family's crises may seem an 'optional extra' that can be detached from the 'core' of the play. There are certainly many examples of successful adaptations of Greek tragedy that have excised the chorus altogether. But the counterpoint between the collective and the individual perspectives on disaster was at the heart of the ancient experience of tragedy, as recent directors (especially since Karolos Koun's pathbreaking

FIG. 1.4. Theatro Technis' *Persians*, directed by Karolos Koun (1965), reproduced courtesy of the APGRD.

*Persians*; see Fig. 1.4) have begun to appreciate, and this has much to do with the context in which it was performed and the audience for which it was designed.

The chorus speaks as well as sings, and sometimes functions as an 'umpire' between warring parties in a debate (*Medea* 567–8). Sometimes it is sworn to collusive silence (*Hippolytus* 710–12). Sometimes the chorus' songs 'fill in' time while actors change roles, or 'telescope' time while events happen offstage (e.g. *Hecuba* 444–83; *Iphigenia among the Taurians* 1234–82). Often the chorus sings forms of lyric song derived from the world of collective ritual. The ancient Greeks all knew dozens of songs to be sung on certain kinds of socio-religious occasion—far, far more than the 'Auld Lang Syne', 'Happy Birthday', and 'He's a jolly good fellow' that constitute the entire personal repertoire of most twenty-first-century English persons. The tragedians could draw on a vast range of familiar religious songs that their audience knew off by heart, in what was still a lively song-culture. A choral song may be a hymn of thanksgiving, such as the ode in *Antigone* expressing gratitude to Helios, Zeus, Ares, and Dionysus for the

Theban military victory of the day before. It may be a hymn of praise, like the 'dithyrambic' hymns to Dionysus sung by his followers in *Bacchae* (e.g. 64–166, 370–431), or a 'summons' which asks for a god or gods to make their presence felt by helping to solve the problems the chorus are witnessing. The first choral ode of *Oedipus Tyrannus* summons the help of numerous gods to help rid Thebes of the plague (151–215). The hymn to Apollo was traditionally called the *paian*, and was a song of relief often performed after an illness had been cured, or a victory secured in battle: the chorus of Euripides' *Electra*, on hearing of Orestes' victory over Aegisthus, encourage her to 'dance, jumping lightly for joy, like a leaping fawn', while they raise a victory cry and perform a chorus to the sound of the *auloi* (859–65, 874–8).

Yet the tragedians created irony by fusing or contrasting joyful types of song, such as the paean or wedding song, with elements from much more sinister genres. In *Iphigenia in Aulis* the trick played on the heroine is reflected in the macabre ode which evolves from a marriage-song into a funerary lament (1036–97). One of the favourite types of choral song developed the traditional funeral dirge, and these feature in a large majority of the plays (see below, pp. 69–79). But through their 'synthetic' method, by which choruses blend elements from more than one type of ritual performance, they can fuse a song in praise of a hero's achievements with funereal grief for his demise, as the chorus of Euripides' *Heracles* lament his assumed death by recounting his labours (348–51).

Other choral songs may be rooted in a less obviously ritual way in the time of the action taking place, but likewise offer valuable contextualizing material. In the unusual first song of *Iphigenia in Aulis*, the chorus of women breathlessly catalogue the famous heroes they have been lucky enough to see assembling at Aulis for the expedition against Troy (164–302). The bellicose, brooding Greek army is a forceful unseen presence in the tragedy, and it was a brilliant stroke to present the audience with a description of the famous leaders—Ajax, Diomedes, Achilles, and so on—seen from the admiring and slightly eroticized perspective of a group of ordinary women.

Some choral odes, however, are more philosophical or contemplative in orientation, and meditate in general terms on the issues which have been explored in the concrete situation of the play's previous episode. Thus the chorus of *Antigone* concludes the scene in which Haemon tries to save his betrothed by meditating on the potentially destructive power of sexual passion (781–805). Other odes offer a series of mythical parallels to the situation developing in the play, such as the poetic catalogue of figures who have suffered enforced incarceration in the next ode in *Antigone* (944–87). Some of the most beautiful odes present a narrative functioning as a form of memory; early in *Iphigenia among the Taurians* the Greek chorus traces the curse on the heroine's family back to her ancestor Pelops (179–202), and in a lovely later ode recalls the sacking of their city (1088–152). All three tragedians excelled in this technique; the chorus' memories of the sacrifice of Iphigenia in *Agamemnon* has a dreamlike pictorial quality (see below p. 212), while in Sophocles' *Women of Trachis* the chorus relate the terrifying events of the fateful day long ago when Heracles and the river-god Achelous, in bovine form, battled over Deianira (517–24):

> Then there was the noise of rattling fists, clanging weapons,
> And butting bull's horns, all mixed together;
> Their bodies grappled at close quarters, their foreheads
> Struck deadly blows, and both of them were groaning.
> But she, so delicately lovely, sat on a distant hill,
> Awaiting her bridegroom.

The poets of Greek tragedy were astoundingly versatile. Few dramatists today can dream of producing such exquisite lyrics as well as exciting dialogue and imposing rhetoric.

## CELEBRATING DIONYSUS

With the parts to be delivered by the chorus and each of the actors in each of their roles fundamentally settled (although revisions presumably continued right up to the performance), the tragedian handed over some of the responsibility to the performers as *their* real work finally began. Through the long Athenian winter, the young men who made up the chorus trained hard, under a special *chorodidaskalos* ('chorus-trainer'), in singing and dancing the many odes—perhaps as many as fifteen or even more—that they would have to perform over the course of a tragic tetralogy in the festival competitions. They will have become increasingly nervous as the competitions approached and they had to rehearse alongside famous actors; these will often have been considerably older as well as much more experienced. The actors had to learn their lines, and since there were normally only three actors available to each tragedian, they all had to perform a number of parts. Both actors and chorus-men will have needed to rehearse with the pipe-player, meet with the costume designers and mask-makers, and learn to perform in several different masks during the course of a production.

The tragic poet himself may well have had to alter his script in consultation with actors as rehearsals progressed; the *chorēgos* will have become alarmed as the invoices for costumes, masks, and maintenance of the chorus piled up. By the time the competition actually arrived, the sense of anticipation amongst the choral performers will have been just as high as amongst their prospective audiences, which (besides the most important men in Athens and significant foreign visitors) will have included school-mates and playground enemies as well as close family and neighbours.

For the classical Greeks, dancing was so central to worship of the gods that it could symbolize the practice of religion, which in turn meant reciprocal engagement with divinity: when the chorus of Sophocles' *Oedipus Tyrannus* wonders whether Apollo's oracles are really to be trusted, they ask why they should *dance* any more (896). Greek tragedy in performance was part of a divine festival for Dionysus, and a sizeable proportion of the poetry in Greek tragedy was designed to be performed to the accompaniment of dancing, in which the god of wine and theatre took particular delight. There are a few solo songs which definitely involved choreographed movement, such as Cassandra's crazed wedding dance in *Trojan Women* (308–41), and some actors specialized in this kind of role, including Aeschylus' son Euaion. But most of the dancing was performed by the chorus, whose training ensured that they could sing with ease at the same time as they danced.

There has been a new interest in ancient dancing recently, both amongst scholars and amongst directors of performances.[28] They have been taking inspiration from ancient vase-paintings of dancers in action as well as from non-western traditions of dance theatre such as the Wali (sacred dances of Indonesia), or the Xhosa dances of South Africa, with their emphatic shoulder movements. But it must be admitted that we know distressingly little about dance in the classical period, let alone dancing in the theatre. As one dance historian has recently put it, we 'cannot recreate with assurance a single step of choreography: there was no ancient system of dance notation'.[29]

Our picture of the dancing in the theatre is one suggested only by accumulating evidence and illustrations from different sources and juxtaposing them. There are vase-paintings of dramatic choruses in action, and of scenes from plays in which the postures and gestures of some figures imply choreographed movement. Tragic choruses make suggestive references to the sun, sky, and the earth, which would make best sense if accompanied by movements in upwards or downward directions. The hands and arms are also often mentioned by choruses. In Aeschylus' *Persians*, a play about a sea-battle, Xerxes tells the chorus to 'row with their arms', as if plying the oars of a warship (1046). Although there is an unresolved debate about whether the chorus danced primarily in a circular formation or a rectangular shape echoing military drill, the poetry of choral lyric itself implies that the choreography was varied and flexible. The verb for communicating through gesture, *cheironomein*, is used in Herodotus, who is contemporary with the tragedians (6.129); it is tempting to believe that the classical Athenian chorus-men may already have deployed a wide vocabulary of hand movements signifying both objects and actions of the type that we associate, for example, with the Kathakali dancing of southern India.

The importance of dance to tragic theatre is one reason why almost all scholars assume that the genre grew out of religious ritual, although the precise type of the ritual has been contested. In one sense the debate is sterile, since we know so little about the Athens of the period which invented tragic drama in the sixth century BCE. The 'popular' tyrant Pisistratus, who ruled Athens for many years in the mid-sixth century, took control of the communal activities of warfare, building, and sacrifices, and imposed an income tax on the Athenians in order to support this programme (Thucydides 6.54.5). He was anxious to build up Athens' reputation as a cultural centre, and it is to his reign that the institution of the drama competitions in the city of Athens is traditionally dated (534 BCE). More than this we do not know, although it is quite possible that the early plays may have been much more concerned with tracing mythical genealogies for Athens and its aristocratic families than with engaging ordinary citizens—who did not yet hold the sovereign power— in political debate. It is equally possible that Pisistratus shrewdly saw that participation in the cult of Dionysus was not only popular, since this god demanded a great deal of wine and partying, but also a great leveller. Worshipping Dionysus could foster a sense of community identity that temporarily transcended class distinctions; the god's attendants, the satyrs and maenads, 'were ideally projected in myth as an undifferentiated harmonious collective'.[30]

Yet the 'origins' debate itself tells us something about the sheer complexity of the tragic medium. Because the plays involve figures who are long dead, some have proposed that tragedy grew out of ritual laments sung within hero cults at heroes' tombs. Athenian citizens certainly did perform rituals in honour of heroes such as Ajax, and there may have been some overlap in form and content between what went on in such cults and in plays about their recipients. In ancient Greece there were also 'oracles of the dead', where Athenians could go to consult a dead relation, and after undergoing the correct rituals may have been regaled with puppets or other simulacra. Waiting for the physical appearance of a long-dead hero in the theatre of Dionysus might have shared something with the psychological process of raising a ghost at an oracle of the dead.

In the mid-fourth century BCE, in his *Poetics*, Aristotle stated that both tragedy and comedy developed out of the hymns sung to Dionysus (ch. 4, 1449a 10–13). The technical term for a hymn to Dionysus is a *dithyramb*, a genre which may originally have narrated stories to do with Dionysus rather than the other gods. We have some notion of the content of dithyrambs from Euripides' *Bacchae*, where the Asiatic chorus of Dionysus' worshippers perform choral songs in the dithyrambic tradition (135–50):

What joy there is in the
Mountains, when the worshipper,
Wearing the sacred fawn-skin, falls to the ground,

While his companions run on;
He hunts for the blood of the goat that is slain, the rapturous
Devouring of raw flesh, hurrying on the mountains of Phrygia, Lydia,
The leader of Bromios' [Dionysus'] rites! *Euoi!*
The ground is flowing with milk, flowing with wine,
Flowing with the nectar of bees.
The Bacchic one, raising the blazing flame of the pine torch,
Fragrant like the smoke of Syrian frankincense,
Lets it stream from his fennel wand; with running and dancing
He spurs on stragglers, rouses them with his calls,
His soft locks rippling in the wind.

The Aristotelian connection of tragedy with Dionysus seems inherently plausible. Indeed, the earliest visual image of Tragedy personified herself, on a vase from about 440 BCE, portrays her as an elegant, well-dressed maenad, holding a cute baby hare, at a divine party held by Dionysus (see Fig. 1.5).[31] The plays continued to be performed at festivals of Dionysus, and his cult included some cross-dressing rituals that may have inspired the transvestite convention in Greek theatre. The case has been made that the key is the act of animal sacrifice, as performed within the cult of Dionysus, since so many plays involve the sacrifice-like slaughter of one human by another. At the moment of violence, similes and metaphors sometimes compare characters with crazed maenads, the traditional female attendants of Dionysus.[32]

Dionysus was the god of the vine, of viticulture, of the constructive collective drinking not only at his own festivals but at the symposia that were such an important feature of Athenian social life. Perhaps because he was the divinity who presided over the psychological and emotional changes that drinking induces, he was also the god associated with mysterious transformations. One of his own archaic *Homeric Hymns* (7.38–53) relates the myth of his escape from pirates who had abducted him in his true shape—that of a handsome youth. Dionysus first made the ship sprout vines and ivy, and then himself changed into a lion and a bear, before turning his adversaries into dolphins. It is no coincidence that it was in the context of the worship of this shape-shifting god that theatre was invented at Athens in the sixth century BCE. All performances of theatre were felt to be touched by his presence, and actors regarded

FIG. 1.5. Tragedy attends Dionysus' drinking party on an Athenian red-figure vase now in Compiègne, c.440–430 BCE. Photo reproduced courtesy of the Musée Antoine Vivenel.

him as their special patron. When professional theatre companies began touring the ancient Greek world in the third century BCE, they called themselves what else but the 'Artists of Dionysus'.

Aristotle believed that tragedy and comedy both originated in the worship of Dionysus, but from different elements within it. He said that comedy developed out of the phallic processions rather than the dithyramb (see above, pp. 23 and 49). There are some important differences between tragedy and comedy, and it is worth thinking about them here since they can throw light on what was meant by the word 'tragedy' in ancient Greece. The masks and costumes used in tragedy seem to have aimed at aesthetic beauty, whereas those in comedy were grotesque, exaggerated, and often absurd or caricatured. Other body-related elements that are central to comedy—eating, drinking, scatology, and sexual innuendo—are all avoided on stage in tragedy, and for the most part in narratives of offstage activities as well.

The relationship between the worlds created in the two genres and 'reality' was certainly different; in some ways tragedy was, paradoxically, much more realistic, since it is not a world in which frogs can sing onstage or dung-beetles can fly to Olympus. Indeed, Euripides prides himself with some justification in Aristophanes' *Frogs* on having taught the Athenians what 'actually happened' (1052). Acting styles seem to have become increasingly naturalistic during the fifth century, and one tragic actor, Callipides, became famous for his impersonations of lower-class women (see above p. 26). Nor is it a simple matter of one genre being funny and the other serious, since there are many episodes in tragedy that seem designed to produce a wry smile in the audience if not an actual belly-laugh. These include scenes with lower-class characters such as Cilissa the nurse in *Libation-Bearers* and the guard in Sophocles' *Antigone*. Some scenes involving mistaken identity are truly hilarious, above all Ion's second encounter with Xuthus in *Ion*; the middle-aged Xuthus embraces the young stranger, thinking he is his long-lost son, and Ion misunderstands entirely the reason for the attempt at physical contact (517–30). Euripides' *Helen* and *Orestes* are consistently amusing; his *Trojan Women*, perhaps the very darkest of his plays, also contains his best one-line joke, when Menelaus enquires why Hecuba is anxious for him not to transport Helen on his own ship away from Troy (1050). Has she put on weight, he asks?

The setting of the plays might help to distinguish the genres. All the tragedies are set in the past, although in the case of one of them, Aeschylus' *Persians*, it is not the very distant past. With the same exception, all the tragedies deal with mythical figures that the audiences will have known something about from other poetry, although we know that one lost tragedian, Agathon, did attempt a tragedy, entitled *Antheus*, with entirely invented new characters (Aristotle, *Poetics* ch. 9, 1451b 21). Another important difference is that the tragedies face death head-on, whereas death hardly ever occurs in comedy, and is scarcely even envisaged. Yet it is not the case that tragedy was generically obliged to end sadly, since many plays, by all three tragedians, have fundamentally upbeat endings (Aeschylus' *Eumenides*, Sophocles' *Philoctetes* and *Oedipus at Colonus*, Euripides' *Iphigenia among the Taurians*, *Helen*, and *Ion*). But perhaps the most outstanding difference between the two genres is the relationship between the people in the play and their audience.

Tragedy had a fundamentally different cognitive contract with its spectators from the one that was mutually understood in comedy. Characters in comedy are often aware of their audience, at times address them directly, and also break the 'illusion' by crossing the boundary between stage world and real world, as for example when in *Peace* the hero Trygaeus hands over the actor personifying Festival to the council members sitting on the front row of the theatre (881–908). Such an action is unthinkable in tragedy, where characters and choruses, almost without exception, do not address the audience directly.[33] They may deliver speeches and choral odes in a reflective way that assumes no listener external to their own meditative internal worlds; several Euripidean prologues strike a slightly curious note from the 'illusion' point of view, as if the character understands that their identity and whereabouts need somehow explaining. But address the audience by name or title these prologists do not.

This 'closed-off' quality of the world conjured in tragedy, which after all was thought to be set in the distant past, has not, however, prevented critics over the last two decades from seeing theatrical self-consciousness—usually labelled 'metatheatre'—in many Greek tragedies.[34] But 'metatheatre', if carefully defined, is thin on the Greek tragic ground, however fashionable it has been to identify it. Explicit metatheatre falls into five essential categories: plays within plays, generic self-reference, performed rituals, role-playing within roles, and self-conscious intertextual allusion.[35] While in Greek tragedy there are manifold examples of the performance of ritual, some of overt role-playing within roles (for example when a character appears in disguise, like Orestes in *Libation-Bearers*), and a few of indisputable intertextual allusion, the two primary types of metatheatre—plays within plays and overt generic self-reference—simply do not occur. Taplin was absolutely correct in identifying ancient Greek tragedy's lack of overt self-referentiality as one of its definitive differences from Old Comedy.[36] The quest for 'self-consciousness' is only useful insofar as it throws light on the serious and dangerous issues which are really at stake in tragedy.

No terminology which is exclusive to *theatrical* literature, poetry, or performance conventions appears in Greek tragedy. Terms for dramatic genres are never used: tragedy is not named, nor comedy, nor satyric drama. Nor are there found in tragedy the words for dramatic actor—*tragōidos* (tragic actor), *kōmōidos* (comic actor), *hupokritēs* (speaker in a drama). The word for theatre (*theatron*) does not appear, nor the theatrically specific technical terms that are found in Old Comedy referring to props, stage machinery, dance-floor (*orchēstra*), entrance routes, and even rows of audience benches.[37] The word by the fourth century used for stage (*skēnē*) means, in extant tragedy, a tent in a military encampment or at a religious festival, or a curtained caravan on wheels (Euripides, *Hecuba* 1289, *Ion* 808; Aeschylus, *Persians* 1000). The word for 'face' (*prosōpon*), which certainly by the fourth century could also mean 'mask' or '*dramatis persona*', is perhaps the best candidate for the bearing of explicit metatheatrical meaning, above all in *Bacchae*. Here the ambiguity of the term *may* have been exploited by Euripides if Pentheus' character mask was indeed used to represent his decapitated head in the Agave scene: at 1277 Cadmus asks her, 'And whose face (*prosōpon*) are you carrying in your arms, then?'[38] But the term never exclusively means 'mask', let alone 'theatrical mask' in extant Greek tragedy. The moment where arguably the material presence of the actor's mask is with most force brought to the audience's conscious attention does not involve the word *prosōpon* at all, but rather the notion of paint overlaid on a three-dimensional, sculptural image: in *Helen* the loveliest woman in the world, desired by Menelaus, Paris, and now Theoclymenus, blames her suffering on her beauty. She wishes that, as on a statue, the paint which made her lovely could be obliterated, and replaced by ugly features (262–3).

Appreciating the remoteness and elevation of the heroic world which the dramatists sought to create in their tragic dramas involves acknowledging their generic *avoidance* of overt reference to the theatre, whether as a social institution, a physical location, a material presence, or an aesthetic experience. This avoidance must result in part from a desire to avoid anachronism—the playwrights, aware of the relative newness of their medium, were staging the heroic world portrayed in epic and archaic lyric narrative, which know nothing of theatre.[37] But if the tragedians had wanted to discuss *explicitly* the role that the heroic stories they dramatized would one day play in the theatre, they could have found ways to do so. What they preferred to do was talk about music, poetry, painting, and sculpture, art forms which had preceded tragedy and which had all contributed to its total effect as a complex multi-medial form of story-telling.

The visual sign that the theatrical performer had changed his identity was in classical Athenian theatre signified by his mask. The masks were painted, and by convention most of them were beautiful to look at, in contrast with the deliberately grotesque masks of Old Comedy. Many scholars have observed the similarities between the beautiful visages of classical Greek sculpture and those of tragic characters represented in the visual arts. Like the statues contemporary with them, the facial contours of the masks worn in tragedy seem to have been softly rounded, rather than using sharp angles and planes to represent three dimensions. For a production like the original *Oresteia*, with its three tragedies plus its concluding satyr play *Proteus*, the twelve chorus-men will have required four masks each: one of an old Argive male citizen for *Agamemnon*, an Asiatic slave woman for the *Libation-Bearers*, an Erinys for *Eumenides*, and a satyr for *Proteus*. In addition to these forty-eight masks for the chorusmen, the tragedies of the *Oresteia* require a mimimum of twelve different masks, distributed between the three actors (for the watchman, Clytemnestra, a herald, Agamemnon, Cassandra, Aegisthus, Pylades, Orestes, Electra, the nurse, the priestess of Apollo at Delphi, possibly Clytemnestra's ghost (unless she retained the mask she had worn when alive), Apollo, and Athena). This is not to count the silent on-stage characters (slave women and guards in *Agamemnon*, Hermes in *Eumenides*), nor the minimum of two roles—Proteus and presumably Menelaus—for the satyr play. This means that for each tragedian at the competition, the contracted mask-maker had to provide well over sixty masks every year.

Although theatrical masks carved in stone became popular in ancient ornamental sculpture (Fig. 1.6), actors' masks needed to be much lighter in weight. They were actually made of fabric rags, soaked in plaster and dried. They came with hair attached, and may

FIG. 1.6. Marble mask of Dionysus, crowned with ivy berries (1st–2nd century CE), reproduced courtesy of the Trustees of the British Museum.

have been fixed to felt caps. Attempts by modern mask-makers to recreate examples in which it is feasible to speak, sing and dance have shown that linen soaked in plaster (the equivalent of the 'stuccoed linen' used nowadays to make medical casts to encase broken limbs), or stiffened with glue and coated with plaster, can be moulded over what is called a former (a basic convex form of the mask, made in clay or wood, which can be moulded or carved into smooth contours); alternatively, it can be built into a negative, concave mould of the former. That these procedures would have presented little challenge to the advanced ancient techniques of casting from moulds is evidenced in the mass production of pieces in terracotta and bronze.

A single former could be used repeatedly if a whole chorus needed similar masks, if one actor found a particular former produced masks that enhanced his performance and fitted comfortably, or if there was a requirement for a likeness between two individuals. A probable example occurs in Euripides' *Electra*. The old man is scrutinizing the disguised Orestes. Orestes asks Electra why he is doing so (559), 'as if examining the bright impress on a silver coin. Is he finding in me a likeness to somebody else?' But the face painted on the dried rags-plaster laminate, once dried and removed from the mould, could vary enormously in appearance. Aeschylus traditionally pioneered the use of elaborately painted, colourful masks, for example for his repulsive Erinyes, that could in themselves inspire strong reactions in spectators.

The performers of a group of plays will have needed as many costumes as masks, and more in the case of characters who change their garments in the course of a play, as the family of Heracles changes into funeral robes in *Heracles*, or Pentheus changes into the robe of a Bacchant in *Bacchae*. The costumes worn by tragic characters were usually long-sleeved, which distinguished them from the everyday wear of Athenians. This may have helped them not only to make male actors, some of whom were of considerable age, able to impersonate even young females, but also to indicate a character's status and ethnicity as well as his or her ritual standing. For example, the chariot-borne Queen in Aeschylus' *Persians* originally wears sumptuous robes that identify her as Persian royalty, but after a change of clothes later returns on foot, dressed in the simpler gown suitable for pouring a libation, to consult the spirit of her dead husband Darius at his graveside.

Hundreds of yards of beautiful textiles must have been required to equip a chorus and actors with costumes for an entire tetralogy. The descriptions of finery in the texts, and the theatre-related vase-paintings, suggest a medium where spectacular costumes were expected and relished by the audiences. Costume played a significant role in theatrical semiotics, not only as an indication of age, ethnicity, gender, and status, but in creating ironic, subversive, or ominous effects, for example when Cassandra appears dressed as a bride in *Trojan Women*. Since weaving was primarily a female activity in classical Athens, as it was in the whole Greek world, this must be one area of tragedy in which the creative efforts of women made, at one remove, a definitive contribution to the tragic productions. The sheer amount of labour at looms that was required for the shows at every City Dionysia did also, if indirectly, affect the plots of Greek tragedy, which is partial to portraying women who use cloth and clothes in lethal stratagems.[38] Clytemnestra asks Agamemnon to tread the carpets to his death (*Agamemnon* 908–13); the heroine of *Medea* sends her love rival a wedding dress anointed with a lethal drug; Deianira in Sophocles' *Women of Trachis* does the same, although involuntarily, with the ceremonial robe she sends to her husband Heracles.

Other significant props woven by women in Greek tragedy are less destructive: Orestes can recognize his adult sisters by being reminded of special items of their girlhood handiwork. Electra's weaving 'with beasts in the design' is displayed on stage in *Libation-Bearers* (231–2), and in *Iphigenia among the Taurians* Orestes proves his identity to his sister by describing her picture, woven in fine linen, of the golden lamb over which their grandfather Atreus and great-uncle Thyestes had fought; she had added a picture of the sun averting its face from the dreadful conflict (814–17). But with the discussion turning from mask and costuming strategies in tragedy to its allocation and portrayal of gender roles, it is time to turn from the equipment used by the performers to their portrayal of social issues.

# 2
# Community Identities

## GATHERINGS

Athenians loved performing together in single-sex choruses. Girls and women performed choruses at weddings (see e.g. *Iphigenia among the Taurians* 365–8) and at the parties that celebrated the birth of a child to a citizen. But boys were trained on a much more public basis to sing and dance together, both in the course of worship and in civic competitions. These collective performances were an integral part of the democratic culture: when in 405 BCE the Athenians faced defeat at the hands of the Spartans, one of the things they most feared losing was their distinctive public choruses (Aristophanes, *Frogs* 1420). Two years later, when the city was enduring the reign of terror of the so-called Thirty Tyrants at the end of the Peloponnesian War, the prominent democrats of Athens were in exile. They raised an army and won a victory, after which their spokesman Cleocritus addressed the defeated aristocrats in a speech which shows how the shared experience of public activities lay at the heart of the Athenians' sense of group identity (Xenophon, *Hellenica* 2.4.20):

Fellow citizens, why are you keeping us out of Athens? Why do you seek our deaths? For we have never done you any harm. We have taken part alongside you in the most hallowed rituals and sacrifices, and in the finest festivals. We have been your co-dancers in choruses and co-students, as well as your co-soldiers. We have been in dangerous situations with you on both land and sea in defence of our mutual security and freedom.

Joint participation in festivals such as the City Dionysia, and performing together in choruses, are thus seen as two of the primary activities which create intense bonds between the citizens that no civil war should ever jeopardize. Cleocritus' speech proved effective, and the democracy was soon restored. He had the advantage of a beautiful speaking voice and was already known to the citizens as the herald who made announcements during the rituals at the Eleusinian Mysteries, a ceremonial role which will have lent him public authority. In Athens, therefore, politics, military training, religion, and choral performance, the last two categories of which are inseparable from the drama competitions, were interlinked as *community* activities.

Gatherings of citizens took place often and routinely, usually in the open air, as at the theatre of Dionysus. These gatherings were an essential social mechanism in shaping group opinion. In his *Republic*, Plato makes Socrates describe the Athenians thus: 'they sit down together in the assemblies or the law courts, or the theatres or camps ... and proceed with great noise to find fault with some of the things that are being said or done and to praise others' (6.492b 5–c 1). The noise included shouting and booing, wolf-whistling, cat-calling, hissing, heel-drumming, and hand-clapping. Such noises were regarded by Plato as having been taken to such extremes in the drama competitions that they had established over the poets a 'dictatorship of the spectatorship' (*theatrokratia*, *Laws* 3.701a 3). For besides the festivals of Dionysus, there was a considerable number of collective events in which the citizens participated, and in which they made an enormous amount of noise.

The gathering about which least is known is actually meeting to hear speech-making in military camps (see below, pp. 109–10). In terms of religious festivals, the only one at Athens more important than the City Dionysia was the Panathenaea, held in summer every year, with an especially major celebration every fourth year. Like the Dionysia, the Panathenaea was an occasion on which the whole city would have been inundated with visitors from other Greek city-states, and featured spectacular ceremonies in Athena's honour. But it also offered the opportunity to watch a variety of competitive events in athletics and music, including the performance of choruses and above all the rendition of the great Homeric epics by some of the most distinguished rhapsodes in Greece. It is no coincidence that theatre was invented in Athens in the sixth century under the 'popular tyrant' Pisistratus at the same time that the city was first enjoying regular, formal recitals of Homer at public festivals; the *Iliad* lies behind the popularity of episodes from the Trojan war in tragedy, and the *Odyssey*'s fascination with disguise and role-playing must have proved a stimulus to the new art of theatrical imitation.[1]

Many other, local festivals and Attic rituals are mentioned in tragedy, as we shall see in the discussions of individual plays, including the Eleusinian Mysteries at which the ardent democrat Cleocritus performed the role of Herald; the sanctuary of Demeter and Persephone at Eleusis is the setting for Euripides' *Suppliant Women*. But the religious life of the Athenians also included long-distance travel to attend the major Panhellenic cult centres elsewhere in Greece. In *Women of Trachis* an important oracle was produced by the sacred oak trees at the sanctuary of Zeus in Dodona in north-west Greece. The cult of Hera at Perachora in the Gulf of Corinth is Medea's next destination at the conclusion of Euripides' *Medea*. It took Athenian citizens five or six days to get to Zeus' great sanctuary at Olympia, one of the major sites of ancient athletics, and imagery from several events—wrestling, boxing, running and chariot-racing—appears in Greek tragedy. Indeed, one of our best sources of information about chariot racing is the exciting messenger speech in Sophocles' *Electra*, which (although entirely false) recounts in detail how Orestes died in an accident during a race competing with other charioteers at the games for Apollo at Delphi (720–30):

> Keeping his horses near the pillar at the end,
> Each time he grazed the post; giving his right-hand trace horses room
> He tried to block off his pursuer.
> At first they had all stood upright in their chariots,
> But then the hard-mouthed colts of the competitor from Aenia
> Carried him on despite his resistance. At the turn
> Between the sixth and the seventh rounds
> They smashed their foreheads against the chariot from Barce ...
> And then the whole plain was filled with the wreckage of chariots.

But it is the actual oracle of Apollo at Delphi, rather than the races held there in his honour, that dominates the theology of several plays (notably those about Oedipus and Orestes), and provides the backdrop of the first part of *Eumenides* and all of Euripides' *Ion*. In both these plays an important role is played by the august Pythian priestess herself, who sat on the tripod absorbing the vapours that became transformed into Apollo's cryptic oracles.

In *Eumenides*, the moves and counter-moves by prosecutor and defendant in the trial of Orestes are likened to a series of throws and holds in a wrestling match (589). A legal interrogation, compared to moves in an athletics contest, is thus enacted in the poetic dialogue of a drama. The fusion of these three activities seemed natural to an audience in classical Athens, where a similar shape and overall character characterized court cases, athletics competitions, and drama festivals. They had all developed out of the tradition of the aristocratic competition, the *agōn*. The shape of the actual trial was reminiscent of a social drama in which both defendant and prosecutor learned roles, and enacted a competition in front of the democratically selected jurors, who were equivalent either to the listening, responsive chorus, or to the audience.[2]

In crime, and what to do with the criminal, dramatic contests shared their subject-matter, up to a point, with legal trials. The dramatist and the writer of legal speeches each had to create convincing roles to be played by the major players; law-court roles needed to be believable in terms of each individual's family history, just as in tragedy the hero's parentage and ancestry could be a decisive factor in his presentation. The main difference between drama and the law is that, for the courts, two different authors usually wrote the scripts—the two leading litigant's separate but interacting 'parts'— instead of one. It is not surprising that Greek tragedy had a close and complicated relationship with the law, intriguingly indicated by the fact that the word for actor—*hupokritēs*, from which we derive the word *hypocrite*—means both an actor and a respondent in a trial. Some ancient Greek tragedies actually include trials. The lost plays of Aeschylus' tetralogic *Danaids* included a trial at Argos, and Orestes is tried onstage in Aeschylus' *Eumenides* as well as off it in Euripides' *Orestes*. In the contemporary world, trials that are televised—like the notorious trial of O. J. Simpson in 1995—still raise questions about where reality ends and fiction and entertainment begin. Scholars have long recognized the impact on ancient Athenian drama made by the development, under the democracy, of legal language, concepts, and procedure, and especially by the advent of the teachers of rhetoric.

Trials and tragedies shared formal aspects, such as performance in the open air, since litigants in murder cases were required to plead their cases under the sky. Jurors seem to have taken their seats, as they did at the theatre, in rows at varying distances from the rostra (Dem. 43.18). By the end of the trial the platform might become crowded, as could the tragic stage. Political allies were often introduced in large numbers to vouch for their performer's good name; it was also customary to arrange one's family, especially children, on the platform in a social display (see e.g. Demosthenes 21.99, Aeschines 2.152). Failure to produce family members, just as in today's North American presidential campaigns, could cast doubt on the unity of one's household. Interestingly it is a tragedy, and an early one, which best describes the demeanour suitable for children soliciting social approval and sympathy from the platform. When in Aeschylus' *Suppliants* the asylum-seeking Danaids are about to supplicate Pelasgus, their father instructs them to look modest, piteous, and humble, and to speak the kind of words that elicit pity and that are mild and succinct (191–203).

Politically speaking, the most important gathering of the Athenians was that of the *dēmos*, the sovereign body, at the Assembly (*Ekklēsia*) itself. These meetings were held on the Pnyx Hill not far from the theatre, where the citizens deliberated and voted, after listening directly to some of the most famous statesmen in ancient history: Pericles, Nicias, Cleon, Alcibiades, and almost certainly Sophocles himself. There was a sense of competition in terms of oratorical performance; Demosthenes compares the assessment of an orator's skill with the judgements passed on playwrights, choruses, and athletes (18.318–19). There are several episodes in tragedy that reflect the proceedings in the Athenian Assembly more or less directly. Theseus consults his people in Sophocles' *Oedipus at Colonus*, and in Euripides' *Orestes* the parliament at Argos that votes to execute the hero is clearly modelled on the Athenian Assembly.

The tragedians' interest in the psychology of decision-making was also fed, indirectly, by the real-life experience of deliberation undergone by their Athenian citizen spectators in the Assembly and the Council. It was the Council (*Boulē*) where the hard work was really done. In the theatre of Dionysus, the most privileged front-row seats were bestowed on the members of the *Boulē*, most accurately translated as the 'Deliberatory'; it was on this committee that selected citizens deliberated for long hours on policy. The work done in the Council is the aspect of the Athenian political system that has most relevance to tragedy, which repeatedly stages or describes scenes of decision-making—should the Argives grant asylum to the Danaids? Should Agamemnon revoke the order to execute Iphigenia? Sitting on the Council was seen as the highly responsible form of service to the state that it certainly was. Men had to be in their thirtieth year in order to serve on the Council (Xenophon, *Memorabililia* 1.2.35),[3] and it seems that in practice men over fifty years old were given some precedence by the herald in the queue of men wanting to address the Athenian Assembly (see e.g. Aeschines, *Against Timarchus* 23, 49).

Deliberation means the entire process of giving and receiving advice, acquiring information, weighing up alternatives, and decision-taking. It is part of what Aristotle insists is the third most important constituent of tragic drama (preceded only by plot and character), namely the representation of 'intellectual activity' (*dianoia*), which he says is associated with both a political sense and with rhetoric (*Poetics* ch. 6, 1450b 6–8). Its importance in terms of the decisions made by the city is underlined by the speed with which the oligarchs who took power in 411 ousted the democratically elected Council, and even took over the building where the people's councillors had met to serve as their own centre of power.[4] The *Boulē* required no fewer than five hundred citizens to serve, proportionately selected from each deme. From the mid-fifth century, or even earlier, they were replaced every year, by lot:[5] at any one time it 'could thus have contained a fair cross-section of the citizen body'.[6] Since no man could serve more than twice in his life (*Athenian Constitution* 62.3), the chances that any particular citizen would serve at some point in his life (once he had reached the qualifying age) must have been high, especially after pay was instituted in the later fifth century to encourage poorer citizens to participate.[7] The Council met almost every day (Xenophon, *Hellenica* 2.3.11), and it considered matters relating not only to the state's finances and the scrutiny of magistrates, but the Athenian cults, festivals, navy, building programme, and care for the sick, disabled, and orphaned. To serve as a councillor required accumulating information, assessing past actions and deliberating about future ones *virtually all day, every day*. The 'quality of attention' required by service on the Council seems breathtaking compared with what is today required of politicians, let alone ordinary citizens.

Greek tragedy offers a training in decision-making. From the Persian Queen's request for advice from her elders on how she should react to her dream and the omen she has seen in *Persians* (179–245), to Iphigenia's articulation of her (limited) alternatives (i.e. whether to die willingly or unwillingly) in *Iphigenia in Aulis*, the corpus of fifth-century tragedies offers many characters engaged in deliberation, both in soliloquy and in dialogue. Aeschylean characters deliberate less than those in the other two tragedians, since his characters are more 'embedded' in the actions represented in his dramas, and their fates more 'externally' determined;[8] this implies that the representation of deliberation in tragedy became more sophisticated and extensive in parallel with the development of deliberation by citizens in the Council and Assembly. Euripides seems to have been interested in how rhetoric, where the impulse to control 'how things seem' supersedes the impulse to discover truth, can interfere with good deliberation and persuade people into immoral actions. But deliberation as a mental *process* seems to have been most important to Sophocles, the only tragedian amongst the 'big three' who himself held important public offices. At least one crisis in most of his extant tragedies is precipitated by the inability of a character in a quandary to listen to good counsel, to discount bad, or simply to spend sufficient time considering potential outcomes: Oedipus fails to hear Tiresias, neither Ajax nor the Atridae demonstrate much ability to anticipate the consequences of their actions, and Creon substitutes bluster for deliberation when faced with cogent arguments framed by both Antigone and Haemon.

Indeed, in Greek tragedy, there are few wholly competent deliberators: the scene where Aethra advises Theseus in Euripides' *Suppliant Women* is an outstanding counter-example (286–364). Most deliberation scenes are compromised by facile prejudice or strong emotion, but some do, if only in passing, reveal sophisticated distinctions between knowledge and opinion, advanced reasoning from precedent, or careful assessments of likelihood. But, as Thucydides' Athenian general Nicias realizes, the trouble is that although it is incumbent upon citizens to deliberate extensively, it is ultimately more important that they enjoy good luck (6.23.3). The need to have good luck as well as to practise expert deliberation becomes apparent to many tragic protagonists. No amount of even the best possible deliberation could prevent a man from suffering the sort of bad luck that afflicted Philoctetes or Oedipus. Yet it is certainly up for discussion whether more effective deliberation could have prevented Agamemnon from sacrificing Iphigenia at Aulis, or Deianira from sending the robe in *Women of Trachis*, just as it might have prevented Creon from refusing to listen to his niece and son in *Antigone*.

Women deliberate just as much, if not more, than men in Greek tragedy. In the imagination of a community, feminine figures can play symbolic roles that differ from the roles allocated to them in daily life. Within a particular society, the representation of female minds sometimes has more to say about 'referred' or displaced class identity than about the contingent views on gender. The eighteenth century's dominant ideal of femininity, with its emphasis on feeling and morality, for example, was a powerful factor in establishing a more general middle-class identity. The emergence of female-dominated sentimental literature at that time really demonstrated 'an evolution of a particular ideological construction of a new class identity, displaced into a discussion of female virtue'.[9] Perhaps the female deliberators in Greek tragedy might be 'referred' or displaced democratic subjectivities. They are part of what Pat Easterling has called Greek tragedy's 'heroic vagueness', the special idiom created by settings in the distant past and elevated poetic language, which 'enabled problematic questions to be addressed without overt divisiveness' and certainly without creating an artform in which 'hard questions are avoided or made comfortable because expressed in these glamorous and dignified terms'.[10]

If a performance of tragedy is considered as a site where the Athenian democratic subject flexed his intellectual muscles, figures such as Creusa in *Ion* or Deianira in *Women of Trachis* could be seen as mythical surrogates of the civic agent receiving advice, attempting to deliberate, and coming to a decision. This proposition stands even if the issue that the woman is deliberating is not so transparently political as, for example, whether or not a man perceived as a traitor should be given a burial (the issue in *Ajax* and *Antigone*). There have been some excellent challenges published recently to the idea that there was anything fundamentally 'democratic' about tragedy as an art-form, since it originated in Athens before the democracy was established, and since many of the political concepts it examines are also pertinent to other, undemocratic, city-states.[11] But the focus on deliberation, entailing audience scrutiny of characters who are deliberating about action, constitutes an important way in which Athenian tragedy was certainly 'to do with' the democracy: in the tyrant Pisistratus' day the characters in tragedy may indeed have deliberated, but the audience that watched them was not yet the body with decision-making and executive powers—that was Pisistratus himself.

The relevance of democratic deliberation to tragedy is conveyed by Thucydides in the several scenes in which he describes the citizens being led by emotions to take precipitate decisions in the Assembly, with life-or-death consequences. These accounts underline how the Athenians acquired for themselves the name of 'mind-changers' and 'hasty deciders' (Aristophanes, *Acharnians* 632, 630), and why they quoted (although did not obey) the proverbial saying that it was best to 'deliberate at night'—that is, take one's time over a difficult decision and 'sleep on it'.[12] Indeed, in the second debate on Mytilene in the mid-420s, the statesman Diodotus opened his response to the bellicose Cleon with the famous statement that the two things most inimical to good counsel are speed and passion (Thucydides 3.42.1). Since they were not characters in a tragedy, on this occasion the Athenians did, fortunately, have the chance to 'deliberate at night'. Diodotus' reproof was delivered one day after the Athenians had taken an outrageously hasty decision to slaughter the entire male population of the city of Mytilene on the island of Lesbos, and within hours had sent a trireme sailing off over the Aegean to carry out the mass execution. The extreme volatility of the *dēmos*' temper is shown by what happened the next morning: after 'a sudden change of heart', they called a second Assembly. At the end of the second debate, which was of extreme intensity, they voted—narrowly—to rescind the measure taken the day before, and managed, more by good luck than good deliberation, to get a second ship to Lesbos in the very nick of time (Thucydides 3.49).

The Athenians here deliberated badly but enjoyed good luck: most tragic decision-makers deliberate badly but suffer *bad* luck. Greek tragedy could theoretically have pursued a different route in which good deliberators suffered solely—and therefore more unfairly—on account of ill fortune, like Job in the Old Testament. But that did not happen. The Greek tragedians seem to have chosen, by and large, to opt for bad deliberators meeting bad luck, or, rather, for deliberators who are put in a position which *through pressure of time and emotion* makes the incompetence of deliberations inevitable. The pressure of time is often expressed through imagery placing the deliberator on the edge of a razor, or in the pan of a set of scales, which are not comfortable places from which to review alternatives thoroughly (see e.g. *Antigone* 996, *Women of Trachis* 82).

Clytemnestra in *Agamemnon* is relatively unusual in that she has been planning her revenge for many years. Most tragic characters act much more precipitately. How many of them take or are offered the opportunity to deliberate without haste, passion, or at night? The answer must be, 'scarcely any'. Tragedy may, in fact, in some cases contrast the sensible decisions to which deliberators have come during protracted night-time thought and those that they take precipitately within the timescale of the play's action. Phaedra's great monologue in *Hippolytus* is an example: a lengthy process of deliberation in the long watches of the night has allowed her to understand why people are not always able to carry out what they know is right, and also has helped her to arrive at the view that the best course of action entails silence and self-control (Euripides, *Hippolytus* 373–99). It is only the intolerable stress which Aphrodite has imposed on her that has now made her resolve on death as 'the most effective plan' (403).

The proverb 'deliberate at night' also illuminates the normal practice of Greek tragic dramaturgy to confine the time enacted to less than a single day, the notorious 'unity of time' that has had such an extraordinary effect on western drama—and literature more widely—ever since. Although there are some signs of attempts to compress significant actions into single revolutions of the sun in Homeric epic, the mysterious origins of the distinctive temporal unity of ancient tragic drama have never been properly explained. The idea that deliberators ideally need to sleep on their decisions may at least explain why the compressed temporal dimensions of tragic theatre proved so long-standing a convention.

The vision of the world implicit in Greek tragedy suggests that there is much about human life that cannot be controlled even by the most competent of deliberators. But it would be incorrect to say that this vision is fatalistic. It entails deliberators failing to take the most obvious precautions and establish the most crucial facts through enquiry, as well as failing to consult relevant parties and allow time to calibrate likelihood. These failings allow a fissure to open up in the action suggesting that, with more careful thought, many of the great catastrophes of myth could have been averted even at the last minute, or, at the least, their consequences in terms of collateral damage ameliorated. The democratic sense of authority—that the Athenians had seized control of their own destiny—thus manifests itself, however highly mediated by the vocabulary of myth and the form and sensibility of tragic drama, even when tragic characters deliberate disastrously and take their mistaken decisions. Greek tragedy may be metaphysically pessimistic, but it is, socio-politically speaking, suggestive of a self-confident, optimistic, and morally autonomous Athenian democratic subject.

## DEALING WITH DEATH

At a tense moment in the earliest extant tragedy, Aeschylus' *Persians*, the Queen of Persia and her chorus of counsellors need to take a decision on how to react to the news from Salamis, and so they summon up a ghost from the Underworld. They intend to consult her husband and their previous king, Darius. By pouring a libation, scratching and drumming at the earth until it resounds, and singing a long wailing hymn full of inarticulate noises, invocations, and appeals to the Underworld gods to release Darius' spirit, they succeed in talking directly to the dead man. The actor playing Darius appears from below in regal finery, perhaps having lain concealed in a stage tomb or perhaps through a trapdoor, but certainly amidst a cloud of mist (see Fig. 2.1). We should not underestimate the inventiveness of the special effects department in the ancient theatre. But the reason the chorus gives for the presence of that sinister 'Stygian mist' is that 'all our young men have recently perished' (667–70). The waters of the Styx, the river that divides the world of the living from the world of the dead, have recently been disturbed by an unprecedented number of new arrivals.

There are two further ghosts who appear in the plays (see above, p. 2), and numerous other rituals performed to honour the recently deceased or propitiate the long departed. Many plays contain a messenger speech in which a death is described; many others display at least one corpse to public view. Talking to (and about) the dead was a constant activity in Greek tragedy, which is rooted in death and dying as no other artistic medium. Even the Homeric *Iliad*, which is fundamentally an aesthetic evocation of the death of

FIG. 2.1. George Romney's illustration of the ghost scene in *Persians* (1778–9). Photo reproduced courtesy of the Walker Art Gallery, Liverpool.

handsome warriors on the battlefield, contains nowhere near as varied and as vivid accounts of killing, suicide, death throes, accidental death, death rites, funerals, spectres, and dialogues with the departed.

Some people must have died on their own in the ancient Greek world, and the deaths of even more—especially slaves—will have gone virtually unremarked and unlamented. But what happens when someone dies in tragic theatre is a series of responses, from the other characters in the drama, the community represented by the chorus, and the external audience in the theatre. It is not Death as any abstract principle or ontological state that fascinated the Greek tragedians, but how a particular death or deaths is experienced by the victim, the killer (if there is one), the bereaved, and the wider community. The tragedies ask what goes through the head of someone who knows they are about to die, and how do they express it? What does a dead body look like before it is prepared for burial, and what rites are due to it? How does a death impact subsequently on the surviving individuals and community? Can the powerful emotions of despair and rage be contained and channelled in constructive group activity? How can the sudden rupture in the social fabric be healed? What rituals or language, private or public, can ever be appropriate to the shocking murder of the innocent, for example Heracles' slaughter of his children in *Heracles* by Euripides, which makes the appalled chorus wonder what honorific dance for Hades they can possibly perform (1027)? Why can some of the dead rest in some kind of peace, while others wander the world of the living, seeking retribution? What role do the dead play in the consciousness of the living and in the creation of social memory?

The description of fatal violence is often entrusted to a messenger, such the account in *Bacchae* of the gruesome death of Pentheus, torn to pieces on the mountains. But the artistic representation of the physical processes undergone by a victim of violent death offered great potential to the Greek tragedians, who had visual and musical as well as poetic resources, and a variety of voiced agents on whom to call—the victim, the killer, the witness, the next-of-kin and the dependants and subjects. The screams of the dying Heracles, being eaten alive by skin-devouring toxins, echo around

FIG. 2.2. The scholar Jane Ellen Harrison as Alcestis in an Oxford production (1887), reproduced courtesy of the APGRD.

the theatre in *Women of Trachis*. Euripides' Alcestis (see Fig. 2.2) slips into unconsciousness, surrounded by her children and husband, as Death—who has, uniquely in tragedy, himself physically appeared in the opening dialogue of the play—abducts her soul by mysterious means. Medea's children call for help from backstage as their mother assaults them with a deadly weapon in Euripides' *Medea*. The dreadful chariot crash of his *Hippolytus*, caused near the sea by the panic of his horses at the supernatural bull that Poseidon sends from underwater, is described in horrific detail by his attendant (1235–9):

> The wheels and axle-pins were hurtled skywards
> And the poor miserable man himself, entangled in the reins,
> Tied up in a knot that could not be undone, was dragged along.
> He smashed his poor head against the rocks,
> Tearing his flesh, as he shouted things terrible to hear.

Hippolytus' suffering is far from over (see Fig. 2.3). He is carried back to the palace, where the audience see his 'fair hair and young

FIG. 2.3. *The Death of Hippolytus* by Lawrence Alma-Tadema (1860).

flesh all mangled' (1343–4) and he writhes in agony. They know that death is imminent when he says that he can actually see the gates of the Underworld (1447).

Yet many of those whose deaths are portrayed in the war-torn world of Greek tragedy die on the battlefield. Descriptions of death in combat occupy a great deal of Aeschylus' *Persians*, and his *Seven against Thebes* is the earliest of several plays which bring war dead—the corpses of Eteocles and Polynices—into the theatrical space to be lamented. The burial of war dead is the fundamental issue at stake in Euripides' *Suppliant Women* as well as, more obliquely, in *Antigone*. This reflects a major concern in ancient Greek life, where there was in the later fifth century a distressing breakdown in the protocol that after battle the dead should be returned to their own side and treated with respect. This led to incidents such as the aftermath of the battle of Delium in 424 BCE, when the Boeotians refused to return the Athenian bodies during negotiations that lasted for nearly three weeks, while the bodies putrefied. Such negotiations were conducted through heralds, figures granted inviolability in enemy territory, whose importance is reflected in several scenes of diplomacy in tragedy.[13]

During the decades when the surviving Greek tragedies were composed, the people of Athens annually conducted ceremonies in honour of the war dead at a public funeral, financed by the state and held in mid-winter. This gathering fleetingly created a real community identity which more closely resembled the one imagined in tragedy than most of the Athenian public gatherings, since the state funeral officially included women and resident foreigners in its rites. Indeed, it was perhaps the only occasion in the civic calendar when women were officially exposed to extended oratory by a statesman, and its importance in terms of the creation of group identity for the whole state can therefore scarcely be overestimated.

Three days before the ceremony and the oration, the bones of the dead were laid out in a special tent (probably erected in the marketplace), and their kin came to pay their respects and bestow offerings upon them. On the third day the people of the city gathered for a funeral procession bearing the bones in cypress coffins, one for each tribe, with an additional, empty coffin to represent the unrecovered bodies of the missing. The procession was open to all citizens, resident foreigners, and women, the traditional performers of sung lament. The procession wound its way to the city gate and out into the cemetery in the 'most beautiful' part of the city, the Kerameikos, where the bones were interred in the public sepulchre. A statesman chosen for the his high moral reputation and beautiful voice delivered the speech that served as the collective farewell to the dead and manifesto for the living, praising the city, the principles for which the dead had sacrificed their lives, and offering some comfort to the bereaved.

The experience of the public funeral and its associated patriotic oration exerted a considerable influence on tragedy, where death on the battlefield is a constant theme, and funeral processions and rites, both for dead soldiers and civilians, provide a recurring source of conflict, spectacle, and pathos. But the world portrayed in tragedy, which is chronologically set hundreds of years before the Athenian public funerals, still presents the lamentation for the dead as a primarily female activity, and is unafraid to show women rending their clothes, gouging their cheeks, and beating their breasts in despair. In reality, legislation had been passed in the sixth century which curtailed excessive practices of self-mutilation and other displays of grief by women, probably to prevent aristocratic families competing with each other in expenditure on funerals. The earliest surviving Athenian oration from a public funeral, delivered by Pericles at the end of the first year of the Peloponnesian War, sternly enjoins the women of the city to control their lamentations and keep quiet, and remember that the greatest glory of a woman is not to be mentioned in public at all (Thucydides 2.45). But tragedy allowed the men of Athens collectively to watch old-fashioned ritual dirges of untrammelled wildness and intensity.[14]

The obligation to ensure the proper conduct of non-state funeral rites for private individuals, in any case, continued to fall on their close male kin, ideally on a son who was also the legitimate heir. Harsh criticism was incurred by sons, both natural and adopted, who shirked this responsibility;[15] spectators at Greek tragedies will have scrutinized each funeral portrayed to see whether such a son was available for the dying hero or heroine, as Hyllus is able to oversee his father's death rites in Sophocles' *Women of Trachis*, and in his *Ajax* the hero's half-brother Teucer ensures that Ajax's son, although still a small child, is present to honour his dead father. In Euripides' *Suppliant Women*, which enacts funeral rites in considerable detail, the sons of the slain are present alongside the aged mothers at the funeral.[16] But in the distorted, dysfunctional world of tragedy, there is often no son available to take care of an individual's obsequies, which heightens the sense of gloom and disorder. Agamemnon in the *Oresteia* has received no proper funeral, and Antigone is forced to take the initiative with respect to Polynices' corpse because he has no living male relative to take responsibility.

The staging of death and funerals in Greek tragedy must have conformed, to an extent, with standard practice. Where the action involves noticeable deviations from expected procedures, it must have generated additional meanings that would be picked up at some level by the audience. In a private funeral under normal conditions, the body would be bathed, perfumed, and dressed in special robes, which were traditionally white, and crowned with a wreath of foliage or gold. Cleansing and making the body presentable were duties that fell by ancient custom on the women of the family, in preparation for its display on a couch to other relatives and friends. This wake or *prothesis* ('laying-out ceremony') is regularly denied to the bloodied, disfigured corpses of murder victims in Greek tragedy, who may be exposed to the public view without being touched by any female next-of-kin, nor dressed in fresh garments. Under normal circumstances, precautions would be taken to protect participants in the wake from the pollution that death caused, including a jar of water standing at the door for sprinkling purposes, but in tragedy pollution is often the last thing on the minds of murderers or the bereaved.

The real-world wake entailed the bereaved assembling around the corpse and mourning it with loud laments and wailing, although extremities of self-mutilation were discouraged at Athens, where the law also dictated that the *prothesis* had to take place indoors. This, again, must have made the extreme mourning rituals performed in public spaces within the world of tragedy seem all the more jarring and discordant. In the case of a real-world death, the funeral itself, which was called the *ekphora* ('carrying out'), took place the next day, usually soon after dawn. The people in the mourning procession that accompanied the bier wore dark clothes, and sometimes cut their hair or shaved their heads; the men traditionally led the way. The funeral was followed by a private family meal, and further ritual visits to the tomb on the third, ninth, and thirtieth days after the interment.

Greek tragedy teems with death rituals. In Euripides' *Trojan Women*, the different ways in which the untimely deaths of Polyxena and subsequently Astyanax are treated are crucial to the shifting emotional landscape of the play. Hecuba and the other widows focus almost entirely on their individual grief and terror at their separate futures as slaves in the earlier scenes. But soon the chorus begins to identify their collective grief at the destruction of their whole community as a joint emotional focus; in a desolate song they dwell on the mental picture of the children of Troy clinging to their mothers' robes as the city was invaded (557–9). At this point the captive Andromache appears on a wagon, surrounded by the weapons of her dead husband Hector, with her little child Astyanax in her arms. She has been awarded to Neoptolemus, the son of her husband's killer. In this agonizing scene Astyanax is taken from her to be executed. But Andromache also has news for Hecuba: she saw the corpse of Polyxena, who had been sacrificed by the Greeks, and managed 'to cover it with robes and lament it' (627). Polyxena's body had apparently been left shockingly exposed, but Andromache has at least performed actions representing in a rudimentary way both the traditional preparation of the corpse by female family members, and the *prothesis*. For most of the Trojan dead, there are apparently to be no funeral rites at all. It is implied that many corpses are exposed as carrion (599–600).[17]

The funeral rites for Astyanax therefore have immense symbolic value, since they are surrogates not only for the mourning of both Hecuba and the community for Polyxena, but also for all their Trojan dead, and indeed for their living children from whom they are to be separated forever as they go off to their different fates in slavery (1089–99). How the corpse of Astyanax is treated becomes a matter of overwhelming emotional significance. This is Troy's sole chance to see a body properly tended and to create, one last fleeting time, the group solidarity and consolation that death rites offered. The body arrives from the direction of the Greek fleet, with or already on Hector's shield. Andromache has been unable to bury it herself, since Neoptolemus' fleet has set sail, but the body has already been washed for burial in the river Scamander, and Talthybius is making sure that a grave is dug.

Under pressure of time, with the moment for the fleet to depart pressing ever closer, Hecuba takes the boy's body in her arms and delivers an unexpectedly formal speech to him in her capacity as his closest available next-of-kin (see Fig. 2.4). Some of this consists of rhetorical assaults on his killers and regrets for the shortness of his life and for the perversion of the natural order by which the grandchild should bury the grandparent. But Hecuba also lingers on parts of his body, his head, hands, and mouth (1173–86), noticing resemblances to her dead son (also the boy's father), Hector. The warrior is represented symbolically by his shield, on which the boy is at some point placed. The shield itself bears the physical marks of the beloved man—the grooves in the arm-band where his fingers had gripped, and the sweat on the rim where his beard had brushed (1194–9). Through the evocation of parts of his body, Hecuba seems to be preparing her son for burial at the same time as she prepares her grandson.

After this address, Hecuba tells her women to fetch what adornment they can muster in order to array the little corpse, and then makes the final preparations for burial. She dresses the body in Trojan robes that are not specifically funeral robes, although the customary wreaths are provided for both him and his father's shield. She and the chorus then perform a short antiphonal lament, during which she attempts to dress the disfiguring injuries and make the body decent for interment. Astyanax's funeral, however makeshift and terribly rushed, does at least allow Hecuba and the women of Troy to recreate, one last time, their joint identity as wives of Trojan men, symbolized by Hector's shield, and mothers of Trojan children.

In almost all Greek tragedies, there is something 'not quite right' about the way the dead are treated, and the dysfunctional rituals underline and crystallize, on a theatrical and symbolic level, the dysfunctional nature of the family of the deceased. In the *Oresteia*, for example, Aeschylus uses the perversion of death ritual not only to signify the problems in the family of Atreus, but instrumentally in ways that advance the dramatic action and emotional development. The chorus of the *Agamemnon* already see that by killing her own

FIG. 2.4. Sybil Thorndike as Hecuba in *Trojan Women*, c.1919, reproduced courtesy of the APGRD.

husband, who has no non-hostile male relative left in Argos to take responsibility for his funeral, Clytemnestra may, scandalously, be depriving him of funeral rites altogether (1541–50). In the great scene sung by Electra, Orestes, and the chorus in *Libation-Bearers*, emotions are aroused by lingering on the neglect suffered by Agamemnon's corpse. It had not been prepared for burial by the customary rites, but had its extremities cut off and hung beneath the armpits (439); this form of emasculation was designed to neutralize Agamemnon's power to seek vengeance through a living surrogate.

There was clearly no orthodox mourning of his death by family and friends, since Orestes was absent, Electra was locked up in the house (444–9), and the citizens of Argos were not permitted to attend the funeral and perform laments (430–3). The lamentation continues for so long now because it has never previously reached its proper consummation in the collective mourning of Agamemnon's death by his close kin and friends. The shape of the collective that engages in the funeral rites, under normal circumstances, would define the shape of the future household and its relationships within the community. This never happened in Agamemnon's household. The household can only 'regroup' now, with the belated sequence of concentrated mourning by Agamemnon's true male heir, Orestes, by his female kin, represented by Electra, and the wider household and friends, represented by the chorus.[18]

Yet the great *kommos* (sung dialogue) between the mourners evolves into a vengeance catechism, a psychological preparation for reciprocal violence. One of the features of the lament for the victims of violence in traditional societies has always been to define the death as unjust and untimely, and to transform grief into concentrated rage. When the lament is repeatedly performed over a period of time, as Electra has sung her dirges for a decade and more, it functions to keep alive the memory of the deceased and the wrathful emotions until such time as the killing is avenged. Until recent times, such laments could still be heard and recorded in remote parts of Mediterranean culture. The role of 'memory keeper' for a dead man through performance of lament is indeed traditionally taken by women, his surviving dependants. The enormous amount of lamentation in Greek tragedy is partly a function of the prevalence of revenge as a motive for action—usually further, reciprocal violence.

The Greek word for 'revenge' is very close to the Greek for 'return a favour' and the idea of *reciprocity*, whether it took the form of exchanged acts of violence or exchanged good turns, was fundamental to the fifth-century Greeks' understanding of history and of human relationships. In *Medea*, for example, the dreadful gift that Medea gives Jason in the form of the poisoned wedding dress for his new bride is just the latest in a series of favours and gifts that they have given each other over time. Their great *agōn* amounts to a competition in terms of which of them has done the other most favours. The gift-giving turned into exchange of brutalities when Jason abandoned Medea, and this transformation of their relationship is concretely manifested in the material gift that is simultaneously a deadly weapon.[19] Indeed, gifts in Greek tragedy are almost without exception dangerous. Tragedy's portrayal of the inevitability of revenge in human relationships is consonant with a certain trend in ancient Greek thinking about the cosmos more widely. The concept of reciprocity underlies Greek physics and metaphysics as well as ethics. One of the earliest and most influential of the pre-Socratic philosophers, Anaximander, taught that everything in the universe returns to the element from which it came, in a process of give-and-take across time, like reciprocal compensation for injustice (Anaximander fr. 1 DK). There is a sense in which reciprocal violence is an attempt to impose order on chaos, to make symmetry out of asymmetry, to balance the unbalanced.

The ancient Greeks were more capable than we are of emotional honesty in articulating the drive for revenge and the emotional relief and satisfaction it can bring to the avenger: Thucydides records that in his speech to his Syracusans before battle with the invading Athenian imperial forces, the Sicilian general Gylippus urged them that 'in dealing with an enemy it is most just and lawful to claim the right to slake the fury of the soul on the aggressor ... [since revenge provides] the greatest of all pleasures' (7.68). Aristotle was certainly representing the dominant view when he wrote that avenging oneself is a normal impulse, and not to do so is a sign of a servile personality (*Nicomachean Ethics* 4.5.1126a 7–8). Greek revenge tragedy shows what happens in a world chronologically prior to democratic Athens. In this new civic order, the legislation reflected a general agreement that in pursuit of revenge it was better to raise a lawsuit against the person who had damaged you, even if the damage was physical, rather than to take executive action oneself. There did, however, remain exceptions—it was legally permitted for an Athenian citizen to kill a man whom he discovered having sexual intercourse with his wife, provided he could prove that the killing was not premeditated (see below, pp. 190–2).

Revenge may therefore be seen as a natural phenomenon in the world of Greek tragedy, but it is a problematic one. It is a recurring issue that reciprocal violence is potentially infinite, unless a stop is put to it by another social mechanism such as the court of the Areopagus in Aeschylus' *Eumenides*. Some plays show how the desire for revenge can distort whole lives, which seems to be the point of Chrysothemis' pragmatic perspective in contrast with her embittered sister's emotional trauma in Sophocles' *Electra*. Others show how the wrong people, such as the children in *Medea*, can get hurt when individuals seek restitution for damage. In several plays, the problem of escalation is put centre-stage when more people are killed by the avenger than were killed in the original crime, as Hecuba kills *two* of Polymestor's sons in Euripides' *Hecuba*, as well as blinding him, when he 'only' killed one of hers. These plays all focus on human avengers as they retaliate against a human antagonist. But several others explain human suffering in terms of a god's revenge on a human who has offended him or her, which often involves terrible collateral damage: why should Phaedra be made to suffer by Aphrodite when it is Hippolytus who has disrespected the goddess?

One of the most thrilling scenes of violent revenge in tragedy is Ajax's remarkable suicide scene in his name-play by Sophocles. He curses his enemies the Atridae, calling upon the spirits of vengeance to bring doom upon them and their entire army (835–44). Ajax is angry that he has been disrespected by his own leaders and comrades-in-arms, and is unable to live with the shame of what he has done while insane. His curse will have been heard by the audience in the theatre partly as a prediction of the fifth-century Athenian hostility towards the Atridae's historical descendants in Sparta. Ajax's suicide thus plays a determining role in the public domain of international history. But there are differences between the motives that drive men to suicide in Greek tragedy and those that drive women. Another male suicide, Menoeceus in Euripides' *Phoenician Women*, sacrifices himself to Ares as an act of benefaction to his country. The exception here is Haemon in *Antigone*, who stabs himself primarily for the very personal 'feminine' reason that his beloved Antigone has hanged herself rather than die a slow death by starvation in the cave where she has been incarcerated. The messenger delivers a dazzling speech which relates the only double suicide in Greek tragedy (1220–5, 1231–9):

> In the corner of the tomb
> We caught sight of her, hanged by the neck,
> Caught in a noose of woven linen.
> But he was collapsed beside her, his arms round her waist,
> Howling for the death of his Underworld bride,
> For what his father had done, and for his ill-starred marriage.

When Creon tried to reason with him,

> > The boy glared at him with wild eyes,
> > Spat in his face rather than answering him, and drew
> > His double-edged sword. But he failed to strike
> > His father, who darted backwards to avoid him.
> > Then, enraged with himself, and just as he was,
> > The poor wretch pressed himself against the sword
> > Driving half its length into his side. While still alive,
> > He folded the girl weakly in the bend of his elbow,
> > And spurting forth a fast stream of blood
> > Stained her white cheek.

A modern psychologist would probably also say that Haemon enacts anger that he actually feels against his father on his own body. It is certainly rage against Creon that motivates Haemon's mother Eurydice, after hearing this speech, to stab herself to death; it transpires that she has lost not one but both of her sons through her husband's actions, and in her dying moments she curses him in retaliation (1302–5).

A year after he saw a production of Sophocles' *Antigone* in 1845, Edgar Allan Poe proposed that 'The death of a beautiful woman is, unquestionably, the most poetical topic in the world.'[20] While many have bridled at the apparent misogyny here, it is illuminating to consider how much more interested the Greek tragedians seem to have been in how women died in their plays, by sacrifice, murder, and especially by suicide, than their epic predecessors had been. Since these women are almost always motivated by things that have happened within their own households, their reason for self-destruction is connected with tragedy's interest in intra-familial aggression, rather than the inter-familial or interstate relations that dominate the world of epic myth. Even discounting the young women who volunteer themselves for sacrifice, several women other than Antigone and Eurydice die by their own hand in tragedy, which relates the details in beautiful poetry. After she has inadvertently caused her husband Heracles' death, Sophocles' Deianira stabs herself, in a sexually charged scene, on the marriage bed she shared with him. Sophocles' Jocasta hangs herself, also on her marriage bed, after discovering the true identity of her second husband. Euripides' Phaedra uses the same method, out of a combination of frustrated love for Hippolytus, retaliation against his misogynist tirade, and the need to salvage her reputation for the sake of her own children (419–27).

Some scholars have argued that hanging was a typically female method of suicide, and that women who use weapons against themselves are exceptional, even deliberately 'masculinized' by the poets. It is true that young, unmarried women in tragedy seem to prefer nooses to swords. This is the method threatened by the Egyptian virgins of Aeschylus' *Suppliants*. But there are fewer female suicides in this age group than of more mature, married women, so generalizations are dangerous. Women attempt death in Euripides in strikingly different ways. Hermione in *Andromache* considers a sword, a noose, and a leap from a great height into the sea or a woodland ravine (841–50). Hecuba tries to charge into the fire consuming Troy at the end of *Trojan Women*; Evadne leaps from a rock onto her husband's funeral pyre in *Suppliant Women*; Jocasta stabs herself between the bodies of her sons on the battlefield in *Phoenician Women*.

'Outdoor' deaths such as these may be followed by the display of the bodies in the theatre after they have been brought in by a character and mute attendants: in *Phoenician Women* the corpses are accompanied by Antigone (see Fig. 2.5). But 'indoor' deaths, including the suicide of Phaedra in *Hippolytus*, required the use of

FIG. 2.5. Edouard Toudouze, *Farewell of Oedipus to the Corpses of His Wife and Sons* (1871). École Nationale Supérieure des Beaux-Arts, Paris.

the theatrical device called the *ekkuklēma* or 'rolling-out' machine. This could be used for striking tableaux involving people who are alive, such as Ajax, surrounded by the Greek army's tortured livestock. But often it was used to display gruesome cadavers. In Aeschylus' *Agamemnon* and *Libation-Bearers*, the corpses of two heterosexual couples—Agamemnon and Cassandra, Aegisthus and Clytemnestra—are rolled out of the same palace doors by their respective executioners. In Sophocles' *Electra*, the corpse of Clytemnestra, rolled out and displayed to Aegisthus, itself becomes an instrumental 'luring device' that leads him to his own death (see Fig. 2.6). Euripides' Phaedra is cut down from the beam where she has hanged herself, and rolled out in front of the palace where Theseus finds the suicide note clasped in her hand (857–60). The display of the corpse, a central feature of the funeral in ancient Greece, thus became transformed, through the invention of the *ekkuklēma*, into a central feature of its theatre art.[21]

FIG. 2.6. Benjamin West, *Aegisthus, Raising the Veil, Discovers the Body of Clytemnestra* (1780), reproduced courtesy of the Trustees of the British Museum.

PHYSICAL CONTEXTS

Most Greek tragedies portray a character who has travelled from afar to arrive at his or her destination, whether on horseback, by horse-drawn chariot, on foot, or by sea. The sense of arrival from a different, distant place will have resonated amongst the audiences of the tragedies. For when representatives of numerous Greek city-states assembled in Athens in the springtime to watch heroes and heroines suffering, they had all experienced a journey in order to get there. For some, Athenians who lived within the city walls, the short journey (two kilometres or less) will have been on foot. For the Athenians who lived further away and many mainland Greeks, the journey will have taken a day or several days, and entailed horses, donkeys, and camping en route. For the Athenians' allies from further away, a lengthy journey by sea across the Aegean or Mediterranean will have preceded their attendance at the Dionysia.

Aphrodite opens *Hippolytus* by describing the world which worships her as 'all those who dwell between the Euxine [i.e. Black] Sea and the Pillars of Atlas and look on the light of the sun' (3–4). In Plato's *Phaedo* Socrates says 'I believe that the earth is enormous, and that we who dwell in the area extending from the river Phasis to the Pillars of Heracles inhabit only a small portion, around the sea, like ants or frogs about a pond' (109b). The Greeks seem to have seen themselves as coastal beings, living round the edges of the Black Sea (into which the river Phasis runs from what is now Georgia) and the Mediterranean, bounded to the west by the Pillars of Heracles at Gibraltar. The sea defined the ancient Greeks' sense of geography, and was at its centre, fringed around by Greek civilized habitations. Greek colonizers tended not to found settlements much more than thirty-five kilometres or so—a day's journey—inland. One of the central unifying factors in ancient Greek life, both in reality and psychologically, was sea travel. No wonder the sea scenes in the *Odyssey* were so much loved and marine imagery occurs in so many plays. Oedipus' ship, says Tiresias, sailed into the harbour of a dreadful marriage (*Oedipus Tyrannus* 422–3); Heracles regards his children as little cargo-boats that need to be towed along by their parent ship (*Heracles* 631–2); Pelasgus in Aeschylus' *Suppliants* says that there is need of profound thought, 'like a diver descending into the depth' (408; see also Theseus' figure of speech at Euripides, *Hippolytus* 822–4).

The map drawn by Greek tragedy, which extends from Egypt in the south to the northern coast of the Black Sea and the Caucasus, and from the Peloponnese to Phoenicia (a land where no play is set but which sends a chorus to Thebes in Euripides' *Phoenician Women*) and Susa inside the Persian Empire, was approximately commensurate with the psychological map inside the heads of tragedy's spectators. Many of them will, however, have travelled further west, especially to the Greek cities of Sicily, and it comes as no surprise that there were tragedies, now lost to us, set on that island.

The physical setting of Greek tragic performances underscored the relationship between their content, their audiences, and their performers. Performances of Greek tragedy were not fundamentally illusionist; besides the costumes, masks, and some rudimentary scenery, little attempt was made to disguise the fact that fifth-century citizens were sitting in the open air in a particular sanctuary in Athens. It is therefore remarkable how varied the settings of Greek tragedy are; they could be set on any land on which the same sun shone that illuminated the theatre of Dionysus at Athens. This space was repeatedly transformed, in the collusive experience of the play shared by spectators and performers, into cities or sanctuaries far away in barbarian lands (the Susa of Aeschylus' *Persians* or the Black Sea crags of Euripides' *Iphigenia among the Taurians*), into a remote mountain region, desert island, or coastal region suitable for a military encampment (in *Prometheus, Philoctetes, Hecuba,* and *Iphigenia in Aulis*), or into any other Greek city or shrine that the tragedian's choice of story made appropriate (Thebes, Argos, Delphi). It could also transform itself into a famous site within Athenian territory, such as the sanctuary of Zeus at Marathon in *Children of Heracles*. It could create a doublet of an important civic space that was within a short walking distance of the theatre itself, such as the Areopagus (in *Eumenides*).

There is little evidence external to the texts to help us imagine how scenery design suggested these different locales. In Plato, writing early in the fourth century, there is a suggestion that scenery may have been more sophisticated than other evidence allows us to infer. In his *Republic* one character talks of a stage 'front', and of 'shadow-outlining' (2.365c 2–6), which may mean that perspectival scene-painting, of the kind that can occasionally be glimpsed on vases connected with theatre, was well developed by Plato's day. Indeed, perspective and shading were invented by ancient Greek artists at exactly the time that they were developing the new medium of theatre in the fifth century BCE. It was almost certainly the painting of stage properties—'flats' that represented, for example, wings protruding from buildings—that stimulated Greek painters into experimenting with creating the illusion of three dimensions on a surface with only two.[22]

Greek tragedy, however, relied on its words to evoke a sense of place. Choral odes refer to rivers, mountains, sanctuaries, and other landmarks in the vicinity of the setting of a play, but not necessarily visible to the audience at all.[23] Characters discuss their immediate environment in suggestive ways. When Antigone guides the polluted and exhausted Oedipus into the grove of the Eumenides at the opening of *Oedipus at Colonus*, she describes it thus (14–18):

Father, poor Oedipus, the towers
That crown the city are at some distance, as far as I can see,
But this place is holy, as one may obviously presume from the
Laurels, olive trees, and vines thriving here. And there are many feathered
Nightingales singing beautifully inside.

Such 'programmatic' descriptions of the imagined space are often to be found early in the plays, perhaps to help future scenery designers if and when the plays were revived in other Greek theatres, but mainly to help transport the audience, in their imaginations, to a specific locale. An illuminating example occurs in the opening chorus of Euripides' *Ion*, where in a dialogue between the chorus of Athenian women and Ion, who works at the temple of Apollo at Delphi where the play is set, the images decorating the sanctuary are described in detail—some labours of Heracles and Iolaus, and the battle of the giants, with Athena and Dionysus featuring prominently (190–218). However a modern designer may decide to react to these descriptions, we can't be certain whether they were actually represented in the ancient theatre. Audiences were used to the epic convention of pictorial description of 'ecphrasis', in which they created in their mind's eye an artwork described in the poetry, and perhaps this was how some descriptions of material environments worked in the theatre as well.

The visual arts become more prominent in fifth-century poetry. There are more than a thousand allusions to art objects such as statues and weaving in tragedy alone, which also adds references to paintings, almost unknown in the earlier surviving Greek literature.[24] There are, for example, several instances of a rhetorical figure in which characters say that they have learned what they know about a particular topic from its depiction in paintings—the claim Hecuba makes about ships in *Trojan Women* (686–7), Hippolytus about sexual intercourse (*Hippolytus* 1004–5) and Ion about the ancient Athenian story of Erichthonios and Cecrops' daughters (*Ion* 271). There are also occasions on which characters are *compared* with works of visual art. They are said to look like a painting, a figure in a painting, or a sculpture; alternatively, they are described in metaphors that suggest such a resemblance. In Aeschylus' *Agamemnon* the chorus famously describes Iphigenia at the moment before she was killed (239–43): 'shedding to earth her yellow-dyed robe, she struck each one of the sacrificers with piteous eyes, looking as if she were in a picture, yearning to speak'. The two most striking visual details—the yellow robe flowing to the ground and the beseeching eyes—are emphasized by the poet's request that his audience imagine the scene as a painting. The pathos of the moment is immeasurably heightened by the frustration of the gagged Iphigenia, *forcibly* silenced. In Euripides' *Phoenician Women* the exotic chorus invite the audience to see them as the equivalents of votary images in a precinct (220–1): 'like gold-wrought statues we are in the service of Phoebus'.

Such imagery is linked to casting from moulds and painting, technologies also central to the production of masks for theatrical performances. The artwork comparisons are also culturally specific in another sense; they are symptomatic of the aesthetic training undergone by the Athenian theatregoer. In an influential article Zeitlin argued that it was the Athenian theatre which raised the topic of the partnership between the representational modes of drama and the visual arts to prominence; the development of the figurative arts themselves in the fifth century was virtually coextensive with the evolution of drama. The theatregoer was trained in a stylized mode of viewing which not only aroused his affective responses, but also engaged his skills in evaluating and interpreting the 'visual codes' of what he saw.[25] The early philosophers were also thinking about the visual arts: Democritus wrote a treatise on painting, and Hippias' treatises included both painting and statue-making.[26]

In the fifth century, Athenian public buildings and spaces acquired artworks, paintings and sculptures, that often shared content with tragic drama. In the market-place stood the monument to the ten heroes of Attica, after which its ten tribes were named; the heroes there represented as grand bronze statues included characters who appear in tragedy, such as Ajax and Aegeus. Also in the market-place, along its north side, stood the Stoa Poikile (Painted Colonnade). It was decorated in the mid-fifth century with large murals depicting historical battles against the Persians that are also celebrated in Aeschylus' *Persians*, a battle with the Amazons such as that described by Athena in the same poet's *Eumenides*, and a painting of the sack of Troy which provided the backdrop to so many tragedies. The ruins of the Acropolis left after the Persians had razed its buildings and stolen its statues in 480 BCE would have lingered in the memory of the Greeks and complemented their experience of all the many tragedies where the background is war. But it was the magnificent temples that from the 450s onwards were being built on the Acropolis, towering above the sanctuary of Dionysus, that must have interacted most powerfully with the ways that tragedy was experienced by its first spectators. This adventurous architectural programme was made possible by an immense amount of human labour (probably supplied by both slaves and free men), as well as by Athens' newly acquired wealth as she built up her empire, by the ambition of Pericles, who wanted to achieve a physical transformation of the city that would raise its profile forever, and by the artistic skill of Pheidias, the artist who oversaw the project.

Foremost amongst these temples was the Doric Parthenon. Its decorative sculptures portrayed many stories to which allusion is made in tragedy—fights with the Amazons, or Theseus' heroic labours; its decorative frieze represented the Athenians engaged in procession during a festival of Athena as well as the twelve Olympian gods, several of whom physically appear in tragedy (see below pp. 156–8). Inside the temple there stood Pheidias' enormous gold and ivory statue of Athena Parthenos, over twelve metres high including her base, armed with helmet, spear, and shield. There was another massive statue of Athena by Pheidias standing nearby in the open air on the Acropolis, but made of bronze and emphasizing her warlike nature as Athena Promachos; it is hardly surprising that she was the deity most favoured by tragedians composing a divine epiphany. The Erechtheion was particularly associated with the myths of early Athens celebrated in Euripides' *Ion*, and with the god Poseidon to whom Athena is talking at the beginning of his *Trojan Women*.

Other gods were celebrated in particular shrines on or at the foot of the Acropolis, including Artemis, Zeus, Pan, and Demeter. The theatre itself was part of the sanctuary of Dionysus. But our lack of certain information about the original theatre for which most of the tragedies were written means that we do not know much about its basic features, let alone what specific myths were or were not illustrated in its decorative artworks. A source from later antiquity suggests plausibly that statues of the Persian War heroes Miltiades and Themistocles stood prominently alongside those of the three great tragedians.[27] There is a stone theatre in the sanctuary area at Athens, but its earliest elements date from the late fourth century BCE, and subsequent additions throughout antiquity have made recovery of whatever form the theatre took in the heyday of the great tragedians virtually impossible. The dancing space may have been rectangular rather than round (as it was in the deme theatre at Thorikos in Athens, for example), although neither shape need have limited to either circles or rectangles the formations in which the chorus-men danced. There were almost certainly wooden benches erected in a semi-circle or similar shape, so that the spectators sat with their backs to the slope of the Acropolis looking outwards in a southerly direction. The external evidence from fourth-century vase-paintings and authors does not allow certainty about the original stage buildings, although there was some kind of structure, in its earliest days perhaps only a temporary tent (the primary meaning of the ancient word for stage, which has survived as our word *scene* (*skēnē*), is 'tent'). This provided the entrance to the imagined house, temple, cave, or tent which forms the backdrop to almost all the plays from the *Oresteia* onwards. This stage construction would have needed to be adapted during the course of any one Dionysia to represent the settings of nine different tragedies, three different satyr plays, as well as the comedies, and this makes a preference for light, portable panels inherently likely.[28]

The evidence internal to the texts does suggest, however, that the stage building could support actors performing on an additional, higher level than those represented 'on the ground'. It must have had a flat roof, at least part of which could support the weight of two or more actors. Scenes such as the watchman on the roof who opens Aeschylus' *Agamemnon*, Evadne's appearance on a precipice in Euripides' *Suppliant Women*, Antigone's appearance with an old slave on the walls of Thebes in his *Phoenician Women* (88–192), and that of Orestes, Pylades, and Hermione at the end of *Orestes*, all seem to require actors to appear on top of the stage building. Other scenes, including the appearance of Iris and Madness in *Heracles*, may have used either this upper horizontal level or the crane. The machine seems to have been favoured when the goal was to suggest that a character—in our extant plays almost always a god—was actually flying through the air.

Many of the Attic demes had their own theatres, and performances of plays in them are well attested by the end of the fifth century. They will have taken place at the small, local festivals of Dionysus that had been celebrated before Pisistratus inaugurated the great urban festival, and had never been abandoned. Plato even speaks of theatre enthusiasts who attended as many drama performances at local theatres as they could manage (*Republic* 5.475d; *Laches* 183a–b). By the last decade of the fifth century, travelling star actors began to take their repertoire to any city with a theatre that would pay them to perform there. There are signs of this process already in the fifth century; a few plays were written not for the Athenian festivals of Dionysus but for the rulers of other cities. Aeschylus was commissioned by the Sicilian tyrant Hieron to compose a play for the people of Gela called *Women of Etna*, and also to produce his *Persians* in Sicily (*Life of Aeschylus* 8–11, 18). An ancient scholar who wrote a comment on line 445 of Euripides' *Andromache* said that it was first performed outside Athens; this was probably in Molossia for the young king Tharyps, who believed he was descended from Andromache's child by Neoptolemus, the boy whose life is saved in the tragedy. In the fourth century, theatre spread to the Greek-speaking communities of southern Italy, where the majority of the important theatre-related vase-paintings have been found, and across the Greek-speaking world.

The audiences of tragedy knew that their Greek world was part of a larger world, populated by speakers of other languages, and that the human race who walked the earth were just one part of a much larger universe. Their love of the choral dance as collective activity means that they even conceptualized the planets and other heavenly bodies as revolving around a common central point in an unceasing cosmic dance. Plato, who had seen a great deal of tragic theatre, draws an analogy between the divine creator or choreographer of the universe and the statesman who organizes the choral dancing in the city-state (*Timaeus* 40c).²⁹ The speculations of the pre-Socratic philosophers on the physical make-up of the planets and the spaces between them are occasionally reflected in tragedy, for example Anaxagoras' theories about lumps or 'clods' of celestial matter in Euripides' *Orestes* (984). But far more frequent is the powerful relationship invoked between the doings of humans and the most obvious celestial body, the personified 'all-seeing' Sun. The chorus of Euripides' *Iphigenia among the Taurians*, Greek women stranded in slavery in a north-eastern barbarian backwater, look upwards to the sky and fervently wish that they could fly in the pathway of the Sun-god's chariot back to the choral dances of Greece (1138–52).

In Euripides' *Medea*, Helios is an important behind-the-scenes figure, since he is the heroine's grandfather and lends her his chariot when she needs to escape from Corinth. The Sun is invoked by Aegeus when he swears his oath to her, as it is by many other oath-takers in Greek tragedy, and this reflects standard practice; the regular divinities invoked in oaths were Zeus, the Earth, and the Sun. But references to the sun are ubiquitous in Greek tragedy, for a variety of interrelated reasons more connected with the notions of light and sight. One is psychological; there is a sense that the very intensity of daylight exacerbates pain. The herald in Aeschylus' *Agamemnon* who reports the storm that has savaged the Greek fleet returning from Troy speaks of his emotions, as a survivor, the morning after the catastrophe (667–70):

> Then those of us who had escaped from that marine Hades,
> In white daylight, our trust in luck all gone,
> Herded thoughts of our fresh calamity like sheep around our heads,
> With our fleet wrecked and terribly storm-battered.

Under the clear sun the surviving sailors went over and over in their minds, like shepherds herding sheep, the depth of the suffering undergone by their comrades and themselves. The very whiteness of the light, which seems not to flinch from illuminating the appalling scenes it witnesses, adds to the pain conjured here.

In Cassandra's last speech before she enters the palace to her death later in *Agamemnon*, it is the sunshine she calls to witness that she, a lowly slave, suffers alongside the mighty (1323–6):

> There is one more speech—or dirge for myself—I want
> To perform. I pray to this, my last sunlight,
> That the avengers of this deed take reprisals for my death too.
> Killing a slave girl is an easy victory.

In *Libation-Bearers*, when Orestes reveals to the world both the net in which his father had been murdered and the corpses of his mother and her lover, he calls to witness the god 'whose eye oversees everything, the all-seeing Sun! Let him behold my mother's damned deed' (985–6). There is a sense that the Sun, because he has witnessed the previous murder in the household, can attest, like someone called to give evidence in a trial, to the justice of Orestes' own action. In *Prometheus*, the Sun has the pride of the climactic position in the tortured Prometheus' first lines, the utterance of a figure who is truly 'suffering under the sun' (88–92):

> O divine air and fluttering, winged breezes!
> Founts of the rivers, and of the sea's waves,
> The infinite laughter of Earth, mother of all,
> And the all-seeing circle of the Sun—I call on you!
> Look at me and what I, a god, suffer at gods' hands.

References to the Sun in Greek tragedy remind us continually that the plays were performed outdoors, with the same immortal, 'all-seeing' Sun invoked by the suffering characters in tragedy now high in the sky over the heads of the spectators. The spectators of Greek tragedy share their perspective with Helios, as physically elevated witnesses to suffering played out in the daylight. The suffering is patent, but its causes, however determinedly sought, remain partially obscured. As the Shakespearean scholar A. C. Bradley sensibly said, 'tragedy would not be tragedy if it were not a painful mystery'.[30]

## MYTHS AND THE CITY

This chapter has looked at some of the real communities and group identities that underlay questions asked in Greek tragedy, especially those engendered by civic procedures such as policy-making, decision-taking, and by the performance of death rituals at both state and private funerals. Deliberation and dealing with death are activities to which any fifth-century Greek spectator at the Dionysia will have been able to relate, but their representation in tragedy will have resonated in unusually specific ways for the local Athenian citizen spectators themselves. Indeed, all Greek tragedy reflects an underlying tension between its appeal to any spectator who could understand basic ancient Greek and was familiar with the fundamental elements of Greek mythology, and its special appeal to Athenians, indeed the body of Athenian male citizens, to the exclusion of the women and non-Athenian males who resided in Attica.

The idea that tragedy was the exclusive property of the Athenian male citizen is underscored by Aristophanes' comedy *Women at the Thesmophoria*, in which the heroes are two male citizens, Euripides the tragic poet and his kinsman by marriage. They outwit both the women of Athens and a male, barbarian slave during their extended parodies of Euripides' own tragedies. The two heroes can participate together in the fantastic world of 'paratragedy', subjecting the texts to quotation, travesty, and interpolation, while the woman and the slave entrusted with guarding them fail even to understand what they are doing. When the kinsman announces during the parody of Euripides' *Helen* that he is in Egypt, the female guard insists, quite correctly, that he is actually in the Athenian sanctuary known as the Thesmophorion (878–80); the barbarian archer similarly fails to be drawn into the paratragic experience of Euripides' romantic Ethiopian *Andromeda*, a lost tragedy which was in antiquity reputed to be exceptionally beautiful.[31]

The Athenian men who attended the theatre comprised by far the largest single group within the audience. Each citizen defined himself by his relationships with several other groups, from which he needed to distinguish himself and thus impose some order on his universe. Tragic drama reveals a thoroughgoing preoccupation with defining a self, the male citizen self, which is what is continuously at stake in the Athenian citizens' theatre. The plays may be set in the pre-democratic past, more often than not in a place other than Athens, and the non-divine members of their casts may far more frequently be women, slaves, non-Athenian Greeks and non-Greeks than Athenian males. But the artistic endeavour they represent, however differently it was interpreted by other Greeks beyond Athens in antiquity, is—because of the circumstances of its original genesis—always susceptible to interpretation as an explanation of the world from the perspective of the Athenian male citizen.

Social identity is a complex and slippery phenomenon. Every individual partakes simultaneously in a large number of a distinct (though often overlapping) groups. Which particular group membership is temporarily predominant depends almost entirely on immediate social context. In classical Athens, after the reorganization that Cleisthenes oversaw at the time of the democratic revolution in 507 BCE, the group identity for the citizen male was complicated; he was a member of a household, a deme, as well as other subdivisions of the *polis* ('tribes' and 'phratries'). He also participated in the Assembly and intermittently in other institutions of the democratic state such as juries and the Council. Comedy is profoundly interested in the group identities to which such a complex civic organization gave rise, but tragedy is more fundamental in its examination of identity.

In Sophocles' *Philoctetes* the hero, who has been stranded alone on a desert island for many years, says that being without a *polis* is equivalent to being dead (1018). Tragedy's civic dimension is most apparent in its continuous exploration of the theme of displacement—threatened or actual—from one's *polis*, whether in the form of exile or deportation through slavery. Over and over again the tragedy of the central heroic figures' situations is compounded by the hazard of being rendered, like Philoctetes, totally *apolis*, without a *polis* at all. It is a condition of the tragic Orestes' life, whether in the *Oresteia*, Sophocles' and Euripides' Electra-tragedies, Euripides' *Iphigenia among the Taurians* and *Orestes*, that he is an exile from his homeland; the same applies to Jason and Medea in Euripides' *Medea*, to Heracles and Deianira in Sophocles' *Women of Trachis*, to Oedipus at the end of *Oedipus Tyrannus* and throughout *Oedipus at Colonus*, and even to Euripides' Ion, the man without a genealogy.

Other characters are forced to seek asylum or suffer captivity in alien cities for a variety of reasons: Danaus and his daughters in Aeschylus' *Suppliants*, Heracles' children in *Children of Heracles*, Helen in the Egypt of Euripides' *Hele*n, and Iphigenia in the Black

Sea in his *Iphigenia among the Taurians*. War, the near omnipresent background of tragedy as it was a nearly continuous fact of Athenian life (see the following chapter), displaces numerous female groups and individuals from their own communities, a displacement feared by the chorus of Aeschylus' *Seven against Thebes*, and actually suffered by Cassandra in his *Agamemnon*, the chorus of *Libation-Bearers*, by Euripides' Trojan Women in *Hecuba* and *Trojan Women*, and his Andromache in her name-play. The importance of the *polis* to tragedy, and the stress on the absolute need to be a member of such an organized and regulated community, finds expression in the recurrence of these plots involving displaced persons, in the problems caused by the appearance of exiles from another city-state seeking asylum in your own, and in the development of the themes of displacement, exile, and lack of civic rights in tragic rhetoric.

The Athenian citizen emphatically distinguished himself, as an inhabitant of a city-state, from the primitive peoples and wild beasts without thought or language (see Sophocles' *Antigone* 354–6), who lived in the untamed countryside beyond the boundaries of civilization and the laws of the community; Athenian tragedy draws an emphatic boundary between civilization and the wild. It is a feature of the barbarous Scythians of *Prometheus Bound* that they do not live in settled houses in settled cities, but are nomads, taking their caravans with them (709–10). A building or residence within a city-state or a city-state surrogate such as a military encampment (*Hecuba*, *Ajax*), came to be a standard setting of tragedy, in contrast with the wild, uninhabited by mortals, where only caves provided shelter, which was, however, the standard setting of satyr drama. This genre enacted plots against a background of mountainsides (for example in Sophocles' satyr play *Trackers*), or remote seashores (Euripides' *Cyclops*) where no city-state existed: the Roman architectural writer Vitruvius speaks of these as suitable settings for satyr drama (7.5).

The characters who populate the tragic texts are products of a citizen-centred world-view, and examination of the commoner patterns and generic plot conventions will reveal something about the shared inner life, values, and standards of the group which produced it. Yet tragedy, unfortunately, cannot be used as a document of the realities of everyday life in classical Athens. It is essential to take into account the infinite processes of mediation, the way in which Athenian institutions, social relations, and preoccupations are refracted, distorted, and displaced onto the mythical world. Many things could happen in the real life of Athens which were virtually unthinkable in the tragic universe. This strange world, an imaginative reconstruction of the mythical past, is full of attempts at archaizing but is often anachronistic; it is also simultaneously idealized and dysfunctional, which leads to surprising generic conventions delimiting and defining the nature of social relationships within it. Thus, for example, in reality people could rise socially beyond birth-status (which is almost impossible in tragedy), and Athens was riven by factional in-fighting (but the tragic Athens is an idealized community virtually free from *stasis*). It is also the case that we know very little about 'everyday life' in classical Athens with which we can compare life as it is lived in the plays. Most of the texts which are informative on these issues, especially legal speeches, date from the next century. But what tragedy undoubtedly offers is a document of the Athenian *imagination*. It is not just that sentiments and ideas expressed by its characters, however apparently subversive or at odds with the dominant ideology of the city, can be used as illustrative of *imaginable* arguments heard within the democratic *polis*. More importantly, the very norms of the genre itself are important illustrations of the social preoccupations of the Athenian citizen, and can yield profound insights into the imaginative life of his peer group.

The Athenocentrism of the extant tragedies is manifested in numerous ways. Most obviously, many plays include explicit panegyrics of the Athenians and their city, for example in Aeschylus' *Persians* and Sophocles' *Oedipus at Colonus*. Even the women of Troy, about to be sent off to slavery in Greece, are inclined to express their hopes that the city to which they are to be conveyed is Athens (e.g. *Trojan Women* 208–9). Secondly, even plays with no obvious Athenian focus often include an explanation through myth of the origins of an Athenian custom or ritual: for example, Euripides' *Iphigenia among the Taurians*, an innovative tragicomedy portraying the escape of a pair of Greek siblings from a barbarian community in the Black Sea, startlingly concludes with Athena establishing rituals in perpetuity at cult-centres on Athenian territory, the sanctuaries at Halae and Brauron (1459–69). Thirdly, the tragedians used cities other than Athens, especially Thebes, to build up a picture of an 'anti-city' (a negative image of democratic Athens, which prided itself on its openness, see Thucydides 2.39); the tragic Thebes is closed in on itself and blighted by internecine squabbling, incest, and tyranny. This is especially clear in Euripides' *Phoenician Women* and Sophocles' 'Theban Plays', *Antigone*, *Oedipus Tyrannus*, and *Oedipus at Colonus*.

Fourthly, a group of plays emerged with transparently 'patriotic' myths, concerned with the early history of Athens and Attica, stressing such vital components of the Athenians' identity as the myth of their own autochthony (the notion that they had sprung from their own land and were not external occupiers of it). There is a whole sub-species of tragedy portraying scenes from the Athenians' own mythical past. Archaic poetry had not been conspicuously interested in Athens or Athenians, and some fifth-century tragedy displays a self-conscious project of building up a repertoire of famous incidents to challenge the epic dominance of the Argive/Mycenean and Theban mythical cycles. This new repertoire included Euripides' *Suppliant Women* and his *Children of Heracles*, as well as his fragmentary *Erechtheus*, of which considerable portions survive. This was a patriotic piece which Athenian orators liked to quote, dealing with the struggle over Athens between Athena and Poseidon; it also portrayed the self-sacrifice of Athenian princesses and the death of King Erechtheus when the city was under siege by Poseidon-worshipping Thracian barbarians during a patriotic war. The play was produced between 423 and 421 BCE and was designed to celebrate the building of the Erechtheion, the second largest temple on the Acropolis. One reason why this group of plays has, until recently, been so neglected may be that Aristotle's *Poetics*, which took the Athenian *polis* out of tragedy, at the time when the genre was becoming performed in many other cities (see below), conspicuously ignores them.

Even in plays where Athenian territory is the setting and mythical Athenians are seen in action, it is always in interaction with representatives from other city-states. Some seek to display the superiority of Athenian democratic culture over that of Greek states, especially Thebes or Argos, and imply that Athens is entitled to the role of 'moral policeman' in Greece. The most notable example is Euripides' *Suppliant Women*. In this play Theseus, the mythical founder of the Athenian democracy, is portrayed as a pious and democratically minded monarch, who says, 'When I first assumed leadership, I gave my people freedom and an equal vote, and on this basis instituted monarchy' (352–3). He takes action against the Thebans to impose the 'common law of Hellas' which protects the rights of the dead.

The Athenocentrism of tragedy is most clearly revealed in the manner in which myths involving heroes from other cities are blatantly manipulated to serve Athenian patriotic interests. Until the sixth century Athens had enshrined little of its own local mythology in poetry and art; it had no hero equal in status to Heracles, Jason, Achilles, Orestes, or Oedipus. And although there was a concerted attempt made in the late sixth and in the fifth centuries to develop a nexus of myths around the Athenian king Theseus, who appears in a number of tragedies, the heroes from the old epic cycle remained central to the tragic universe, and are therefore systematically appropriated to the *Athenian* past, in each case conferring on the city some special advantage.

Orestes, for example, is brought to trial by Aeschylus in his *Eumenides*, and the myth is self-consciously altered to make him, rather than Ares, the first figure to be tried at the court of the Areopagus for murder. This means that Aeschylus even had to offer an alternative reason why the hill was named the 'hill (*pagos*) of Ares' rather than the 'Oresteopagus' (685–90). But Orestes does not only cause the Athenians to be blessed with their new court: he also benefits them by pledging on his departure an eternal relationship of peace and friendship between Argos and Athens (762–4), almost certainly a mythical explanation for the thirty-year alliance with Argos pledged by the Athenians in 461 BCE (Thucydides 1.102.4). The play also provides an instance of Athens' fair treatment of suppliant strangers. It is a remarkable feature of *Eumenides* that the poet dared to portray an Athens without a king, even in a play set only shortly after the end of the Trojan war. And as if to emphasize the democratic nature even of the Athens of the heroic age, silent male characters appeared on stage representing male citizens of Athens, the first ever jury at a trial for homicide at the court of the Areopagus. So the audience's direct ancestors mingled before their eyes with the gods, demi-gods and heroes.

Similarly, in Euripides' *Heracles* the greatest hero of Greek legend is kidnapped—or 'myth-napped'—by the playwright and brought to an old age at Athens. An ancient friendship between Theseus and Heracles, resting on the debt Theseus owes the great hero for rescuing him from the Underworld (1169–70), is paid when Theseus dissuades Heracles from suicide and pledges to take him to Athens. There he will purify him, grant him land, and make sure he is honoured after death with sacrifices and stone memorials (1322–33): these perhaps supply an *aition* for the sculptures commemorating the famous deeds of both Theseus and Heracles on the 'Hephaesteum' (a temple in the Athenian agora), datable to between 450 and 440 BCE. The appropriation of a figure like Heracles to one's own *polis* was no small acquisition. As Theseus says, his citizens will win a fair crown of honour in the eyes of Greece for helping a man of such quality (1334–5). But friendship is one of the most recurring themes in this fascinating play, and the mythical celebration of the friendship between Theseus and Heracles also acts as an *aition* for the social institution of friendships between citizens which were a central feature of Athenian democracy, and could even be used as a justification in Athenian law.

In his *Oedipus at Colonus* Sophocles provides a mythical explanation for the nearly permanent hostility between the historical city-states of Athens and Thebes during historical times; he does so in the course of 'myth-napping' the Theban hero to a mystical death at the Athenian deme of Colonus—the poet's own birthplace. The hero is not only welcomed kindly, but formally granted full citizen status by Theseus (636–7). Oedipus promises that if his body is granted burial there, it will confer a great benefit on the city (576–8, 626–8). Only Theseus witnesses his death, and he is to guard the secrets surrounding it and pass them on only to his heir (1530–2). Oedipus explains that his body will always provide for the Athenians 'a defence, a bulwark stronger than many shields, than spears of massed allies' (1524–5). Sophocles' tragedy has thus not only brought Oedipus within the Athenian mythical orbit. It has actually transferred his allegiance, and the special blessings he can confer, wholesale from the city of his birth to the city of the play's production. Oedipus will lend posthumous assistance to the Athenians against the citizens of his own much-hated Thebes.

This play, most unusually, offers as a speaking character a nameless Athenian citizen of the deme of Colonus. He is the mythical forefather of the citizens in the audience. He is the first character to speak after the arrival of the exiles Oedipus and Antigone at the grove of the Erinyes; he is distinguished by his pious regard for the sanctity of the grove, his fear lest it be defiled, and his exemplary respect for the processes of the Athenian democracy. He announces that he would never eject Oedipus from his seat without reporting his arrival to the other citizens, and taking his instructions from them (47–8).

Athenians in tragedy usually display exceptional virtue, piety, respect for the democratic principles of freedom of speech, and treat suppliants honorably. When Athenians do misbehave or act foolishly in tragedy it is conspicuous that they are removed from their city for the duration of their misadventure. In Euripides' *Medea* the Athenian king Aegeus may be no culprit, but he is faintly ridiculous, credulous, and upset about his own infertility. One of the reasons why *Medea* was so unsuccessful in the dramatic competition of 431 BCE may indeed have been that the audience did not appreciate having one of their own mythical ancestors discussing his infertility on stage. But the play is set at Corinth. Theseus in *Hippolytus* is not a bad man, but he is precipitate in judgement and unfair to his son. It is noteworthy that he is residing not in Athens but in Troezen in the Peloponnese for the purposes of the play. Likewise, it is at Delphi that Creusa, the Athenian daughter of Erechtheus in Euripides' *Ion*, plots the murder of the young man whom she believes to be her husband's illegitimate offspring.

Tragedy seems to have become less transparently Athenian in focus at the same time as it began to be increasingly exported across the Greek-speaking world towards the end of the fifth century. By the mid-fourth century Aristotle says that tragedians 'today' write speeches 'rhetorically' rather than 'politically' (*Poetics* ch. 6, 1450b 7; see also *Rhetoric* 3.1403b 31–5). Yet the scraps of later fourth-century and Hellenistic tragedy themselves do not imply that political affairs were of less interest to tragedians—indeed, there seems to have been a revival of interest in the history play. Tragedy did not become any less to do with the government of the *polis*, but it did become less Athenocentric in the sense that there are few signs of the type of play designed to elaborate specifically Athenian mythical history, or the aetiology of exclusively Athenian cults and civic institutions. The sub-species of Athenian tragedy such as *Suppliant Women* seems to disappear, and in his *Poetics* Aristotle (a non-Athenian) does not specify the Athenian Theseus as one of his ideal tragic heroes, alongside his recommended list of the Argive Orestes and Thyestes, the Theban Oedipus, the Calydonian Alcmaeon, and the Tegean Telephus (*Poetics* ch. 13, 1453a.17–22).[32]

Presumably, during the process by which tragedy metastasized over the entire Greek-speaking world, it became inappropriate for its content to be so explicitly designed for Athenians. But there is no evidence that tragedy became less 'political' in a broader sense of the term. Generally defined models of acceptable behaviour in leaders were universally dramatizable, and could be made suitable for viewing in any city with almost any kind of constitution. Greeks will probably have agreed on what makes a good leader, almost regardless of the nature of their polity. Plato's Athenian in *Laws* regarded tragedy as an effective form of political communication; he says that tragedians are rivals and competitors in presenting alternative and by no means equally proper representations of the *polis*. The powerful political effect that tragedy could produce made him insist that state censorship was essential: tragedies should be scrutinized before they were granted permission to be performed (7.817b–c).

# 3

# Confrontations

## WAR

In every Greek tragedy there are conflict and dissent; confrontations between warring characters, and sometimes between a character and a chorus, are the raw material from which the poet made his play. Moreover, the context of most of the plots is a recent or ongoing war. Male characters in tragedy are often dressed for battle. Choruses sometimes consist of soldiers or sailors. Items of weaponry and armour (swords, shields and bows) are crucial props, possession of which can both cause and resolve tragic conflict. Arguments rage over the conduct of armies and whether burial can be afforded to the enemy slain. Nervous choruses sing while battle rages nearby off-stage. Gore-streaked, lacerated corpses from the battlefield are carried on to be lamented. Four of the exceptional plays, which are not connected with a war, are (perhaps surprisingly) amongst the most famous—Euripides' *Medea*, *Hippolytus*, and *Bacchae* and Sophocles' *Oedipus Tyrannus*. In all of these the violence that erupts contrasts with the quietude of the townscapes in which it occurs.

Fifteen plays deal with the Trojan war and its aftermath (the three plays of the *Oresteia*, Sophocles' *Ajax*, *Philoctetes*, and *Electra*, Euripides' *Hecuba*, *Trojan Women*, *Andromache*, *Helen*, *Iphigenia* plays, *Orestes*, *Cyclops*, and *Rhesus*). As an intercontinental war involving many Greek states besieging a non-Greek empire, this group has potential for revival at any time of international conflict. Five plays dramatize episodes related to the 'civil' war that afflicted Thebes and spilt out to involve another Greek city, Argos (Aeschylus' *Seven against Thebes*, Sophocles' *Antigone* and *Oedipus at Colonus*, Euripides' *Suppliant Women* and *Phoenician Women*). Less familiar wars inform other plays, including the war declared on the Argives by the Egyptian herald at the end of Aeschylus' *Suppliants*, Heracles' sack of Oechalia which precipitates the tragedy in *Women of Trachis*, the Argive invasion of Attica in Euripides' *Children of Heracles*, and a war between Athens and Euboea which created the marriage central to his *Ion*.

'War is the father of everything, and king of everything, too,' said the philosopher Heraclitus (fr. 53 *DK*), and as a fifth-century Greek he had good reason. The history of the decades that produced the plays discussed in this book is one of more or less continuous warfare. The earliest surviving tragedy, Aeschylus' *Persians*, already emphasizes the tightness of the relationship between war and tragedy. It was performed in 472 BCE, just eight years after Xerxes, the Persian King, had invaded Greece with a massive army, and had won at the battle of Thermopylae. He had then sacked Athens, only to be defeated at Salamis and Plataea. This was the second time in a decade that the Persians had invaded Greece, since Xerxes' father Darius had himself had to withdraw after an unsuccessful campaign in 490 BCE. Since ordinary Athenian citizens had rowed and fought in the Persian Wars, and their wives and children had been hurriedly evacuated, the audiences of tragedy would have retained *direct* memories of these momentous events for at least another sixty years, until the last of them had died.

No sooner had the Greeks collectively fought off the threat from the Persian Empire in the early decades of the century than they began to compete for power and revenue between themselves. The tension led to the second great fifth-century war, between Athens (along with her 'Delian League' of allies), and the Spartan dominions, based in the Peloponnese. This catastrophic power struggle occupied the Athenians almost continuously between 431 and 404 BCE. The fatalities during this war proved unmanageable, especially those incurred in the year 413 as a result of the failure of the Athenians' ill-fated aggressive expedition to Sicily. The leaders were slaughtered, a significant proportion of the entire citizen male population of Attica died a pitiful death from exposure, hunger, thirst, and disease when imprisoned in the Sicilians' roofless quarries under the scorching sun, and the survivors were sold into slavery (Thucydides 7.85–7).

Even during the earlier decades that intervened between the two great wars, the Athenians were almost always engaged in military campaigns both overseas and nearer their own borders. The Delian League lost at least a hundred triremes during operations around Egypt in 454 BCE, causing many thousand fatalities amongst Athenian men alone, and dozens from a single tribe, the Erechtheids.[1] Bereavement on a massive scale was normal at Athens. Inter-state rivalry expressed in intermittent military confrontation was seen as a fact of life: the fictional Cretan legislator in Plato's *Laws* denies that peace is possible, since every city-state of Greece is *by nature* engaged in a permanent, if undeclared, war on every other (1.626a 2–5). He would certainly have concluded this from what was depicted in the theatre.

Although naval warfare was central to both the defence of Athens and her imperial policies, and some Athenian citizens served as rowers and cavalrymen,[2] at the heart of the Athenian citizen's upbringing was training as an infantryman, a hoplite. Equipped with a long spear and a huge shield, the men on the front line of the hoplite phalanx smashed into their opponents, trying to force a way through or encircle them. Failing that, the battle turned into a violent pushing contest. Hoplite battles were brutal and short, the soldiers 'knee pressed in the dust, and spear splintered in the onset' (Aeschylus, *Agamemnon* 64–5). As the Persian general Mardonius is made to say by the historian Herodotus, the Greeks 'wage their wars in the most nonsensical way. The minute they declare war on one another, they look for the finest and flattest ground, and go there to do battle. As a result, even the victors suffer extreme fatalities. Needless to say, the losing side is annihilated' (7.9.2).

The classical Greeks' extraordinary way of war can be associated with the all-or-nothing destinies dramatized in Greek tragedy, where prosperity and life itself can be taken away in a single day. 'A citizen of a Greek city-state understood that the simplicity, clarity and brevity of hoplite battle defined the entire relationship with a man's family and community, the one day of uncertain date that might end his life but surely give significance to his entire existence.'[3] Some have emphasized the relationship in the specifically *Athenian* mind between politics and pitched battle.

In the democracy, the men who voted for a war were committing themselves to fighting in it to defend their own right to vote. Hoplite battle aimed at a speedy, unequivocal result. 'Better the risk of death tomorrow, but the chance of a victorious return home the day after, than the interminable, deracinating, and wealth-draining uncertainties of guerrilla warfare.'[4] Athenian tragedy is suffused with imagery expressing the notion that an individual or city's fate is in the balance of a scale or on a razor's edge, hovering between death and glory—the same sense that the hoplite must have shared before every battle he entered.

War was certainly the father of the new genre of history-writing, since Herodotus and Thucydides recorded the history of the Persian and Peloponnesian Wars respectively. Yet the brutality of the battlefield is not something that either of them describes in any detail, which is more surprising since most ancient Greek men had experience of battle, and some a great deal of experience. Paul Fussell has commented on how few precise descriptions can be found of the true physical suffering experienced by soldiers in World War I; narratives of that war do not often contain words, he writes, like 'blood, terror, agony, madness, shit, cruelty... legs blown off, intestines gushing out over his hands, screaming all night'. The reason is that soldiers know that nobody is very interested in the bad news that they have to report.[5] The most detailed ancient Greek description of a battlefield is the account by an eyewitness, the Athenian mercenary Xenophon, of the aftermath of the battle of Koroneia (*Agesilaus* 2.14):

Once the fighting was finished, you could see, where they had smashed into each other, the discoloration of the earth with blood, comrades and enemies lying dead side-by-side, shattered shields, broken spears, unsheathed short swords—some on the ground, some stuck in bodies, and some still clutched in the hand.

In these terse phrases, there is little sense that those bodies had belonged to individuals who had suffered an agonizing death from the wounds which had emitted that blood.[6]

In tragedy, however, which allows individuals to express their subjective experience of traumatic events, the desperate suffering caused as a result of military conflict achieves rather more exposure.

This is especially the case with Aeschylus, who had fought at Marathon himself, as well as losing his brother, who had died as a result of having his arm hacked off (Herodotus 6.114). The messenger in *Persians* reports how Xerxes' heavy infantrymen

> Were struck repeatedly by stones thrown from Greek hands,
> And arrows shot from the bow-string fell on them,
> Destroying them. In the end the Greeks, rushing against them
> At a single cry, struck them, butchered the poor men's limbs
> Until they had all been deprived of life. (459–64)

The chorus of *Seven against Thebes*, who, as women, are facing rape and enslavement if their besieged city falls, describe the physical reality of awaiting the assault of the seven enemy contingents: the pounding hooves, the rising dust, the clash of shields, the rattling of harness, the creaking axles, the clashing and clanging of bronze-bound shields at the gates of the city (78–87).

The hoplite shield, nearly a metre in diameter, and supported by the left arm alone, was extremely heavy. Constructed out of solid wood, bronze facing, and leather lining, it weighed between seven and nine kilograms. The first thing any man fleeing the battlefield did was discard his shield to enable him to run. Ordinary soldiers complained about struggling under the weight of their shields while their superiors relaxed on horseback (Xenophon, *Anabasis* 3.4.47–8); conservative older men complained that decadent modern youths could not even hold their shields up properly (Aristophanes, *Clouds* 987–9). The mighty warrior Ajax's shield was even heavier than normal, since its defensive wall was made out of no fewer than seven compressed ox-hides (*Iliad* 7.219–20). This knowledge lends potency to the scene in Sophocles' *Ajax* where the hero insists that his son Eurysaces, on whom he has bestowed a name that means 'Broad Shield', learns to wield the massive object (574–6). Ajax is clear that the child, who is still young enough to be carried, must early be 'broken in' like a colt to obey his father's 'stern code' (548–9). While this scene may well be related to the cults of Ajax and Eurysaces, who was himself worshipped a hero in at least one Attic deme, it draws what must have been even to its first audience a telling contrast between Ajax's toughness with his son, and Hector's tenderness to Astyanax in their farewell scene at the end of *Iliad* book 6.

Many of the men in the audiences of tragedy will have faced dangers and dire discomforts on campaigns, and the multivocal form of Greek tragedy allows the disgruntlement of the ordinary soldier to be expressed on several occasions. The ageing Peleus, although an aristocrat, seems to be speaking up for the common man when he complains to Menelaus in Euripides' *Andromache* that in war the generals take all the credit, even though it is the ordinary troops who face the hard labour and suffering (693–705). In *Agamemnon* the herald recounts in painful detail the ordeal undergone by the ordinary soldiers at Troy (555–69)—the cramped quarters, squalid bedding, and crawling insects, the harshness of the rain, the winter cold and the scorching sun in summer. The chorus of Sophocles' *Ajax*, Salaminian soldiers, also reflect on their ordeal at Troy (600–7):

> It is for ages now, countless months, that I, poor fellow
> Have camped on the grasslands of Ida,
> Worn by the passing of time
> With the grim prospect of coming some day yet
> To the ruthless destroyer, Hades.

The military chorus of *Rhesus* (attributed to Euripides) are heard criticizing their leader Hector's decision, and stating that they do not approve of generals who put their men in unnecessary danger (132). In the same play there is a lively debate between Hector and a Trojan shepherd on the intellectual capacities of country people in contrast with military men. Hector is contemptuous of the humble shepherd and his like (266–70), but the shepherd turns out to be an acute observer of military matters, and bilingual (284–316).

The strongest flavour of military rhetoric is conveyed by Eteocles' speech to his compatriots as they await a siege at the opening of *Seven against Thebes* (30–5):

> So all of you, rise and man the battlements and the doors
> To the fortifications! Hurry to arms!
> Throng the parapets and take up position
> On the turret platforms! Take heart and
> Stand your ground at the exits from the gates,
> And don't be afraid of the alien rabble.
> God will be on our side!

The several tragedies set in military camps can usefully be read alongside Thucydides' *History of the Peloponnesian War*; this former general offers vivid accounts of the types of harangue delivered by military leaders to their men, and the dangerous moods that could arise in response. Sophocles' *Ajax* as well as the Euripidean *Hecuba*, *Trojan Women*, *Iphigenia in Aulis*, and *Rhesus* all convey a powerful sense of a near-mutinous soldiery just out of sight in the plays, whose louring and volatile presence affects the behaviour of all the characters and the chorus.

## ETHNICITY AND CLASS

Greek tragedy scrutinizes relationships between people of different ethnicities—between Greeks and Persians, Egyptians, Phrygians from Troy and the west coast of Asia Minor, Thracians and Taurians from the Balkans and Black Sea. The Athenians and most other Greeks called people who did not speak Greek 'barbarians', a word which originally referred to the unintelligibility of their languages, but soon acquired the more negative connotations which the word bears in English. Greek identity, as opposed to an ethnic identity attached to a particular city-state, became important in an unprecedented way during the Persian Wars; its fundamental constituents, according to the speech by Athenian envoys in Herodotus explaining why they could never come to terms with Persian rule, were shared blood, language, religion (defined as attendance at recognized joint cult centres and shared sacrificial practices), and way of life (8.143). Greek tragedy, with its complex mythical genealogies for Greek royal families and civic communities, and focus on religious practices, consolidated the Greek identity of its audience, which at the Dionysia consisted of Greeks from many different places. The other constituents of Greekness, identified here as language and way of life, turn out to be just as central to the tragedians' agenda.

Philoctetes, stranded on the uninhabited island of Lemnos for many years, can hardly contain his joy at hearing his own Greek language spoken again (234–5). Pleasure in the poetic and theatrical possibilities of their own tongue must have been a bonding factor at the drama competitions. Aeschylus' *Persians* and *Suppliants*, with their barbarian choruses and characters, show that the earlier tragic theatre found in the Greek confrontation with the ethnically different, however 'racist' in modern terms the effect may be, a rich seam to mine. The Persians of course speak Greek, but it is an exotic, colourful Greek, with flat 'a' vowel sounds chosen to create an 'eastern effect', strings of foreign-sounding names, and unintelligible interjections in the choral odes which suggest an alien discourse. The Egyptians of *Suppliants*, similarly, enunciate strings of 'a' sounds (difficult to convey in translation), use some exotic vocabulary, and no doubt the music accompanying their extensive choruses supported the barbarian ambience. It is with mounting excitement, therefore, that in *Agamemnon* the audience must have waited for the barbarian Cassandra to desist from silence, although it turns out, as she says, that she knows Greek all too well (1254).

In Euripides, the Greek spoken by barbarians is indistinguishable from that of the Greek characters (although in lyric passages the music may well have created a foreign atmosphere), but there is a recurring discussion of barbarian ways of thinking and talking in a more abstract sense. Agamemnon orders the overwrought Thracian Polymestor to cast the 'barbarian' element out of his heart and speak like a rational man (*Hecuba* 130–1). In Euripides, indeed, the polarity between Greek and barbarian is subject to examination and gives rise to powerful rhetorical and ironic effects. These reveal that an underlying stereotype of the barbarian underpinned Greek ideology in the fifth century, which assumed that where Greeks were manly, courageous, intelligent, and law-abiding, barbarians were the opposite—effeminate, cowardly, unintelligent, and either despotic or anarchic. Euripidean speakers therefore often play on these assumed distinctions between the Greek values and 'way of life', and the customs observed in barbarian communities. Jason blames Medea's bad behaviour on her alien provenance, and insists, patronizingly, that he was doing her a favour in bringing her to the advanced civilization of Greece (537–41). The Spartan characters in *Andromache* throw anti-barbarian insults at Hector's captive widow. In *Helen* the brother and sister Theoclymenus and Theonoe personify the twin extremes of the Greeks' complex vision of

Egypt—one is a violent, rapacious pharaoh, while the other a spiritual and pious high priestess.[7]

The invention of the idea of the barbarian stretched a long shadow over the Greek tragic stage. Greeks who were misbehaving could now be portrayed as turning, psychologically and ethically speaking, into barbarians. In Aeschylus' *Agamemnon* Clytemnestra, who wants to imply that her husband's sojourn in the East has gone to his head, performs a prostration before him like a Persian courtier before the Persian king (919–20). In Euripides' *Orestes* Menelaus has indeed come back from Troy with an effeminized gait and despotic tendencies (348–50). In his *Iphigenia among the Taurians* the irony is stressed that while the Black Sea barbarians sacrifice intruders into their country, the Greeks commit matricide and execute their own daughters at shrines of Artemis. In *Bacchae*, the polarity between Greece and barbarian becomes a metaphor for something very different—attitudes to the altered states of consciousness that can be accessed by Dionysiac religion.

The barbarians of the Greek tragic stage had their real-life counterparts in Athenian society. Amongst the resident foreigners classified as 'metics', there were undoubtedly individuals with a barbarian upbringing, or, if they had been born in Athens, an ethnic identity informed by barbarian parentage and possibly bilingualism. Metics may have been present in some numbers at drama competitions, at least at those held at the Lenaea, where they were even allowed to fund choruses. They are not known to have been excluded from at least *watching* plays at the Dionysia. Moreover, although evidence is thin on the ground (not least, presumably, because a naturalized citizen would be unlikely to want to draw attention to foreign origins), it was at least possible for a metic to become a citizen.

Yet the largest category of non-Greeks in Athens was undoubtedly constituted by slaves. Indeed, it is difficult to over-stress the intimacy of the connection in the ancient mind between ethnic difference and suitability for slavery; the idea may have reached its most developed theoretical exposition in the first book of Aristotle's *Politics*, but it is implicit in much of the discussion of slavery prior to that. It is certainly an issue, for example, in Plato's *Lysis*, where Socrates emphasizes that a young citizen boy has less liberty than a slave. Indeed, he is ruled by a slave in the form of his *paidagōgos*, a word which used to be translated 'tutor' but which actually designates a 'minder' with some responsibility for the education of the youth he attends. Socrates remarks that it is a terrible thing for a free man to be ruled by a slave (208c–d). At the end, he remembers (223a–b),

there arrived the *paidagōgoi* of Lysis and Menexenus, like supernatural beings, bringing with them the boys' brothers; they called out to them, telling them it was time to be off, for it was already late. At first both we and the bystanders tried to drive them off, but they took no notice of us at all, and became annoyed and carried on calling out in their barbarian speech. They seemed to us to have become a bit tipsy at the Hermaia.

The elevated Greek conversation is thus contrasted with the drunken barbarisms of the boys' slave-class minders, theatrically—and ironically—presented like gods suddenly appearing on stage: the word used of their speech implies that they had a pronounced foreign accent. Yet if these semi-barbarian *paidagōgoi* could move freely around the town, and attend the festival of Hermes, god of the gymnasium, who is to say that they were necessarily excluded completely from any of the public festivals of Dionysus?

Slavery was a central institution of the classical Athenian *polis*: only the most impoverished citizen could not afford a slave at all. Slavery affected the Athenians' conceptualization of the universe at every level, a process reflected in their metaphors, for the citizen perceived analogies between his relationships with slaves and his relationships with women and children. He could use slavery to express the terrible pressures on men in power: in a neat rhetorical inversion of the real power structure, Agamemnon in *Iphigenia in Aulis* reflects that low birth (*dusgeneia*) has its advantages, for the obligation of the highborn to preserve their public dignity means that they are metaphorically 'enslaved' to the crowd (450). Slavery was even used to express the perception of fate: Heracles realizes after his madness that men are 'enslaved' to fortune (*Heracles* 1357).

It is always a struggle to remind ourselves of the ubiquity of slaves in classical Athens, and what must have been the theatregoer's daily experience of dealing with individuals who were not Greeks and who were institutionally powerless. The boundary between Greek and barbarian was less a 'vertical' curtain encircling the areas of the Mediterranean and Black Sea mainly populated by Greek-speaking communities than, in Athens at least, a 'horizontal' slicing across the heart of the community, both within the city walls and beyond them in more rural demes. Slavery imposed an intellectual pressure on the class of owners, forced to create elaborate rationales to justify the everyday conviction that one ethnic group was either naturally, or culturally, more slavish than another (see below). The level of emotional pressure that slavery imposed both on slaves and on masters is most devastatingly illustrated by the assumption in Plato's *Republic* that the slaves of a rich man would instantly kill him, together with his wife and his children, if they were given the opportunity to do so (9.578d–79c). The property confiscated by the state from the Athenian metic Cephisodorus in 425 BCE remains one of the most eloquent reminders of the type of slave being transferred from one owner to another in classical Athens at the time when Euripides and Sophocles were writing their tragedies.[8] Among his possessions, he had counted women, men, and children from Thrace, Caria, Syria, Scythia, Lydia, Colchis, and elsewhere. This ethnic mixture would have been approved by the venerable Athenian in Plato's *Laws*, who regarded it is an important principle of slave management to keep apart slaves who could speak the same barbarian language (*Laws* 6.777c–d).

Indeed, the participation of both slaves and ex-slaves in the consumption of classical Greek theatre is a topic that deserves more consideration. Some scholars have argued that Socrates is only talking hypothetically when in Plato's *Gorgias* he describes tragedy as a form of rhetoric that aims solely at giving pleasure, as much to slaves, women, and children as to the male and free (502 b–d). But Theophrastus implies that by the later part of the fourth century, at least, it was standard practice for any Athenian citizen who could afford it to be attended by a personal slave who placed the cushion on his seat at the theatre (*Characters* 21.4), as well as for the habitual sponger to trick other people into subsidizing a seat at the theatre for his children's *paidagōgos* (*Characters* 9.5). Much earlier, in the late fifth century, there were almost certainly state slaves such as the Scythian archers present at the City Dionysia, because one of their official roles was the regulation of crowd behaviour at large gatherings of people in public spaces. They may not have paid close attention to the performances, but the question of their responses, especially when they were themselves impersonated in comedy, can scarcely be dismissed altogether.[9] Slaves were often skilled musicians: we simply do not have the evidence to prove whether or not an attested slave pipe-player (*aulētēs*), known to have been active in Athens in 415 BCE, had ever experienced the representation of any barbarian character in any of the performance arts (Andocides 1.12). The most important group, however, is constituted by the slaves who were emancipated as a reward for rowing alongside Athenian citizens in 406 BCE.

Nor were the opportunities to react to theatre restricted to actual full performances at festivals. Plays needed to be rehearsed for weeks—indeed months—before performances, and were much discussed after them. Speeches from tragedy were, by the time of Aristophanes' *Clouds* (1371–2), being recited at symposia; scenes from drama, or myths regularly enacted in drama, were painted on the vases from which slaves served their masters, and Sian Lewis has recently reminded us that vase-paintings were 'an open form of communication, available to every gaze', and their meanings were therefore construed in the minds of slaves as well as in those of free people.[10] It is of course impossible to be sure how an individual metic or slave might have responded to Aeschylus' savage Egyptian herald in *Suppliants*, to Euripides' obtuse Crimean monarch Thoas, or to the loyal pedagogue in Sophocles' *Electra*. But that does not mean that we should avoid asking the question. If the male slave from Colchis belonging to Cephisodorus who we know was sold at Athens in 414/13 (see above) ever witnessed, or heard about, a production of Euripides' *Medea*, or even saw a vase on which this tragedy was painted, can his reactions to her and her nurse have been identical to those of an Athenian Greek? The largest group of barbarian slaves at Athens came from Thrace: at least one Thracian slave, Sosias, was in a position of importance as supervisor of other slaves working in the mines, in 420 BCE (Xenophon, *Poroi* 4.14); this was just four or five years after the Thracian king Polymestor's shocking scenes in Euripides' *Hecuba*, and probably the famous *Tereus* by Sophocles, in which another Thracian monarch had raped and mutilated a freeborn Athenian princess.[11] The play-scripts of Athens only acquired their multiplicity of original meanings at the point that they were realized in the mind of each spectator, even if the vast majority of these spectators, like the authors, were indeed free and enfranchised citizens.

The civic male consciousness at the heart of the theatrical experience defined an identity shared by poor Athenian craftsmen, shopkeepers, and labourers with a smaller elite group of enormous wealth. While social class was complicated at Athens, since even the citizen body was divided into ranks, in tragedy almost all 'lower-class' people are actually slaves. There are some exceptions in minor roles, such as some anonymous heralds and messengers and the guard in Sophocles' *Antigone*. Yet it is one of the paradoxes of this democratic art-form that the crises it represented virtually always afflicted persons of aristocratic social status. Social class is not itself a prominent issue equivalent to that of either ethnicity or slavery. Although we know of one experimental tragedy in which the characters were all 'invented', and not familiar figures from myth (Agathon's *Antheus*, see Aristotle's *Poetics* ch. 9, 1451b 21–3), there is no evidence whatsoever that any tragedian ever attempted a tragedy in which the central characters were ordinary citizens of a *polis*. This was the privilege, apparently, of comedy, where non-too-wealthy citizens usually take the leading roles (Strepsiades in *Clouds*, Trygaeus in *Peace*, Praxagora in *Ecclesiazusae*).

If this paradox is to be understood it is important to remember that the mythical legacy which the tragedians inherited from the poets of archaic epic and lyric, the 'forests of myths' as Herington, paraphrasing Baudelaire, calls it, centred almost exclusively on the deeds and sufferings of royal houses. The tragedians' project was to reinterpret such myths for contemporary purposes, to dignify the present by marshalling in its cause the weight and solemnity of the past. But from another perspective we can see the royalty of classical tragedy as operating at a high degree of abstraction from social reality, encoding the newly discovered political freedoms and aspirations of ordinary men in the metonymic language of pre-democratic political hierarchies. Every citizen, free and autonomous, joint holder of the sovereign power under the democracy, and subject to no other single individual, saw himself in some sense as a monarch. As Northrop Frye astutely observed, 'princes and princesses may be wish-fulfilment dreams as well as social facts'.[12] The Athenian citizen liked to imagine his tragic self through the depiction of aristocrats.

Yet real aristocrats in real-life Athens still had considerable influence, and their own private lives and personal dramas were still played out, to appreciative audiences, on the public stages of the law-courts. There was still a widely held belief that high birth went hand in hand with both virtue and intelligence. Old and wealthy families still held a near-monopoly on the higher offices of state, and continued to use the claim of *eugeneia*, or superior pedigree, to justify their preeminence: in fifth-century legal and political discourse *eugeneia* appears as 'the wellspring of those qualities of mind and spirit that made a nobleman a superior person. Intellectual and moral proclivities are traced back to character, which, in the final analysis, is determined genetically'.[13] This contemporary social question is reflected in the frequent discussions of the inheritability of virtue in tragedy. On balance the statements are surprisingly reactionary, for example the kind of argument used by Iolaus complimenting Demophon in Euripides' *Children of Heracles*, where he says that 'children have no finer endowment than to have been begotten by a noble and brave father' (287–8).

Yet the exploration of the meaning of 'good birth' can no more be separated from the institution of slavery than can the issue of ethnicity. One of the most frequent forms of 'reversal' is actually reversal of status. Numerous characters, especially in plays treating the fall of Troy, lose previously aristocratic status and become slaves, a fate regarded in the tragic universe as particularly hard to bear (see e.g. Euripides, *Trojan Women* 302–3). This was the fate which women did actually meet if their cities were sacked in the historical period of tragedy: when the islanders of Melos surrendered to Athens in 416/415 BCE, the Athenians 'put to death all the men of military age whom they took, and sold the women and children as slaves' (Thucydides 5.116). Whether it is Cassandra in Aeschylus' *Agamemnon* or the chorus in *Libation-Bearers*; Tecmessa in Sophocles' *Ajax* or Iole in his *Women of Trachis*; Hecabe, Cassandra, Andromache, or Polyxena in

Euripides' *Hecuba*, *Trojan Women*, and *Andromache*, slave women, once royal but 'won by the spear', bitterly lament their catastrophic fall from high estate.

There is a crucial distinction to be drawn here. While heartbreaking descriptions of life under slavery are frequently rendered by tragic characters, most devastatingly by Hecuba in *Trojan Women* (see e.g. 190–6, 489–510), they are virtually all in relation to those once free who have lost their freedom. This seems to have been regarded as considerably more 'tragic' than to have been born into a whole life in servitude: as Menelaus says in *Helen*, a person fallen from high estate finds their lot harder to bear than the long-time unfortunate (417–19). Deianira can tell merely from the appearance of the enslaved Iole in Sophocles' *Women of Trachis* that the young woman is well-born, for she seems more shocked by her experiences than the others (309). The form of tragedy reinforces the distinction between the enslaved aristocrat and the slave from birth, for the medium of lyric song is denied to characters of low birth status, while enslaved aristocrats, in common with their free counterparts, often express their emotions in song.

Moreover, the once-free can regain their freedom. This is what happens to Andromache in her name-play, and to Sophocles' Electra, who is originally treated like a household slave, but has her status restored by her returning brother. Male characters who by accident of fortune lose high status usually recover it: in Euripides' *Ion* the servant-priest of Apollo at Delphi is upgraded to his birthright as heir to the Athenian throne. The disguised hero of Euripides' lost *Telephus* spent time in service as Clytemnestra's porter before his true identity was revealed to be the son of Heracles and an Arcadian princess. While tragedy can envisage the opposite social movement, from seeming aristocratic to actual servile birth status, it never actually happens. Oedipus in *Oedipus Tyrannus* considers the possibility that his natural mother was 'a third generation slave' (1062–3), and Ion indulges in similar speculations about his mother's class position (556, 1477), but in both cases their mothers turn out to have been aristocrats by blood.

In the case, however, of the never-free, slaves from birth, the tragic texts everywhere assume that the slave/free boundary is as natural and permanent as the boundary between man and god.

It was necessary to the perpetuation of institutionalized slavery to foster a belief in the *natural* servility of those born into the slave class, and there is no character in tragedy who proposes abolishing slavery. The dominant view probably held by the majority of the theatrical audience was that enunciated by a character in Euripides' lost *Antiope*, who said that 'a slave ought never to form an opinion becoming a free person, nor to covet leisure' (fr. 216 *TrGF*); when slaves do express their own opinions in tragedy they often preemptively apologize for it, as Deianira's nurse in *Women of Trachis* prefaces her advice to her mistress with the precautionary words, 'if it is right to advise the free with a slave's opinions' (52–3). In the tragic universe characters can rarely improve upon the social status into which they were born. Even the free poor peasant to whom Electra is married in Euripides' version of her story, although he is to be made into a wealthy man by Pylades (1287), was originally from an old Mycenean family. The only exception to the inescapability of birth status is represented by the extraordinary claim of Hyllus' slave in *Children of Heracles* that Alcmena had promised him his freedom (888–91). Unfortunately the incomplete state of the text makes it unclear whether this unique promise was fulfilled.

Tragedy is replete with characters of slave status who perform various functions. Almost always nameless, frequently mute, they attend upon royalty, carry out menial tasks such as the arrangement of Clytemnestra's carpet in *Agamemnon* (908–9), or the binding of other slaves on the orders of Menelaus in Euripides' *Andromache* (425–6). The so-called 'messenger', whose function is to report violent incidents taking place within or away from the household, is often a slave. It is most intriguing that tragedy should have granted such lowly figures these privileged speeches, especially since slaves could not even give evidence in Athenian courts. And although modern audiences can find these speeches tediously static, the frequency with which the scenes they describe appear on vases is an indication of their ancient popularity.

Indeed slaves, although formally powerless, can wield enormous power in the world of tragedy through their access to dangerous knowledge. The Theban shepherd in *Oedipus Tyrannus* was born a slave into the Theban royal household, rather than bought in from outside (1123). This man with no name, identified variously as 'shepherd, 'peasant' and 'slave', is the only living person other than Tiresias who knows and has long known the truth concerning Oedipus. Parallels are drawn between the slave and the prophet, who are both reluctant to answer their summonses to the palace. Tiresias was sent for twice, and Oedipus was surprised at how long it took for him to arrive (289): the slave who witnessed the murder of Laius was also summoned twice (see 118, 838, 861), and when he finally arrives, Oedipus remarks in similar language on how long it took him to arrive (1112).

The ageing slave refuses to concede that he gave the baby Oedipus to the Corinthian messenger. Refuses, that is, until he is threatened with the torture to which all slaves were subject by jurisdiction in the law-courts of Athens. Indeed, slave evidence was regarded as virtually inadmissible unless extracted under torture;[14] lying, seen as unbecoming in the free citizen (Sophocles, *Women of Trachis* 453–4), was seen as a natural feature of the slave. Oedipus first threatens the Theban man with pain (1152), and then actually orders his attendants to twist the old man's arms behind his back, in preparation for torture (1154). Finally the victim breaks, and the truth is extracted from him. Thus perhaps the most famous recognition in tragedy, Oedipus' recognition of himself, results directly from the knowledge of a slave.

Many critics have objected to the coincidences which meant that so much dangerous knowledge resided in a single man, in particular that the same slave who was asked to expose the baby survived to be the only living witness of Laius' murder. 'This Theban is the man who took the infant Oedipus to "trackless Cithaeron," who witnessed the murder in the pass, who saw Oedipus married to Jocasta. In other words, astonishingly, wildly improbably, he has been keeping company with Oedipus all of Oedipus' life.'[15] But such criticisms neglect the social structures which meant that slaves, especially those regarded as particularly trustworthy through having been born into the house, must often have known more about their masters and their families than their masters can have known themselves. Is it really so unlikely that a man sufficiently trusted by Jocasta to have been entrusted by her with the exposure of the infant would also have been selected to accompany Laius on his mission to Delphi? The invention of this extraordinary slave-character, whose knowledge kills Jocasta, reflects at an aesthetic level the ancient awareness that the dehumanized slaves who lived cheek by jowl with the free, and were privy to their secrets, sometimes had knowledge with literally lethal potential.

The most interesting category of tragic slave is comprised by the old female nurses and male *paidagōgoi*, who were appointed to attend upon aristocratic figures in their childhood, and remained with them in their maturity. In reality such figures must have been repositories for enormous amounts of information about the households which they served, and the playwrights exploited this knowledge for dramatic purposes: in Euripides' *Medea*, for example, a nurse and a *paidagōgos* between them provide all the background information required by the audience during the opening scene.

The *paidagōgos*, appointed by a child's legal 'guardian' (*kurios*), usually his father, was in reality the *kurios*' agent in his absence, who physically represented his authority and interests. In the two *Electra* tragedies by Sophocles and Euripides the old *paidagōgos* does indeed symbolically extend the authority of the master who had appointed him, even beyond his grave. In Sophocles' version Orestes' *paidagōgos*, whom Electra significantly wants to call 'father' (1361), is an authoritative figure focused on avenging Agamemnon's death. He urges on the two siblings towards the matricide, rebukes them for time-wasting, and facilitates the murder by the brilliant 'false' messenger-speech he delivers, alleging the death of Orestes. Euripides, typically, stretches the convention to its limits. He makes Orestes' *paidagōgos* the man who had reared not only Orestes, but also Agamemnon himself. Thus his authority stretches far back into the past; he is the appointee of Atreus himself. Both nurses and *paidagōgoi* exhibit a profound 'vertical' allegiance to the households they serve, rather than to others of their class: two Euripidean slaves, the nurse in *Medea* (54–5) and the second messenger in *Bacchae* (1027–8), express their attachment to their owners, saying that good slaves share in their hearts their masters' suffering. Even Orestes' old nurse Cilissa in *Libation-Bearers*, while hating Clytemnestra and Aegisthus, remains loyal to the household as represented by Agamemnon's memory and Orestes.

The influence of nurses and *paidagōgoi*, like the knowledge of Oedipus' Theban shepherd, can be potentially lethal. A driving force behind the plot of Euripides' *Ion* is cultural anxiety about the influence of slaves upon free members of the household, in particular women. If there is a crime in this tragedy it is the attempted murder of Ion, whom Creusa, at the time she agrees to it, believes to be an illegitimate child of her non-Athenian husband Xuthus. She believes that Xuthus intends to bring the youth to Athens and thus wrest from her Erechtheid bloodline the throne of the land. The dangerous conversation between the slave and the woman occurs in the emphasized physical absence of her husband: Xuthus, delighted with the apparent discovery of a son, has left (749) for the 'twin peaks' of the mountain to sacrifice (1122–7). Creusa now enters, with her old *paidagōgos*, who was appointed by her father to look after her (725–7); the scene can be taken as implying an unhealthy degree of inter-class trust and intimacy. For Creusa insists that he is her friend although she is his mistress (730–4), helps him physically with his lame struggle onto the stage (739–45), and affectionately hails the chorus as her 'slave-companions' in her weaving (747–8).

The plotting scene which ensues enacts the influence which clever and trusted household slaves might be imagined by any absent male householder to wield over their mistresses. The upshot is that the slave leaves to slip poison into Ion's drinking-cup. But it is important to see how the scene evolves psychologically. The chorus transmits the necessary information (as slaves must often have had to do). But it is the *paidagōgos* who first suggests that the whole affair is a betrayal of Creusa, because Xuthus is contriving a scheme to eject her from the house of Erechtheus (808–11). Xuthus has, suggests the slave, been breeding behind Creusa's back and intends to pass on her inheritance to the bastard child. Meeting no response, the slave tells Creusa that she must kill both Xuthus and Ion, and volunteers to stab Ion himself (844–56).

Creusa ignores all this talk of murder, and spends well over a hundred lines lyrically lamenting her past, confessing to her rape and pregnancy long ago, and bewailing her fate in general (859–922, see further below p. 143). Once again the slave, who is almost preternaturally solicitous about the fate of the royal house, urges her to take action. Creusa, it must be said, does find the moral strength to withstand most of his suggestions. She wisely rejects the notion of burning down Apollo's temple (975). She also refuses to contemplate killing Xuthus (977). However, on the question of Ion's life she yields to the slave and provides the poison herself. But it cannot be sufficiently stressed that it was the slave who raised the question of murder in the first place. He encounters a slave's fate for his pains: he is tortured to extract Creusa's name (1214). But the plotting scene emanates from a social anxiety about the lethal combination of manipulative slaves and susceptible women left alone without free male judgement to guide them.

In Euripides' *Hippolytus* the crisis is caused by a similar interaction in the absence of a husband, between a nurse with a dangerous degree of initiative and a psychically frail mistress. The point, in human terms, at which the lethal machinery of this plot is set in motion, is the precise moment when Phaedra breaks silence and confides her passion for her stepson to her nurse, who is a slave. For it would have damaged none but Phaedra herself had it remained unspoken; she has, in fact, been in love with Hippolytus for some time, since before she and Theseus were required to leave Athens (24-40). Aphrodite informs the audience in the prologue that Phaedra has since been suffering the goads of *erōs* in silence, and adds the intriguing detail, the significance of which will only later become apparent, that 'not one of the household slaves knows of her affliction' (40).

The nurse tells the anxious chorus that Theseus 'happens to be out of town, away from this land' (281). On his arrival it is clear that he has been a visitor to a cult centre or oracle (792), for he comes garlanded with leaves, a sign of an auspicious mission (806-7), just like Creon in *Oedipus Tyrannus*, garlanded from Delphi (82-3). It has been argued that Theseus' visit to the oracle was invented for the present play (in the lost Sophoclean version of this myth he was in Hades, believed dead), and that the choice of reason for his absence was to 'be in effective contrast...with the disaster which greets him'.[16] But this is to overlook the ideologically loaded plot convention by which the husband-figure has to be physically absent while the meddling slave and the emotionally susceptible mistress can between them engender catastrophe.

Phaedra's nurse claims to feel nothing but benevolence towards her charge (698). What she shares with the *paidagōgos* in *Ion* is a loyal devotion to her mistress's position in the household, including her two sons. Her onslaught onto Phaedra's sentiments opens with the statement that Phaedra has a duty to continue living, for if she dies, she will betray them by allowing Hippolytus (an illegitimate older son of Theseus by an Amazon mother) to share their patrimony (304–10). She gradually applies more pressure, implying that the audience believed that slaves were always anxious to gain access to their superiors' secrets (328), and finally beseeching Phaedra with a formal act of supplication (310–33). She persists in the face of Phaedra's protests, and eventually Phaedra reveals that she is in love. But at the climactic moment when Hippolytus is named as the object of her desire, it is, significantly, not in the mouth of Phaedra but of her nurse (352).

Uniquely for one of such low social status, this slave is given the second largest part in this Greek tragedy. Her sinister role in driving the plot, indeed instigating it on the human level, would have been underscored in the likely event that she was played by the same actor who played Aphrodite, the instigator of the action on the superhuman level. The nurse is also dangerously well educated. In the speech designed to persuade Phaedra to act on her desire, she marshals arguments from moral philosophy, appealing to pragmatism and expediency, and also from cosmogonic theory, perhaps even Empedoclean philosophy (447–50). Euripides makes her cite mythical examples of the effects of *erōs* on the gods, whilst simultaneously signalling that the acquisition of such knowledge requires a full-time education in the liberal arts: these tales, she says, are known by those who look at paintings and spend all their time with the Muses (451–3).

The nurse also has too much initiative. In direct contravention of Phaedra's wishes, she decides to intervene with Hippolytus, thus prompting his misogynist rant, unfortunately overheard by Phaedra (see Fig. 3.1). An ideological premise of the plot is that when slaves act independently as moral agents the results can be catastrophic. And the moral boundary between slave and free is further underscored by the contrast between the nurse's breaking of her word to Phaedra, and Hippolytus' refusal to break the vow

FIG. 3.1. Phaedra listens with horror to Hippolytus and the Nurse. Victorian book illustration, unknown origin, reproduced courtesy of the APGRD.

of silence imposed upon him by the nurse (657–60), even when his father curses him. It is left to Phaedra to articulate the underlying premise of the first half of the play, before she departs to commit suicide, by excoriating the nurse for her untrustworthiness and meddling (712–14).

The hazards involved in talking to servants, signalled so conspicuously in Aphrodite's prologue, are made quite explicit in Hippolytus' vitriolic invective. He may well have been voicing the opinion of many in his audience when he states that women should not be attended by servants but by voiceless beasts, for it is communication between unchaste women and their attendants which brings unchastity into the world (65–8). Women devise schemes: their servants carry them into effect. What Hippolytus does not, however, articulate is the overall impression made on those who have watched the foregoing scenes: that trusted slaves can manipulate vulnerable women, and, given a little knowledge, force them into positions at which they would never have arrived alone. It is no accident that the 'boorish man' amongst Theophrastus' *Characters* is recognizable by his habit of confiding the most important matters to his slaves while distrusting his own friends and family (4.2). Aristotle recommends that children, whose moral capacities he regarded as undeveloped, 'spend very little time in the company of slaves' (*Politics* 7.1336a 39–40).

## WOMEN AND MEN

Clytemnestra and Agamemnon, Medea and Jason, Deianira and Heracles—all three tragedians portrayed troubled marriages that engender brutal and untimely deaths. Fear of male domination and rape underlie the predicaments of the Danaids fleeing forced marriage in Aeschylus' *Suppliants*, the women of Troy awaiting allocation to Greek masters in *Trojan Women*, and the terrified captive Iole in *Women of Trachis*. Female choruses have conflicted relationships with male rulers in *Seven against Thebes*, *Bacchae*, and Sophocles' *Electra*. Orestes assaults his aunt Helen and cousin Hermione in Euripides' *Orestes*; Antigone defies her uncle Creon in Sophocles' *Antigone*. Conflict between the sexes is the fountainhead of suffering in the majority of Greek tragedies.

The prominence of such conflict is inseparable from the prominence of women, of which the ancient Greeks were themselves uncomfortably aware. 'There are more females than males in these plays', remarked a character in a treatise, composed in the second century CE, on danced versions of Greek tragedy (Lucian, *On Dancing* 28); in a novel of similar date there is a discourse on the large number of plots which women have contributed to the stage (Achilles Tatius, *Leucippe and Clitophon* 1.8). Only one extant tragedy, Sophocles' *Philoctetes*, contains no women, and female tragic choruses outnumber male in a ratio of more than two to one. This has long been identified by scholars as a 'problem': since women were almost excluded from Athenian public life, it is seen as a paradox that they were so conspicuous in this most public of Athenian art-forms.

Various explanations of the paradox are customary. Women's role in religion, especially in lamentation and sacrifice, must partly explain their presence in a genre where death and killing are central focuses. Others see the Dionysiac origin of tragedy as explaining the emphasis on the feminine (see Fig. 3.2): maenadic frenzy often occurs in metaphors associated with kin-killing in tragedy because of its affiliation with the cult of Dionysus. Zeitlin refers us to the femininity of Dionysus, transvestism in his cult, and symbolic gender inversions in Greek ritual to help explain the role of women as the 'other' of the masculine self which is truly at stake in the theatre.[17] Anthropological symbolism suggests that cultures often use the figures of women to help them imagine their social order, even when they are not particularly visible in public life. Moreover, women were regarded as more susceptible to invasive passions than men (see below, pp. 134, 194), and thus women were particularly plausible vehicles through which to explain the occurrence of tragic events, and particularly effective in the generation of emotional responses in the audiences.

Yet talking collectively about 'women in Greek tragedy' is arguably as absurd as talking in generalizing terms about 'men in Greek tragedy'. The category includes children and ageing widows, nubile virgins and multiple mothers, adulteresses and paragons of

FIG. 3.2. Barrie Ingham as Dionysus in *The Bacchae* at the Mermaid Theatre (1964), reproduced courtesy of the APGRD.

wifehood, murderesses and exemplars of virtue, lowly slaves and high priestesses, maenads, witches, and a girl with a cow's head chased by a gadfly to the Caucasus. There is, nevertheless, a marked tendency in the extant plays to story patterns revolving around women who are transgressive (that is, women who break one of the 'unwritten laws', develop an inappropriate erotic passion, or flout male authority). This generic pattern can be taken as an aesthetic expression of a central feature of the classical Athenian male's world-view. The conventional plot typology can be formulated as follows: women in Athenian tragedy only become transgressive in the physical absence of a legitimate husband with whom they are having regular sexual intercourse. This convention applies equally to virgins and to married women, who transgress only in the absence of their husbands. The opposite rule does not always apply; husband-less women may behave with decorum (Chryosthemis, for example, in Sophocles' *Electra*, and Megara in Euripides' *Heracles*). But every single transgressive woman in tragedy is temporarily or permanently husbandless. This generic convention can be interpreted as a symptom of the Athenian citizen's deep anxiety about the crises which might envelop his household in the event of one of his frequent absences. Greek poetry repeatedly stresses the difficulty of keeping permanent watch over women in order to control their activities.

The pattern is in turn dependent upon the striking prevalence of the type of plot in which the male head of the household enacts a homecoming (*nostos*) during the course of the play. The *nostos*-plot had a masterly antecedent in the *Odyssey*, where chaos also reigns in the hero's absence, although his wife is not in this case the culprit. Perhaps more important archetypes were the *Nostoi*, the epic poems which told of the returns of many heroes from Troy, such as Agamemnon and Menelaus, and the difficulties (at best) they encountered on arrival. A large group of the extant plays involve at least one *nostos* by a prominent male: Xerxes, home from Greece in *Persians*, Agamemnon in his name-play, Orestes in *Libation-Bearers*, Aegisthus in Sophocles' *Electra*, Heracles in his *Women of Trachis*, Theseus in *Hippolytus*, Heracles in *Heracles*, Menelaus in *Orestes*, Pentheus in *Bacchae*, and Jason, back from Creon's palace, in *Medea*. Even Euripides' *Andromache* is a distorted *nostos*-tragedy: throughout the return from Delphi of the householder

Neoptolemus is awaited, but when he arrives, it is in the form of a corpse (1166).

It is indeed a paradoxical feature of surviving tragedy that although it is profoundly concerned with the Athenian's public, collective, identity as a citizen, its plots were set not in the male arenas of civic discourse—the Council, the Assembly or law-courts (see above, pp. 59–69)—but in the marginal space immediately outside the door of the private home, to which men returned from public business. The action takes place at the precise physical point where the veil was torn from the face of domestic crises, revealing them to public view, and disclosing their ramifications not only for the central figures' public reputations but also for the wider community.

This becomes less surprising if the relationship between the household and the city-state, which was no simple antithesis, is considered in its full complexity. The *polis* consisted of multiple households, and it was the place where the citizen body reproduced itself; the citizen's own claim to the rights and privileges of citizenship depended upon his ability to prove that he emanated from a legitimate union in an Athenian household, at least after Pericles had passed a law to this effect in 451 BCE.[18] The ability to produce new citizen males to perpetuate the democracy was to be much desired by any aspiring politician: a public man who wanted to get the confidence of the people or become general was certainly expected, and probably legally required, to own land in Attica and to father legitimate children (Dinarchus 1.71). In writings on political theory, 'public' catastrophes like stasis and revolutions are often traced to 'private' issues affecting eminent individuals, such as love affairs, marriages, and private lawsuits: Aristotle, who catalogues such 'private' causes of public crisis in the fifth book of his *Politics* declares that 'even the smallest disputes are important when they occur at the centres of power', and 'conflicts between well-known people generally affect the whole community' (5.1303b 19–20, 31–2).

A citizen's family life was also a deeply political aspect of his identity. It was important to be seen as the responsible head of a well-ordered household in the lawcourts; it was established practice for a citizen involved in a trial to introduce his decorous children onto the rostrum in a public display to enhance his chances of victory (see above, p. 63). His own treatment of his family was used to assess the way in which he would be likely to treat the Athenians if he were in possession of power: Demosthenes was criticized for dressing in white and performing public ceremonies only seven days after the death of his daughter (Aeschines 3.77). His accuser warns, 'the man who hates his child and is a bad father could never become a safe guide to the people... the man who is wicked in his private relations would never be found trustworthy in public affairs'. Yet it was his own family members' reputations which constituted the public man's greatest liability; political enemies might attack him precisely by targeting his wife or other dependants for litigation, ridicule, or censure.

A central obsession of the tragic theatre was the survival of the household by its perpetuation through legitimate male heirs. The institution of marriage necessary for the production of such heirs is a constant question for rhetorical examination, and it is a constant theme of tragic lamentation that the crises enacted will result in the total extirpation of a family line. Childlessness itself is a concern of men in tragedy; both Aegeus in *Medea* and Xuthus in *Ion* visit oracles out of a desire to produce children. In reality one of the worst punishments which could be visited on a convicted criminal—usually for political crimes—was the total overthrow, the physical razing to the ground of the house (*kataskaphē*), which was symbolically charged as the concrete visual manifestation of the whole kinship line through time. *Kataskaphē* entailed the denial of burial, destruction of family altars and tombs, removal of ancestors' bones, confiscation of property, exile, and a curse applying even to offspring and descendants. Heracles in his name-play by Euripides threatens to raze the house of the usurping tyrant Lycus to the ground in just this way (565–8). It was an attack, therefore, on the whole family line, on ancestors and descendants as well as the living. And the destruction of the household is a major theme of tragic drama. It provides the climax of Euripides' *Trojan Women*, where Astyanax, Priam's only surviving male descendant, is murdered: it is the reason why Medea chooses for Jason not his own death but the death of his new wife, by whom he could create new children, and deaths of both of his sons; it is the cause of Peleus' tragedy in Euripides' *Andromache*, when he hears the news of the death of his only son's only son: 'my family line (*genos*) is no more; no children remain to my household' (1177–8).

One of the most vulnerable aspects of any citizen's reputation was the public perception of his wife. The convention that respectable women were not even to be named in public stems from the same ideal which led Thucydides' Pericles to proclaim that a woman's greatest glory was to be spoken of as little as possible, whether in praise or blame (2.46). One tragic wife, Eurydice in Sophocles' *Antigone*, nearly conforms with the Periclean template of the perfect wife, since she is never even mentioned, either in praise or blame, until nine-tenths of the way through the play. But most tragic women, by emerging from the front door of the tragic household into the public view, are already running risks which most Athenian males would rather their own wives avoided; the more idealized female characters, especially unmarried virgins, are conspicuously made to apologize for their own emergence (e.g. Euripides, *Children of Heracles* 474–7).

A speech by Clytemnestra in Euripides' *Iphigenia in Aulis* sums up the position of women in the tragic universe. When pleading with her husband not to sacrifice their daughter, she argues that she has been a blameless wife, 'chaste with regard to sexual matters, increasing the prosperity of the household, so that joy attends you when you come home, and good fortune when you depart' (1159–61). There is an implicit acknowledgement that although women *were* transferred from household to household (by male consensus in the case of marriage and male violence in the case of war), they were essentially immobilized, in contrast with the unrestricted movements of men. Greek tragedy normally portrays static household-bound women awaiting and reacting to the comings and goings of men.

Arguably the most transgressive woman in extant tragedy is Aeschylus' Clytemnestra. She has not only committed adultery, but murders Agamemnon and Cassandra, and aspires to political power. But even she embarked on her transgressive career in the physical absence of her husband, who left her behind so many years ago to fight for his brother's wife at Troy. There is no suggestion whatsoever that she had transgressed her socially sanctioned role before his departure. Amidst all of her mendacity it is perhaps difficult to believe much that she says, but perhaps we hear echoes of a 'suppressed' female viewpoint in her comments on the fear and loneliness afflicting a woman 'sitting alone at home, without a husband' (*Agamemnon* 861–2).

In extant tragedy the adulterous elopement of Clytemnestra's lovely sister Helen is never actually dramatized. But in the several passages which refer to it, emphasis is often laid on Menelaus' absence from home when the incident occurred. In Euripides' *Iphigenia in Aulis* this is made quite explicit: Paris took Helen away from Sparta when 'Menelaus was out of town' (76–7). In *Trojan Women* it is said that the elopement could occur because Menelaus left the culprits alone in his house and went off on a trip to Crete (943–4). Thus the generic convention of the absent husband structures the construction of female transgression even in narratives of the past.

Deianira, left alone for vast stretches of each year by her husband Heracles, does not kill her husband intentionally. But the manner in which the plot of *Women of Trachis* unfolds, as a *nostos*-play, stresses the dangers inherent in leaving womenfolk alone, to make decisions without male guidance. Deianira's killing of Heracles may be the result of extraordinary panic and stupidity rather than malevolence, but it is conceived by her in isolation from her husband. Medea, living alone and abandoned by Jason, and said to be suffering from acute sexual deprivation, manages to kill Jason's new wife, his new father-in-law, and his children. It is also in the absence of Theseus that Phaedra embarks on the series of events which result in both her death and that of Hippolytus (see above, pp. 123–6).

Euripides' *Andromache* provides another striking example. In this play Neoptolemus' wife Hermione and concubine Andromache are living under the same roof, and Hermione conceives her barbaric plan to murder her rival and her child. Neoptolemus, typically, is removed from his household so that this crisis can occur: he is away at the Delphic oracle. Hermione ultimately regrets her miscreant behaviour, and blames it on 'foul-minded women...they would come to visit me, with their endless chatter: "Are you going to allow that wicked slave-woman to share your house and husband?"' (930–3). This instance exemplifies yet another generic pattern played out in Greek tragedy. While friendship between males of different households is consistently idealized, especially in the relationships between Orestes and Pylades and Heracles and Theseus, no such relationship between two women ever graces either the tragic stage or Greek myth in general. Friendship between females, even conversation between them, is consistently portrayed as a negative force in society, disparaged even by (idealized) wives (e.g. Andromache in *Trojan Women* 647–55).

Euripides' *Bacchae* is formally a *nostos*-tragedy. Thebes is ruled by the young Pentheus, who is away when the catastrophe begins to unfold. Dionysus announces in the prologue that he has sent the sisters of Semele mad, and that they, along with the entire female population of Thebes, are now out on the mountainside. What the audience does not yet know is the whereabouts of the king of Thebes, of for that matter of the husbands of Agave and her sisters. It gradually becomes apparent that the Thebes in which the Dionysiac frenzy has taken hold is surprisingly devoid of men. When Pentheus arrives he informs the audience immediately that he 'happens to have been out of town' (215). Soon the picture of the Theban royal family becomes clearer: not only Agave, but also her sisters Autonoe and Ino, are out on the mountainside. There are several references to Agave's husband and Pentheus' father, Echion, one of the original 'Spartoi' or 'sown men' of Thebes, who sprang from the dragon's teeth sown by Cadmus (265, 507, 995, 1030, 1274). Although it is not actually stated that Echion is dead, he is certainly not present in Thebes. Autonoe's husband Aristaeus is also mentioned (1227); he seems to have made his home abroad. Ino's husband, usually identified as the Boeotian king Athamas, is not even mentioned. Euripides has so structured his picture of the Theban royal house that the only men present, Pentheus' grandfather Cadmus and the prophet Tiresias, are aged and infirm when Dionysus comes to wreak his vengeance on Pentheus through the fragile medium of the psyches of manless women.

Play after play, therefore, portrays the disastrous effects on households and the larger community of emotions such as anger and sexual desire or jealousy, or divinely inspired madness, on women unsupervised by men. What were the social tensions underlying this prevalent plot type? Aristotle explained that the deliberative faculty, which is not present in slaves and is undeveloped in children, is actually inoperative or 'without authority'—*akuron*—in women (*Politics* 1.1260a). The term he uses for 'without authority' derives from the same stem as the term *kurios*, used for the male family member who had to act as legal representative and 'guardian' to every Athenian woman throughout her life. Yet there is more to this question than anxiety about male supervision. Virginity and chastity were perceived differently in the pagan ancient world: unmarried 'spinsters' were regarded as a social liability. More importantly, Greek medical writings suggest that for a woman between menarche and menopause the healthy, normal situation was that she was having regular sex with her husband, and ideally remained pregnant most of the time. Indeed, after puberty women were regarded as liable to physical and psychic disorders under enforced sexual continence. The gynaecology of the Hippocratic corpus frequently prescribes intercourse as a cure for the diseases of women (*On the Nature of the Child* 30.11, 82.6–12); for the Hippocratics 'menstruation, intercourse, and childbirth are collectively essential to the health of the mature woman'.[19]

The biological belief seems to be a contributory factor in the tragedians' portraits of transgressive wives: if Phaedra had consulted a doctor, it is likely that he would have prescribed sexual intercourse (with her husband, of course). Deianira, sing the chorus of *Women of Trachis*, is worn down by sleeping alone, without her husband (109–10). The belief also informs the characterizations of the insubordinate virgins, Antigone and Electra. The author of the medical treatise *On the Diseases of Young Women* regards girls in and after puberty as prone to madness; marriage and childbirth are the recommended treatment. In Sophocles' *Electra*, emphasis is laid on her unmarried status; in Euripides' version Electra is so disturbed that she jointly wields the sword which murders her mother (1225). In this play she is of course married, but the poet seems to indicate that he is aware of the latent generic convention by making characters twice stress that Electra's marriage has never been consummated (43–53, 253–7).

Yet medical beliefs alone are not sufficient explanation. The economic structure underlying gender relationships also underlies this generic pattern. Samuel Johnson once said that 'all the property in the world' depends upon the chastity of women: 'We hang a thief for stealing a sheep; but the unchastity of a woman transfers sheep, and farm and all, from the right owner.'[20] For male anxiety about female transgression, especially female infidelity, has always had an underlying economic explanation where property is transmitted down the generations through the male bloodline. One of the ancient Athenians' greatest fears was that his household would be extinguished by his lack of an heir. Even worse was the idea that his household might be extinguished without him even knowing it— that is, by the introduction of a son he had not himself fathered: in Euripides *Phoenician Women* the Corinthian adoptive mother of Oedipus tricked her husband Polybus in exactly this manner (28–31). Women were sometimes challenged to take formal oaths in front of arbitrators affirming the paternity of children (Demosthenes 39.4, 40.10, see Aristotle, *Rhetoric* 2.23.11). This Greek male preoccupation already found expression in the mouth of Homer's Telemachus, who says that he cannot be sure who is father is, whatever Penelope says (*Odyssey* 1.215–16). A character in a lost play by Euripides expressed the problem even more succinctly: 'A mother always loves a child more than a father does. She knows it is her own: he only thinks it is' (fr. 1015 *TrGF*).

Electra may hate her mother (see Fig. 3.3), but Sophocles' Antigone and Electra are both locked in conflict with their closest male relative of their parents' generation. It is not difficult to identify with the young women emotionally, but it *is* difficult to understand the impact their disobedience would have made on the original audience. From its perspective, the authority which Aegisthus (Electra's paternal second uncle) and Creon (Antigone's maternal uncle) want to wield would have been theirs as of right under Athenian law, at least until these teenage nieces married. When an unmarried woman's father died, her oldest adult brother would become her guardian (*kurios*), or her paternal grandfather if he was still alive. But in the absence of these she would come under the authority of the nearest male relative, beginning with the maternal uncle (as in the case of Antigone and Creon).

FIG. 3.3. The entrance of Clytemnestra in *Electra* at Girton College, Cambridge (1883), reproduced courtesy of the APGRD.

It is difficult to believe that under this system there was never any conflict at all. Is it possible that there was never any strong-willed young Athenian woman who objected to being ordered around by her *kurios*, especially if he was 'imported' in from outside during her adolescence when she was bereaved? Strangely, from our extant sources which ostensibly deal with the 'realities' of daily life, in particular legal speeches, we hear nothing of young unmarried women rebelling against their guardians. But this does not mean that it never happened; citizen men are unlikely to have been willing to admit publicly to such disgraceful and humiliating rebellions taking place in their households. But whatever went on in reality, Sophocles' Antigone and Electra prove that devastatingly strained relationships between an 'imported' *kurios* and a young unmarried woman were by no means beyond the imaginations of the Athenians.

Yet the understandable fascination with women who come into conflict with men in Greek tragedy has perhaps tended to obscure the variety and impact of the women who conduct themselves uncontroversially and with dignity in many plays. The Pythian priestesses in *Eumenides* and *Ion* are august and blameless. Cassandra in *Agamemnon* has never harmed anyone, unlike all the other royal characters. There is something quietly impressive about the sensible, moderate Ismene in *Antigone*, whose instincts are conciliatory but whose loyalty to her living sister eventually drives her into making a stand. Aethra in Euripides' *Suppliant Women* is a remarkable mature woman, intelligent and persuasive, who takes the initiative on a question of religious obligation to the dead and counsels her adult son Theseus wisely and effectively. The heroine of *Iphigenia among the Taurians* has a strong sense of her own moral agency and the wits by which to make it effective; what she wants, as she states, is to do something active to *save* her brother and therefore her family, as if in compensation for her utter helplessness when *she* was the one facing sacrifice at Aulis.

Iphigenia is responsible for thinking up all the details of the plan to remove the image from the temple, with Thoas' blessing, and to secure her escape and those of Orestes and Pylades. To Orestes, an effective lieutenant, she entrusts only the preparation of the ship and crew. Although it is Orestes who points out that she will need to secure the collusion of the chorus, it is Iphigenia who in an elaborate oath scene promises the captive Greek women her personal commitment to making sure, once she has won her freedom, that they are rescued and brought back to Greece as well. These are the plans and promises of an action hero, even if they are couched in the language of female solidarity.

## AGE GROUPS

In Euripides' *Bacchae*, the only mortals who understand what is happening to their city from the outset are two of its most senior inhabitants, the aged prophet Tiresias, and the (apparently retired) king, Cadmus, who is even older (see Fig. 3.4). Cadmus is keen to learn how to dance for the newly arrived god, Dionysus, since the joy generated by worshipping him can help the elderly to forget that they are old (187–9). Tiresias agrees, and asserts that it is not undignified to honour Dionysus, whose religion is totally inclusive (206–8):

FIG. 3.4. Cadmus and Tiresias in *The Bacchae* at the Mermaid Theatre, London (1964), reproduced courtesy of the APGRD.

> For the god makes no distinctions; he does not
> Define the obligation to dance for him as resting on young or old.
> He wants to receive honours jointly from all of us,
> He wants to gather honours from us all,
> To receive praise from everyone united, undivided.

Tiresias is speaking in the context of prehistoric Thebes, but his words apply to all Greek tragedy, which attaches significance to every age group, from young babies to the very old indeed. It does not presuppose that members of any one age group are morally superior to any others: there are several immoral old men, but just as many good ones, and the young range from ruthless hotheads to thoughtful and principled members of the community. There is a good deal of intergenerational conflict, however, even where it is suggested rather than, as it is often, fully developed in the action. The new king of Thebes in *Bacchae*, young Pentheus, would have been adamantly opposed to his grandfather Cadmus' plan to join the Bacchic revels if he had returned to Thebes in time.

Young people were granted much less room to separate from their parents and express their individuality than their equivalents usually expect nowadays. We hear little of domestic relationships in non-citizen families, but citizen boys were expected to grow up to respect their parents, look after them in old age, and serve the state assiduously both institutionally and on the battlefield. Even so, young men were not encouraged to speak up in the Assembly before they were thirty years old, and were actually prevented from serving on the Council until then. Young women, who were granted neither right nor occasion to address large groups in public, except other women at single-sex festivals, would be married in their teens and severely judged if they ever flouted the wishes of their menfolk or even expressed dissent.

Yet young women and young men come into conflict with their elders in many tragedies. No doubt these intergenerational confrontations reflect psychological reality in which the requirement to pass down the family name, status, and fortune as intact as possible put enormous strain on relationships. Even Aeschylus' *Persians*, the 'historical' play set in the recent past, sees the ghost of the dead Darius blame his son roundly for causing the empire such damage (759–86). Orestes, of course, kills his mother in plays by all three tragedians—Aeschylus' *Libation-Bearers*, and the *Electra* plays of both Euripides and Sophocles. In *Antigone*, it is Creon's inability to listen to the younger generation, quite as much as his intolerance of being disobeyed by a woman, that causes the deaths not only of Antigone and Haemon but of his wife Eurydice as well. Creon fails to benefit from several potentially helpful consultants because, as his son Haemon plucks up the courage to point out, he never takes the opportunities that are afforded him to foresee what people might say, do, or criticize. The reason for this is that nobody dares to help him deliberate since his face becomes so frightening to look at when he hears things he does not want to hear (688–91). Haemon is careful not say that he is offering his father formal advice (*bouleuein*), perhaps on account of a widespread feeling in Greek culture that it was inappropriate for the young to *bouleuein* their elders (see below); instead, he concludes with a statement in arguably milder language that since nobody can have complete understanding of every matter, 'it is also good to *learn* from those who speak well' (723). The chorus hastily tries to moderate even this by saying that both Creon *and* Haemon should learn from each other, but Creon demands to know why he, at his age, 'should be taught' by one so young (727).

The tragedians' audiences would have contained old men, even nonagenarians, but the choruses were probably dominated by very young men. It is therefore no surprise that the plays taken as a whole are even-handed in their depiction of age groups, and on occasion strikingly positive about the contribution that the young have to make to community decision-making. In *Women of Trachis* poor Hyllus' advice could well have helped his hapless mother, while the contrast between his reasonableness and his father's insensitivity in the closing scene is breathtaking. Older men are often shown to create their own problems by their quick tempers, such as Theseus in *Hippolytus*, who curses his son precipitately. Admetus' selfish father Pheres in *Alcestis*, although advanced in years, refuses to offer up his life to save his son's.

Yet although intergenerational conflict is ubiquitous in tragedy, there is a rise in the temperature in young people's disaffection in some of the last surviving tragedies, which premiered in the final decade of the fifth century. Euripides' *Phoenician Women* stages a scene where Jocasta desperately tries to reconcile her warring sons to each other. Sophocles' *Philoctetes* studies closely a moral struggle over an impressionable young man's soul. Euripides' *Orestes* stages the conflict which most explicitly uses age-related insults in Greek tragedy, when Orestes rather tactlessly asks his grandfather Tyndareus for help when he is facing prosecution for the murder of Tyndareus' daughter Clytemnestra. Euripides is here certainly expressing issues of enormous current concern at Athens, where private gangs of upper-class young people, bound together as 'comrades' (*hetairoi*) by some special initiation rite or oath, had directly precipitated the oligarchic revolution of 411. After the revolution, the toppling of the rule of the *dēmos* by the aristocracy had led to a general conflation of the concepts of an anti-democrat and a *hetairos*. The clubs terrorized Athenians in dark streets and behind closed doors, resorted to murder, and played an important role in the establishment of the Thirty Tyrants at the end of the war.

One of the main features of the gangs was that the members of each one were drawn from a particular age group, and the intense loyalty between members grew out of a sense of peer group solidarity. The gangs, for whom the democracy symbolized the old, establishment order against which they defined themselves, attached extreme importance to membership: 'reckless daring was held to be loyal courage... the man who decided to have nothing to do with the plots was regarded as an oath-breaker... the club bond was stronger than a blood relationship, because the comrade was ready to dare anything without asking why' (Thucydides 3.82.4–6).

In *Orestes*, the spotlight is on the three disaffected young aristocrats, Orestes, his sister Electra, and his friend Pylades. At the end of his vituperative scene with Tyndareus, Orestes says that at least he can now speak without having to deal with the senile interruptions of his elderly relative; in their dialogue, the large gap between their ages is used to symbolize the vast gulf dividing their ideological positions. Tyndareus insists, like an ageing Athenian democrat, on the importance of the rule of law. But the gang of three repeatedly affirm that 'for this trio of comrades there is one death and one settlement—death for all or life for all' (1244–5). One of the most important ways in which the gang-members helped each other was in litigation, and Pylades supports Orestes at his trial. These three *hetaroi* work themselves up to compound the murder of Clytemnestra with that of her (in this play) silly but relatively harmless sister Helen. This is Pylades' idea, supplemented by Electra's vicious plot to take her cousin, the innocent young Hermione, hostage. This idea occurs to them after considering suicide in a meeting that resembles a secret assignation of vindictive and obsessively loyal *hetairoi*, whose conspiratorial alliance is created out of lethal violence. The play culminates in a massive staged conflict. The three young aristocrats are about to burn down the very house that had until recently been occupied by Orestes' mother, and his uncle Menelaus is leading an army of citizens against them.

Yet with pre-pubescent children in Greek tragedy, there is never conflict, unless it is so extreme that it takes the form of homicidal violence directed against them. Even then the small victims are caught in the crossfire in what is in fact a conflict between the killer and another adult—Jason in the case of Medea's children, and Eurystheus in the case of the deluded hero of *Heracles*. There are no young children on stage in the surviving plays by Aeschylus, which may suggest that the use of children was a later development. Sophocles uses children to great effect in *Ajax*, when the depressed hero tells his little boy that he expects him to grow into a mighty warrior, and at the end of *Oedipus Tyrannus*, when Oedipus is separated from his young daughters. But putting children on stage was perhaps instigated by Euripides, who is certainly the tragedian in whose plays children are used most and most emotively. Indeed, he had discovered by 438 BCE that a weeping child was a promising element in a death scene; when the heroine of his *Alcestis* passes away on stage, her little daughter and son are at her side. The boy, heartbroken, sings as he weeps by her corpse in a profound miniature dirge (408–10):

> I am little, father, but left behind
> By the mother I love, like a lonely ship adrift.
> It is terrible to suffer like this, and you, little sister,
> Suffer alongside me.

Some scholars have argued that adult actors must somehow have performed the role of children (the effect of which, with the aid of masks in a visual field as large as the Athenian theatre, would not have been as strange as it sounds). But children are certainly found performing as actors as well as singers and dancers in later antiquity. Euripides himself had a son who grew up to produce and probably write tragedies; it is perfectly possible that he used him on stage as a child actor, especially if he was a gifted singer. Euripides junior would probably have enjoyed the experience enormously, to judge from the philosopher Epictetus, who watched children playing games in which they pretended to be figures in tragedies as well as wrestlers, gladiators, and trumpet-players (*Encheiridion* 29).

In *Medea*, the children's physical presence throughout some of the earlier action increases the audience's outrage at the verbal violence being committed, and heightens the pain of the scene in which their mother embraces them before sending them inside to die. But their voices are not heard until, interrupting a choral ode, they scream in abject terror, from inside the house, that their mother is assaulting them (1270–8):

> FIRST BOY [*screaming*]: Help me! Help!
> CHORUS: Do you hear that?
> Can you hear the children shout?
> That wretched, dreadful woman!
> FIRST BOY:   Oh no! What shall I do?
> How can I get away from my mother's violence?

SECOND BOY: I don't know, my dear brother.
We're done for.
CHORUS: Should I enter the house?
I ought to stop this killing!
FIRST BOY: Yes—for god's sake, stop her! We're desperate!
SECOND BOY: The sword is fast approaching, like a trap!

Then their young voices fall silent forever. Euripides even adds further to the shock by displaying their bloody corpses in their mother's escape vehicle, the chariot sent by her grandfather the Sun.

Pre-adolescent children also die in *Heracles*, and make poignant appearances in *Children of Heracles*, *Andromache* (the heroine's young son is nearly murdered), and *Iphigenia in Aulis* (the baby Orestes). In *Suppliant Women* Euripides augmented his chorus of mothers of the Argive dead with another chorus of boys, sons of the same deceased warrior. But one play in particular shows that there may have been a connection between Euripides' innovative use of children and his reputation as the 'most tragic' of the poets—the one best at arousing the emotions of pity as well as terror. This was illustrated in antiquity by the singularly upsetting *Trojan Women*. In this play the infant Astyanax is torn from his mother Andromache's arms in full view of the audience, hurled from the walls of Troy, and then brought onstage to be prepared for burial by his devastated grandmother Hecuba (see above pp. 76–8). Some spectators have always found these two scenes unwatchable (as I have since I became a mother). A wicked northern Greek tyrant named Alexander, for example, who quite happily tortured and murdered on a large scale, had to leave a production of this play because he burst into tears 'at the sorrows of Hecuba and Andromache', and dared not demonstrate psychological weakness in front of his populace (Plutarch, *Life of Pelopidas* 39.4–6).

Euripides fleetingly raised the possibility that Clytemnestra might be pregnant in his iconoclastic *Electra* (626; see below p. 264); Greek tragedy, so focused on death, does have an interest in childbirth. Babies are inherently part of the Dionysiac sphere, the repertoire of images related to this god's myths, cults, and poetic narratives, for example in the description of the neonate Theban mothers who leave their houses, their breasts bursting with milk, for the mountainsides in Euripides' *Bacchae*

(699–702). There was at least one Dionysiac festival at Athens in which not only small children but babies who were still at the crawling stage (i.e. less than thirteen months or so) seem to have featured prominently, the Anthesteria. Dionysus has a close affinity in art with very young children, and babies are important in the playful world of his attendant satyrs. Tragedy probably absorbed its babies from a combination of the famous scene in *Iliad* book 6, where Hector says goodbye to his little son before entering battle, and satyr drama, in which birth and babies seem to have been a fundamental theme. This interest may have been connected with the theme of divine birth and infancy characteristic of archaic hymns, especially in the cases of Zeus's children Hermes, Apollo, and Artemis.

From Clytemnestra in *Agamemnon* (1417–18) through to Euripides' *Medea* (248–51) and onwards, appealing to the pain of childbirth had been a rhetorical marker of the emotionally disturbed tragic woman: in *Hippolytus* the more discreet chorus women consider that certain ailments—probably gynaecological ones—are 'unspeakable' and must be treated by women rather than referred to male doctors (293–96). In *Eumenides*, gynaecological speculations underlie the discussion of the rival paternal and maternal claims to ownership of the child when it has left the womb. The myth enacted in Euripides' *Medea* has been connected with ancient Greek belief in demons who threatened women and their offspring around and shortly after childbirth.[21] Nosologists have speculated about the medical identity (malaria?) of the 'Fever-god' causing women's 'barren pangs' in the plague-beset Thebes of *Oedipus Tyrannus*. Loraux's study of the conceptual equivalence between men who died on the battlefield and women who died in childbirth included discussion of dramatic texts, especially Medea's preference for standing three times by her shield than giving birth once (Euripides, *Medea* 248–51). Athena's announcement at the end of *Iphigenia among the Taurians*, that the clothes of women who died in childbirth will be dedicated to Iphigenia at Brauron (1462–7), has attracted attention both because of the availability of inscriptions listing garments donated to Artemis at Brauron, and because Athena's ordinance misrepresents known cult practice. In *Ion* Creusa's memory of her lonely labour has been shown to be implicated in the Athenian myth of autochthony; the first stasimon has been shown to violate the female language of prayer for good birth associated with Athenian cult.

Women generally began to have children so young in classical Athens that it is dangerous to attempt to give an age to the older women and female choruses of Greek tragedy. The women who have adult sons in battle in Euripides' *Suppliant Women*, for example, need not be any older than their mid-thirties. But the grandfather figures and choruses of old men who are explicitly said to be too old to fight are a rather different matter, since in many states, including Athens, it was normal not to be released from military service until the age of sixty. The choruses, therefore, of Aeschylus' *Persians* or *Agamemnon* and Euripides' *Heracles*, whose advancing years are repeatedly stressed, were indeed imagined as old-age pensioners by modern standards.

When the chorus of Euripides' *Heracles* enter the theatre in response to the pleas for help of another old man, thus providing a stark visual contrast with the three little boys huddling as terrified suppliants at the Theban altar of Zeus, each describes themselves thus (107–15):

> Leaning on my walking-stick,
> Singing a doleful lament like a bird that has gone grey,
> My only power the power of speech,
> An apparition such as comes in nocturnal dreams,
> Shaky with age, but meaning well.

A little later, when they witness the brutal new tyrant of their city threaten Heracles' family with death, they complain bitterly that old age is stopping them from taking up arms and intervening (252–74). They have a counterpart in the man to whose aid they come, Amphitryon, Heracles' father, who has the largest role in the play. But by giving his chorus memories that extend far back into the past, Euripides is able to inspect his hero in a way that similarly stretches back over many years, giving the play a philosophical depth which has been remarked upon frequently. It gives the authority of men who were alive at the time of the great labours that Heracles has had to endure, from the slaying of the Nemean lion to Hades, where he is currently believed to have travelled. It also heightens the celebration of manhood at its physical peak, a phenomenon admired above all else by the ancient Athenians, who even held contests in male comeliness.[22] But the point is not entirely a cerebral question. The chorus' poetry explores the effects of old age on the male body, in language that must have been accompanied by careful choreography (119–24):

> Don't overdo things as you drag your heavy limbs
> Like a colt under the yoke, exhausted from pulling
> The weight of a wheeled wagon up a rocky slope.
> Grab someone's hands or clothes
> If your feet stumble.

But youthful bodily excellence is at the same time a prime symbol of mortality, since, once lost, it can never be recovered. This theme, indeed, is explored by this chorus in one of Euripides' most arresting lyrics (637–48):

> Youth is forever desirable to me, but old age
> Hangs over my head, a heavier load than the crags of Etna,
> Shrouding my eyes in darkness.
> Not even the wealth of an Asian potentate,
> Not even palaces crammed with gold
> Should be seen as equivalent in worth to one's youth,
> Which is the greatest blessing, whether you are rich or poor.

The generation of tragic emotion often relies on the idea that it was somehow a perversion of nature for a father or indeed grandfather to bury a member of a younger generation. The importance of grandfather figures in tragedy reflects the need of Athenian society to represent the father–son relationship, a need which Strauss argues has been central to all patrilineal societies until very recently indeed: 'The uncertainty (before the modern technology of verification) of paternity makes it necessary for a culture and the individuals within it to construct, discursively, the ties that bind father and son.'[23] Those ties, which can be explored 'discursively' by dramatizing them in a play, are both more complex and more fragile than the patently physical bond between birth mother and her infant.

Greek tragedy was an arena in which to affirm the ties that bind the *oikos* across the generations of *men*. As Fowler has succinctly put it when discussing ancient Greek genealogical thinking: 'In patrilinear societies the male line is cohesive and extends ideally in both directions forever.'[24] The independent nuclear household, rather than the extended family, dominated the architecture and economy of classical Athens.[25] It is against this background that we need to understand the predominance of the nuclear *oikos* in classical Athenian ideology and therefore also in the theatre. The importance of the *grand*father—apparent in the scrutiny of candidates for citizenship and the archonship ([Aristotle], *Constitution of the Athenians* 52–5)—and the continuity of the intergenerational male line, are therefore fundamental to the confrontation of the generations in tragedy.

But this sociological approach does not tell the full story. In a play where the young meet untimely deaths, the choice of an elderly chorus adds greatly to the pathos. Surviving when younger, healthier people do not, and telling the story from a viewpoint freighted with experience of suffering, is part of the Greek tragic vision. No Greek choruses and only a minority of the Greek tragic heroes die at the end of the plays: they are what we now call *survivors*. In the judgemental, Christian world of Renaissance tragedy, most perpetrators (and indeed victims) of murder, rape, incest, and so on, die before the end of their plays. But in Greek tragedy the bereaved women of Troy, the blinded, polluted Oedipus, the filicidal Agave and Heracles, and the disgraced and lonely Creon all stagger from the stage at the end of their dramas leaving their audiences wondering how they can possibly cope with their psychological baggage. When the survivors are grandparents and can personally remember the events of two or three generations previously, the tragedy is further compounded: Cadmus, driven from Thebes at the end of *Bacchae* after watching his daughter realize she had killed her son, Amphitryon, left behind in Thebes to bury small corpses at the end of *Heracles*, or Hecuba, foiled in her attempt to commit suicide by running into the flames burning Troy at the end of *Trojan Women*. Perhaps this is the most important of all ways in which Greek tragedy has resonated with the obsessions of an age that has itself only just survived the man-made horrors of the twentieth century. They are now seen as grown-up heroes for a modern age, trying to accommodate their guilt, their shame, their bereavement, and their trauma.[26]

## TRAGIC INCLUSIVENESS

The polyphonic tragic form, which gives voice to characters from such diverse groups, continually challenges the very notions that it simultaneously reaffirms. Some of the most thrilling moments in Athenian tragedy are created when women, foreigners, slaves, the very young, and the very old challenge the dominant value-system, and tell us how it felt. This did not go entirely unnoticed in antiquity. Plutarch complains that tragedy put specious arguments into the mouths of women, while the Christian writer Origen said that Euripides was regularly lambasted in comedy because he put philosophy into the mouths of slaves, women, and barbarians.[27] Some classical Athenians were already aware of tragedy's hazardous capacity to give voice to the citizen's subordinates.

On frequent occasions in the tragic texts themselves even the most virtuous of women, such as Andromache, are rebuked for speaking too freely and too antagonistically to men (Euripides, *Andromache* 364–5). If proof were needed of tragedy's radical potential for giving voice to the oppressed it is to be found in the third book of Plato's *Republic*. Socrates correctly argues that the major difference between drama and other kinds of poetry is that it consists entirely of speeches in the first person, that is, in direct 'imitation' of characters, to the exclusion of narrative in the authorial voice. He then suggests that the actual impersonation of 'inferiors' such as women and slaves, bad men and cowards, has a deleterious moral effect on the characters of those doing the impersonating, and it is clear from much else of his literary theory that he was as much concerned about the ethical damage done to the audience as to the actors.

Tragedy consists of pure and multiple antiphony. No genre is so definitively dialogic, nor erases the authorial persona to such an extreme degree. Interestingly, *mythical* poets and bards figured much more as characters in their own right than the extant plays would lead us to suppose. Orpheus was a central character in Aeschylus' lost *Bassarids*; both Aeschylus and Sophocles composed plays named *Thamyris* dramatizing the singing competition between this bard and the Muses; Euripides' *Hypsipyle* portrayed Eumaeus, the citharode and founder of an Athenian clan of musicians;

his *Antiope* included a debate between two twins over the benefits which poets can confer on a community (fr. 182b *TrGF*).[28] Yet the authorial voice of the tragic poet has been more completely erased from the genre than from any other ancient literary form, including comedy. The views of the speaking characters are thus subjected to no moral evaluation, except by other characters.

Even the laudatory tone with which Athens is usually discussed in tragedy is occasionally subverted. In Euripides' *Medea*, for example, the whole plot-type by which non-Athenian heroic figures could find sanctuary in Athens is subverted by the addition to their ranks of Medea, the murderous barbarian sorceress, who ends the play, unpunished and unrepentant, flying off on the chariot of the Sun to Athens, 'to live with Aegeus son of Pandion' (1385). And the panegyric effect of the famous choral lines in this play praising Athens (824–45) is undercut by its occurrence after the scene in which Medea has dominated the Athenian king Aegeus and wheedled the promise of sanctuary out of him. Perhaps the best example is embodied in the figure of Demophon in Euripides' *Children of Heracles*. On a superficial reading this play seems to follow the standard lines of the 'patriotic' tragedies relating events in Athens' own mythical past. In this play the children of the deceased Heracles, who are being persecuted by the Argive king Eurystheus, have arrived at the temple of Zeus (god of suppliants) in the Attic district of Marathon, a particularly patriotic site for the Athenians ever since the Persian Wars. The suppliants are received by the old men of Marathon with politeness, pity, and pledges of protection. The play abounds in praise of Athenian democratic institutions, especially the rights to free speech, impartial judgements in the courts, and to sanctuary. Yet various ambiguities suggest that in this play the Athenian king Demophon is not quite the exemplar of virtue the audience might have become accustomed to expect in the portrayal of an Athenian king in tragedy; he is made, for example, to threaten the herald Copreus with violence, an act of great impiety, as he is reminded (270–1). And later it is implied that he is by far too susceptible to the unreliable advice of oracle-tellers (a group who were often the target of condemnation in tragedy), when he heeds their admonition barbarically to sacrifice a high-born female virgin (399–409).

The idea that all Greeks were superior to all barbarians, however important a plank in Athenian imperial propaganda, was undermined and challenged in tragedy, especially in the case of the Trojans. Although they had been re-identified as Phrygians, and therefore barbarians, in early tragedy, their heroic portrayal in the *Iliad*, and the pathos of their situation, led the playwrights to grant them an exceptional status that lies between Greek and barbarian, and often to point out how savage and uncouth the Greeks themselves could be. Thus Andromache in *Trojan Women* bitterly addresses the murderers of her child, as 'Greeks, inventors of barbarian evils' (764).

By giving voice to persons of much lower social status than their aristocratic masters, tragedy also contains some remarkable imaginative representations of the experiences and perspectives of the lower classes. The military life and the personal experience of war of the ordinary soldier and sailor recur as topics of discussion, though their first-hand experience may be voiced through an upper-class figure: Peleus, for example, gives a fascinating speech in opposition to the militaristic Menelaus of *Andromache*, which despite his own personal high status permits the audience to hear a grievance which must often have been felt by the ordinary citizen, that the glory for victory in battle goes always to the general and never to the thousands of soldiers who laboured under his command (693–8).

By offering so many enslaved former aristocrats, tragedy can express some fascinating 'worm's-eye' views of the social system of slavery. The captive heroine of Euripides' *Andromache*, when attacked by her mistress, laments that as a slave she cannot hope for a fair hearing, and that people hate to be worsted in argument by their social inferiors (186–90). On a very few occasions even slaves from birth are allowed to express something of their life experience. Menelaus' loyal slave in *Helen* proudly declares (728–31),

> Even though I was born to serve,
> I would like to be regarded as a noble slave.
> I may not have the title of a free man,
> But I have his mind.

Later in the play a slave of Theoclymenus offers to die instead of the princess Theonoe, thus displaying virtues singularly lacking in his master; with great irony, he is made to say that it is a great honour for 'noble slaves' to die on behalf of their masters (1640–1). And Cilissa, the nurse in *Libation-Bearers*, speaks with remarkable freshness across the centuries about the labour and responsibilities involved in the care of infants: in her speech we are privileged to hear as authentic a description of the experiences of servile wet-nurses as survives from classical antiquity. We learn how as a baby Orestes disturbed her sleep with his urgent cries; we hear of his hunger, his thirst, and even his 'call of nature', which often meant that she had to launder his linen (749–62). Unusually, Cilissa also expresses to the chorus displeasure at the conduct and orders of her mistress, a truly 'suppressed' voice released by the imaginative capacities of drama, for the voices of the real discontented slave women of classical Athens are forever silent.

Moreover, the manner in which aristocrats treat their subordinates is an important means by which their characters are 'tested' in tragedy. Menelaus' cliches about the importance of the free not tolerating insolence from slaves in *Andromache* (433–4) are subverted by his own brutality and cynicism. The central function of the guard in *Antigone*, besides bringing the factual news of the two burials of Polynices, is to elicit responses from Creon suggesting how heavy-handed and impetuous a ruler he is turning out to be. The guard's fear that as bringer of bad news he will be punished summarily for a crime of which he is innocent (228), turns out to be more than justified, and Creon threatens him with torture unless he and his fellow guards find the culprit: they are all to be strung up alive (308–9). The herdsman who delivers the first speech in *Bacchae* serves a similar function with respect to Pentheus' tyrannical proclivities. He asks Pentheus whether he may speak freely (670–1),

> Or if I should trim my words.
> I fear your hastiness, my lord, your anger,
> Your all too potent royalty.

Similar language is used by the old female porter in Euripides' *Helen* who is terrified of bringing bad news to her master Theoclymenus (481–2).

Many tragic speakers disrupt the received assumptions about women. Euripides was aware that the poor reputation of women in myth could be blamed on the male poets who had created them (*Medea* 420–30). Euripides' *Medea* includes a supremely negative portrait of a vituperative, vindictive, and murderous female which could only be the product of a patriarchal society. Yet by giving Medea a voice, and *imagining* the emotions of an abandoned wife, it allows her to deliver the most remarkable account of the second-class status of women in the *polis* to be found in ancient literature (214–66), a speech whose explosive political potential caused it to be read aloud at meetings in support of women's suffrage (see Fig. 3.5). And all this is in a dense poetic language enhanced by highly wrought rhetoric (231–5, 244–9):

> Of all creatures who breathe and have a brain
> We women are the most miserable.
> First, we have to buy a husband, a master
> Of our bodies, at an extortionate price.
> The most difficult issue we face is whether we get

FIG. 3.5. Sybil Thorndike as Medea outside Christ Church Library, Oxford, reproduced courtesy of the APGRD.

A bad husband or a good one. For divorce
Brings disgrace on a woman, and she can't refuse her husband...
When a man is bored with the company at home
He goes out and relieves his vexation
By socializing with a male friend or someone of his own age,
While we can only resort to a single person.
And they say that we live a danger-free life at home
While they fight with the spear. They are wrong.
I would rather stand three times in battle with my shield
Than give birth a single time.

Medea was not alone: a striking example is Procne's denunciation of women's experience of marriage in Sophocles' famous *Tereus*. In this play Procne's husband had raped and mutilated her sister. Procne complains as follows on behalf of women (fr. 583 *TrGF*):

When we reach adolescence and full understanding,
We are packed off and sold, far away from our ancestral gods and parents.
Some of us go to the houses of complete strangers, others to foreigners,
Some to houses who know no happiness, others to hostile ones.
And once we have been yoked to our husbands on our wedding night,
We are compelled to speak well of our situation and maintain that all is well.

Tragedy's medium of communication operates at a more heightened level of reality than everyday speech. The same language is shared by all the characters, whatever their ethnicity, gender, or class. Tragic language is a democratic property owned collectively by all who use it; in tragedy individuals whose gender, status, or ethnicity would debar them from public debate in democratic Athens paradoxically get the chance to speak in front of the massed Athenian citizenry. The elevation of the tragic diction used by Medea and all the others, moreover, actually permits it to elicit responses beyond those achievable by the mere communication of content. It is clear, then, that only a bifurcated reading, sensitive both to underlying ideological import and its explicit verbalized subversion, can hope to do justice to texts of such complexity.

Moreover, if the texts are read in a manner sensitive to their portrayal of relations between men and women, there are signs that male disrespect towards women in the sphere of the household met the same disapproval in the theatre as in reality. For however pervasive the sexual double standard in tragedy, as in Athenian life, which allowed men multiple sexual partners while severely punishing female adultery, there is an immanent rule discernible in the genre by which the installation of a concubine *in the marital home* is strictly censured. Every man who attempts it in tragedy suffers death shortly thereafter: Aeschylus' Agamemnon, who brings back Cassandra from Troy, Heracles in Sophocles' *Women of Trachis*, who does much the same with Iole, and Neoptolemus in Euripides' *Andromache*, who has outraged his young wife Hermione by introducing Andromache to his marital home. As Orestes remarks in that play, it is a bad thing for a man to have two women he shares a bed with (909): in the world of Greek tragedy it is apparently not only bad, but fatal. The ideology underlying this story pattern is a refraction through a mythical and poetic prism of the same culturally endorsed notion which leads the orator Apollodorus to praise Lysias for having refrained from bringing his girlfriends home out of respect for his wife and old mother ([Dem.] 59.22).

From our twenty-first-century perspective, the Athenian democracy was not democratic at all. Women, slaves, foreigners, and the young had no political power and no right to participate in the public discourse of the city. Tragedy reveals at every level the sexist, hierarchical, and racist ideas and values which were necessary if the system were to perpetuate itself. And yet the fictional form of tragedy, with its juxtaposition of diverse voices, goes beyond the narrowly restricted notions of democracy and right to free speech that mark our documents of Athenian reality, such as inscriptions, historiography, and legal speeches.

Greek tragedy does its thinking in a form which is immeasurably more politically advanced than the society that produced Greek tragedy. The human imagination has always been capable of creating egalitarian models of society even when they are inconceivable in practice, such as the communistic utopias of 'golden age' myths. In tragedy the Athenians created a public dialogue in an egalitarian *form* beyond their imagination in reality. Its multivocal form and socially diverse casts suggest an implicitly inclusive vision whose implementation in the society that produced it was absolutely inconceivable. Tragedy postulates in imagination a world rarely even hoped for in reality until relatively recent times. It is a world which is indeed 'democratic' in something like the modern sense; it is a world in which characters of diverse ethnicity, status, and gender all have the same right to express their opinions and the same verbal competence with which to exercise that right.

Aristophanes seems to have been prophetically aware of our modern sense of the term 'democratic' and its relevance to tragedy. He gives his Euripides an extraordinary claim in his contest with Aeschylus in *Frogs*. Euripides actually says that he has made his tragedy democratic (*dēmokratikon*) by keeping his females and slaves, young girls and old women, talking alongside 'the master of the house' (949–52). Although it is to misrepresent the case to imply that Euripides was the only tragedian to have done this, since important roles are given to women and slaves by Aeschylus and Sophocles as well, this instance of the term 'democratic' deserves close attention. Its inclusive reference, extending to women and slaves, and encompassing age groups, has no parallel in Athenian literature. The people (*dēmos*), who exercised sovereignty (*kratos*), is elsewhere always exclusively defined as the adult collective male citizenry of the city-state. But the Aristophanic context in which the term is used inclusively is of course a discussion of *tragedy*. Despite the genre's prevalent tendency to sustain the social *status quo*, it does give voice to those debarred by their gender or class from what *we* would call their democratic right to free speech. It grants them temporarily, in imaginative scenarios enacted under the Athenian sun, the rights and freedoms normally enjoyed only by citizen males. Greek tragedy's claim to have been a truly democratic art-form is therefore, paradoxically, far greater than the claim to democracy of the Athenian state itself. The tension between its egalitarian form and the dominantly hierarchical world-view of its content is certainly one of the reasons for its constant rediscovery in the culture of the modern world.

# 4

# Minds

## THEOLOGY, CULT, AND RITUAL

Greek tragedy, as an enquiry into the reasons why humans suffer, addresses human relationships with the powers that run the universe. In the minds of most fifth-century Greeks, these powers were conceived in the form of the Olympian religion. For twenty-first-century minds trained to explain the world in secular or scientific ways, this can be difficult to understand. It also poses problems to people brought up in a religion with one supreme god, such as Judaism, Christianity, or Islam. But polytheism (which simply means worship of a plurality of gods) was what the classical Greeks practised, and it is fundamental to the action and meaning of their tragic drama.

Gods do actually make appearances on stage. Aeschylean tragedy offers speaking roles to Apollo and Athena in *Eumenides*, as well as to Hephaestus, Ocean, and Hermes in the play that is usually attributed to him, *Prometheus Bound* (see Fig. 4.1). Gods who appear in Sophoclean plays include Athena in *Ajax* and the immortalized Heracles in *Philoctetes*. Euripides' plays are frequently opened or closed by divinities, who include Apollo, Death, Aphrodite, Artemis, Athena, the Dioscuri, Thetis, Hermes, and Poseidon; in his *Heracles* Madness appears, terrifyingly, mid-action, and Dionysus is almost omnipresent in his *Bacchae*. This means that ancient actors had to dress up as and impersonate gods as well as kings, queens, shepherds, and slaves.

There are also certain conventions about the way in which gods are portrayed. They can arrive in a chariot, as Athena does in Aeschylus' *Eumenides*, without appearing arrogant in the way that chariot-borne humans do, such as Agamemnon in his *Agamemnon*.

FIG. 4.1. A transvestite Mercury/Hermes in a Victorian burlesque of *Prometheus Bound* (1865), reproduced courtesy of the APGRD.

In Sophocles and Euripides gods also have access to the theatrical crane in which they can physically appear in order to address mortals from above; no mortal ever appears in the crane unless they are dead (Medea's children), turn out in the end to be semi-divine themselves (Medea), or have been plucked from the world of mortals and be about to be turned into a constellation (Helen in *Orestes*). When gods mingle with mortals, at stage level, even if they are visible to the audience, they have the power to make themselves invisible to the on-stage characters (as Athena is at the beginning of Sophocles' *Ajax* and Artemis seems to be at the end of *Hippolytus*), and recognizable only by other sensory means—their voice or smell. They also do not normally sing lyric odes, the medium of heightened sensibility, misery, and madness, since displaying varied emotional states (except anger and vindictiveness) is not one of their theatrical tasks.

Yet gods, whether visible or not, do have other identifiable functions in Greek tragedy. The first is to take the lead in a personal relationship with an individual hero or human that affects the latter's experiences irrevocably. Hera persecutes Heracles because he is her husband's son by another female and is too successful for her liking. Another example is the relationship between Apollo and Cassandra, which is important in both Aeschylus' *Agamemnon* and Euripides' *Trojan Women*. Cassandra caught the eye of this particular god, and their troubled relationship underlay her prophetic gift, which in turn causes her crazed songs in the two tragedies in which she appears. Another example is the intense relationship between Artemis and Iphigenia; it is Artemis who demands a human sacrifice in the numerous plays which discuss Iphigenia's death, and it is at a temple of Artemis in the Black Sea that *Iphigenia among the Taurians* is set.

The audiences of tragedy were living in a world where individuals' own status in terms of their sex, age group, and what would now be called their place of work profoundly affected their relationship with the gods. Women gathered together all over the Greek world to worship Demeter and Persephone, while metal-workers formed guilds whose divine patron was Hephaestus. The second important function of the gods is in their bearing of a portfolio of universal, Panhellenic (i.e. 'all-Greek') responsibilities. Women facing physical rites of passage, especially childbirth and death, asked for help from Artemis. Wherever you were in the Greek-speaking world, you were likely to call upon Apollo for help with most other medical problems, as the chorus of Sophocles' *Oedipus Tyrannus* ask Apollo as Healer to rescue them when stricken by a plague (154). Apollo was also the Olympian helper of poets and prophets of all kinds (see e.g. Euripides, *Medea* 426–9). Choruses singing about catastrophes in war tend to blame Ares, the god of berserk behaviour on the battlefield (see below, pp. 212–13). Greeks about to thieve or use trickery needed the help from Hermes which the chorus of Aeschylus' *Libation-Bearers* asks the cunning god to bestow on Orestes as he assassinates Aegisthus (812–14). Hermes had other functions as well. He is often invoked by people praying for safe travel, since he was the divine 'escort' (*Medea* 759). This role takes on an intense form when he is invoked as his role of 'escort of souls', to lead the spirits of the newly dead down to the Underworld (Sophocles, *Ajax* 831–2). But the god whose Panhellenic function was most important was the top god of Olympus, Zeus himself.

Zeus supervised the implementation of the taboos and imperatives which constituted Greek popular ethics, and which repeatedly drive the plots of Greek tragedy. His primary assistants in this awesome task were his one-time consort or daughter *Themis* (whose name means 'The Right [way of doing things]' or 'Natural Law'), and his daughter *Dikē* ('Justice'). The taboos and imperatives took the form of boundaries defining what was traditionally acceptable or unacceptable behaviour; they are called by Sophocles' Antigone the 'unwritten and unshakeable laws of the gods' (*Antigone* 454–5), and by characters in Euripides 'the laws common to the Greeks' (e.g. *Children of Heracles* 1010). These laws regulated human relationships at every level. In the family they proscribed incest, kin-killing, and failure to bury the dead, all crimes that are repeatedly committed in Greek tragedy. At the level of relationships between members of different households and cities, these laws ascribed to Zeus the protection of three vulnerable groups: suppliants, recipients of oaths, and parties engaged in the compact of reciprocal trust required by the guest/host relationship. Traditionally minded Greeks believed that if they disrespected a suppliant, broke an oath, or killed the person offering them hospitality or receiving it from them, then Zeus might blast them with a thunderbolt or exact retribution another way.

If you were a person in a situation of extreme vulnerability, as many characters are in tragedy, then you could pray for help to a particular god, or the gods collectively. But prayers in Greek tragedy are not often answered.[1] A last resort available to the desperate was supplication. Characters in tragedy could put themselves in the hands of a god by taking refuge in his or her temple, preferably actually physically sitting on an altar or holding a statue, as the Egyptian women of Aeschylus' *Suppliants* take refuge in the Argives' sanctuary, and the chorus tell Creusa to sit on Apollo's altar in Euripides' *Ion* (1255–60). The other alternative was directly to supplicate the human being who had them in their power. The god who oversaw these procedures was Zeus in his function indicated by the title *Hikesios*, 'Zeus of suppliants'. Supplication is a formal entreaty, accompanied by ritualized touching of knees, hand, and chin, which puts the recipient under a religious obligation to accede to the suppliant's requests. Supplication characterizes numerous crucial scenes in tragedy. In *Medea* it is only by supplicating Creon that the heroine gains the crucial extra twenty-four hours' grace during which to exact her revenge (324–47). In *Hecuba* Odysseus, shockingly, rejects Hecuba's supplication when she appeals to him for Polyxena's life, even though, as it is revealed, Hecuba had acceded to Odysseus' pleas as a suppliant many years ago (245–53). In *Iphigenia among the Taurians* Iphigenia supplicates Orestes (1067–71), but also recalls desperately supplicating her father as she begged him to spare her (361–4); this terrible scene is actually enacted in *Iphigenia in Aulis*, shortly after Clytemnestra has supplicated Achilles (1216–17, 908–10).

When trying to control the behaviour of others in situations where secular sanctions were of questionable efficacy, promises and oaths were another useful expedient that came under Zeus' jurisdiction as Zeus *Horkios*. Oaths were considered extremely important as social 'glue' in Athens: Lycurgus the fourth-century orator said that it was oaths that held the democracy together (*Against Leocrates* 79). Several important oaths are taken in Greek tragedy; some of the more spectacular include the promise that the dying Heracles extracts from Hyllus that he will marry his father's concubine Iole (*Women of Trachis* 1179–90), Aegeus' oath to offer asylum to the heroine of *Medea* (746–55), and Pylades' promise to Iphigenia in *Iphigenia among the Taurians* that he will convey her letter to Orestes (744–58). Characters in Greek tragedy who are justifiably accused of perjury are all punished for it; they include Eteocles in Euripides' *Phoenician Women* and Jason in his *Medea*.[2]

Zeus *Xenios*, however, watched over how humans behaved in tricky situations of vulnerability created by entering the sphere of another's jurisdiction, or by receiving a stranger in one's own. The Greek tragedies, almost all of which portray at least one character entering an alien community (see above pp. 110–11), repeatedly explore how the principle of mutual respect during such encounters (*xenia*) is properly upheld or violated. The chorus of Aeschylus' *Agamemnon* is clear that Paris had offended Zeus *Xenios* (60–1). Permanent relationships of guest-friendship were formalized by rituals of gift-giving and divine invocations, and these rituals inform the growing trust between Philoctetes and Neoptolemus on the island of Lemnos in *Philoctetes*.[3] The relationship between Admetus and Heracles in Euripides' *Alcestis* revolves entirely around how a *xenia* relationship is affected by a death in the host's family, and in *Iphigenia among the Taurians* Thoas demonstrates the wrong way of receiving strangers by slaughtering visitors to his country.

The third function that gods performed was as the resident or patron deities of particular locations and communities. Each mountain and river had its own divinities, and these are mentioned in the hymns of tragedy, but each city-state also had its favourite gods and goddesses. Theban characters in tragedy may talk of the Theban river Dirce, but Dionysus and Ares are the ancient divinities of their town, and this is reflected in the poetry of the plays. Hera was the tutelary deity of Argos, as well as the goddess who, everywhere in the Greek world, oversaw the social transitions in women's lives, from unmarried woman to bride, mother, and widow. She therefore plays an important role in tragedies connected with Argos, above all Euripides' *Electra*, which actually takes place during her festival. The history of religion seems to have fascinated all three tragedians, who include in their plays numerous 'aetiological' explanations of the origin of cults and festivals. The whole of *Bacchae* is an aetiological explanation for Dionysus' cult in Greece.

The local importance of a particular god can be seen in the Athenian tragedians' obsession with Athena, the only divinity to take the stage in surviving plays by all three of them. In Aeschylus' *Eumenides* she announces the foundation of the Areopagus (see below pp. 225–6), having arrived in Athens directly from Troy (397–8) (see Fig. 4.2). In Sophocles' *Ajax* she opens the play, making

FIG. 4.2. Athena arrives to arbitrate in *Eumenides*; drawing of a 4th-century South Italian vase, now in the British Museum.

savage fun of the great Attic hero Ajax, destined to become such a benefit to her people. She is Euripides' favourite god, who appears with the second most important Athenian god, Poseidon, at the beginning of his *Trojan Women*, individually *ex machina* to explain matters of theology in *Suppliant Women*, *Iphigenia among the Taurians* and *Ion*, and, more mysteriously, behind the scenes, in his *Heracles* (1002–6). None of these plays is set in her city, but the audiences clearly felt that her perspective on a mythical event was usually worth their attention.

Special relationships, spheres of competence, and topographical affiliations all affect the way that the gods are presented in tragedy. Each play draws on all three types of divine interest in humans, and it is worth thinking about one example in detail. In Euripides' *Medea* the heroine has special relationships with her grandfather the Sun, whom she names when devising her schemes (406) and who lends her his chariot so that she can escape to Athens at the end of the play. She also has an intense personal bond with Hecate (see below). Jason, however, is quite clear that the divinity who especially favours him is Aphrodite (528). The theology of the play is very traditional, and the key divinity is Zeus in his capacity as *Horkios*, overseer of oaths, along with his designated partner in oath-protection Themis, and the elemental gods Earth and Sun, by whom oaths were conventionally sworn. The chorus intuitively feel that a woman whose husband has broken his oaths will be protected by Zeus (158–9), and say that Medea calls on (208–10)

> Themis, daughter of Zeus, goddess of the oaths
> which carried her across the ocean
> to Hellas, through the dark briny sea.

Indeed, when Medea finally realizes that she needs to kill the boys, after her dialogue with Aegeus has stressed to her what pain childless men undergo, she calls unambiguously on her 'friends' to help her triumph over her enemies, and the friends she lists are 'Zeus, and Justice (*Dikē*), child of Zeus, and flaming Helios!' (764). When she gloats at the stricken father of her children from the safety of her chariot, she reaffirms that 'father Zeus' knows what has really passed between them (1352–3), and what god would listen to 'a man who doesn't keep his promises, a man who deceives and lies to strangers?' (1391–2), thus implying that Jason has offended Zeus as both *Horkios* and *Xenios*.[4]

Yet the theology of the play also involves cults that were specifically associated with Corinth and its surrounding areas. Aphrodite was the most important god at Corinth as well as Jason's patron, and the chorus of Corinthian women sing an ode to her (627–41). Most significantly, at the end of the play Medea says she is flying to the cult centre of Hera Akraia, across the Corinthian Gulf at Perachora (one of the wealthiest sanctuaries ever to have been excavated in Greece). She will bury the boys and thereby found a Corinthian ritual (1378–83), which will atone in perpetuity for their deaths. The Doric temple of Hera Akraia was ancient and spectacularly adorned with marble tiles; everyone in Euripides' audience will have known of it. Moreover, the large number of votive objects that have been found there by archaeologists (amulets worn by pregnant women, and figurines) show that it was visited by individuals anxious about the health of babies and young children.[5] The killing of Medea's children was therefore presented by the tragedy as the charter myth for a specific set of cult practices in the Corinthian area. Greek myth and religion often exhibit this 'dialectical' tendency, where opposites are united in the same figures: seers are blind, the feared Erinyes become benevolent, and here children who have been destroyed are somehow to protect other children from destruction.

All over the Greek world, Hera was the deity who represented women's social status as respected wives, as well as the angry wife of Zeus permanently disgruntled at his infidelities. As such she shares some important features with Medea in a less specifically Corinthian way. But a discussion of the religion in this play is not complete without Medea's special relationship with the goddess Hecate, whom she names just once, when no men are in earshot, calling her 'the mistress I serve before all others, my chosen collaborator, who resides in the inmost recesses of my hearth' (395–7). It was probably as a result of this passage that Hecate came to dominate ancient literature's scenes of female witchcraft. But Euripides' portrayal of Medea was exploiting the real anxieties of Athenian men, who feared women with expertise in lotions, potions, and incantations. This is shown by the evidence relating to the real-life trial of a woman named Theoris in the fourth century, who was executed, along with her whole family, for the use of 'drugs and incantations'.[6]

Most of the religion portrayed in Greek tragedy is the religion practised by the tragedians' contemporaries as seen from a specific angle, which is public and sanctioned by the state. The rituals are conducted in public, many of them in the open air, and accessible to everyone or to specific groups (for example, the festivals of Heracles which excluded women). The personal religious beliefs, practices, and superstitions of the individuals in fifth-century Greek society are a different matter. There are fleeting moments in tragedy where we can glimpse a rather different world, where individuals, perhaps especially women and slaves, who held less official power, practised rituals to further their own interests that are often described as 'magic' or 'sorcery'. One example was the laying of a curse on an enemy before a confrontation with him in a court of law (see below pp. 220-2). Another is the secret use of what we could call pharmaceuticals with aphrodisiac or lethal effects, combined with undercover rites. The use of an aphrodisiac, in conjunction with a material object in which Hippolytus had been in contact, is the course of action recommended to the lovelorn Phaedra by her aged nurse.

The question of what the audience of tragedy really 'believed'— whether in the existence of the Olympian gods, the universality of certain standards of behaviour, or the efficacy of magic—is further complicated by the critique of traditional religion by some of the thinkers who will be discussed in the next section. A few characters in tragedy, especially in Euripides, do express some views that must have appeared advanced or sceptical to his audience. Cadmus in *Bacchae* tells the vindictive Dionysus that gods *ought* to be less susceptible to anger than humans (1348), and Iphigenia stoutly denies the tradition that the goddess Artemis could favour human sacrifice (*Iphigenia among the Taurians* 380-91). Orestes thinks that even the supposedly omniscient gods are as blind, confused, and ignorant as humans, and that sensible people must rely upon their own judgement (*Iphigenia among the Taurians* 570-5). Other characters express views that will have sounded modern and 'scientific'. They depart from traditional theology by attributing the workings of the universe either to physical causes or to the power of the human mind. In *Trojan Women* Hecuba wonders whether Zeus should be addressed as 'Necessity of nature or the mind of man' (884-6). In one lost play a character asserted that 'the mind that is in each of us is god'; in another that the first principle of the cosmos was Air, which 'sends forth the summer's light, and makes the winter marked with cloud, makes life and death'; in a third Air was explicitly equated with Zeus.[7]

Consequently there has always been a critical tendency to see Euripides as seeking to overturn or challenge traditional religion, especially belief in the arbitrary, partisan, and often malevolent anthropomorphic Olympian gods of the Homeric epics. It has been argued that in figures like the vengeful Aphrodite of *Hippolytus*, Dionysus of *Bacchae*, and the bloodthirsty Artemis of *Iphigenia in*

*Aulis* he included the most uncompromisingly 'archaic' and self-interested of all Greek tragic gods precisely to undermine them. According to this view, his theatrical divinities are a literary throwback to the old anthropomorphism, constituting a consciously reductive enactment of the commonly accepted personalities of the Olympians. Alternatively, Euripides is interpreted as a humanist who denies any but human motivation to human action and whose works operate on a similar principle to Thucydides' rationalist and atheological determination that it is human nature, *to anthrōpinon* (3.82.2), which drives and conditions history. Critics have even seen Theonoe in *Helen* as a proselyte advocating a new Euripidean doctrine: her striking statement that Justice has a great shrine in her heart (*Helen* 1002–3, see also *Trojan Women* 886) offers, allegedly, a completely new religion of peace and justice, which Euripides is urging should replace the old Olympian cults.

Yet it is mistaken to confuse Euripidean characters' more innovative theological opinions with his own (unknown) personal views. Moreover, many of the expressions of scepticism are more complicated than they seem. One rhetorical function of scepticism is to *affirm* the belief being doubted simply by raising it to consciousness. Orestes may doubt that the gods know what they are doing, but his scepticism brings his tense relationship with Apollo into sharp focus. This helps the audience to appreciate the play's underlying argument, which emphatically reaffirms the infallibility of the Delphic oracle.[8] It is true that Aphrodite in *Hippolytus*, Artemis in the *Iphigenia* plays, and Dionysus in *Bacchae* are unusually brutal and demanding, even by the standards of ancient Greek gods. But the deaths of Hippolytus and Phaedra caused by Aphrodite provide the basis for rites that will in perpetuity bring comfort to young girls about to enter marriage (1423–30), and Artemis still provides a shrine where families can dedicate the clothing of their women who died in childbirth (*Iphigenia among the Taurians* 1466–7). Dionysus brings joy as well as terror, and the songs concluding *Iphigenia in Aulis* help to prepare Iphigenia and the community for losing her. Ritual brings group consolidation and profound consolation, as a human response in the face of catastrophe. In *Heracles* something constructive is to emerge even from the terrible suffering of the hero and his family, when Theseus promises that after Heracles' death the city of Athens will unite in honouring him with sacrifices and a monument of stone (see above p. 101), and indeed Heracles was an important figure in Athenian religion.

The overall impact of Euripidean tragedy does no more than Aeschylean and Sophoclean drama to disrupt the three fundamental tenets of Athenian religion as practised by its citizens: that gods exist, that they pay attention (welcome or unwelcome) to the affairs of mortals, and that some kind of reciprocal allegiance between gods and humans was in operation, most visibly instantiated in rituals, especially sacrifice. Greek tragedy is fundamentally built around this view of divinity. The tragic performances were framed by the elaborate and substantial sacrificial rituals of the Dionysia, and ritual fundamentally informs tragedy's action. The libation scene in Aeschylus' *Persians* evolves into a scene where the ghost of Darius is raised through elaborate ritual (see Fig. 4.3). The chorus of demesmen of Colonus in Sophocles' *Oedipus at Colonus* prescribe in detail the ritual libation by which Oedipus can atone for polluting their sacred grove (he sends Ismene to perform it in his place). Water fetched by undefiled hands from a fresh spring is to be placed with honey but no wine into carved wooden bowls, and its handles crowned with the freshly shorn wool from a yearling lamb. The performer of the libation must then face East, and pour three streams of the liquid, the last of which is to drain the bowl completely. The earth where the libation has been poured must then be dressed with twenty-seven sprays of olive, using both hands, and a prayer offered in a whisper to the Eumenides (466–94).

The imagery of the tragedies is also informed everywhere by ritual practices. A study of wedding and funeral motifs has shown how they become conflated into sinister variations of the figure of the 'bride of death' when young women, especially young unmarried women, die.[9] The motif of the sacrifice that has been corrupted or mishandled is fundamental to the *Oresteia*.[10] When characters are roused to violence, the imagery of animal sacrifice is recurrent, and crazed killers like Heracles are sometimes likened to maniacal dancers or Bacchic figures through the use of suggestive language (see below pp. 184–5). Yet Heracles, more than any other Greek tragic hero, makes it necessary to focus on the confusing category of

FIG. 4.3. The libation scene in *Persians* in a performance at Bradfield School, England, reproduced courtesy of the APGRD.

'demi-god'. The tragic world, peopled by individuals some of whom have a divine parent or more remote divine ancestry, contains many liminal figures who are neither completely mortal nor precisely divine. Medea, granddaughter of Helios, turns out to have supernatural powers and to be exempt from some of the limitations that constrict ordinary mortals, even if she is not exactly on a par with the Olympian and chthonic immortals. Achilles and Helen, who as children of Zeus are half-divine, are both credited with a cult or an unusual life-after-death. The deceased Achilles can demand that a young woman be sacrificed to him, or he is imagined inhabiting his Black Sea island of Leuke (*Iphigenia among the Taurians* 435–8); Helen is taken up to heaven by Apollo and turned into a constellation (*Orestes* 1636–7). Several heroes with cults in the fifth century BCE, even if their parents were both mortal, are seen in their final hours in tragedy (Oedipus, Ajax). But by far the most significant figure here is Zeus' son Heracles, who in the ancient world became so identified with the genre of tragedy that his iconic accoutrements—lionskin and club—were actually sometimes worn by personifications of the tragic genre in Roman imperial statuary.

In the third century BCE, a Greek champion boxer also pursued an alternative career on the stage. Although today the phenomenon of sportsmen who recreate themselves as actors is not unknown, their favoured medium tends to be popular cinema rather than tragedy. An important inscription from Tegea, in the Arcadian heart of the Peloponnese, reveals, however, that this ancient boxer supplemented his victories in sports competitions with prize-winning performances as male heroes in tragedies, mostly by Euripides, which included the masterpieces *Heracles* and *Orestes*.[11] This information is important to the study of Euripides' plays because it reminds us that the ancient theatre was as robust and spectacular as it was intellectual and emotional. The boxer–actor also reinforces the point that Heracles' physical stature was as crucial to his ancient popularity as to the Disney animated blockbuster *Hercules* (1997, directed by John Musker).

Two centuries earlier, during the fifth century BCE, Heracles appeared in scores of dramas, including Euripides' *Alcestis* and *Heracles*, Sophocles' *Women of Trachis* and *Philoctetes*, and Aristophanes' comedies *Birds* and *Frogs*. Heracles was an important hero at Athens, where he was worshipped in exclusively male festivals that brought together men and boys, and symbolized male friendships that connected different households. Yet the ancient theatre survived to dominate Greek and Roman cultural life not only until Hellenistic times, when our champion boxer starred in revivals of Euripidean classics, but for at least another millennium. The empires of the Macedonians and subsequently the Romans saw theatres built in almost every corner of the known world, from Austria to Turkey and Afghanistan, from Carthage to St Albans. Where there was a theatre there was always Heracles; in the first century CE an epigram dedicated to the tragic actor Apollophanes lists his props, giving primacy to Heracles' club (*Palatine Anthology* 11.169). To the same century belongs the most famous amateur actor of antiquity, the emperor Nero, whose preferred tragic roles included the mad Heracles (Suetonius, *Nero*

21). But Heracles was also central to satyr play, to comedy, and to pantomime, a serious genre of musical theatre in which ballet dancers performed myths familiar from spoken tragedy. Episodes from Heracles' life were favourites: one dancer, when playing the mad Heracles, was famous for a stunt in which he aimed arrows into the audience (Macrobius 2.4).

The staying power of Heracles in the ancient theatre was a result of his complex ontological status, which allowed him to bridge, as no other figure in ancient myth, the world of the gods and the world of human beings. Through Heracles the Greeks could explore almost every aspect of their condition and their relations to the inscrutable workings of the universe. Heracles was worshipped in every corner of their world as both a god and a hero, but experienced his tribulations as a man. He is of course the most physically impressive of all ancient heroes (his boxing, wrestling, and archery render him more versatile than the hoplite warrior Achilles). His series of arduous physical labours, celebrated in tragedy, were and are some of the most well-known and important of all myths from the ancient Mediterranean. His physicality is also reflected in his comic characterization (apparent in his portrayal in Euripides' tragicomic *Alcestis*), which always stressed his phenomenal appetites for food, wine, partying, and sex. Yet it cannot be sufficiently stressed that the red-blooded, carnal Heracles is also, paradoxically, found at the heart of the Greeks' exploration of more metaphysical concerns. In *Alcestis* he also cogently argues for the pursuit of happiness in the face of the transience of human existence (780–802), and in *Heracles* he calls into question fundamental tenets of traditional theodicy, the system by which the Olympian gods were conceived by the Greeks as administering justice (1340–6).

The cerebral Heracles of serious literature, whose heightened metaphysical consciousness arises from his dual divine and human status, allows humans, through him, to transcend the limitations of their mortal existence and adopt a perspective more than mortal. He also offers them the hope of life beyond the grave. For Heracles actually conquers death: his own return from the Underworld, and his miraculous ability to rescue others from it (Alcestis, Theseus), are connected with his role in mystery religion and its promise of a blessed afterlife; he was regarded as the first initiate of the most important of such cults to the ancient Athenians, the Eleusinian Mysteries. He was the mythical prototype of all who shared in their secret knowledge.

The tragedians' attraction to Heracles was not lost on his contemporaries. The most powerful evidence for the impression that the Heracles of the theatre made on his original public is Aristophanes' comedy *Frogs*, first produced in 405 BCE, shortly after both Euripides and Sophocles had died. The protagonist of the comedy is Dionysus, the tutelary god of drama, who decides to retrieve Euripides from Hades and bring him back to Athens. In Euripides' *Heracles* the hero returns, alive, from the Underworld: in order to brave the terrors of Hades, the comic Dionysus knows that he must borrow this hero's costume and equipment. For Heracles was crucial to the tragedians' confrontation of their audience with questions as different and as huge as the nature of genre, of virtue, of heroism, of mortality, immortality, and even of the divine. In *Heracles* the audience is not only asked whether Heracles is an international terrorist or saviour of the human race, but whether traditional gods exist at all, whether humans must ultimately take ethical decisions without divine guidance, whether murderers are really physically polluted, and whether adoptive parents can be better than biological ones. It would be wonderful to know to what uses Euripides put Heracles in the several other tragedies, now lost, in which this incomparable hero also featured, including *Alcmena* (in which Heracles may have been born), *Auge* (a scandalous piece during the course of which Auge gave birth in a temple to Heracles' son), and, intriguingly, the complex plot of the Euripidean *Antigone*.

## PHILOSOPHY

It is no coincidence that Greek tragedy arose at the same time as the type of systematic and self-conscious thinking that came to be labelled *philosophy*, or 'love of wisdom'. Over the last few decades, neither scholarly works on Greek tragedy, nor the majority of productions, have been primarily concerned with the philosophical questions it asks. They have tended to be attracted primarily by its social and political content—gender, race, war—or the anthropological and theatrical interest of its form. This emphasis has run the slight risk of presenting Greek tragic theatre as a primal, even primitive, presentation of mythic material. But the searching questions asked in the plays relate to every aspect of the human experience that exercised Socrates and the other thinkers working in fifth-century Greece, especially Athens, and to most of those that still exercise philosophers today.

The philosophers who just preceded or were contemporary with the tragedians have traditionally been put into three rather arbitrary groups, the pre-Socratics, the sophists, and Socrates himself. The ideas and argumentative techniques of all three are reflected extensively in tragedy. The pre-Socratic philosophers of the sixth and earlier fifth centuries BCE included Heraclitus, who was fascinated by the problem of change, and seems to have believed that the whole universe is in a constant state of transformation or flux. The inevitability of change is perhaps the central topic of tragedy, which asks how happiness is overturned. Another pre-Socratic, Democritus, stressed the material basis of the universe and the difficulty of understanding things through sense-perception; many tragic characters express bafflement at trying to understand from their eyes or ears the truth that underlies their situations. Aeschylean tragedy, if not directly influenced by pre-Socratic philosophy, certainly asked similar questions and used similar images. Some people in antiquity even said that Aeschylus was a follower of the esoteric ideas of Pythagoras (e.g. Cicero, *Tusculan Disputations* 2.10), perhaps because his plays feature a good deal of numerical imagery, and often a rather mystical atmosphere. The ideas of other pre-Socratics sometimes appear in plays by the other two tragedians (see above, pp. 93, 124).

Perhaps the most important intellectual advance of the entire era was the introduction of 'relativism'. Is there a single right way of doing things, or does it all depend on the perspective of the individual human, their gender, social class, civic affiliation, or indeed whole ethnic group, defined internationally? This kind of thinking developed as a result of two factors, of which the first was the emerging science of comparative ethnography. As the Greeks compared their own customs (*nomoi*) with those of other peoples, such as the Persians and Egyptians, a process which was well developed by the middle of the century and underpins Herodotus' *Histories*, they inevitably began to ask whether one way of organizing a community was *inherently* or in nature (*physis*) superior to any other. The other reason was the end of hereditary monarchy in many Greek city-states. If sovereign power was no longer devolved directly by Zeus onto the successive fathers and sons of a particular bloodline, but could be contested according to the merits and strategic manoeuvres of an individual (who could become 'popular tyrant') or a much wider group of citizens (who could instal a 'democracy'), then many of the old religious and social beliefs needed to be reformulated or abandoned altogether. The *Iliad*, with its presentation of inherently different value systems—the aristocratic divine right of kings, embodied in Agamemnon, contrasted with the meritocratic right of the best warrior to due rewards, embodied in Achilles—already foreshadows this clash of ideas.

The introduction of relativist thinking into tragedy allowed the dramatists to develop the conflicts between different viewpoints which are so fundamental to the impetus and fabric of the plays. It is completely up for discussion in Aeschylus' *Agamemnon* whether the titular hero deserves to suffer in the way he does on account of the sacrifice of Iphigenia. Neither her mother's viewpoint nor that of the chorus is likely to coincide with Agamemnon's. But in tragedy, despite the opening up by relativist thinking of an intellectual space in which to explore different perspectives on the same events, the overall ethics invariably reaffirm universal imperatives. In Aeschylus' *Suppliants*, the aggressive Egyptian herald may say that he does not have to heed Greek gods because his gods live beside the Nile, but the audience would certainly have seen his disregard for the sanctity of the Argive shrine as sacrilegious regardless of his ethnicity (922). Euripides' scandalous *Aeolus* stretched relativism to its logical extreme by asking whether one of the ultimate taboos—incest—was wrong in an absolute and natural sense, or only if your culture and education happened to make you think it was. In this tragedy Macareus, son of Aeolus, impregnated his own full sister Canace, and delivered a notorious speech defending his right to marry her on the radically relativist ground that no action is inherently shameful—it only becomes so if it is so deemed.[12] According to tradition, this speech so infuriated the anti-relativist philosopher Socrates when he saw the play in the theatre that he rebuked Euripides, declaring that 'what is shameful is indeed shameful, whether so deemed or not!'[13] But he need not have been so concerned, since the play ended up with the incestuous couple and their baby emphatically dead. Greek tragedy asks radical questions, but tends to give conservative answers.

The Introduction to this volume suggested that a working definition of tragedy is that it constitutes the dramatized expression of an enquiry into suffering, an aesthetically articulated question mark written in pain. It has an inherently interrogatory quality. It was this status as a form of enquiry that has made it important to some schools of philosophy subsequently, especially in nineteenth- and twentieth-century Germany and France. The German poet Friedrich Hölderlin, whose translations of Greek tragedy are still used in theatres today, actually defined tragedy as an artistic transposition of an 'intuition' that was fundamentally intellectual.[14] For tragedy, while representing an instance of suffering in dramatic form, is philosophical because it asks *why* it has occurred.

The answers to the question of cause can belong to any of the three main branches of the emergent fifth-century intellectual enquiry. The first of these was Ethics, which asked the basic question 'how should we live?', and originally included social and political theory. The suffering might have been caused by an ill-considered choice by an individual who is not fundamentally an immoral person. Examples would include Creon's edict banning the burial of Polynices in *Antigone*, and Phaedra's decision to leave a note falsely accusing Hippolytus of sexual assault on her in *Hippolytus*. It might, however, have been caused by the act of an evil individual (for example, Eurystheus' persecution of Heracles' children in Euripides' *Children of Heracles*). Perhaps it resulted from a pragmatic decision that attempted to secure a good outcome for the majority, while ignoring the suffering of an individual or individuals, such as the decision taken long ago to dump Philoctetes on the island of Lemnos in *Philoctetes* (Fig. 4.4). On the other hand, the cause might be partly caused by a social force, such as the pressure placed on Agamemnon by the opinion of the ordinary

FIG. 4.4. *Philoctetes on the Island of Lemnos*, engraving (1785) by Francesco Rosaspina after a painting by James Barry, reproduced courtesy of the Trustees of the British Museum.

soldiers in his army in *Iphigenia in Aulis*, or a political one, such as the outbreak of civil war in Thebes.

The second major branch of philosophy was Epistemology, which asked 'how do we know things?' The problem of knowledge, and the difference between true knowledge and mere opinion, underlies or contributes to the suffering in a large number of tragedies. Perhaps the hero, like Oedipus, had no way of knowing that the woman he married was his mother; indeed, all the evidence pointed the other way. Creusa in *Ion* would not have tried to assassinate Ion if she had not believed, quite incorrectly, that he was the son of Xuthus. One of the reasons that the tragedians like staging psychotic delusion (see below) is that it allowed them to explore false belief: the child-killers Heracles and Agave in Euripides' *Heracles* and *Bacchae* both believe that the sons they slaughter are not their sons at all. The erroneous opinion that causes the suffering may have been held by the community at large: the Theban people would not have elected Oedipus to the role of leader if they had known that he had killed Laius, nor would Agave's fellow Theban women have supported the killing of Pentheus if they had known who he was. On the other hand, the tragedy may be caused by an individual's deliberate falsification of information.

In Euripides' *Medea*, if Jason had not believed Medea's temporary pretence that she had accepted the position he had imposed upon her, and her lies about her gift to his new wife, several deaths might have been avoided altogether. In *Iphigenia in Aulis*, Agamemnon deceives his wife and daughter into travelling to the Greek camp by telling them that he has arranged a marriage for her. In Sophocles' *Women of Trachis*, if Lichas the herald had not deceived Deianira about her husband's sexual interest in Iole, she might not have taken the girl in and been panicked into acting as rashly as she did. But it is not just downright mendacity that causes the misunderstandings or mistakes of fact that lead to or compound suffering. The chorus of Aeschylus' *Agamemnon* simply do not understand what Cassandra is clearly telling them about the intergenerational nature of the bloodshed in the house of Atreus. In *Hippolytus*, Theseus does not seek out the witnesses and additional evidence that would prevent him from believing Phaedra's letter and cursing his son so precipitately. In *Ion*, despite an intense dialogue, the mother and son fail to recognize each other on their first encounter because they do not ask the right questions. In *Antigone*, the suffering is made inevitable by the limitations of language to explicate different concepts of principle; words for 'law' and 'edict' abound, but Creon and Antigone mean quite different things by identical terms.

The third question asked by the philosophers—*what is being?*—was known as 'Ontology', from the same root as the Greek verb 'to be', and was in due course, along with the study of the gods entailed by theology, subsumed under the general heading of the study of the non-physical world, or the world beyond the one which can be materially seen—that is, 'Metaphysics'. These philosophical questions often overlap with questions addressed in a more directly religious idiom, as we have seen in the previous section. But all the more abstract questions about 'the meaning of life' are broadly metaphysical, since they deal with the world that can't be physically experienced. Characters who are suffering agony of one kind or another tend to be provoked into asking these very questions. Why are we here? Is human existence actually desirable? What is the point of human suffering in an unknowable universe? Is death better? What happens after death? Is it possible to fathom the future through oracles or divination? Are there gods? Can the gods be controlled by prayer and sacrifice? Is fate the same thing as the gods? Are there cosmic forces to which even gods are subject?

Troy formed the centre of the mythical map by which archaic Greeks sought proto-philosophical routes through their experiences, and in Euripides' repeated use of the mythical figure of Helen of Troy we can see how a mythical figure, in fifth-century hands, could become a benchmark for philosophical questions. In the three surviving tragedies in which Helen appears, the issues raised by her presence fall under the headings of Ethics, Epistemology, and Ontology respectively. In *Trojan Women* (415 BCE), Helen's role is to complicate the ethical dimension of the play and its quest to find the individual—human or divine—responsible for the carnage at Troy. In *Helen* (412), she is to be found in Egypt, where she has resided throughout the Trojan War, while a substitute image of her eloped with Paris. Her presence raises epistemological questions about how the true Helen can be identified. Is she the apprehensible, material individual, subject to ordinary laws of cognition, or the mysterious embodiment of her reputation, in the discourse and imaginations of men, that was psychologically manifested in stories and songs at Troy? In *Orestes* (408), the question becomes baldly ontological and metaphysical: Helen literally vanishes in supernatural circumstances, is elevated to the machine in which only gods could conventionally appear, and is turned, finally, into a constellation. This Helen confounds any rational probing of the nature of being Human, or of the human Being.

Many tragedies suggest that several causes have combined to create the suffering that they represent. It is not always easy to distinguish the metaphysical from the ontological, or the ethical from the epistemological. Some tragedies, notably *Oedipus Tyrannus*, even make allocation of responsibility itself not only a symptom of suffering but the direct cause of more. Laying blame exacerbates the pain of the titular Trojan women, and yet it is one of their main activities, since nearly all the characters as well as several gods are sooner or later held responsible for the carnage at Troy.[13] Their other activity is suffering, which the play potently synthesizes with the 'why' question that it also asks, especially when Hecuba's bereavements are consummated by the Greeks' murder of her grandson Astyanax. Few episodes in world theatre can rival the emotional impact of the scenes in which the infant is torn from his mother Andromache's arms, and later laid out by his heartbroken grandmother, a tiny corpse on his dead father Hector's shield (709–98, 1118–251—see above, pp. 76–8).

The generation of philosophers who succeeded the pre-Socratics and flocked to Athens from the 440s onwards are known as the sophists. The oldest of them, who must have been born around the same as Sophocles and Euripides, was the northern Greek Protagoras, who was also by far the most significant sophist in intellectual history. He is important to a study of Greek tragedy because two of the major ideas that he expounded are crucial to some of the most important plays. His most famous sayings were that 'man is the measure of all things', and that the existence of gods is an assumption that cannot be verified (Protagoras, fragments 1 and 4 *DK*). It is interesting to find Aristophanes' caricature of Euripides including the charge that Euripides' tragedies had persuaded people 'that the gods do not exist' (*Women at the Thesmophoria* 450–1). By later antiquity it was believed that it was at Euripides' house that Protagoras, the great relativist and agnostic thinker, read out his famous treatise on the gods. Characters in both Sophocles and Euripides consistently wrestle with the fact that the only judgement they can rely on is that of themselves and other humans; they are not given unambiguous instructions or signs from any other, let alone higher authority. Characters in desperate straits, like Hecuba in *Trojan Women*, do indeed start to question whether the gods can exist at all. Oedipus in *Oedipus Tyrannus* and Creon in *Antigone* might both have been listening to Protagoras when they assume that they can rely exclusively on their own, human intelligence in order to solve major problems of statecraft.

In *Antigone* there is preserved one of the three great examples in the plays of 'Protagorean' thought. At the crucial moment in the play when the guard has announced that someone has tried to bury the corpse of Polynices, and the chorus suggest to Creon that perhaps the gods have intervened (278–9), the guard leaves to try and identify the culprit, and Creon goes into the palace. While we wait to see whom the guard arrests, the chorus sing a beautiful ode, which describes how humans have conquered nature (332–41):

> Many things arouse awe, but none is more awesome than man.
> He crosses the white ocean, under the winter wind,
> Cutting a path through the heaving waters that surround him,
> And he works away at Earth, the highest god, immortal and enduring,
> As his ploughs turn and counter-turn from year to year,
> Breaking up the soil with the breed of horses.

Further stanzas celebrate the human invention of hunting, fishing, speech, thought, political institutions, shelter, and medicine. The amazing power of man's ingenuity has allowed him to build an advanced civilization, which the chorus celebrates along with the philosopher Protagoras, but with a Sophoclean conservative religious sting in the tail (365–71):

> Intelligent beyond all hope is his skilful ingenuity,
> And it brings him disadvantages as well as advantages.
> When he observes the laws of the land, as well as the justice
> Of the gods sworn on oath, then his position in the city is high.
> City-less is the man who does wrong for the sake of gain.

That same intelligence can be used either for good or ill. An individual who fails, in this advanced civilization, to retain respect for both law and divine justice, jeopardizes his entire community. Although they do not specify Creon, his treatment of the guard in the previous scene makes it impossible not to think of him here.

Ancient Greek thought accommodated simultaneously the 'lapsarian' myth of the fall of the human race from a blissful utopian golden age, articulated in Hesiod's *Works and Days* 109–26, and the idea of the ineluctable technological progress that had allowed humans to emerge from the cave. Humanity was on the rise or in decline depending on your point of view. Tragedy generally has an upbeat view of human progress, preferring the Protagorean to the Hesiodic view of the past, but with the proviso, emphasized by the chorus of *Antigone*, that it is crucial to practise caution and all due respect for the gods and traditional ways of propitiating them while human progress continues. The tension between the human intelligence on which the Athenian democracy prided itself, and the traditional religious outlook, underpins all Greek tragedy in subtle but fundamental ways. As Albert Camus suggested in a famous lecture, tragedy as a genre becomes prominent in a community which is half-way between a sacred society and a society built by man; effective tragedy is created by the contrast between these viewpoints.[15]

In his *Philoctetes*, Sophocles explores Protagorean ideas from a rather different perspective. By putting his hero on a desert island, entirely alone, he is able to examine how human beings had to survive before the invention of all the technologies enumerated by the chorus of *Antigone*. Philoctetes is unable to construct a ship to escape the island, till its soil, heal his damaged leg, or talk to anyone, let alone practise statecraft. He can just about manage to avoid the worst weather by sleeping in a cave, and hunt with his bow for food. But this puts him on the level at best of Neolithic man, at least on a purely practical basis.

Protagorean historical anthropology probably also lies behind Theseus' exposition of man's acquisition of intelligence, language, agriculture, navigation, and trade in Euripides' *Suppliant Women* (201–10). Protagoras' vision of the distance travelled by humans from cave-dwelling to the city-state is also a major interest in a fourth play, the *Prometheus Bound* attributed to Aeschylus. But in this play, as probably in the beliefs fostered in the Athenian cult of Prometheus, humans were taught not only the use of fire but *all* their fundamental arts and crafts by the philanthropic Titan, as he proudly states himself (506). To the sympathetic chorus of daughters of Ocean, he describes his work (450–9):

> They did not know how to use bricks to build houses
> Facing the sun, nor anything of carpentry,
> But lived in sunless caves underground, like swarming ants.
> They had no way on which they could rely of marking winter,
> Or flowery springtime, or fruitful summer, but handled everything
> Unscientifically, until I taught them the difficult art
> Of detecting the rising and settings of the stars.

Prometheus subsequently adds arithmetic, writing, medicine, augury, and metallurgy, as well as the use of beasts of burden and sailing, to his impressive list of benefactions. The Greeks had several 'technology' heroes, and elsewhere attribute the invention of writing to Palamedes, one of the Greeks at Troy. But in Prometheus' great speeches in this tragedy, the Protagorean vision of the Ascent of Man receives its grandest articulation.[16]

If human inventiveness, and pride in that inventiveness, could result in either good or evil, so could the new science of rhetoric, or 'persuading others to do or think what you want them to'. Protagoras was not the only sophist whose work affected tragedy profoundly; many characters in Euripides' plays, and some in those of Sophocles, speak as if they have been attending lessons with the thinkers who specialized in persuasion, above all Gorgias the Sicilian (see also above, pp. 36–8). Most fifth-century Greeks will not have seen any difference between the study of rhetoric and the study of philosophy, and indeed neither could have developed without the other. Euripidean characters are drawing on both when they adopt the new philosophical *methods*: they subtly argue from probability and relativism, and formulate their points as antilogy, proof, and refutation. But, as Socrates seems to have insisted, rhetoric was only interested in changing opinion, not in whether that opinion was actually true. The goal of tragedy as an enquiry into the causes of suffering is, like philosophy, interested in discovering the truth, however painful, so it was perhaps inevitable that rhetorical displays came to be used so ironically in the medium.

## PSYCHES, MADNESS, AND MEDICINE

This book has so far discussed many ways in which the characters in tragedy look outwards as they relate to other humans, as well as to the gods and other forces in the universe. But there are interior 'selves' portrayed in these plays, selves who think, speak, feel, and suffer as individuals. There has always been a good deal of controversy about the extent to which we can talk about 'character' in Greek tragedy, since masked acting in huge spaces made psychological naturalism, where emotion is conveyed through subtle changes in facial expression, out of the question. Moreover, the psychological vocabulary available in the fifth century was still small and crude, and the idea of an autonomous individual will that acts independently of relationships with others was only just beginning to emerge. The stylized poetic speech in which everyone communicates in tragedy means that suggesting character by verbal idiosyncrasy was not an option.

Yet it is nonsense to say that by the end of tragedies the audience members did not have a clear idea what types of people they had been watching—whether they were stubborn or malleable, brave or cowardly, rash or cautious, harsh or kind, selfish or self-sacrificing, indecisive or decisive, exhibitionist or modest, irreligious or pious, argumentative or conciliatory, liars or truth-tellers. Moreover, these fundamental if rather polarized typologies will have reflected how the audience perceived other people's personalities in reality. The important point is that the character is *revealed by the play* to have these characteristics, as he or she is seen in a crisis, reacting to and instigating events.

Tragedy's fascination with the way that the self takes decisions was called by Aristotle its interest in portraying intellect or *dianoia*, the mind in operation, which he believed was so important to tragedy that it was only beaten into third place as a constituent by plot and character (*Poetics* ch. 6, 1450b 4). Individuals in moral quandaries inspired the tragedians to think of poetic language in order to suggest their dilemma. Aeschylus, for example, was fascinated by the metaphors that expressed the activity involved in deliberation about action: he compared it with the skills of steering a ship (*Suppliants* 438–41) and herding a flock of thoughts (*Agamemnon* 669).[17] The difficulty for modern readers, trained to see thought and feeling as a function exclusively of the biological brain, as something which takes place entirely in the physical head, is that the Greeks had not yet split the mind from the material body in a manner to which we would be able to relate. There are two words used for what makes a person who they are in a non-material way. In *Antigone* the chorus says that the young *nous* suffers terribly when upset (767), and *nous* is best translated as 'mind' or 'sensibility'. In some later plays the word often translated 'soul', *psuchē*, comes to mean something like a 'personality': Electra's intelligence is part of her psyche (*Orestes* 1180).

Other bodily organs were involved, all located in the upper torso, where humans still feel many of the physical sensations of grief, anxiety, fear, and stress (racing heart, panting, queasiness, 'gut' reactions). Characters in tragedy say, as we still do, that they feel some emotions in the heart: Polymestor's savagery, says Agamemnon, needs to be pushed out of his heart (*Hecuba* 1129) when he needs to calm down and 'discuss rationally' the fact that his children have just been murdered and he has been blinded! Yet when Medea considers murdering Jason and his new love, she imagines creeping into their marriage bed and stabbing through the liver, which was, however incongruous it may seem to us, the organ associated with erotic desire (378–9).

The modern actor is challenged by the psychosomatic nature of the Greek tragic body: Phaedra's infatuation is clearly taking its toll on her body as well as her mind since the chorus can actually see its effects (*Hippolytus* 267–70). This body, moreover, has two crucial sentient organs in addition. One is the rather unlocatable *thumos* or organ of courage, anger, and pride, which can make the sufferer act in extreme ways. 'Temper' is too mild and limited a translation; it is Medea's *thumos* that, she says, has overcome her ability to deliberate rationally even though she is conscious that what she is doing is wrong. The other sentient organ, found everywhere in Greek tragedy, is the *phrēn*, often found in the plural as *phrenes*, 'wits' or 'private way of thinking'. This was located in the midriff. Hippolytus says that he may have sworn with his tongue, but his *phrēn*, his private intellect and thought-world, remains unsworn. The *phrenes* were supposed to enlarge as humans became older and wiser: Creon insultingly complains that Oedipus has not even developed his *phrenes* in old age (*Oedipus at Colonus* 804). Careful thought took place in the *phrenes*, and disturbed individuals are unable to use this organ well.

Another problem with understanding the minds portrayed in Greek tragedy is that emotions and impulses, which we tend to feel well up or spring up from deep inside us, were felt by the Greeks to invade their sentient organs from outside. Eros attacks the lover through the eyes; Helen is said to have been struck out of her *phrenes* by the sight of Paris in his dazzling barbarian attire (*Trojan Women* 992). Such 'altered states of consciousness' are fundamental to Greek tragedy. Here, again, there are significant differences between the way that we talk about madness and psychosis and the ways that they were conceptualized by the classical Greeks. They were fascinated by what we would call psychotic delusion, and several of the most pitiable actions in Greek tragedy are committed when the perpetrators are completely mistaken about the identity of their victims. Heracles kills his children in Euripides' *Heracles* while fantasizing that they are the children of his archenemy Eurystheus. Agave in *Bacchae* kills her son Pentheus while imagining that he is a mountain lion. Ajax assaults cattle and sheep because he thinks that they are his new enemies the Atridae. Orestes is blighted with agonizing illusions by the Erinyes, in contrast, *after* he has killed his mother. But these instances of madness, although all effected by a divine agent exterior to the individual rather than arising from inside his or her psyche, have different causes.

A terrifying epiphany occurs in Euripides' *Heracles* when Madness (here named Lyssa) herself appears with Iris, the messenger of the gods, and announces that the jealous Hera has sent her to drive Heracles insane (858–66):

> I call on the Sun-god to witness that what I do here is
>     done against my will.
> But if I am compelled to serve you and Hera straightaway,

> And attend you in full cry as hounds follow the hunter,
> Then that is what I will do. Neither the ocean, with its
>     violently groaning waves,
> Nor an earthquake, nor the thunderbolt with its agonizing
>     blast, compare
> With the races I shall run into the breast of Heracles.
> I will smash into the building and plunge into his house,
> Killing the children first. Their slaughterer will not realize
> That it is his own children he destroys, until he is released
>     from my insanity.

Lyssa does her worst, and then describes to the audience the physical symptoms that Heracles, behind the palace facade, is now suffering (867–70):

> Look at him! Even at the starting-post he is tossing his head,
> And rolling his eyes ferociously but without a word.
> His panting breath is out of control;
> Like a bull in act to charge, he bellows dreadfully.

Sudden madness can attack arbitrarily, force entry into the body even of a superhero, send him into a wild state with physical symptoms of derangement, terrify him, wreck his cognitive skills, and make him destroy the things he loves the most. But the word translated here as 'Madness' is a specific sort of madness, Lyssa, which designates the berserk state of mind into which warriors enter on the battlefield. It is the appropriate type of madness for a trained, professional killer.

When in *Bacchae* Pentheus dresses up as a maenad, and when Agave kills Pentheus, the madness is not Lyssa but the mania that worshippers of Dionysus experience when he sends it upon them (the word *maenad* is related to the term *mania*). This is an ecstatic state of emotional liberation, involving altered perceptions. It is directly related to the worship of Dionysus, his mysteries, the drinking of alcohol, and the illusions conjured up in theatre itself. Pentheus can see two suns when under the Dionysiac spell (918), which perhaps makes the audience think about the relationship between the Theban world created in the play as well as their own Athenian sanctuary of Dionysus where the fictional environment was being created. Women are particularly vulnerable to Dionysiac madness, and in *Bacchae* the audience watches as Agave is brought out of this deluded state by her father Cadmus; the true recognition in this play is when she recognizes what she had believed to be the lion's head is her own son's, and that this is the work of Dionysus (1296): 'Now I understand. Dionysus has destroyed us.'

The most painful dramatization of a god inflicting insanity on an individual is the opening scene of Sophocles' *Ajax*. Here Athena, whom Ajax has previously disrespected, explains to his enemy Odysseus that she has stopped him attacking both Odysseus and the Atridae. But she has also humiliated him by making him act out the assault, with ludicrous vengefulness, on sheep and cattle instead (51–60):

> I held him back, casting on his eyes
> The grievous fantasies of his incurable state of ecstasy,
> Turning him instead against the flocks
> And the war booty of mixed livestock, as yet unallocated,
> Under the herdsmen's guard.
> Then he launched himself against the many horned beasts around him,
> Hacking at them and slicing through their spines.
> At times he thought he had cornered the two sons of Atreus
> So he could kill them with his own hand; at others
> He thought he was assaulting one of the other commanders.
> I goaded the man into frenzy with waves of insanity,
> Driving him into hunting nets of evil.

Athena then summons Ajax from his tent, where he has taken some more livestock to torture, and ensures that his vision is further altered. He cannot see Odysseus, and so is unaware that his humiliation is being compounded by merciless baiting in front of his deadliest rival.

In the case of Orestes, the Erinyes cause slightly different symptoms in the several plays in which he is portrayed after murdering his mother. In the *Oresteia*, his speech and thought processes seem to become disjointed almost immediately afterwards, along with the visual appearance to him of the Erinyes. In Euripides' *Iphigenia among the Taurians*, the barbarian herdsman who witnesses an onslaught of madness upon Orestes, reports it to Iphigenia thus (282–300):

> He stood and tossed his head up and down,
> And groaned, his arms trembling to his fingertips,

Convulsed with onslaughts of madness, and shouted like a hunter:
'Pylades, have you noticed this one? Can't you see
This she-serpent from Hades, who wants to kill me,
Brandishing her fearsome snakes at me?
This one is breathing fire and gore from inside her robes,
Beating her wings, holding my mother in her arms,
A weight of rock to hurl at me. Oh no! She'll kill me!
Where can I escape?' ...
He drew his sword, and like a lion rushing
Into the middle of our herds, hacking at their flanks and
    ribs with the metal,
So that the sea-swell blossomed with blood.

This Orestes' visual competence is compromised in a similar way to Ajax's in that he mistakes cattle for his enemy—in this case, the Erinyes. The fits from which he suffers in *Orestes* are very similar; he is convinced that he can see the Erinyes that are invisible to Electra, and indeed tries to shoot them with his bow and arrows (268–74).

The explanations for human suffering offered by tragedy can put the responsibility primarily on the gods, as we saw in the first section of this chapter, or investigate the moral agency of the human beings involved and the mistakes they make in what they say and do. An important term which is related to 'popular ethics' and appears in analysis of disaster within tragedies is the term for 'error', *hamartia*, or the verb related to it, *hamartanein*. This concept appears in Aristotle's statement that tragic heroes suffer a reversal of fortune 'on account of some mistake' (*Poetics* ch. 13, 1453a 9–10). It is originally a metaphor from archery, and means letting forth an arrow that fails completely to hit the target. The best translation in contemporary English is probably 'to screw up'. It can mean in tragedy a mistake of fact, or a mistaken decision (Creon chose the wrong course of action, as he finally admits at *Antigone* 1265, 1269). But either kind of mistake can lead to tragic suffering.

In Aeschylus and Sophocles, there is a gap between these two levels of explanation that can only be filled by concepts which function as intermediaries between these two spheres. Aeschylean tragic characters are vulnerable to something exterior to themselves called *Atē*, 'Calamity', 'Ruin', 'Curse', or 'Destructive Delusion', which makes Xerxes decide to invade Greece (*Persians* 113). *Atē* often takes the form of temptation to greed or self-aggrandizement. It was part of an age-old nexus of ethical beliefs that underlie Greek tragic story patterns, most succinctly expressed by Darius when he says that the Persians' defeat at the battle of Plataea is proof of a universal moral law (820–2):

> Mortals must not think thoughts above their station;
> For *hubris* flowered and produced a crop of calamity (*Atē*),
> And from it reaped a harvest of lamentation.

*Hubris* is not respecting the proper hierarchies that define and regulate power and status relationships in society; it is something that you do to someone of equivalent or equal status by disrespecting them. Xerxes was offending the gods as well as the Greeks by invading their land. Xerxes got above himself, committed hubris, which produced ruin (*Atē*) and therefore suffering. In *Agamemnon*, the pattern seen by the chorus is a variation on this theme (758–71): an old act of hubris produces another act of hubris, which leads to recklessness 'and for the household, black curses' (the plural of *Atē*).

*Atē* involves a degree of delusion, of not assessing the situation accurately. Tragedy, ultimately, does not draw so very hard and fast a line between people in their 'right minds' and those that are deluded. The state of prophetic ecstasy into which Cassandra enters in Aeschylus' *Agamemnon*, although it is ultimately caused by Apollo and is clearly abnormal, is not one of delusion. Cassandra uses bizarre images, and can, in this condition, see things clairvoyantly that are invisible to 'normal' human eyes, but what she sees is true. She can see the truth more clearly than anybody else in Argos. The shock of bereavement, again, can cause extreme or uncharacteristic behaviour in otherwise calm individuals, but this state is not necessarily to be classified as delusional. The strange behaviour is in its own terms rational, as an extreme response to extreme pain. The honest facing of trauma explains the preponderance in tragedy of lamentation, the ritual task of which was precisely to contain and regulate those extreme emotions. In Euripides' *Suppliant Women*, the widowed Evadne arrives, to celebrate (as she puts it) her victory over other women in bravery, by committing suicide on her husband's pyre. She is clearly neither completely deluded nor in normal control of herself (990–1003):

What light, what radiance did the Sun-god's chariot convey,
And the moon in the darkness of the sky, the swift stars around her,
The day of my wedding, when the city of Argos raised the
Joyful marriage song for me and mail-clad Capaneus? Aahh!
Now I have come to you, running, crazed like a Bacchant, from my home,
To share with you the flaming fire and the same tomb...

The shock of relationship breakdown can have similarly destabilizing effects upon the psyche. Euripides' Medea is quite clear that she knows that what she is going to do in murdering the children is morally wrong, and yet her ability to take sensible decisions has been overmastered by her rage (1078–89). She is very severely provoked in the early scenes of the play, both by Creon and by Jason, and in court today, in some jurisdictions, she could make a case that the provocation was so severe, and her reaction so instantaneous, that it lessened her culpability. *Medea* is the only surviving Greek tragedy where a murder is committed in this entirely ambiguous moral terrain (see Fig. 4.5). Clytemnestra's murder of Agamemnon in Aeschylus' *Agamemnon* has been planned for many years, and is therefore absolutely premeditated. Heracles in Euripides' *Heracles* and Agave in his *Bacchae* kill their children while demonstrably deluded and insane. The nearest parallels to Medea are offered by two other parents in Euripides. Creusa in *Ion* is persuaded into making an attempt on the life a youth she does not know is her son while she is sane but distraught. Agamemnon in *Iphigenia in Aulis* authorizes the sacrifice of his daughter when clinically sane but psychologically confused and under pressure.

Several contemporary forensic psychologists have argued that when parents separate, children are acutely vulnerable to violence from the abandoned party, but that in most cases this extremely volatile and dangerous period only lasts for about one week. Children are at terrible risk during the first week after their parents separate, even if those parents would never normally be violent at all. This is how explosive the emotions are at this critical time. An important issue here is the speed at which the events in Euripides' *Medea* develop: the children's parents have indeed only just split up.

FIG. 4.5. George Romney, *Medea Contemplating the Murder of her Children* (mid-1770s), reproduced courtesy of the Trustees of the British Museum.

Medea's state of psychological shock at being abandoned may be a day or two old, but she is banished and then argues violently with her husband *immediately* before the murders she commits: they may indeed be 'premeditated', but the 'premeditation' is compressed and abridged; alternatively, it could be argued that Euripides has stretched the precise definitions of 'sudden' violence in response to unbearable 'provocation' to their absolute limits. Euripides' Medea not only deconstructs the psychic categories of 'male' and 'female', but rivets attention on the blunt instruments that Criminal Law, both ancient and modern, must utilize.

Provocation in Criminal Law is a ground of defence found in many legal systems. This defence attempts to excuse a crime by alleging a 'sudden' or 'temporary' 'loss of control' (as opposed to a plea of insanity) in response to another's provocative conduct. In the UK and some other Common Law jurisdictions it is *only* available against a charge of murder and only acts to reduce the conviction to voluntary manslaughter. In the United States of America the absence of premeditation is one of the ways of distinguishing second-degree murder from first-degree murder. Yet in some states of the USA, premeditation has been seen as requiring *only a few seconds' deliberation* before the murderous act, while in others it can be seen as requiring *several hours*. How long has Medea got? In England, the crucial terms are in Section 3 of the Homicide Act 1957:

Where on a charge of murder there is evidence on which the jury can find that the person charged was provoked (whether by things done or by things said or by both together) to lose his self-control, the question whether the provocation was enough to make a reasonable man do as he did shall be left to be determined by the jury; and in determining that question the jury shall take into account everything both done and said according to the effect which, in their opinion, it would have on a reasonable man.

The 1957 Act changed the Common Law in Britain which had previously provided that provocation *must* be more than words alone and had to be some form of violence committed by the victim upon the accused, subject only to two exceptions—a husband discovering his wife in the act of adultery; and a father discovering someone committing sodomy on his son! Instead, the new Act provided that provocation can be by *anything* done or said without it having to be an illegal act; the provoker and the deceased can be third parties. If the accused was provoked, *who provoked him is irrelevant*.

The distinction between provoked and unprovoked murder was acknowledged in the legal system of Euripides' own day. There has survived a speech by the Athenian lawyer Lysias, called *On the Murder of Eratosthenes* (Lysias 1). This is the defence speech of a man on trial certainly within a few decades of the premiere of *Medea*. He admits that he has killed a man named Eratosthenes, but asks to be acquitted because Athenian law allowed a man to kill another whom he found in bed with his wife. No entrapment was allowed and the occasion had to arise spontaneously. But the killer did *not* have to prove that he had only just discovered that the affair was going on. The man on trial says that his slave girl had told him about the affair, and he had gone home, with witnesses, to find the man standing naked on his own marriage bed beside his wife. It was at this sight that he became angry and struck the lover. The implication is that killing a man found in this sexual situation with your wife was entirely understandable!

If Medea were a classical Athenian male, who could prove that she had murdered her spouse's lover at the moment their affair was discovered, then she would have been acquitted at least of that crime. And Medea, of course, for much of the time thinks of herself in very masculine terms, using the language—including the term *thumos*—appropriate to Homeric warriors such as Achilles. She feels she is an important person who has been publicly humiliated. That is the emotional background to the plot. Yet Medea's status as a responsible and morally autonomous legal agent, since she is female, is fundamentally anomalous. According to ancient Greek men, female brains, especially the parts of them that take ethical decisions, *can* only operate safely under male supervision (see above, p. 134). Women need constant moral supervision. Jason and Creon were stupid to leave Medea unsupervised. Euripides' tragedy therefore raises questions not only about Medea's own stated view that she is acting, as an autonomous agent before the law, with full moral understanding, competence, and time to consider her actions, but also about the gendering of Medea's psyche and the degree to which *as a woman* she is capable of moral deliberation.

It is in the context of this confusion about female thinking abilities that we need to read Medea's great speech in which her 'divided self' debates whether or not to kill the children (1021–79). Although this speech may have been extended and developed by ancient actors enjoying the rhetorical potential of Euripides' text, he obviously designed it to show the struggle she is undergoing to make up her mind and steel herself to action. She changes her mind no fewer than four times, before concluding that her *thumos* has overcome her ability to deliberate. This speech reveals Euripides experimenting with an unprecedented degree of 'interiority' in the way he portrays his characters articulating how they make or have made decisions, and confiding the innermost dialogues in the presence of the audience. It requires a particular engagement of the actor with the listener, and represents a major development from Aeschylus' Orestes, whose tragic dilemma is represented by a picture of the tortures that will be visited on him externally, by madness, disease, and the Erinyes, if he does not avenge his father (*Libation-Bearers* 554–78).

Other Euripidean heroines with important scenes of psychological interiority are Phaedra in *Hippolytus*, in her monologue describing how she has made up her mind to die (see above, pp. 32–3), and Creusa in *Ion*, pouring forth her memories of being raped and giving birth as a young teenager (891–904):

> You seized me by my white wrists
> You—a god who took me sexually in the cave—
> As I screamed aloud, 'O Mother!'
> You committed an act of homage to shameless Aphrodite.
> In my misery I gave birth to your boy child
> And hurled him into the place of our union
> Where you had raped me and brought about my despair.
> Oh, the pain and the trauma!
> And now he is gone, my child and yours,
> Carrion for winged birds to feast on.

Intimacy with a character's repressed memories, fears, or inner thought-world, is sometimes achieved in tragedy by the report of a dream. Euripides conceived a brilliant opening for his *Iphigenia among the Taurians* when he introduces the audience directly to his lonely heroine's innermost feelings, by bringing her out of her gloomy temple to mull over last night's dream, in which she was transported by her mind's eye home to Argos (44–55):

> The earth's surface seemed shaken by a tremor;
> I escaped and stood outside, and saw the cornices collapse
> And the whole roof, shaken by the earthquake,
> Fall in ruins from the top of its pillars to the ground.
> Just one column of my ancestral home was left,
> As it seemed to me, and from its head
> Grew auburn hair, and it took a human voice.
> Then I, observing the ritual of stranger-sacrifice
> I tend to here, sprinkled it, as if it were about to die,
> With drops of water, while I wept.

Iphigenia reads the dream as meaning that her brother Orestes, represented as the sole remaining pillar of the palace, has died, leaving her without a male relative. She is not far wrong, for the dream correctly predicts that she will come within an inch of sacrificing her own brother. Almost all dream-interpretation in the ancient Greek world was based on the assumption that it was a form of divination, whereby the dreamer was granted a glimpse into the future, and the dreams in tragedy follow this principle. Aeschylus' Clytemnestra is shaken into taking ritual action when she dreams that she gives birth to a snake, but the dream is fulfilled when her own son turns into her killer (*Libation-Bearers*, 527–33). In Sophocles' *Electra* Clytemnestra has a dream with the same predictive force, but different imagery, in which Orestes is a tree: Agamemnon, 'restored to the sunlight', recovered his sceptre from Aegisthus, and planted it at the hearth. A tree sprang from it, the shadow of which was cast over all the land (417–23).

Despite the charioteer's 'ambush' dream of wolves on horseback in the Euripidean *Rhesus*, almost all the dreamers in Greek tragedy are female. This corresponds with the general tendency to see women as emotionally vulnerable and expressive. Since the seats of emotion were bodily, women's allegedly different psychological make-up was explained in part from physiology and medicine, which had begun to develop as a distinct science by the fifth century. The earliest texts attributed to the ancient doctor Hippocrates, in which case-based empirical study of symptoms were discussed in ways that increasingly excluded religious explanations, date from the same era as tragedy. There is a strong interest in the symptoms caused by the plague in Sophocles' *Oedipus Tyrannus*.[18] There are no identifiable doctors in Greek tragedy, besides the elderly physician of the dying Heracles, who attends him in *Women of Trachis*— the only treatment he is able to recommend is sleep (978–81). Yet some of the ways in which women behave in tragedy, especially virgins and married women with absent husbands, can be explained in terms of contemporary medical views of the female body (see above p. 134).

A connection between the temple cult of the healing hero Asclepius and the theatre seems to have developed in the fourth century BCE; both at Epidauros and Corinth theatres are built in or close to his sanctuaries. A few suggestive passages in the philosophers suggest that choral performances were used in the formal treatment of the sick; the nurse in Euripides' *Medea* wishes that songs could be invented that could really 'cure' human suffering (see above p. 10). But the association between the theatre and the practice of medicine is not discernible in the fifth century, despite the tradition that Sophocles himself was involved in the installation of an Athenian cult of the healing hero Asclepius in 420 BCE. More important are the numerous ways in which medicine informs the imagery of tragedy, as its crises are likened to bodily disease and injury. This imagery is crucial in some plays, including Euripides' *Orestes*. The analogy can be political: in *Antigone* the problems in Thebes are likened to a sickness (1015). But it is often the individual person in trouble who is seen in medical terms. In *Prometheus Bound*, Strength (*Kratos*) insists that pity provides no 'remedy' for Prometheus' plight, while the chorus say that Prometheus, so good at helping others, is like a bad doctor who has no drugs to prescribe himself when he falls sick (472–5).

How did the altered mental and physical states depicted by the selves in tragedy affect the 'selves' in the audience? According to a character in a fourth-century comedy by Timocrates, the process was one of identification with suffering, which led to consolation. If a spectator gives conscious thought to individuals suffering worse cases of their own problems, he can reap benefits. Thus an indigent spectator is comforted by the extreme poverty of Telephus; a sick one by the ravings of Alcmaeon; one with bad eyesight by the blinded sons of Phineus; one whose child has died by Niobe (fr. 6.5–19 K-A). Even the ancient *sub*conscious seems to have been impressed by the sufferings of individual figures in tragedy and the way they dealt with them. A modern psychoanalyst will scrutinize the fictional characters with whom a client identifies; in the second century CE, the dream interpreter Artemidorus of Daldis was already convinced that his science required understanding of the stories 'about Prometheus and Niobe and all the heroes of tragedy', because they were 'well-known and believed by most people' (4.47). Agave made an impression on one mother, who killed her own three-year-old son after dreaming that she was a Bacchant, 'for such is the story of Pentheus and Agave' (4.39). Another domestic tragedy was caused by the replication of the relationship between the two leading roles in Euripides' *Andromache*, when a slave woman dreamt that she recited the part of the Trojan captive: her jealous mistress, like Hermione in Euripides' play, subjected her to cruel mistreatment (4.59).

For theorists of child development, it is each individual's dramatization of *self* and *other* that is crucial to maturation. The seminal works on identity have all stressed that it is through dramatization of roles that children and teenagers develop their self-images, thus expanding their control over reality. This has always been the case: empathizing with the individuals in epic or the theatre—or alternatively fearing and hating them—was essential to the creation of the individual ancient Athenian's identity. Perceptions of others have always been mediated by the experience of their dramatic substitutes in a culture's collectively experienced fictional and literary characters.

A great role well acted can actually add a whole new individual permanently to a culture's functional imaginary population. If an Athenian woman was indicted for murdering her husband, it created an opportunity to claim that she had been acting out the role of Clytemnestra (Antiphon 1.17). When Demosthenes wanted to undermine the popularity of Aeschines, a former tragic actor, he implied that playing the role of the tyrant Creon in Sophocles' *Antigone* had rubbed off on his rival (Dem. 18.129, 19.247).[19] Drama radically affects the way people behave, especially in unusual circumstances of which they have no experience *except* through staged enactment (and its modern equivalents, which are often screened). It may be difficult to believe the claims of Aristophanes' Aeschylus that his Patroclus and Teucer (warriors who appeared in plays that have not survived) 'inspired every male citizen to live up to their example whenever he heard the trumpet sound' (*Frogs* 1041–2), but war offers stark examples of people taking comfort in dramatic role models under extreme circumstances, as witnessed by this American veteran of World War II:

Combat as I saw it was exorbitant, outrageous, excruciating and above all tasteless, perhaps because of the number of fighting men who had read Hemingway or Remarque was a fraction of those who had seen B movies about bloodshed. If a platoon leader had watched Douglas Fairbanks, Jr.,

Errol Flynn, Victor McLaglen, John Wayne, or Gary Cooper leap recklessly about, he was likely to follow this role model.[20]

Analysing any culture gains from studying its shared cast of characters—its equivalents of the role of Patroclus or those played by John Wayne; much public discourse assumes not only acquaintance with these imaginary beings, but familiarity. It is with this in mind that we now turn to Aeschylus, the poet who made his audiences, according to Aristophanes, enthusiastic to fight in patriotic wars.

# 5
# Aeschylean Drama

Aeschylus, son of Euphorion, was born in around 525 BCE. His family was wealthy and upper-class. There may be no truth in the tradition that when he was a child the poet had been visited in a dream by Dionysus, who found him asleep in his father's vineyard, and ordered him to compose tragedy (Pausanias 1.21.3). But Aeschylus was certainly prolific (he produced more than ninety plays), successful, and took the genre to an entirely new level of artistic brilliance and prestige. We are fortunate to be able to date all the surviving plays that are attributed to him except *Prometheus Bound*, which he may not in fact have written. He first competed at Athens in his mid-twenties in 499 BCE, and won the competition for the first time in 484, after which he was victorious at least twelve times. The winning tetralogies included those containing his *Persians* of 472 BCE, *Seven against Thebes* in 467, *Suppliants* of 463 and also his last Athenian production, the *Oresteia*, in 458. Aeschylus visited Sicily twice, once in around 470, and once after the *Oresteia* victory, for he died at Gela in 456. His *Persians* was revived in Sicily, and he wrote plays for performance there. For more than two and a half decades he was, overwhelmingly, felt to be the most important tragedian not only by the Athenians but amongst the ancient Greeks in general.

When Aeschylus was growing into manhood he witnessed some of the most exciting events in Athenian history—the tyrannical rule of Pisistratus' two sons, the assassination of one of them, the expulsion of the other (Hippias), and the jockeying for position between rival aristocratic factions that had culminated in Cleisthenes' assumption of leadership and his democratic reforms of 507 BCE. There is no reason to believe that the tragedian was not a patriotic and loyal supporter of his city-state and all its democratically agreed domestic and international policies. His fellow citizens had been involved in military operations against the Persians from at least as early as 498 BCE, when they had sent ships to Ionia to aid in the revolt which ended so catastrophically with the Persians' subjugation of Miletus in 494 (Herodotus 5.97), an event which must have shocked and terrified them.

The fledgling democracy had to face a momentous challenge with the Persian invasion of 490 BCE, and Aeschylus was in his physical prime—about thirty-five—when Darius finally invaded mainland Greece, bringing the deposed Athenian tyrant Hippias with him. The poet himself almost certainly fought at the battle of Marathon; his brother died as a result of a wound inflicted there (Herodotus 6.114). The decade between the Persian invasions, marked by turbulent internal politics at Athens, was however dominated by the permanent threat of a fresh offensive from the East. When it finally came in 480, Aeschylus was witness to the crumbling of the Greek defence in Boeotia, the terrifying march of Xerxes on Athens, the evacuation of the civic centre, its subsequent sacking, and the eventual Greek victories at Salamis, Plataea, and Mycale. Aeschylus had then lived amongst the ruins of his terribly devastated—but free—city.

The colour, scale, and magnificence of Aeschylean theatre seem somehow appropriate to the enormity of the events that took place during his lifetime. He was in antiquity universally credited with having effected a crucial transformation in the genre, as the first tragedian 'to make tragedy more grand by means of nobler emotions. He decked out the stage and stunned his audience with brilliant visual effects, with paintings and machines, with stage props such as altars and tombs, with trumpets, ghosts, and Erinyes' (*Life of Aeschylus* 14). The historical encounter with the Persians' vast armies profoundly affected his theatre, not only in his vision of the Persian court or members of the Egyptian royal family in *Persians* and *Suppliants*, but in the 'other country' that is constituted by the past. The colour and grandeur of Aeschylus' archaic and aristocratic Argos and Thebes in the *Oresteia* and *Seven against Thebes* are informed on every level by the fifth-century Athenians' encounter with barbarian monarchies. Aeschylus' language is also magniloquent, suffused by epic echoes, ornamented with exotic vocabulary, crammed with long, newly coined, compound words, and often experimental; Aristophanes could raise a laugh by suggesting that this poet's diction could knock the listener into unconsciousness (*Frogs* 962).

The sheer scale of his theatrical effects and poetry is reflected in the magnitude of his conception of history and of the universe. The underlying philosophy of all his plays is that the progress of civilization, although god-ordained, necessary, and magnificent, is bought at the cost of terrible suffering. The suffering may be the bereavement of the entire Persian people as a result of Xerxes' imperial strategy, the terror of young women who fear violent assault and rape, or the dark emotional deadlock afflicting successive generations of the family of Atreus in the *Oresteia*. But it is always underpinned by a sense of inevitability, and a hope that the reason for the suffering in terms of divine purpose may eventually be explained. In the *Oresteia* this tension between suffering and progress is conveyed as much through imagery as through action and argument. The humans at the infantile stage of social development depicted in *Agamemnon* find it almost impossible to conceptualize the universe they inhabit without resorting to analogies with the law of the jungle, or at the very least to the law of the farmyard and of the hunt (hound, ox, eagle, lion, foal, mosquito, snake, lioness, raven, spider, cockerel, bull, swallow, nightingale, swan).[1] All these images suggest that in the primitive mythical world of Argos, before the human race had learnt through suffering, humans could also only think about one another in the images of the bestiary, like insults thrown around a playground, or the animal figures in children's fables and nursery rhymes.

The Athenians knew that Aeschylus was a titanic cultural figure. His plays were honoured, most unusually, by being posthumously restaged in the context of drama competitions. He was read less than Euripides and Sophocles in later antiquity, when his lyric virtuosity and obscure idioms of poetry were found inaccessible. But his plays inspired countless adaptations and rewritings, in Latin as well as Greek, well into the Roman Empire. When he was finally translated into modern languages in the later eighteenth century, somewhat after the other two Greek tragedians, his elevated lyrics and dazzling imagery had an incalculable effect on the rise of Romantic aesthetics. The *Oresteia*, from Wagner's concept of cycles of myth-based festival opera to the early twenty-first century performance avant-garde, has exerted an incomparable influence on the evolution and intercultural transformation of western theatre.

## PERSIANS (472 BCE)

The earliest surviving Greek tragedy, the only one on a historical theme, and a key text in the history of western images of Asia—Aeschylus' *Persians* could scarcely be more foundational. It was first funded by a young aristocrat named Pericles, who was destined to become the most famous of all Athenian leaders. It was the second tragedy in a prizewinning group of apparently unrelated plays, comprising *Phineus*, *Persians*, *Glaukos Potnieus*, and a satyr play about Prometheus. It was written to commemorate the battles of the Persian Wars—Thermopylae, Marathon, Salamis, and Plataea—that led to the Greek victory over King Darius of Persia and subsequently his son and successor Xerxes. It is set throughout in the Persian capital city; its exclusively Persian cast, dressed in elaborate oriental costumes and slippers, practise ceremonial court rituals.

The chorus, elderly counsellors of the court, open by singing of their concern that they have had no news of the progress made by the mighty Persian army in Greece. The Queen (who is not named in the play, but whose name we know was Atossa) appears and recounts to them ominous and picturesque dreams which have disturbed her. A messenger arrives, and in an extraordinary series of speeches details the appalling defeat that Xerxes had incurred at Salamis (480 BCE); the response of the Queen and the chorus is to consult the ghost of her dead husband, the deified King Darius. In a spectacular ritual, his ghost is summoned from the Underworld, to predict that the Persians will suffer an even worse defeat shortly at Plataea and return utterly humiliated. Finally, Xerxes himself returns, his royal raiment in rags; with the chorus he performs the longest antiphonal lament in Greek tragedy, before processing out of the theatrical space in the direction of the palace.

Since Aeschylus' *Persians* is the only substantial text about the Persian Wars to survive complete that was written by an author with personal experience of them, it has always been mined as a source of evidence for historical 'facts'. But in order to understand the play fully, it needs to be read as a document of the Athenian collective *imagination*: it is beyond all doubt a truthful record of the ways in which the Athenians *liked to think about* their enemy. Critics of the play have usually complained that patriotic eulogy, composed from an unashamedly Greek perspective, is too morally 'low' a purpose for the exalted genre of tragedy. Such interpretations also point to the historical specificity of the subject-matter, which, as Aristotle would say, is less philosophical, less general and universally significant, than poetry on mythical themes dealing with what *might* happen (*Poetics* ch. 9, 1451b 3–7).

Defenders of the play, conversely, argue that it is the very 'universality' of the Persians' experience of defeat which makes it an elevated piece of tragic action. The drama is concerned with all humankind's relation with the gods. It teaches a 'universal' lesson by formulating history in terms of the traditional Greek ethical cycle of arrogance and ruin, *hubris* and *atē* (see above, pp. 187–8). The action, according to this view, is about the character of human destiny in general. The Persians are treated with remarkable 'sympathy' and the ethnic colour is transcended by Aeschylus' sense of human unity. When pushed to its limits, this view regards the play as a conscious warning to the Athenians against imperial expansion.

Aeschylus' plots are often simple, but his poetic structures are complex. Some see this play's structure as dependent on its theological shape, with hubris as the unifying theme. Others have discerned the operation of three movements analogous to those of a musical symphony: realization of foreboding, realization of divine wisdom, and realization of error. Ring compositions appear internally to individual sections, link separate passages, and unite the whole. Through a circular process, the distinctive feature of the inventory of barbarian proper names is enumerated with pride in the opening chorus, but converted into roll-calls of the dead in the messenger scene and final dirge.

Xerxes is one unifying element, for the play is essentially a 'homecoming' drama, and is spent either anticipating or reacting to this

King's arrival. Salamis also offers a focus: discussions of the battle in various different registers and serially by all the characters unite the remainder of the play. It is marked by a high degree of 'double explication', in both speech and song, of the same events and images: the picture of Xerxes tearing his clothes, for example, is described in speech consecutively by the Queen, the messenger, and Darius, and then finally reenacted by the chorus in the lyrics of the closing dirge.

Although beginning 'more or less at the end' of the story of the supposed impact on Persia of the sea-battle at Salamis, the play unloads in passing its antecedents and consequences from the foundation of the empire through to Plataea and the future 'three generations hence' (818). The action underlines the Persians' defeat by its consistent frustration of its characters' intentions. The chorus intend to hold a debate but are interrupted by the Queen; the Queen intends to sacrifice but is interrupted by the messenger; Darius' help is sought to make the situation better, but when he appears he says that it will get worse; the Queen leaves to ensure that Xerxes is not seen in rags, but she loses her 'race against time' as he instead meets the chorus and displays his rags in public. Another unifying feature is the city of Susa itself, ringing with lamentation (119, 1070): the civic location stresses the public nature of the catastrophe.

The play also offers an *emotional* progression, from foreboding, to panic at the news, through to the Queen's resigned pragmatism in the Darius scene, and the exhausting work of grief in the closing dirge. Emotive words describe the Persians' feelings—longing for their men, hatred (notably of Athens), and overwhelming terror. This emotional register is a clue to the complex experience which the play offered its victorious audience; during it they relived the arrival of Xerxes at Athens, the battle of Salamis in which many of them had rowed or fought hand-to-hand, the loss of their own dead, hatred of the enemy, and absolute terror. Despite their own construction in the play as invincible killing machines, the unique psychological process offered by the theatre allows them vicariously to work through the difficult emotions which they had themselves experienced. Yet the *displacement* of those emotions onto the enemy (a process psychoanalysts call 'projection') simultaneously permits them to retain the comfortable identity of unemotional

Greeks maintained by the text. They could simultaneously enjoy patriotic pride, a sense of ethnic superiority, confirmation of their own masculine self-image, the thrill of victory, *and* the covert exorcism of their own psychological pain. No wonder the play has been, and is still, so consistently revived in times of international warfare.

## SEVEN AGAINST THEBES (467 BCE)

If in *Persians* Aeschylus produced the first tragedy in the western repertoire about international war, in his next surviving work, which dates from five years later, he created the foundational dramatic treatment of the effects of *civil* war on an individual community. The play stages the trauma of Thebes—represented by a chorus of terrified local women who have every reason to think they are about to be raped and enslaved—when Oedipus' sons Eteocles and Polynices fight to the death for the kingship of the ancient city. Thebes was by far the most powerful in Boeotia (the territory that bordered on Atttica to the North), a fortified settlement that had first arisen from the hot, flat Boeotian plain way back in the Bronze Age.

The mutual slaughter of the two warriors is the prime Greek example of the fratricide story which is found in the mythical systems of most world cultures, whether Cain and Abel, Set and Osiris, or Romulus and Remus. But in Aeschylus' hands this instance of tragic intra-familial violence is also chief paradigm of the strife that afflicts the entire Theban aristocracy, by extension the whole of the Theban community, and indeed spills over into other cities in Greece. By the time of this civil war, the family of Laius has borne witness for three generations to the interconnectedness of the fate of their 'Labdacid' clan and that of their city.

The Theban king Laius had impregnated his wife Jocasta, in defiance of an oracle warning that he would die at the hand of his own son. Despite an attempt to destroy the baby, he survived infancy and grew to manhood as Oedipus, who in due course did indeed unwittingly kill his father and marry his mother. When the truth came out, Oedipus quarrelled with the sons whom Jocasta had borne him, Eteocles and Polynices, and delivered the curse that is fulfilled in *Seven against Thebes*—that each should die by the other's hand. The ancient scholar who wrote the hypothesis (introductory note) to a copy of the play, inscribed on a papyrus roll, is the source of our information that Aeschylus won first prize at the City Dionysia of 467 BCE with a tetralogy that covered much of this ground—*Laius*, *Oedipus*, *Seven against Thebes*, and *Sphinx*. Many scholars have assumed that this tetralogy was a fairly simple tragic reworking of the ancient *Thebais*, the foundational lost epic on the myths of Thebes.[2] But even if the connections between the epic and the play were strong, to stress them runs the risk of underestimating the huge number of decisions that the dramatist needed to take. He was radically rewriting a long narrative poem, which had been designed for performance by an individual, unmasked bard, by turning it into a collective script to be performed by a singing, dancing chorus and two actors who each wore a series of different masks. Moreover, these decisions needed to be made anew for each tragedy in the tetralogy.

Whatever roles had been assumed by his actors in *Laius* and *Oedipus*, Aeschylus had to decide on the figure who would deliver the prologue of his *Seven against Thebes*, the individuals with whom that prologist should interact, and what was to be the identity of the chorus. It was Aeschylus who decided to make Eteocles open the play, to portray his tense relationship with the women of the city for whose welfare he was responsible, but to have this Theban king's role overshadowed by the sheer poetic force of the speeches describing the hostile army encircling the city—poeticized military dispatches delivered by an unnamed messenger. It is unfortunately not so certain that it was Aeschylus who decided on the conclusion of the play as it stands in the text. In this Antigone, the sister of Eteocles and Polynices, enters with the fourth sibling, Ismene, laments her brothers' demise, and forcefully repudiates the civic edict that Polynices, as a traitor, should be denied burial. Later in the century, this plotline would famously be dramatized in Sophocles' *Antigone* and also features in Euripides' *Phoenician Women* (see below, pp. 305–9 and 282–5); it seems likely that the version of *Seven against Thebes* that we possess is the result of alterations to its original form, perhaps made by actors preparing a revival within decades of the play's premiere (see above, pp. 192). Nevertheless, there is an emotional logic and aesthetic balance to the play's movement from the inaugural, masculine oratory of Eteocles and the warlike descriptions delivered by the messengers, all focused on public expectations of civic duty, to the feminine lamentation at the close of the play, and Antigone's expression of her private duty to her domestic dead. Regardless of whether the play is not all the work of Aeschylus, it can be most effective in performance.

The shade of Aeschylus in Aristophanes' *Frogs* himself describes this play as 'full of Ares', brimming with the god of war himself (1021), which suggests how fifth-century audiences saw the play. Ares is indeed its commanding divinity. The Greek war-god was far less significant among the Olympians than his Roman equivalent, Mars, and indeed in Homer's *Iliad* is notorious for his impartial love of violence for the sake of it. Where the other gods line up in support of either Trojans or the Achaeans, Ares jumps into the fray wherever it is most exciting and bloody. Since in *Seven against Thebes* he signally fails to protect either brother, his true epic personality might indeed be thought to receive here its most significant theatrical exploration. The Argive army, in their camp beyond the walls, are swearing an oath to Ares and Bloodthirsty Terror as they dip their hands in newly shed bull's blood poured into an upturned shield (45)—one petrifying picture of masculine militarism amongst dozens painted through language during the course of the play. Yet Ares, as the chorus complain, should be looking after Thebes rather than its enemies, since Thebes was one of the few Greek states where his cult was extremely important.

Part of the play's fascination lies in its status as prime source for the myth of the seven warriors, a motif which, like fratricide, appears in stories told across the planet. The Greek legend may well have been closely related to a far more ancient Akkadian myth, the story of Erra, the destructive god of plague, and the seven underworld demons called upon to destroy Babylon.[3] The Guarani legends of the indigenous peoples of Paraguay featured at its core seven monsters with special powers. There are seven lucky gods in Japanese mythology as well as seven Samurai in the epoch-making film by Akira Kurosawa (1954). But the seven mighty warriors who marched against Thebes, although described in thrilling detail by the messenger, are never physically seen. They are only visualized, in menacing detail, by the terrified city under siege and the audience in the Athenian theatre.

## SUPPLIANTS (463 BCE)

Ancient Egypt exerted a fascination over the classical Athenians, who recognized the antiquity of the Nilotic culture, and elaborated myths about the longstanding relationship between Greeks and Egyptians.[4] Chief amongst these was the tradition that the Peloponnesian town of Argos had once been ruled by an Egyptian called Danaus, himself ultimately descended from a Greek princess named Io, beloved by Zeus, who had been turned into a heifer and pursued to Africa.[5] Danaus had fifty daughters, and by the fifth century a story had emerged that it was they who had originally brought the important female fertility festival of Demeter and Persephone, the Thesmophoria, from Egypt to Greece (Herodotus 2.171). Aeschylus' *Suppliants* concerns the shared history of the Argive Greeks and the Egyptians, but at its psychological heart lies the dramatization of violent ethnic confrontation. In its discussion of physical appearance, skin colour, and clothing, as well as in its comparisons of religion, behavioural codes, and political culture, the dialogue richly reflects the interest that mid-fifth-century Greeks had in the different peoples with whom they shared the Mediterranean litoral.

The fifty beautiful black Danaids, whose continuous physical presence overwhelmingly dominates the play, have fled with their father from their home in Egypt to occupy an important sanctuary outside Argos in the Peloponnese. They plead with the Greek king, Pelasgus, to grant them asylum, on the ground that they are distantly related to his people through a joint ancestress (Io). They are fleeing enforced marriage with their fifty first cousins, the sons of Danaus' brother Aegyptus, and are so desperate that they threaten to commit suicide unless they are allowed to stay in Greece. Pelasgus is sympathetic, but concerned about what his people will have to say on the matter, and leaves to consult the Argives with due process. At the emotional climax, the girls are left alone, unarmed and undefended, and entirely vulnerable to rape or abduction.

The crisis now occurs as a barbarous Egyptian herald arrives from a ship, probably with supporting warriors, to announce the imminent arrival of the Egyptian would-be bridegrooms, and to make terrible threats of assault and indeed death against the girls should they refuse to comply. In desperate sung responses they resist, clinging on hysterically to the cult images. The tension that underlies the whole play has suddenly erupted, and it is not now ethnic but emphatically sexual. With the arrival of the Argive king and his retinue, and the promise to protect the girls, the obnoxious herald is forced to withdraw, but only after declaring outright war on the opposition. The play may end with a brief respite from conflict, but there is no doubt that much more violence is to come. There is not only an impasse but total chaos and a sense of irresoluble antagonism. If the suppliant women were impersonated by as many as fifty Athenian chorus-men (rather than fifteen or twelve), which is perfectly possible, the effect will have been even more striking. It is certainly the large *corps* of maidens that drew the late eighteenth-century composer of the opera *Les Danaïdes* (1784), Antonio Salieri, to the story, which he ornamented with impressive balletic interludes.

The long odes in this tragedy lend it a lyrical tone in places, and more even than other Greek tragic poetry it alludes to the senses, to touch and hearing as much as to sight. This sensory richness begins with the chorus' invocations and evocations of the marshland round Argos, the clear water of its river, and Danaus' account of the dust and creaking axles of the approaching Argives. With the description of the images of Zeus' eagle, of Poseidon, and of Hermes, the sanctuary setting and the olive branches with which the Danaids adorn it are tangibly created in the poetry: it is from these statues that they describe themselves being dragged, like horses, by their clothes and headgear; it is from these statues that they threaten to hang themselves, creating in the mind of the spectator a terrible image of fifty corpses swaying in the sacred air.

Until a papyrus find published half in 1952 proved that it premiered in 463 BCE,[6] for centuries the play confused admirers of Aeschylus and Greek tragedy. They found it so 'primitive' that they assumed it was the earliest of all Greek plays. Their consternation largely resulted from its problematic status as one play in a tetralogy from which no other survives. It is not even certain whether *Suppliants* was the first or second play. Its story is left certainly incomplete: the Danaids did indeed marry their cousins and then murdered them on their wedding night. The vulnerability of the suppliants of this strange play needs to be read ironically against the knowledge that they are capable of violent murder—all except one of them, that is, since the Danaid Hypermestra spared her husband Lynceus. The final tragedy involved a trial and adjudication, included a speech by Aphrodite on sex and fertility, and a resolution of the fraught relationship between the Egyptian immigrants and their Greek hosts. Danaus became king. But the available information does not allow us to see what, in the surviving play, the central problem really is for the Danaids.

Structural analyses have shown that the action (the earliest of several surviving Greek 'suppliant dramas'[7]) falls into a triadic pattern which exactly mirrors the structure of the ritual of supplication. Images of despair and flight are followed by formal dialogue between suppliant and designated 'saviour', leading to the first physical crossings of tangible boundaries as agreement is verbally reached. But this triad also reflects the deep structure underlying ancient Greek marriage rituals, which began with ritually encoded erotic pursuit and ended with the bride's removal across thresholds to her new home. Such a structure is appropriate to a tetralogy of which a central interest was clearly marriage—both how and how not to do it.

The Danaids may be fleeing their cousins because of the close blood relationship (although even some half-sibling marriages were permitted in Athens—see below pp. 222–3). Perhaps their father has instilled in them an aversion to sex because an oracle has determined that he will be killed by a son-in-law. Possibly they have pledged their virginity to Artemis. Their primary objection may be that the sons of Aegyptus have pressed their suit violently against women who, as kin, they would be expected to protect against violence.[8] In recent years it is indeed the brutal idiom and psychological directness of this imposing drama that have been rediscovered in the theatre, mainly on account of its interest in ethnic conflict, in the rights of the asylum-seeker, and the problems involved in arranged marriages, especially those to close family members. Danaus' role still resonates as he engages in international diplomacy only to disguise personal ambition. It is even more significant that the ethical questions asked by Pelasgus are still of acute relevance today: to what degree is any one state or indeed family entitled to intervene in the affairs of another, even the customs regulating the status of women and sexual relationships? At what point do terrified, vulnerable asylum-seekers begin to look more like antisocial threats to state security?

## ORESTEIA (458 BCE)

Aeschylus won a famous victory with this tetralogy. The three tragedies constitute our sole surviving example of a linked trilogy, conceived to be performed sequentially. Sadly, the final play, the satyr drama *Proteus*, has not been preserved. It took a light-hearted look at a journey home from Troy, by another member of the same family, since it dramatized Menelaus' meeting in Egypt with the sea-divinity Proteus, recounted in the *Odyssey* book 4. But the tragedies explain the history behind the original foundation of an important political and legal institution in Athens, the court of the Areopagus (which means 'the rock of Ares', the hill of Ares adjacent to the Acropolis). In Aeschylus' day there had been controversy about the rights and duties of this court, and it had been reformed. One of its main duties was to hear and adjudicate in cases of homicide, and the *Oresteia* stages an aetiology that traces its foundation to the trial of Orestes for the murder of Clytemnestra.

Clytemnestra and Orestes were from the royal family of Argos, where the first and second plays are set. These two plays are also (unlike all the other Aeschylean examples) the first extant tragedies to be located outside the door of the familial home. They provide a powerful sense of the private domestic recesses just concealed by the palace facade—Agamemnon, wheeled out dead with Cassandra on the *ekkuklēma*, has been murdered at his most vulnerable, naked, in the bath; Aegisthus, Clytemnestra's lover, tends the hearth at the heart of the home (*Agamemnon* 1435); Clytemnestra's screams when she suffers nightmares can be heard issuing from the inmost chambers of the women's quarters (*Libation-Bearers* 35–7). Psychic interiority, the terrible pain that the chorus of *Agamemnon* says drips on their hearts as they sleep (*Agamemnon* 179–80), is replicated in the intense domestic interiority suggested by secretive behind-the-scenes activities in the trilogy.

The poetry of the *Oresteia* is infused with proverbial wisdom. The moral sayings 'the doer will suffer' and 'blood for blood' resound through its choruses. Perhaps the most significant is the phrase 'learning [comes] through suffering'. The trilogy portrays how society changes in response to the things people suffer. This is echoed in the shift from private to public space. It is only in the final tragedy, *Eumenides*, that the scene changes first to the Delphic oracle of Apollo, and then to a public space in the centre of Athens. These settings link the old story of the Atridae and their family curse not only to the most important centre of prophecy in the Greek world, but to the city-state that was, at the time of the play's production, laying claim to imperial leadership of much of that world. The settings also allow the trilogy to suggest what had been the real historical development of the archaic Greek city-state from the constitutional monarchy apparently portrayed in *Agamemnon*, through to the tyranny maintained by Clytemnestra and Aegisthus in *Libation-Bearers*, and thence to the Athenian democracy in *Eumenides*. This last play, uniquely in Greek tragedy, portrays a city that can govern itself without either tyrant or king.

## Agamemnon

Argos, run since Agamemnon left for Troy by his wife Clytemnestra, hears that the war has been won and he is returning. Tension builds while the audience is offered different perspectives on the situation at Argos and the implications of the death of Iphigenia long ago at Aulis. These are the perspectives of the palace watchman, the chorus of elderly citizens, Clytemnestra, and a herald respectively. Agamemnon returns, in a chariot, exhibiting his prize Cassandra, princess of Troy. Clytemnestra persuades Agamemnon to enter the palace up a richly coloured carpet, and after a scene in which the clairvoyant Cassandra sees into the past, present, and future,

Clytemnestra appears, exultantly, over the corpses of both Agamemnon and Cassandra. The chorus try to drive her into exile, but Clytemnestra, a lone woman confronted by twelve angry men, says that she is prepared to fight with any one of them in single combat (1422–5). The chorus subsequently almost join battle with her lover Aegisthus' bodyguards, but she persuades all the men to calm down, and announces that she and Aegisthus are now officially the joint heads of state. Their *coup d'état* is complete.

The exceptional qualities of the roles Aeschylus created for both women in *Agamemnon* (see below) have distracted attention from the Argive king himself, whose slaughter provides the yardstick by which all the other crimes in the trilogy are measured. The fundamental question is whether he deserves to die. The answer to this simple enquiry is complex, not least because Aeschylus ensures that Agamemnon's wife is every ancient Athenian male's worst nightmare incarnate—mendacious, intelligent, powerful, adulterous, and politically ambitious. The outrageous cold-blooded murder Clytemnestra executes could not be cast in a more negative light (see Fig. 5.1). But this does not mean that Agamemnon's own moral stature is not scrutinized minutely, and found to be wanting.

The most important reason offered for why he dies is his responsibility for the death of his daughter Iphigenia. The chorus recall the dreadful moment long ago at Argos when he 'strapped on the yoke of necessity' and undertook an action that was outrageous and immoral (218–20). Kin-killing was in contravention of the most basic laws, and Agamemnon had never yet been punished for it. Clytemnestra also intimates that Agamemnon's wellbeing would be jeopardized if he has committed sacrilege at Troy and disrespected its divine sanctuaries (338–42), and his guilt in this regard is confirmed by the herald, who says that Agamemnon has uprooted Troy, and obliterated 'the altars of the gods and all their shrines' (527–8).

Additionally, Agamemnon is unpopular because he instigated a war which has cost innumerable lives on his own side. In a lyric which resonates down the centuries to every war-bereaved community, the chorus describe the despair in each household which has lost a man: the god of martial violence, Ares, they sing (437–43),

FIG. 5.1. Fragmentary 4th-century Lucanian vase in Basel, probably depicting Agamemnon and Clytemnestra, reproduced courtesy of the Herbert Cahn Collection, Basel.

>     barters gold
> For soldier's bodies. He tips the scales
> In battles of the spear, and then sends back from Troy
> Weighty shipments of ashes,
> Cremated dust instead of men
> Crammed into urns for the families to lament.

The chorus go on to say that anger and resentment against the Atridae are on the increase, and they connect the resentment of the people with the ratification and fulfilment of curses (456–7). Another reason that Agamemnon has to die is that the curse on the family of Atreus cannot be evaded. Crimes committed in a previous generation have never been expiated: the seduction of Atreus' wife Aerope by his brother Thyestes, and the subsequent murder of two of Thyestes' children by Atreus, who served them up to him at a dinner party and made him eat them. Their surviving brother Aegisthus, grown to manhood and now replicating his father's crime by sleeping with Agamemnon's wife, gloats over his cousin's corpse by asserting that his death fulfils the curse Thyestes had called down at the cannibalistic 'feast' after 'vomiting up the butchered flesh' and kicking over the table (1593–602). The curse is also linked, in some obscure way, with the wealth that the family has accumulated and which Clytemnestra displays immoderately by carpeting the palace entrance. The chorus warn that it is easier to practise virtue in the grimy houses of the poor; virtue is incompatible with 'gold-encrusted mansions' (773–80).

Agamemnon's taste for exhibiting his worldly possessions is made concrete in the figure of his war spoil, Cassandra. The only human males who enter on chariots in Greek tragedy are hubristic and shortly to die; non-pedestrian entry signified theatrically that mortal characters were getting above themselves. But riding on a chariot was not in itself a crime. Nor was a sexual relationship with a war captive, even for a married man, although death also faces all men in tragedy who tactlessly bring their sexual partners to the marital home rather than keeping them at a discreet distance from their wives (see above pp. 153–4). Clytemnestra sees the relationship with Cassandra, and her own humiliation at the way the captive has been publicly displayed, as providing additional justifications for murdering Agamemnon (1438–47).

His self-important agreement to tread the carpets betrays an arrogance that comes uncomfortably close to sacrilege. Putting carpets instead of shoe leather between his feet and the earth has metaphysical ramifications. The gods, even Agamemnon realizes, do not like to see humans honoured in such ways (918–25). Clytemnestra activates another, more political meaning in the treading of the carpet. She throws herself to the ground and performs a *salaam* before her husband, in a manner that the Greeks despised when they saw it practised by the courtiers of the Persian king. She reminds him that Priam, an Asiatic king, would in Agamemnon's position happily have walked on carpets. And despite his professed misgivings, Agamemnon allows his footwear to be removed, and walks like a god, or a tyrant. Clytemnestra's strategy has been designed to demonstrate something important about Agamemnon to the Argives. By forcing him to play the role of a man who fancied himself equivalent to a barbarian autocrat, she is attempting to add political legitimacy to his death—to present it as a political assassination. In Athens, a citizen could be acquitted of murder if he could prove that his victim had been intending to overthrow the democracy. Perhaps Clytemnestra is trying to rouse popular support for a deed really motivated by her personal feud with her husband.

Clytemnestra's role as stage-director in this scene supplements her status as consummate actress, word-perfect in the 'role' of a loyal wife. The transvestite actor who played Clytemnestra faced a challenge. He needed stamina: Clytemnestra is the only character to appear in all three plays of the *Oresteia*. He needed to be versatile: in *Agamemnon* Clytemnestra is in the ascendant; in *Libation-Bearers* she is a frightened tyrant whose authority crumbles; in *Eumenides* she is a wandering phantom urging on the Erinyes. But since her poetry is some of the most elaborate and vivid in ancient Greek, the actor also needed to have a gift for declamation, as well as a complex physical presence. Clytemnestra has to be acted convincingly as a woman, the sister of the gorgeous Helen of Troy, a mother of several children, and lover of Aegisthus. Some of Clytemnestra's forcefulness stems from conventionally 'female' forms of exercising power. She and her women stood in different places throughout the city, 'shrieking' the women's conventional victory cry as they sacrificed (594–8).

Clytemnestra also has distinctively masculine qualities. She has a mind that 'thinks like a man's' (8), and keeps control by the force of her language, which refers unsettlingly to the wider world beyond the female sphere of the household. She alludes to disturbing myths about the violent hero Heracles (870, 1040), and uses images drawn from worlds of which no aristocratic woman should have had much experience: hunting, and the farming of the deepest oceans (1375–6, 958–60). When denying that she has committed adultery, she says, sinisterly, that she knows as much of it as 'of dipping bronze' in cold water to solidify the molten liquid (612). Her speech describing the relay of the beacons she has personally organized contains picturesque details of geography and topography (312). She even knows ancient Egyptian poetry. Her bizarre speech in praise of Agamemnon, where she calls him the watchdog of the stables, forestay of the ship, the pillar of the roof, only child to a father, land appearing to sailors bereft of hope, the fairest day after a storm, and spring-water to a thirsty traveller (896–901), is actually a paraphrase of an Egyptian hymn to a King of the Middle Kingdom.[9]

Yet Agamemnon's wife is very nearly upstaged by Agamemnon's concubine. Cassandra, a powerless young woman, and captive in a foreign land, is the only figure who disobeys Clytemnestra, and maintains an independence from the action. The minute Clytemnestra has entered the palace, Cassandra bursts into a terrible song to Apollo. In her prophetic frenzy she describes, only minutes before his actual death cries are heard, Clytemnestra's preparations for the murder of Agamemnon. Her ravings also encompass laments for the fall of Troy, a prediction that Agamemnon will be avenged, and a repudiation of Apollo, who has inflicted such suffering on her. In the end she asserts what little autonomy she can by entering the palace to certain death, of her own free will. But the impact of her unforgettable scene, which left a profound impression on the literature of subsequent antiquity, has much to do with its relationship to the experience of the theatrical spectator. Like each and every audience member, Cassandra can see far beyond the palace facade, into the past and the future; like them, she knows that something terrible is happening inside in the immediate present. But she is as helpless in the face of Agamemnon's suffering as any spectator, and, like them, is a mortal subject to death herself. Her last lines, which equate human life with a painted image that can be wiped away at any time by a wet sponge, are a crystallization of all tragic metaphysics (1327–30).

Cassandra can see with terrible clarity the problem that is undermining the very foundations of the Argive royal family. She points to the spectres of the little children served up at the Thyestean feast, diminutive ghosts who died in and haunt the house that forms the scenic background to the tragedy. 'Do you see those young creatures', she demands of the chorus, 'beside the house, like figures in dreams? They are the children slaughtered by their own kindred; their hands are full of the meat of their own flesh; they are clear to me, holding their vitals and entrails, which their father tasted' (1217–22). Inter-reacting with Cassandra's vision of the ghostly, cannibalized sons of Thyestes, numerous metaphorical and symbolic children haunt the imagery and figures of speech characterizing the tragedy as a whole.[10]

The tragedy extends the imagery of childhood and infancy to encompass its cosmic and ethical themes. The omen of the eagles and the pregnant hare (104–37) thematically prefigures the death of Iphigenia. It also makes concrete the overarching theme of the child-destroying family curse, a curse which affects children born to the household even before their birth. The chorus believe that 'It is the evil deed which thereafter begets more evil deeds, in breed like itself' (758–60). The chorus' metaphorical family of parent crimes and child crimes then almost imperceptibly mutates into the physical reality of a human family: the doer of the evil deed begets further doers of evil deeds. With another slide between concrete and metaphorical families, the doer then becomes the deed again: an act of hubris in the past, the chorus continue, 'begets' an act of hubris in the present; the 'children' of hubris curse the household, but are in fact replicas of their hubristic parents (763–6). While the idea of an inheritable curse may seem alien and primitive to us, it is worth thinking in terms of modern theories about the adverse effect on children of bad parenting and of poor parental examples. Dysfunctional families do often produce dysfunctional children, who are sometimes destined to reproduce, when they become parents themselves, the maladjusted behaviours of their own inadequate parents.

## *Libation-Bearers*

In her prophetic frenzy in *Agamemnon*, Cassandra predicts that Orestes will one day come home to avenge his father's death (1280–1), and the second play of the trilogy opens with two young men, Orestes and Pylades, arriving at Agamemnon's tomb. After long years in exile, Orestes places a lock of his own hair upon the tomb in a traditional sign of mourning. He and Pylades then retreat into a hiding-place on the approach of Electra and the chorus of slave women. Something peculiar has happened; Clytemnestra has herself ordered that a libation be poured to the spirit of the husband she murdered, since she has suffered an ominous dream. This ritual attention to Agamemnon is apparently the first of its kind that he has received; Electra has to be tutored by the chorus in the words to speak as she pours the libation (105–23). Orestes and Electra are reunited, and perform, along with the chorus, a protracted lament for Agamemnon that turns into a rallying cry for revenge.

Orestes in *Libation-Bearers* is the earliest surviving tragic hero who is torn between conflicting imperatives that place him in a terrifying moral dilemma (see lines 269–90). He is certainly the first traumatized revenge hero in the long line that leads to Hamlet and beyond. When it finally comes to the dead, it transpires that Orestes has insufficient personal enmity against his mother, and can only bring himself to kill her with difficulty and with help. And well might he hesitate, because in the nightmare world of ceaseless chains of reciprocal violence which the Erinyes supervise and symbolize, as soon as his mother is dead, it is vengeance for *her* death, rather than for Agamemnon's, that becomes their primary concern. As the proverbial wisdom of the trilogy has it, *the doer will suffer.*

In many ways the twin killings in *Libation-Bearers* reflect the killings in *Agamemnon*: they take place behind the same palace door, and the bodies of the couple are displayed as a pair on the *ekkuklēma*. As if to underline the parallelism, Orestes has the hunting net in which Clytemnestra had trapped Agamemnon displayed, stretched out in a circle, to the Sun, 'so that he may bear me witness on the day of judgement, when it comes, that it was with justice that I carried out this killing' (985–6). Yet *Libation-Bearers* conjures up a sense of danger and menace that is unlike that of *Agamemnon* or anything else in Aeschylus. In *Agamemnon* Clytemnestra is defending space that has become hers, but Orestes and Pylades are vulnerable intruders into enemy territory, where Orestes immediately prays to Hermes to 'preserve' him (2). Throughout most of the play he remains in extreme danger from the regime installed by Aegisthus and Clytemnestra, which is so tyrannical that their household slaves and subjects live in a permanent state of misery and fear (75–83). When Orestes sets out his plan, to enter the palace in disguise accompanied by Pylades, and kill Aegisthus instantly if he finds him inside, he has only women—his sister and the chorus—to act as lookouts on his behalf. Aegisthus, on the other hand, has an armed bodyguard, as the last scene of *Agamemnon* made clear. Orestes and Pylades do indeed enter the house, having deceived Clytemnestra about their identity, but it takes until three-quarters of the way through the play for the audience to learn, from the nurse, that Aegisthus (fortuitously) is away. Clytemnestra is sufficiently rattled to send him a message urging him to return with his soldiers in attendance. It is only the chorus' quick thinking that enables Aegisthus to be lured, without his guards, back to the palace and his death.

In these complex scenes of intrigue and deceit, where the chorus saves Orestes from Aegisthus' private army by 'thinking on their feet', something wholly new in Greek tragedy is seen developing—the exciting 'adventure' plot. The effectiveness of this play depends to a great extent on the degree of suspense achieved. The question of whether this dangerous mission can be accomplished by stealth and rapid responses must have kept the original audience on the edge of their wooden benches. Aegisthus does return, enters the palace, and is almost immediately executed. But the continuing danger to Orestes is signalled by the sudden appearance of a slave loyal to Aegisthus, who shouts that Clytemnestra's life is now also under threat. The complex counter-coup is still far from over. Moreover, in a brilliant touch, Aeschylus makes Orestes' nerve fail him at the last minute. When his mother reveals the breast with which she says she nursed him, and begs for her life, he hesitates, asking Pylades (who has never said a word previously) whether he should kill her or not. It is only when Pylades reminds him of Apollo's injunction that he finally does the deed.

Indeed, Orestes has needed a great deal of support and encouragement to fulfil his vengeance mission, especially from Electra and the mysteriously interventionist chorus (551–3). The need to arouse the necessary feelings of aggression explains the length of the great triangular dirge that occupies much of the first half of the play. Later, Orestes' long wait on stage for something to happen is filled by a song in which the chorus trigger in him the intuitive misogyny of all ancient Greek men by listing all the dreadful crimes that women such as Clytemnestra have committed (585–651). When he takes Clytemnestra inside to kill her, they continue in their moral support, with a triumphant song declaring the liberation of the house of Atreus (935–71). Yet it is this same chorus that but one speech later, when Orestes reveals his bloody handiwork to his citizens, entirely changes its tune. The man who has been in such mortal danger from others has suddenly become the polluted murderer himself. Their last words to the woman they hated show how quickly revenge turns culprits into victims (1007–9):

> Alas, alas for woeful work!
> Hateful the death by which you have been destroyed!
> Alas, alas! And for him that survives, suffering now comes into flower.

## *Eumenides*

In *Eumenides* the divine forces that run the universe, the gods and Erinyes who have communicated only through strange signs and obscure prophecies in the earlier plays, are spectacularly revealed and mingle, undisguised, with mortals on the level of the main stage. So do ordinary citizens of Athens (the direct ancestors of the play's first audience), as they vote in a trial in which an Olympian god and chthonic beings compete. Such, it is implied, was the environment of Athens in the glorious days when its institutions were first founded: gods and men walked and talked together under the Attic sun.

After fleeing Argos at the end of *Libation-Bearers*, Orestes, himself now polluted with matricide, travelled to the Delphic oracle of Apollo, the god who had commanded him to kill his mother. It is at that shrine that the final tragedy opens. He has been pursued there by the Erinyes, who are obeying the ghost of Clytemnestra (Fig. 5.2). Apollo, however, tells Orestes that his future will be decided by the goddess Athena. In a most unusual change of scene, Orestes is next found in Athens, where he seeks refuge with Athena's statue and we learn that he has now been ritually purified and is no longer polluted. But this does not solve the problem that there has been as yet no requital for the murder of Clytemnestra, and it is this problem which the physical presence of the Erinyes, who continue to pursue Orestes, represents. In a long and terrifying ode, they set out their theological manifesto, claiming the eternal right to torture kin-killers by filling their heads with agonizing delusions. This was the Erinyes' 'ancient privilege', bestowed on them by the gods, and they will not lightly relinquish it. The ode also reflects an ancient form of magic whereby litigants in trials

FIG. 5.2. George Romney's illustration of the ghost scene in *Eumenides* (mid-1770s), reproduced courtesy of the Trustees of the British Museum.

wrote down curses on special tablets, several examples of which have been found that date from classical Athens.[11] The procedure aimed to gain an advantage over opponents by inhibiting their mental acuity in court.

Athena announces that she has summoned the best of the citizens, who will adjudicate in the trial of Orestes, examining evidence and witnesses under solemn oath (482–9). After another long song, in which the Erinyes contemplate the moral anarchy that they fear will ensue if their ancient responsibility is taken from them, the trial begins. The issue is not whether Orestes committed the crime, but the relative importance of the duty that he owed to his father and to his mother. The Erinyes insist that it is more important for the killing of a mother by a son to be avenged than the killing of a man by his wife, since the marital bond is not one based in shared blood. But Apollo counter-attacks with the bizarre argument that mothers do not actually contribute to the creation of a child. Their womb is just a receptacle in which the father's seed is first germinated (658–66). The jurors' vote, enacted and counted on stage, is split half in half, but Orestes' acquittal is ensured by the deciding vote of Athena—the motherless, childless, virgin deity who sprang from her father's head.

Great significance attaches to the outlandish nature of Apollo's denial of a blood bond between mother and child. Some scholars have said that it would not have sounded so peculiar to Aeschylus' audience as it does to us, since there is a possibility that one of the pre-Socratic philosophers had taken Apollo's line.[12] Even if this is the case, it might seem strange for an Olympian deity to use an avant-garde biological theory in such a solemn context as a murder trial. But, more importantly, we know for certain that Apollo's argument ran counter to the intuitive, 'commonsensical' view of most Athenians as enshrined in their laws regulating marriage. Brothers could marry their half-sisters in Athens, provided that they had different *mothers*. Children born of the same mother, grown in the same womb, if they mated, would be regarded as committing incest. These rules prove that the Athenians felt that half-siblings nurtured by the same mother were actually biologically far closer to one another than children born by different women to the same father. The blood bond that united mother and child was a deeply felt and obvious fact of life. For Aeschylus to give such a casuistic and counter-intuitive argument to Apollo, and indeed the entire male 'side' in the gender conflict of *Eumenides*, therefore raises the possibility that he was demonstrating that trial by jury, with orators presenting arguments, could in practice be dangerous. No wonder he decided in his version of the Orestes myth that the vote had been split rather than a resounding, unanimous verdict.

One of Aeschylus' favourite theatrical techniques is to introduce an idea or image in poetry, and later to make it concrete and visible on stage in material terms. The unforgettable Erinyes of *Eumenides* had been heralded by the imagery of monsters, dogs and snakes in *Agamemnon*, as well as by the spectral chorus Cassandra had been able to see dancing (1186), and the Erinyes only Orestes could see, wreathed with snakes and with blood dripping from their eyes, at the end of *Libation-Bearers* (1048–50, 1058). *Eumenides* is actually opened by the Pythia, the priestess of Pythian Apollo at Delphi, outside the very doors of this most revered of Greek temples. She enters the temple to take up her oracular seat, but staggers out, aghast at the sight she has just seen: a man with bloodied hands and a sword is polluting the shrine, surrounded by disgusting supernatural creatures. She and subsequently Apollo describe them as something like Gorgons or Harpies, but without wings; they are dark, old women or 'ancient children'; they swallow and spew forth clots of human blood they have sucked, and their eyes ooze mucus (47–54, 69, see also 183–4). They pollute everything they touch. There must have been great pleasure involved for each chorus-man, who had played the much more sedate roles of old men and slave women in the previous two tragedies, to dress up in the costumes and masks of an Erinys and leap about in a repugnant way. The horrid appearance of this chorus was so famous in antiquity that a tradition developed that women who witnessed it suffered spontaneous miscarriages (*Life of Aeschylus* 2).

The chorus is in a sense the tragic hero of the play. Like several important male characters in Euripides and Sophocles—Heracles, Ajax, Oedipus—they undergo a process of transformation leading to hero status. They are uprooted and dishonoured, before being rehabilitated and granted a cult that will ensure them a place in the

Athenian pantheon. Aeschylus is probably here combining two types of ancient goddess in the new cult that is given an aetiology in the trilogy. The Athenians had probably long worshipped 'Revered Goddesses' (*Semnai Theai*) in a cave on the Acropolis; these goddesses promoted fertility and ensured that 'the fruits of the earth and the offspring of flocks flourish for the citizens, flooding forth for all time to come' (907–9). In *Eumenides* it is suggested that they began as the Erinyes, whose primary function was to pursue crimes in the family, but were pacified and took up permanent residence as revered goddesses of Athens. They are to retain, however, some responsibility for the punishment of crime (910).

Some ancient sources state that Athena renamed the tamed Erinyes 'The Kindly Ones', or 'Eumenides'. The word does not appear in the play, which may originally have been entitled *Erinyes*, but it did come to be called *Eumenides*. Some scholars have therefore long believed that a line must have dropped out of the text in which this renaming occurred. It might have been in Athena's last speech, when she sends the procession of her own attendants forth to instal the Erinyes in their new cavernous residence (1021–31):

> I commend the pronouncement of these prayers
> And by glowing torchlight shall send
> You to the regions below, beneath the earth,
> Attended by the women who guard my statue,
> As is right. For the pride of Theseus' entire land
> Will come forth, an illustrious parade
> Of children, women, and aged women
> *[Missing line in which the goddesses are renamed Eumenides?]*
> Honour them, the goddesses clad in scarlet robes,
> And let the fire of torchlight advance,
> So that these guests in my land may from now on be benevolent
> And make our men conspicuously brave.

The religious aetiology that *Eumenides* provides for the cult of the revered goddesses of the cave beneath the Acropolis is balanced in the play by the new aetiology that it offers for the political institution of the court of the Areopagus. This took its name from the place it was held, on one of the other high peaks in the Athenian city centre, the rock (*pagos*) of Ares. Many modern productions interpret the play as staging the foundation of the first murder court, in which the state took over responsibility for murder cases from families and tribes, and replaced blood vendettas with trial by jury. But the specific history of the Areopagus is important to understanding the play.

If the Areopagus' sole function was as a homicide court, then it would be a more accurate reading of the play to see it as celebrating trial by jury as an ideal of universal relevance. But the responsibilities of the Areopagus as an institution had been fiercely contested during the decade prior to the *Oresteia*. This was a response to the domination by the Areopagus of the political scene in the period after the Persian War. It was then a council from which ordinary Athenian citizens of the lowest class (*thetes*) were excluded. But a radical democrat named Ephialtes had led a movement to divide the aristocratic old body's powers up between the Assembly (which was open to all make citizens), the Council which advised it, and the law-courts for which the juries were drawn from every citizen class. There had been terrible conflict in the city over these measures, bloodshed in the streets, and an oligarchic plot to destabilize the new system of government. Ephialtes himself was assassinated in 461 BCE. Athena's several commands to cease all internal violence and civil strife in *Eumenides* must have really meant something to Aeschylus' audience just three years later.

As a result of Ephialtes' reforms, the rights of the Areopagus were severely restricted, but it did still retain jurisdiction in murder cases. How we interpret the play politically comes down to a relatively simple question: does it protest against the reforms of the Areopagus by celebrating the idea that it was a sacred institution, with unique authority, founded according to Zeus's will by his daughter Athena? Or does it take the democrats' side by celebrating the Areopagus primarily as a court of law that adjudicated in homicide trials? This question has been debated for many years, and scholars have tended to pick sides according to whether their own politics are conservative or more progressive. But there is a third answer to the question, and it becomes attractive if we consider the nature of Aeschylus' audience. He wanted to win the drama competition, and succeeded in doing so. The judges in the competition chose the tragedian whose works they approved most highly, but they were most unlikely to vote against what seemed to be the popular choice. Aeschylus has clothed his primeval Areopagus in mythical and poetic dress which is so consciously *ambiguous* that it can sustain any interpretation. By these means he seems to have achieved the difficult task of portraying Athenian constitutional history in a way that pleased people of all political persuasions in his audience.

When Athena founds the Areopagus, she describes its future function (690–7):

> The citizens' veneration for this court,
> And inborn fear, will prevent them,
> Both by day and night, from committing crimes,
> Provided that the citizens themselves
>    do not make innovations in the laws.
> If you pollute bright water by pouring evil and mud into it
> You will never be able to find something to drink.

By talking in the enigmatic symbolism of mud and bright water, Athena makes any single reading impossible. Innovation in the laws could refer to actions taken by either party in Athens in the 450s, which had seen a whole series of reforms, counter-reforms, and reactions. What comes over with real force is the idea that Athena's city is run by the rule of law, as she emphasizes in the following lines, which commend a system that is 'neither anarchic nor despotic', but a middle form of constitution in which justice can prevail.

The mythical explanations for the cult and the Areopagus that are provided in *Eumenides* are part, according to an influential interpretation that may have first been fully appreciated by Simone de Beauvoir, of its much broader function as a sociological aetiology, or 'charter', for men's domination by women. When Athena votes with Apollo and Orestes, effectively dismissing the suffering of Iphigenia and Clytemnestra under patriarchy, the subordinate place of women in Athenian society is defined and given a divine seal of approval. The *Oresteia* argues that democracy is superior to monarchy or tyranny, that Olympian religion needed to replace a more earthy primeval religion, and that law-courts are superior to vendettas. But it also argues that fathers are more important than mothers, that men are more important than women, and that if women have a public role at all, it is in religion rather than politics, legislation, or law enforcement. Clytemnestra may well therefore have been designed to demonstrate what happens in a nightmarish city where women with manlike hearts stake a claim to power and offer to compete for it on equal terms with the other sex. The *Oresteia* trilogy, taken as a whole, prescribes clearly the 'correct' spheres for women's activity. A good woman will be a faithful wife, a mother of legitimate children, and a respected participant in the rites of the city-state. Indeed, the *Oresteia* concludes with the women of Athens. These 'ideal' women, in their religious procession, are excluded from the 'political' arenas in the city—they are not to make or implement laws, or to have political power. But the trilogy's interest in defining the 'correct' role of women in society begins long before, with the discussion in *Agamemnon* of the proper way to be a woman.

## PROMETHEUS BOUND (NO DATE)

In theatrical terms, this magnificent drama is unique amongst Greek tragedies because its cast is exclusively superhuman, since even the mortal princess Io is being turned by the gods into a heifer who can give birth to heroes (see Fig. 5.3). Prometheus the Titan has outraged Zeus by stealing the gods' prerogative of fire and bestowing it upon mortals. Zeus, who has taken over Olympus recently, is determined to make an example out of Prometheus. In the astonishing opening sequence he is therefore hammered to the rocks of the Caucasus by the reluctant smith-god Hephaestus, under pressure from divine personifications of Strength and Violence. This elemental drama is also the only surviving tragedy with no sign of a household or household substitute such as a tent or cave, or even a human building such as a sanctuary. The scene designer needed to supply little more than a rock and fetters, perhaps situated centrally in the dancing space.

The question asked by the play on the most fundamental level of plot is whether the shackled Titan will break under torture on his desolate crag and accept Zeus's absolute authority. He is visited by

FIG. 5.3. Io in a Greek production of the *Prometheus Bound* of the 1950s, reproduced courtesy of the APGRD.

an airborne chorus of sea-nymphs, the daughters of the marine god, Ocean, who have been able to hear his groans even from their submarine cave. They suggest that he could at least compromise. Ocean then flies in on a similar mission, but is told in no uncertain terms that surrender is not an option. Prometheus' next visitor, Io, was once a mortal girl, but has been partially transformed by supernatural means into an gadfly-maddened cow: to her Prometheus reveals the secret knowledge about the child Heracles who will be born from a family line she founds, and who will be connected with future events that will determine whether Zeus retains or loses his hold on power. The last arrival at the site of Prometheus' bondage is Hermes, the messenger of the gods, and here particularly of Zeus. The play ends as Prometheus, who has refused to compromise with the supreme Olympian, is swallowed up by an earthquake for a period of interment that will be followed by the eagle-torture.

The myth enacted in *Prometheus* is an ancient one, and the plotline is strikingly simple. But to an audience whose own collective memory founded their democracy on the myth of liberation from a harsh tyranny—that of the sons of Pisistratus (see above, pp. 198–9)— much of the play's fascination must have lain in the play's presentation of the struggle between Prometheus and Zeus as the defiance of a representative of freedom and progress against a vicious despotic regime. The characters and the chorus in the play, although superhuman, reveal a series of different experiences of an unrelenting autocrat: Hephaestus obeys Zeus, but most reluctantly; the sadistic Strength actually seems to enjoy implementing cruel commands; the Oceanids advise the rebel to apologize, but feel sorry for him and by the time of their departure are stoutly supporting him; Ocean is a pragmatist whose only advice is that Prometheus refrain from making things any worse for himself;[13] Io is a fellow victim who is persecuted without ever even having rebelled; Hermes is a despicable henchman of Zeus simply because it is in his own best self-interest.

The poetry of *Prometheus Bound* is sonorous and forceful, as befits its cosmic scope. The dominant images are connected with disease and medicine, restraints, bonds, and harnesses, and with the elements. Prometheus' monologues are some of the most influential passages of virtuoso verse in western theatre. This most static of tragic heroes, unable to move from the Caucasian peak to which he is fettered, ranges with unprecedented verbal energy through time and space. To the chorus he traces, as the school of thought associated with the sophist Protagoras did, the rise of humans with the help of technology, agriculture, and trade from primordial squalor to civilization (see above pp. 178–81), and the battles of the gods from the defeat of the Titans to some day in the far distant future when he and Zeus will ultimately be reconciled. To Io he describes in detail the cartography of a trek that will take her across the known world from the Russian steppes to Egypt, where the poor, tortured creature will finally find rest. There is no Greek tragedy which concentrates so hard on physical suffering. The two victims of Zeus—Prometheus and Io—writhe in agony before the audience's eyes. Prometheus is the prototype in one sense not only of every tragic sufferer, but in another of every spectator: he is all-knowing, conscious of the meaning of his torment, and yet totally unable to prevent it. His understanding is divine; his physical vulnerability to confinement and torture make him seem all too human.

Aeschylus wrote several plays about Prometheus, including his *Prometheus Unbound* in which Heracles freed the Titan generations after the action of *Prometheus Bound*, and at least one satyr play about the original theft of fire. He may have written a tetralogy of which our extant play is the only surviving constituent. *Prometheus Unbound*, through Shelley's synonymous lyrical drama (1820, inspired by what he had learned from the fragmentary remains of the ancient tragedy), has been one of the most influential lost plays in cultural history.

Many scholars have doubted that the wonderful play that we *do* have is by the same poet responsible for the other plays attributed to Aeschylus. The proportion of the play performed by the chorus is indeed much smaller than in the other Aeschylean tragedies; the Oceanids perform a percentage of the verse which we would expect in one by Sophocles. There are also differences from the rest of Aeschylus in the way that dialogue and verse forms are handled, as well as stylistic idiosyncrasies; in terms of content, it has been argued that the picture of Zeus is incompatible with that in the *Oresteia* and that the Protagorean influence on Athenian thought— usually thought to have commenced in the 440s—postdates Aeschylus' death in 456 BCE. But none of these supposed objections to Aeschylean authorship is insuperable, since a good poet can change his style to suit his subject-matter, and we know almost nothing about the intellectual culture of the 450s. The sheer cosmic scale of the thinking in the play certainly parallels that of the *Oresteia*, as does the grandeur of the imagery and diction. I suspect that we have a play by Aeschylus that may have been radically revised in performance, like most Greek tragedies, before they were finally written down in what was intended to be canonical form late in the fourth century BCE.

# 6
# Euripidean Drama

Euripides wrote at least eighty plays, and possibly ninety-two. Nineteen have been transmitted from antiquity under his name. Of these *Cyclops* is a satyr play, and *Rhesus* is probably not by Euripides himself. The biographical information is however regrettably unreliable. Aristophanes and the other contemporary Athenian comic poets, who wrote what is now known as 'Old Comedy', caricatured Euripides as a cuckolded greengrocer's son, but their portrait offers little more truth value than a scurrilous cartoon. The student of Euripides also has access to a late antique 'Life' (*Vita*), a fragmentary third-century biography by Satyrus, and the 'Letters of Euripides'. These five dull epistles purport to be addressed to individuals such as Archelaus (King of Macedon) and Sophocles, but were actually written in the first or second century CE. Collectively these documents provide the first example in the European tradition of the portrait of an alienated artist seeking solace in solitude. This Euripides is a misogynist loner with facial blemishes, who worked in a seaside cave on the island of Salamis, and retired to voluntary exile in Macedon as a result of his unpopularity. Unfortunately, however, this poignant portrait is demonstrably a fiction created out of simplistic inferences from Euripides' own works or from other sources. Beyond what is briefly detailed below, the only aspect of the 'Euripides myth' almost certain to be true is that he possessed a large personal library (see Aristophanes, *Frogs* 943, 1049).

The lack of evidence for a political career, in contrast with Sophocles' attested appointments to high office, may suggest a neutral emotional detachment from public affairs. But Euripides was thoroughly engaged with the intellectual and ethical questions which underlay the policy debates in the Athenian assembly. Intellectually, he was a child of his time. Every significant field studied by the sophists in contemporary Athens surfaces in his tragedies: ontology, epistemology, philosophy of language, moral and political theory, medicine, psychology, and cosmology. There is thus a kind of truth in Aulus Gellius' statement that Euripides studied physics with Anaxagoras, rhetoric with the lexical specialist Prodicus, and moral philosophy with Socrates (*Noctes Atticae* 15. 20. 4); in the first version of Aristophanes' *Clouds* (fr. 401 *PCG*) it was even alleged that Socrates provided Euripides with the ideas for his clever tragedies!

Providing some antidote to the unreliable biographical tradition, there are fortunately several certain dates in Euripides' life and work. He first competed in the drama competition in 455 BCE, and was first victorious in 441. More than half of his surviving plays are firmly dated. He came second in the competition with the group including *Alcestis* in 438 BCE, third with the *Medea* group in 431, was victorious in 428 with the group including *Hippolytus*, came second in 415 BCE with *Trojan Women,* competed with *Helen* in 412, with *Phoenician Women* between 411 and 409 (probably 409), and with *Orestes* in 408. He won a final victory with the posthumous performance, probably in 405, of *Bacchae* and *Iphigenia in Aulis*. We can also be sure that *Hecuba* was performed before 423 BCE. But that leaves *Children of Heracles, Suppliant Women, Heracles, Electra, Iphigenia among the Taurians,* and *Ion,* as well as *Cyclops* and *Rhesus*.

In the early twentieth century a brilliant eastern European scholar, Thaddeus Zielinski, noticed that (with the important exception of *Bacchae*) the firmly dated Euripidean plays allow an incrementally greater degree of licence in one feature of their spoken iambic verses: the long syllables are increasingly often 'resolved'—that is, replaced by two short ones.[1] Introducing more rapid-fire syllables into a line in this way creates a less formal, more relaxed and conversational style, which is also somewhat suggestive of the comic poets' use of the same metre. Desperate for any new certainty in Greek tragic chronology, almost all scholars subsequently have accepted without much demur that all the undated plays can now be put in a chronological order according to the number of 'resolved' iambics they contain. In the absence of any other rationale for the order in which this chapter discusses them, I have somewhat reluctantly followed the order suggested by Zielinksi's estimates, except in the case of *Cyclops*, which as a different, funnier type of drama than tragedy simply cannot be put in any kind of metrically dated order, however speculative. But where the date is unknown I have not attributed one, since I am sceptical about metrical dating as a method. Besides the fact that *Bacchae* does not fit the scheme, it requires us to make two unreasonable assumptions. One is that the plays were invariably *written* in the order they were performed. The other is that Euripides was incapable of intuitively choosing a particular metrical style to suit a particular tragedy, when the plays suggest the contrary. Two examples are the austere *Bacchae*, which keeps us at a strange psychological distance from its chief sufferers, and the the outstandingly comic and colloquial tone of much of *Orestes*.

The Greeks and Romans, who did not feel the need to count his resolved iambic feet, were passionate about Euripides. A character in a comedy announced that he would be prepared to hang himself for the sake of seeing this (dead) tragedian.[2] Aristotle's formalist discussion of tragedy complains about Euripides' use of the *deus ex machina*, his unintegrated choruses, and the 'unnecessary' villainy of some of his characters. Yet even Aristotle conceded that Euripides was 'the most tragic of the poets', meaning that he was the best at eliciting pity and fear.[3] Besides Euripides' impact on the literature of succeeding generations—especially Menander, Ennius, Virgil, Ovid, Seneca, and oratory—his plays are everywhere apparent in the *visual* culture of the Mediterranean. Homer apart, no author stimulated the arts more; the Romans painted Euripides' scenes on their walls and carved them on their sarcophagi.

All Euripides' poetry is marked by exquisite simile and metaphor; his 'picturesque' style was much admired in antiquity ('Longinus', *On the Sublime* 15.1–4). Euripides' songs were extremely popular. The ancients believed that some Athenians in Sicily saved themselves after the disaster at Syracuse in 413 BCE by singing some of his songs to their captors (Plutarch, *Life of Nicias* 29). In a lost comedy named *Euripides-Lover* a character discusses people who hate all lyrics but those by Euripides.[4] But it was the Euripidean characters' distinctive way of talking that made the greatest impact. Alexander the Great, no professional actor, is supposed to have been able to perform a whole episode of Euripides' lost *Andromeda* verbatim (Athenaeus, *Deipnosophists* 12.537d–e); the most significant reason for Euripides' astonishing ancient popularity was really the accessible and *memorable* poetry in which his characters expressed themselves. Princesses and paupers, demi-gods and warriors, practitioners of incest, human sacrifice, and murder: he made them all 'speak like human beings' (see Aristophanes, *Frogs* 1058). Aristotle affirms that it was not until Euripides wrote roles using language drawn from everyday conversation that tragedy discovered natural dialogue (*Rhetoric* 3.2.5). This ordinary quality to his characters' language attracted emulation by able poets within his lifetime, yet in Aristophanes' *Frogs* Dionysus dismisses such authors as insignificant 'chatterers' in comparison (89–95). Euripides had achieved something difficult in making his unforgettable characters speak 'like human beings'. Thus the author of an encomium to Euripides in the *Palatine Anthology* justifiably discourages the aspiring imitator (7.50):

> Poet, do not try to follow Euripides' road;
> It is hard for men to tread.
> It seems easy, but the man who attempts to walk down it
> Discovers it is rougher than if it were implanted with pitiless stakes.
> If you even attempt to scratch the surface of Medea, Aeetes' daughter,
> You shall die forgotten. Leave Euripides' crowns alone.

## *CYCLOPS* (DATE UNKNOWN)

During the fifth century BCE, hundreds of satyr plays were performed after tragedies in the Athenian Theatre of Dionysus. Satyr plays featured heroes like Odysseus in *Cyclops* and Heracles, whose physical appetites made him the most popular hero of the genre; he starred in numerous lost examples including Euripides' own *Reapers*, *Syleus*, and *Busiris*. These heroes interacted with the satyrs in humorous visitations of the same kind of myths that supplied the plots of tragedies. Favourite satyric plot motifs included servitude and escape, eating and drinking, sexual pursuit, hunting, athletics, and inventions. In *Cyclops* the theme of servitude and escape reaches a climax in the Sicilian rustic symposium as a result of which the one-eyed giant Polyphemus can be blinded.

The ancient critic Demetrius defined satyr drama as 'tragedy at play' (*On Style* 169), and this playful piece is of great interest to the history of theatre as the only fully extant example of an ancient satyr drama. It shows how in this genre the tragedians added a chorus of satyrs and their father Silenus to well-known mythical narratives: in an adaptation of one of the most famous of all Greek myths, Odysseus' escape from the Cyclops (familiar from *Odyssey* book 9), the satyrs help Odysseus to blind Polyphemus and escape the Cyclops' island along with him. In adding satyrs and a theatrical dimension to the old story, Euripides supplies new dialogue, removes the other Cyclopes, truncates Odysseus' adventures in the cave, reduces the number of sailors eaten by Polyphemus to two, and extends the farcical baiting of the blinded giant at the end of the action. Instead of escaping by the ruse of tying themselves to the underbellies of sheep, Euripides imagines a Sicilian symposium, complete with homoerotic escapades: Polyphemus, a self-confessed homosexual (583–4), gets drunk and grabs Silenus, whom he mistakes for Ganymede, the boy Zeus loved. He charges into his cave to rape the ageing satyr, thus giving Odysseus the opportunity to blind him. The exclusively male plot therefore revolves around alcoholic intoxication and morally unquestioned violence enacted against an outright villain who happens to be a homosexual rapist. Such a plot is slight, cruel, and unedifying, but fortunately the plot is not the point: what is at issue is the satyrs' perspective on the world and satyr drama's relationship with its twin sister, tragedy.

The minor adjustments to the action of the Cyclops episode in *Odyssey* book 9 are nothing in comparison with the intellectual transformation of the material that has been engineered by Euripides. With the sole exception of the tragedy named *Rhesus* attributed to Euripides (but almost certainly not by him), which is a dramatic retelling of an episode in the *Iliad*, the accidents of transmission mean that no surviving tragedy can be compared in detail with the treatment of its story in a surviving epic prototype. This makes the modernization of the Cyclops story, and in particular the transformation of Polyphemus from a primitive cannibal into a personification of radical ideas propounded by some of the late fifth-century political theorists, all the more suggestive and fascinating. In Euripides Polyphemus is more like a mortal and less like a fantastic giant. He is a slave-owner, a cattle-rancher, and a man of some substance, like most fifth-century Athenian gentlemen. He is also a careful, even cultivated, cook, whereas in Homer he eats men raw, like a mountain lion. But, most importantly, he has a considerable intellect, and is given an important debate with Odysseus which undoubtedly parodies some distinctive currents in contemporary philosophical circles. Odysseus articulates a democratic Athenian perspective, based on the rule of law; Polyphemus' position caricatures some strains in contemporary anti-democratic ideology, especially his view that riches (here taking the form of comestibles) can substitute for divinity (316, 336), and that man-made rules and laws are redundant (338–40). Polyphemus is strongly reminiscent of Callicles in Plato's *Gorgias*, who argues that civic laws are devised by the weak majority: natural law dictates that strong individuals should satisfy their desires at the expense of such man-made legislation.

It may be that its intellectual sophistication made Euripides' *Cyclops* an unusual example of its genre. It certainly replays serious controversies about human society identical to those explored in tragedy, albeit in a more boisterous key. There is no evidence of quite such pointed parody of philosophical argumentation in the other important evidence for satyr drama, the large fragment of Sophocles' satyric *Trackers*, which has now been incorporated, in English translation, into Tony Harrison's drama *The Trackers of Oxyrhynchus* (see below p. 339). It remains difficult to generalize about this nearly lost genre, but it seems that it is indeed the traditional world-view of the satyrs that Euripides is exploiting when in *Cyclops* he uses them as representatives of a particular political philosophy: as practitioners of pre-industrial, rustic communism they provide an important counterpoint to Odysseus the urban modern democrat and Polyphemus, who is (in Athenian terms) an oligarchic sympathizer, a monadic proponent of the view that only Might is Right.

Yet viewing dramatic satyrs from an anthropological perspective, as representatives of an early stage in human social development, runs the risk of reducing the magic of these complex and charming creatures. Like their master Dionysus, satyrs confound many of the polarities by which the Greeks organized their perception of the world. They are nearly human, yet are touched with the divine and have tails, animal ears, and often hooves. They are cowardly yet violent. They are often bald and yet always childlike. They are sly and knowing, but simultaneously naive and innocent. They are often involved in the gods' inventions of the arts of civilization (in *Trackers* the lyre), but live in remote, uncultivated countryside. The Roman architect Vitruvius recommends that the scenery for satyr drama be decorated 'with trees, caves, mountains, and other things associated with the countryside' (5.6.9).

The one boundary satyrs do not cross is that demarcating male from female. They are exaggeratedly male from the biological point of view (erections are a recurrent feature of satyr drama), and decidedly *homosocial*—they live with members of their own sex, and spend their time on male collective male pursuits— hunting, athletics, drinking, and chasing nymphs. In the female-free environment of *Cyclops* the satyrs can only fantasize about rape, but in many other satyr plays the plot revolved around sexual aggression against females. It may be that it is the masculine and sexualized viewpoint of satyr drama that can help explain why it was deemed an aesthetically, socially, and psychologically important way of concluding a tragic performance. For the final play in a tetralogy, it seems it was conventional if not actually compulsory for the chorus-men to lay aside their tragic robes, so often feminine, and don the costume of a libidinous satyr, a graphic signifier of testosterone (see Fig. 6.1). Most hold that the satyr play must have functioned to create a sense of release or relief from the psychological tension of the foregoing tragedies. More recently it has seen stressed that the satyrs bring drama closer than heroic tragedy can to its tutelary deity, Dionysus, and therefore to its performance context at the Athenian festival of Dionysus. Satyr drama also sends its spectator out to the festival not only laughing rather than crying, but reassured of his place in a joyous, sexualized, male collective.[5] Satyr drama is not only tragedy at play: it is also the collective male Athenian democratic citizenry defining itself, in a utopian register, during its worship of Dionysus.

FIG. 6.1. Athenian chorusmen dress for a satyr play on an Apulian vase, 400-380 BCE, reproduced courtesy of the Nicholson Museum, Sydney.

## ALCESTIS (438 BCE)

In antiquity, and from the Renaissance until the late nineteenth century, *Alcestis* enjoyed an extraordinarily high reputation. Its central attraction was its portrayal of a perfect mother and wife. Yet Euripides' self-abnegating exemplar of ideal femininity nearly disappeared from the public consciousness in the second half of the twentieth century, which could not tolerate the implicit assumption that a woman's life is worth less than a man's; it is only in recent years that the appearance of occasional revivals, notably Ted Hughes' *Alcestis* (2000; see Fig. 6.2), show that it is once again possible to revisit this important text without our responses being intolerably distorted by contemporary sexual politics.

The action of *Alcestis* is simple. A Thessalian queen sacrifices her own life to save that of her husband Admetus; but his friend

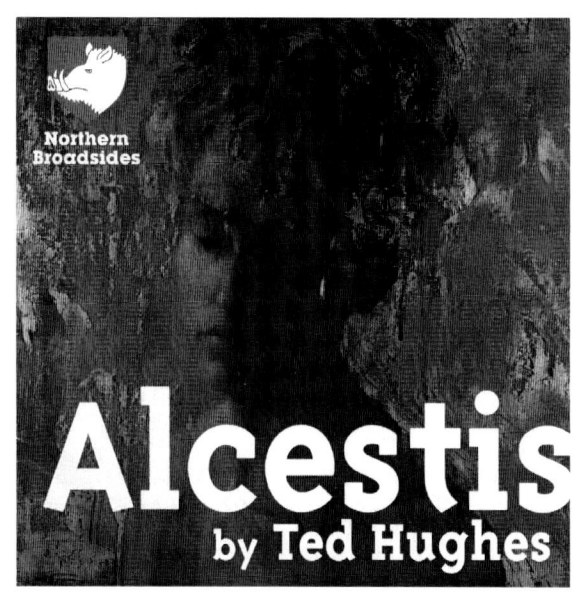

FIG. 6.2. The programme for Ted Hughes' *Alcestis* performed by Northern Broadsides (2000), reproduced courtesy of the APGRD.

Heracles rescues her from Hades and restores her alive. The play is little interested in its own mythical background, in the dealings between gods and men which produced the preposterous scenario in which Admetus could bargain with Death. It is rather more concerned with his outstanding performance as an employer (of Apollo) and as host (of Heracles); it is, indeed, the particular virtue of hospitality for which Admetus is so richly rewarded. Modern critics, for whom hospitality is no longer a fraught and potentially dangerous issue, need reminding that this play asks a serious practical question about competitive social obligations. The question counterposes duty to dead kin with duty to living friends. Although seeming now an odd theme for drama, the question must have arisen often enough in a pre-industrial society: is it right to offer a friend bed and board, however many days' distance he may be from alternative accommodation, when you are newly in mourning?

The answer might depend on the behaviour your guest was likely to exhibit. When the fun-loving Heracles appears in *Alcestis*, before the heroine has even been buried, he precipitates a violent clash of rites, sensibilities, and genres—symposium or funeral, hilarity or woe, comedy or tragedy. The fascinating tonal dislocations which ensue are connected with the play's position in its tetralogy. As the fourth and last, following three tragedies, Alcestis occupied the position which was normally taken by a satyr drama (see above pp. 234–8). Aware of its unusual status, scholars ancient and modern have applied the label 'pro-satyric', but such terminology can actually hamper appreciation of the play's distinctive qualities. Generic labelling occludes the play's intellectual stylishness, especially the sophistic wisecracking of Apollo and Death in the opening scene; more importantly, it obscures the prevalent melancholy of the emotional register, a melancholy little alleviated by the audience's knowledge, from the opening scene onwards, that Alcestis' life will be saved (65–71).

The sadness derives from the play's fascination with thanatology. It is the only ancient drama to portray Thanatos (Death) himself, a sarcastic, peevish, status-conscious god, wielding his sword to shear hair from his victims (74–6), and jealous of his prerogatives. Admetus longs for the 'tongue and music of Orpheus' in order to entrance Persephone and Hades and so recover his wife from the Underworld (357–62), mythical references which draw attention to the play's nature as a 'return from the Underworld' (*anodos*) myth-type familiar from other stories. But before her sinister, silent resurrection in the closing scene, the action of the play is dominated first by a dying woman and then by her cadaver. The verse speaks of shrouds, of veils, of pyres, corteges, and gravestones. It is an extended representation of the process of dying and a painful examination of the social repercussions and aesthetics of death. Indeed, the tightly scripted death scene remains unsurpassed in European theatre. Alcestis' entrance has been prepared by her maidservant's observations that she is wasted, limp, and has difficulty breathing (203–5); once on stage, she visibly undergoes increasing weakness. She hears Charon calling to her from his two-oared boat, sees Hades himself, winged and dark-browed, coming to take her 'to the halls of the dead', senses darkness shrouding her vision, and collapses as her legs fail her (253–7, 259–63, 267–90). But it is the deathbed presence of her children that renders this scene so compelling. Euripides used children more adventurously than Sophocles (Aeschylus, as afar as we know, did not use them at all). By the time of *Medea* and *Trojan Women* he was extracting maximum pathos from the deaths of children, but in *Alcestis* the emotion is generated by a little boy's parting from his dying mother (see above, p. 141).

Euripides deftly explores the emotions inherent in this situation. Alcestis' death is premature (as Death gloats in the opening scene, 55); the early demise of young wives and mothers occurred much more frequently in Euripides' society than in our own, and many in his audience will have been in emotional situations identical to Alcestis and her family. She is bitter that Admetus' own parents refused to die in his place, and terrified that if he remarries his new wife will be unkind to her children (290–10). Her greatest anxiety is for her little daughter, who, she believes, will receive no help in finding a suitable husband, and (a typically Euripidean detail) will have to undergo labour deprived of the traditional support of her own birth mother (318–19).

Admetus imagines having a statue of his wife placed in the marital bed where he can embrace and address it (348–52). This morbid notion underlines the play's own status as a beautiful artwork memorializing a beautiful woman. Other ancient ideas about non-physical immortality are surveyed; death can be transcended by a lingering reputation (323–5). This theme is stressed in the dead Queen's choral obituary; she will be remembered for time immemorial at festivals in both Sparta and Athens, 'For in dying you have bequeathed to poets a rich theme' (445–54). But the play suggests that the legacy of her death, although the death sentence itself is rescinded, will also be emotionally disturbing. The happy ending cannot erase Admetus' questionable earlier decision to allow his wife to die in his place. Euripidean tragedy is exceptionally attuned to the notion that certain traumas inevitably involve a life sentence of psychological suffering. Early in the play Alcestis' maidservant says that Admetus will suffer 'sorrow so great it will never leave his heart' (198). Neither Alcestis' fame, nor the superficially happy ending, can erase the uncomfortable atmosphere and the implication that there will be sorrow still in the heart and house of Admetus.

## MEDEA (431 BCE)

At a superficial level *Medea* is the simplest of all Euripides' tragedies: the action consists of little more than its implacable protagonist's revenge on her treacherous husband by murdering his new bride and his sons. Nor was its status as a masterpiece immediately apparent: its group came last in the tragic competition in 431 BCE. Perhaps the play seemed stiff and old-fashioned, for it includes no solo singing in purely lyric metres, and is visually austere until the final, overwhelming epiphany of Medea, aloft in the sky-borne chariot. Euripides chose, moreover, to make a play which could be performed by only two actors: there is no complex scene with a 'triangular' requirement for three speaking actors, unlike all the other surviving tragedies by Euripides and Sophocles. This simplicity serves to throw the dominating figure of Medea into grander relief, by stressing that in her serial bipolar encounters with men—Creon, Jason, Aegeus, Jason, the tutor, the messenger, and Jason again—she repeatedly extracts by sheer rhetorical power or by psychological manipulation whatever result she requires.

*Medea* may have failed to please because it ends with the barbarian murderess flying off to take up the offer of a safe haven in Athens that she had earlier extorted from Aegeus. Nor may the audience have enjoyed watching one of their ancestral kings expatiate on the subject of his infertility: the Athenian tragedians tended to take care to portray mythical Athenians with dignity (see above pp. 98–103). Moreover, the international situation in 431 BCE meant that Athens was in no mood to see any refugee from Corinth, even in myth, demanding favours or asylum. The play must have been ethically shocking. Medea stands alone amongst tragic felons in committing her offence with impunity. In extant Greek tragedy no other kin-killer reaches the end of his or her plays similarly unpunished. Euripides slightly ameliorates this situation by suggesting that Medea, as granddaughter of the Sun, is not mortal and thus not entirely accountable to ordinary theological rules. Indeed, we never fully understand whether she is mortal or divine, a wronged and sympathetic wife or an agent of divine justice, for Euripides has confusingly given also given her and Jason some of the most 'human' dialogue in ancient Greek. The play at one level is but 'a bourgeois quarrel between an obtusely selfish man and an over-passionate woman'.[6] The vengeful, competitive and sexually honest Medea, in escaping without punishment, was any Athenian husband's worst nightmare realized (see Fig. 6.3).

Medea had been previously implicated in murder on the Euripidean stage, in his *Peliades* of 455 BCE. But the shocking effect of the actual filicide (infanticide denotes the killing of *any* child, whereas killing one's own child is technically *filicide*) was exacerbated because Euripides almost certainly invented it. His Medea is also the first known child-killing mother in Greek myth to perform

FIG. 6.3. Eileen Herlie as Medea at the Edinburgh Festival (1948), reproduced courtesy of the APGRD.

the deed in cold blood; the others (Ino, Agave, Procne) seem always to have been given the 'excuse' of temporary madness. This permits Euripides the opportunity to introduce the extraordinary soliloquy where Medea has difficulty steeling herself to the slaughter (1019–80, see above p. 35). But it also leaves the most disturbing crime in extant Greek tragedy apparently premeditated,[7] its culpability undiminished even by mental disturbance. And in this play Euripides can be seen developing his wholly original stage use of children. We see them long before we see Medea, and their off-stage death cries, which interrupt a choral ode, represent one of the most heartbreaking moments in western theatre (see above, pp. 142–3).

The emotional motor of Euripides' *Medea* renders it one of the more apparently 'timeless' of ancient tragedies: the despair, humiliation, and vindictiveness of a woman traded in by her man in favour of a younger model speak loud across the centuries. Yet there are features specific to Euripides' Athens in the second half of the fifth century BCE, in particular the question of Medea's acceptability, as an alien, to her new city-state. At Athens the possession of citizenship was tied to the biological descent group, and guarded with paranoid anxiety. In 451/0 BCE the statesman Pericles had initiated a law excluding from privileges all but those who could prove that both their parents were members of Athenian citizen families (see above, p. 129). In 431 BCE Jason's plight may have elicited understanding if not actual sympathy from some members of its male audience: Medea stresses that a barbarian wife could cause embarrassment (591–2). One way of looking at Jason is as a man trying to make a life in a xenophobic new city, while burdened with a wife who was not only not a local girl but not even Greek. From an Athenian perspective, Medea's ethnicity must have cast doubts even on the legitimacy of the union's unfortunate offspring.[8] Medea's difference from the women of Corinth must have been emphasized, moreover, by her clothing and appearance: Euripides was almost certainly the first poet to turn her from a Corinthian into a barbarian.

But the unenthusiastic original reception of this play cannot be wholly dissociated from Medea's betrayal of 'femininity'. She fundamentally repudiates the gender role asssigned to her as a woman in fifth-century Greece. From her very first monologue (which also marks her first exit from the 'feminine' sphere of the house), and its extraordinary focus on the 'masculine' notions of 'cleverness' and citizenship, we know this is no ordinary woman. She combines in one psyche the 'feminine' qualities of compassion and maternal love with the 'masculine' heroic values of honour, status, and revenge. Yet by the end of the play the inadequacy of the existing sociolinguistic distinctions between public and private, friend and foe, and especially between woman and man, has been unmasked through the characters' failure to communicate except in the most dislocated of linguistic modes. If Euripides' characters did indeed speak 'like human beings', then human beings undergoing marital breakdown have not changed much, after all.

## *CHILDREN OF HERACLES* (DATE UNKNOWN)

In one of the most extraordinary moments in Greek tragedy, a miracle near an Athenian sanctuary of Zeus transforms an old man into a muscular young warrior. The decrepit Iolaus, former companion and nephew of Heracles, is awarded this supernatural rejuvenation by Zeus and Hebe, god of youthfulness and consort of the now deified Heracles. The renewed strength of Iolaus allows him finally to arrest Eurystheus, the villain who has been tormenting Heracles and his family for several decades. The miracle is without parallel in surviving Greek tragedy. Outside the genre-subverting *Alcestis*, Euripides' profoundly tragic humans, although interfered with and despotically governed by immortals, are not usually offered supernatural or miraculous opportunities to evade the misery of ageing and of death.

In myth Heracles fathered numerous children in addition to those by Megara whom he kills in *Heracles*. In *Children of Heracles* the sons and daughters who survived him are in mortal danger. Under the supervision of their senescent cousin Iolaus and grandmother Alcmene, they have fled from Argos in order to escape death by stoning, a punishment decreed by their father's old persecutor, Eurystheus. They have now taken refuge at the temple of Zeus in Marathon, in Athenian territory on the eastern coast of Attica. This creates a religious and diplomatic crisis. The Athenians, led by their king Demophon (Theseus' son), decide to defend the suppliants, but events take a terrible turn when Persephone demands a human sacrifice as the Argives invade Attica. These problems are superficially resolved when the eldest daughter of Heracles heroically offers herself for sacrifice and the Athenians defeat the Argives in the offstage battle prior to which Iolaus is rejuvenated. Eurystheus, the arch-enemy of both Heracles' family and now of the Athenians, is captured and brought before Alcmene, Heracles' embittered old mother. The last scene revolves around the question of whether Eurystheus should be summarily executed, and, if so, what should be done with his body.

This potent dramatic situation reverberates loudly today. A family of asylum-seekers, with a valid case for being offered protection, nevertheless presents an increasingly onerous burden to their host country. The refugee family is already a liability in terms of foreign policy, but their own unpredictable behaviour exacerbates the problem: their volatile leader allows one of his young charges to be slaughtered, demands to be allowed to fight when physically unfit, and strips a temple of dedicated war trophies; their senior female is revealed to be a voluble and vindictive embarrassment, with scant regard for either local or international law. The apparently honourable course chosen by the host country, the protection of innocent refugees, turns out to involve thoroughly dishonourable abuses of human rights, including the sanctioning of human sacrifice and the execution of a prisoner-of-war.

Iolaus' sudden physical transformation, and the unpleasant developments in the ethical situation, are symptoms of the chimerical power of this unique drama. Nearly everyone involved in the action undergoes a sudden metamorphosis, whether in nature, status, or situation. Demophon seems to be a strong and decisive moral presence, but is helpless in the hands of the despised class of soothsayers. Even a lifelong slave, uniquely in Greek tragedy, is offered emancipation. Alcmene changes from victim into aggressor, object of pity into a pitiless avenger: only just released from captivity and the threat of death, the final scene depicts her arguing maliciously for the immediate and dishonourable execution of her newly captive enemy Eurystheus. But this villain, official enemy of the Athenians and instigator of an act of military aggression against them, at the last minute turns into their benefactor; he promises that his corpse will act as their talisman, a safeguard against any future aggression from the children of Heracles (i.e. the Spartans, who traced their descent from this hero). The theme of sudden reversal and transformation thus underlies the play's distinctive project. No other Greek tragedy offers a 'twist in the tail' quite as surprising as *Children of Heracles*.

Despite its special qualities, however, it is probably Euripides' least familiar tragedy today. One reason is that the text is certainly incomplete (although there is disagreement about the nature and extent of the difference between the Euripidean text used for the original performance and that found in the manuscript tradition). It is suspicious that no reference is made to Heracles' slaughtered daughter subsequent to the sacrifice scene; there can be no doubt that the ending of the tragedy as it stands is not just abrupt but actually lacunose. Yet these problems of transmission alone do not account for the neglect the play has suffered, since a large part of the ending of the hugely popular *Bacchae* is also missing. The real obstacle facing the modern reader of *Children of Heracles* is the play's strong interest in somewhat obscure religious aetiology. Several of the turns taken by events in this highly charged political drama meant a great deal more to the original audience than it is possible to reconstruct with any confidence today; the rejuvenation of Iolaus was almost certainly linked to his cultic connection with young people, for example, and the graves of the maiden and of Eurystheus may actually have been visible in the Marathon area. This aetiological dimension makes *Children of Heracles* a vital document for historians of ancient hero cult and Athenian religion, but prevents it from being fully appreciated as drama.

This is a pity, not only on account of the dramatic finesse demonstrated in the radical reversals of expectation, but also because several speeches and episodes are individually striking: the shocking initial confrontation between the frail Iolaus and the thuggish herald, where physical violence explodes over one of the Athenians' most sacred sanctuaries; the human sacrifice sequence, where Euripidean irony expertly dissects the fictions on which young people are fed when they are asked to die in the name of high-sounding causes; the subtlety of the interchange where Iolaus is shown all too hastily licensing this outrage while insisting on his affection for the girl; the scene in which he demands to enter battle, which includes a Euripidean experiment with the essentially comic stereotypes of the belligerent old man and the cheeky slave; and above all Eurystheus' scandalous but disarmingly frank account of his descent into moral depravity. The strange, painful, immoral world of *Children of Heracles* combines a dark ethical realism similar to that in *Hecuba* with experiments in absurdity, comedy, and sudden surprise. The play may be an enactment of an episode important to the local myths and religious beliefs of Euripides' audience, but it is also emotionally complex, theatrically innovative, morally honest, and psychologically penetrating. In a modern world all too familiar with the phenomena of asylum-seekers and teenagers volunteering for patriotic suicide, *The Children of Heracles* has been successfully revived by Peter Sellars, and may yet prove to be a tragedy whose time has come.

## HIPPOLYTUS (428 BCE)

Euripides' *Medea* did not find success in the dramatic competition; nor did his first attempt at a dramatization of the story of Phaedra and Hippolytus, which has survived only in fragments. Phaedra in the first *Hippolytus* loved shamelessly and lied blatantly, staying alive to bear false witness against her stepson. It is therefore tempting to see Euripides as deliberately changing strategy in the surviving revised *Hippolytus* of 428 BCE, the most 'Sophoclean' of all his plays. This time all the characters are trying to do their best within their individual moral frame of reference, and acting within an unusually perfect literary structure emphasizing the parallels between the two deviant characters who die in it. The play has even been interpreted as an eloquent manifesto of the humanist principle that virtue has its own reward in the face of apparently arbitrary suffering and death: this message is supposed to have spoken loudly to the Athenians in 428 BCE, when they were scarcely beginning to recover from the ravages of an unusually terrible plague.

Judaeo-Christian tradition includes several examples of the wife who becomes sexually obsessed with a younger man, and who responds to rejection with persecutory behaviour. The Old Testament offers the passion of Potiphar's wife for the young Joseph: the *Iliad* tells how Bellerophon was pursued by his host's wife (6.156–90). Euripides himself dramatized Bellerophon's story in yet another lost tragedy, *Stheneboea*, spectacularly featuring the hero astride the winged horse Pegasus. It was probably produced in the 420s, not long either before or after *Hippolytus*. But Greek culture distrusted stepmothers in particular. In a society where childbirth was extremely hazardous, and widowers remarried, there were proportionately more families in which a new wife was introduced to stepchildren often no younger than herself. The Athenian legal speeches attest to the domestic conflicts to which this could lead. But it could also cause sexual confusion, and the canonical Greek articulation of the illicit love of a married woman for a single man, the famous love of Phaedra for Hippolytus, is compounded by the quasi-incestuous connotations of the step-parent/step-child bond.

The legend the play dramatizes may have functioned as a ritual narrative helping to prepare brides psychologically for marriage, expressing with the extremism characteristic of myth the polar notions of sexual aggression and repudiation of sexuality. It certainly constitutes the most powerful enacted articulation of the ancient Greek perception that *erōs* is the most dangerous of all psychosomatic forces and puts under threat the very boundaries of the autonomous self by subjecting it to the magnetic desire for another being. Both Phaedra and Hippolytus deviate from socially endorsed models serving to delimit the power of *erōs*, and both are outsiders who owe their deviance partly to genetic inheritance. She, as the play stresses, is a Cretan princess, daughter of the lustful Pasiphae who bore the Minotaur, and granddaughter of Aerope who adulterously slept with her own husband's brother: Cretan women in tragedy are unusually susceptible to transgressive erotic impulses. Hippolytus inherits his rejection of sexual maturity, repudiation of marriage, and extreme antipathy to the opposite sex from his mother's origin as the Queen of the Amazons, the matrilineal race of warrior women who spurned 'normal' conjugal relations and roamed the virginal wild.

The central characters in the play are strangely locked into their separate fantasy lives, each escaping in their imaginations to beautiful, mysterious, watery locations where they feel the numinous power of the play's presiding deities. Hippolytus praises Artemis' 'inviolate meadow', visited only by bees and irrigated by purest freshwater streams (73–8); Phaedra wants to escape from her sickbed to the mountains to hunt like a maenad and to Artemis' 'salt lake' (215–30); the nurse praises Aphrodite, who flutters in the air 'and haunts the waves the sea' (447–8). Even the chorus want to fly like a bird, far, far away to the West to the surf-beaten shore of the Adriatic sea into which the blue-black river Eridanus flows (732–42). But these images of escape into another element, which represents to each of them different kinds of freedom from social restraints and responsibilities, are ironically juxtaposed with the deadly threat posed to Hippolytus' young life by the supernatural bull who appears from the sea to destroy him. The beautiful hymn-like poetry of much of the play can do nothing to prevent the malice of the gods whom it honours. Yet on a human level, the plot emphasizes the power of language not to evade or wish away the truth but to reveal it, alongside the power of silence to conceal. Phaedra's passion would have damaged none but herself had it remained unknown. If she had not been pressurized by the nurse into confession, if the nurse had not told Hippolytus, if Hippolytus had not articulated his misogyny, if Phaedra had not inscribed her stepson's death warrant into her suicide note, and if Theseus had not cursed Hippolytus, then instead of tragic words and tragic action there would only have been a mutely tragic situation: a frustrated wife, a preoccupied husband, a maladjusted youth.

A feminist reading can hardly fail to see the drama as a charter text for patriarchy, a 'male-bonding' play: its plotline validates male authority by sidelining the female family member and celebrating relations between men. Phaedra was forced into the loneliest of deaths, in order to try and salvage her reputation. A structuralist reading emphasizes the dualities embodied in the goddesses, and the symbolic likenesses and antinomies in the natural world which they represent. Yet the most distinctive feature of *Hippolytus* is the stark dualism with which the action delineates human responsibility and divine determination for the catastrophe.

Euripides makes us serially watch each one of the four equally important main characters (they have similar numbers of lines) make a decision or take an action which will bring disaster closer. But he has also made us learn from Aphrodite that she is responsible for everything that will ensue. *Hippolytus* thus juxtaposes two alternative views of the causation of human action, much as Sophocles' *Oedipus Tyrannus* probes the relationship between Oedipus' precipitation of his downfall by his personality and actions and the predetermination of Apollo. Greek thought was inherently dialectical: Greek myth includes blind seers, benevolent Curses, and a virgin who presides over maidens' passing from virginity into marriage. It could also cope with humans choosing actions which gods have preordained. Theseus is ultimately left alive and alone, doubly bereaved, knowing both that he has himself contributed to the catastrophe and that it was part of Aphrodite's grand design. Euripides' mortals help to define Athenian morality by deviating from its ideals. Yet there is no possibility of deviation from the tragic paths they choose but which are simultaneously decreed for them by his vindictive gods.

## *ANDROMACHE* (DATE UNKNOWN)

This tragedy looks at one of the women whose lives were wrecked by the Trojan War, Hector's widow, and reveals what happens to her in her life as a slave in Greece. It thus shows how war informs the lives of its victims even in times of peace. The conflict in *Andromache* is not international combat, but a domestic dispute—the bitter war waged by a man's wife against his mistress. The husband is Neoptolemus, killer of Priam and son of Achilles; the wife is Hermione, daughter of Helen; the mistress is the widow of Hector. It is little wonder, then, that the ghosts of the Trojan War haunt the triangular psychological landscape of the drama. Andromache, for example, warns Hermione against trying to outdo her mother Helen 'in the love of men' (229–31).

Fundamentally the plot is similar to that of the *Odyssey* and many Greek tragedies: it is a 'homecoming' play, in which the male householder is away but awaited, and a crisis develops in his absence. In *Andromache* Euripides stretches to extremes this familiar plot-type by making his audience wait for the hero (who could return from the Delphic oracle at any moment to discover Spartans throwing his mistress and son into deadly jeopardy) until three-quarters of the play have passed. Moreover, when Neoptolemus finally makes his long-awaited entrance, it is on a funeral bier (1166). Yet his name and absence have dominated much of the foregoing action, thus lending emotional coherence to the play's two earlier movements: the persecution of Andromache and her rescue by Peleus, followed by Hermione's fear of persecution and her rescue by Orestes. The 'Hermione' sequence is itself a 'mirror' scene, offering a distorted reworking (complete with her own nurse and exaggerated laments) of the foregoing 'Andromache' sequence. This complex structure, which used to dismay unitarian critics, has recently been better understood as one of Euripides' subtler experiments with plot-type—or rather, with his audience's *expectations* of plot-type: *Andromache* mutates from suppliant drama to escape play to a tragedy of divine vengeance for human misdemeanour. Within this fluid structure, the action pushes emotional crises and rhetoric to their limits: the poets strains for striking effects produced by the distortion of character and exaggerated situations.

The play is set in a relatively remote district in Thessaly, known as 'Thetideion' because the goddess Thetis lived there with her mortal husband Peleus before she abandoned him (19–20). Marriage—or rather, marital breakdown—is a crucial theme: Neoptolemus' marriage to Hermione is disastrous; he finds her sexually unattractive (157), and she has failed to become pregnant by him. In terms of the immanent 'rules' of Greek tragedy, Neoptolemus has courted disaster by expecting his wife and concubine to share one roof: all the men in the genre who do so (the other two are Agamemnon in Aeschylus' *Agamemnon* and Heracles in Sophocles' *Trachiniae*) are dead by the end of their plays. As Orestes says here, it is a very bad thing for one man to live with two women he sleeps with (909, see also 464–6). This seems to reflect Greek popular ethics: although male adultery was not condemned, an Athenian legal speech attributed to Demosthenes praises a man for keeping his mistress away from his marital home out of respect for his wife and old mother (59. 2).

Neoptolemus actually dies at the hand of his rival for Hermione's hand—the young Argive murderer Orestes. Other ill-omened marriages featuring prominently include Menelaus' union with the adulterous Helen (680–6) and Agamemnon's even more catastrophic marriage to Clytemnestra (1028–30). It comes as a relief, therefore, when the play concludes on a note slightly less pessimistic about matrimony: Thetis bestows immortality on the husband she once forsook, thus effecting a type of reconciliation, and moreover implies that Andromache's forthcoming marriage to the Trojan exile Helenus will at least be uneventful (1231–49).

Euripidean tragedy was performed by men before a male audience, and it is therefore striking to find him writing a scene where a wife and a mistress quarrel in front of a female 'internal' audience (the chorus). Such theatrical 'eavesdropping' on the secluded and excluded sex is a typical Euripidean technique: in *Hippolytus* Phaedra and her nurse discuss matters of the heart; the heroine of *Electra* has a terrible argument with her mother. But no other Greek tragedy features what today might be termed a 'cat-fight', an altercation between two women, unrelated by blood, over a sexual partner. Indeed, this quarrel is almost without parallel in ancient literature until the Augustan Roman elegist Propertius. He describes, in comic vein, how his mistress Cynthia gatecrashed a party where he was finding solace with two foreign women, attacked them, chased them away, and returned to upbraid her two-timing boyfriend (4.8.59–80).

For humour was one option open to ancient authors, including the versatile Euripides, when dealing with strong 'feminine' emotions. Hermione, a spoilt teenager with pathologically extreme reactions, verges on the laughable. Sexual jealousy makes her lambast Andromache with preposterous rhetoric, until she senses danger to herself and lurches into terror and self-recrimination. Threatening suicide by several means, teetering on the edge of insanity, she is rescued from emotional breakdown only by the appearance of Orestes, a murderous young man to whom she seems to be ideally suited. Yet Hermione's emotional incontinence, comical and dangerous by turns, nevertheless conforms with the beliefs held by Euripides' contemporaries about the effect of puberty on the female psyche. The gynaecological texts attributed to Hippocrates show that young women between the menarche and their first pregnancy were regarded as vulnerable to all manner of physical and psychological disorders; a doctor of Euripides' day would have suspected that Hermione's womb was wandering through her body, causing her to become literally 'hysterical' (the word in Greek signifies a disorder of the uterus). The treatment prescribed would undoubtedly have included sexual intercourse and serial pregnancies (see also above, p. 134).

This dark fantasia on the theme of marriage entails a series of head-on rhetorical collisions between Greek characters from Thessaly, Sparta, and Argos, in addition to Andromache and her nurse, who are not Greek at all. An interest in ethnic provenance is signalled in the entrance song of the local Greek chorus, who tell Andromache that they want to help her 'even though' she is Asiatic (119); the play subsequently demonstrates how personal hatred is often conflated with and expressed by what would today be called 'racial prejudice' and 'racial abuse'. Hermione alleges that Andromache's sexual relationship with Neoptolemus is a sordid quasi-incestuous sexual deviation typical of barbarians (170–6); to Menelaus Andromache expresses a trenchant denunciation of the Spartan character (445–53), a theme which Peleus vituperatively elaborates, with a focus on the promiscuity of Spartan females (595–601). The prominence of the ethnicity theme may in turn be connected with the circumstances of the play's composition. According to an ancient piece of testimony, *Andromache* was not originally performed in Athens. Scholars have suggested various venues, including Argos and Thessaly, but the most probable answer is that the play was written for the royal house of the northern kingdom of Molossia, and thus may represent a unique example of an important sub-genre of ancient tragedies commissioned by patrons outside Athens.

At the end of the play the goddess Thetis announces that Andromache's child (called Molossos in the ancient cast list) will go to Molossia and there found a dynasty of kings (1247–8). In the 420s the ruling member of that dynasty was the young king Tharyps, who was keen to 'Hellenize' his semi-barbarian country and came to Athens for an education, where he was granted citizenship.[9] It is not unlikely that *Andromache* was intended to pay Tharyps a theatrical compliment. For it enacts a myth which bestows upon him a genealogy going back not only to one of the greatest Greek heroic lineages—Peleus, his son Achilles, and his grandson Neoptolemus—but also, through Neoptolemus' 'interracial' union with Andromache, to the royal house of Troy.

## HECUBA (BEFORE 423 BCE)

One of the bleakest of all Euripides' dramas, *Hecuba* is a study in the repercussions of international war on individual families. In the immediate aftermath of the fall of Troy, it brings the Greek king Agamemnon, the Thracian warlord Polymestor, and the Trojan queen Hecuba into a perverted form of intimacy born of reciprocal brutality. While Hecuba's former friend Polymestor becomes her bitterest enemy, and her deadly opponent Agamemnon becomes a temporary ally, the tragedy emphasizes the volatility of loyalties and coalitions in such times of crisis. As the chorus comment, it is strange how 'the laws of necessity determine men's relationships, making friends of bitter enemies and enemies of those who were once friends' (846–9). This vicious triangular plot is played out on the harsh, snowy, marginal region of the Thracian Chersonese, where Asia turns into Europe across the straits from the Trojan mainland; by a type of pathetic fallacy this atmospheric setting seems reflected in the tragedy's major psychological interests: in the processes by which humans harden themselves to commit crimes of chilling barbarity, in the darker edges of the self, in the disintegration of social boundaries, and in strange mental and physical transformations. *Hecuba* places the psyche of the Trojan queen under a theatrical microscope: already multiply bereaved, she is confronted with two further excruciating losses which precipitate her own mutation into a vindictive aggressor. The first part of the play dramatizes her reactions to the news that her daughter Polyxena must be sacrificed to appease the ghost of the Greek Achilles; the second part presents her with the corpse of her son Polydorus (who has been murdered by Polymestor, king of the wild Thracian land where the play is set), and enacts the dreadful reprisal she exacts. The ancient Greeks were more capable than we are today of emotional honesty in articulating the human drive for revenge (see above, pp. 79–82). Thucydides' account of the Peloponnesian War draws repeated attention to the importance of this impulse in the shaping of history. No Greek tragedy concentrates to such a degree as *Hecuba* on the psychology of revenge, or rather on the psychological *process* by which a victim turns into an avenger, a process some psychoanalysts would call 'the internalization of the oppressor'.

The Greeks in the play, with the single exception of the herald Talthybius, display a casual brutality as shocking to the audience as to their victims on stage. Although Hecuba once saved Odysseus' life, he is responsible for persuading the Greeks to carry out the sacrifice of Polyxena, and makes his most shameful appearance in ancient literature when he arrives to justify arresting her. Agamemnon, to whom Hecuba turns for assistance against Polymestor, is a self-serving moral invertebrate, quick with a platitude on the nature of virtue but incapable of virtuous action. He agrees to turn a blind eye to Hecuba's actions against Polymestor, while refusing, lest he incur the disfavour of his army, to provide her with any active support. The Thracian Polymestor is one of the most unmitigatedly unpleasant characters on the ancient stage—a barefaced liar, a cynical opportunist, and the only tragic villain whose crime is motivated solely by avarice. And Hecuba herself, although she has far more excuse than the male characters for her atrocious behaviour, is transformed by her psychological trauma into as culpable a villain as any of them; she instigates not only the blinding of Polymestor, but also the killing of the two sons with whom he was unwise enough to enter the women's tents. The penalty exacted for the life of Polydorus is not one but *two* lives: it as if Hecuba's need to avenge Polyxena is displaced into Polymestor. This is a brilliant piece of psychology on Euripides' part: it is the Greeks who are responsible for by far the greatest part of Hecuba's suffering, but they are too powerful for her to oppose, and the psychological violence she has endured simply has to find expression somewhere.

The play includes several passages which show why Euripides was regarded by Aristotle as the absolute master of the tragic emotion of pity: the last parting of Polyxena from her mother is one of the most painful moments in western theatre. Indeed, it can be argued that this play makes its audience consciously meditate upon the tragic aesthetics of pity. Unlike the drama of the Renaissance, Greek tragedy did not use 'metatheatrical' figures of speech, such as 'all the world's a stage', perhaps because its authors were attempting to avoid anachronism in their portrayal of a Bronze Age world when theatre had not yet been invented (see above, pp. 53–5). But they did use analogies with the visual arts, which force the audience into thinking about the *visual* dimension of tragic theatre. Thus Talthybius' shocking account of the beautiful princess's dignity and courage, as she bared her breast for the sacrificial sword, memorably likens her appearance to that of a beautiful statue (560–1); later, Hecuba asks Agamemnon to pity her, standing back from her 'like a painter' to scrutinize her suffering (807). Passages such as these remind the spectators that they are colluding in the theatrical process precisely by gazing upon anguish and atrocity.

One of the most powerful theatrical moments in the play is the blinded Polymestor's gory entrance on all fours, 'crawling like a four-footed beast of the mountain', and expressing in nearly inarticulate song a bloodthirsty desire to glut himself on the flesh and bones of the 'savage beasts' he deems the women of Troy to be (1056–106, quoted above, pp. 41–2). Polymestor has become as like an animal as a human can, thus not only reinforcing one of the most important images in the play's poetic repertoire, but bodily demonstrating that all the social boundaries dividing human from beast can disintegrate when the human psyche is placed under sufficient pressure. Hecuba, whose children have been slaughtered by Greek and Thracian alike, and who is treated with no more respect than an animal, comes to behave like a beast herself when her emotions get out of control. The process of psychological 'bestialization' culminates in Polymestor's prediction that she will actually be transformed into a dog, and her tomb, 'Poor Dog's Tomb', will serve as a landmark to help sailors navigate (1265–73).

It is not only on an individual level that this play shows the boundaries between human and beast disintegrating. It dramatizes the total failure of those social practices, such as deliberative and judicial procedures, which are supposed to regulate the expression of human passions. The Greek assembly is revealed to be no dignified arena of debate, but an unthinking mob, manipulated into sanctioning the outrage of human sacrifice by Odysseus, 'that cunning-hearted, logic-chopping, sweet-tongued courtier of the people' (131–3). Polymestor's show trial in Agamemnon's 'kangaroo court', so hastily convened at the end of the play, is shown to have nothing whatsoever to do with the administration of justice. Despite Agamemnon's nauseating insistence on the inherent superiority of Greek legal procedures (1129–31, 1248), the trial takes place only *after* Hecuba has taken the law into her own hands and exacted her terrible penalty (see Fig. 6.4).

As if to underline the emotional isolation inflicted upon Hecuba by serial atrocities, Polymestor is condemned to end his days alone on a deserted island. But the play never lets its audience forget the future awaiting Agamemnon, either. The sacrifice of Polyxena is designed to remind the audience of the sacrifice of Iphigenia, especially since it is caused by the becalming of the Greek fleet near Troy, just as they were becalmed ten years before at Aulis. Hecuba discusses Agamemnon's relationship with Cassandra, implicitly reminding the audience of the reception that awaited this couple at Argos (826–32); moreover, the blinded Polymestor infuriates Agamemnon by accurately foreseeing that his real wife, Clytemnestra, will murder him with an axe in his bath (1279–81). Few ancient

FIG. 6.4. Hecuba in Euripides' play on an Apulian vase of the later 4th century BCE, reproduced courtesy of the Trustees of the British Museum.

tragedies culminate in such unmitigated hopelessness for all the principal characters concerned; even fewer imply that the terrible fates awaiting them are quite so richly deserved.

## *SUPPLIANT WOMEN* (DATE UNKNOWN)

This stately, sombre tragedy, the extended mass funeral of the Argives who died besieging Thebes, provides some of the most impressive spectacles in Euripidean drama. Set in Athenian territory at the sacred sanctuary at Eleusis, outside the temple of Demeter, it opens as a group of black-robed women with shorn grey hair supplicate the Queen Mother of Athens. The Argive King Adrastus lies prostrate at the gate, surrounded by several boys. The air is filled with lamentation, but there are no corpses to grieve over. It is not until the climax that the funeral cortege appears (778–94)—another striking spectacle, since it is rare for more than two or three corpses to be seen in the Attic theatre. There is no parallel in Greek tragedy for the scene in which one crazed widow, Evadne, flings herself onto her husband Capaneus' pyre, nor for the choral re-entry of the bereaved boys, tearfully bearing in the bones of their cremated fathers.

Every year Euripides' fellow Athenians gathered to hold a public funeral for the citizens who had died in combat. The bones were gathered in a special tent; this was followed by a procession in which coffins—including an empty one for those missing in action—were borne on wagons to the cemetery (see above pp. 74–5). A prominent citizen delivered an oration to the assembled families (Thucydides 2.34), a unique occasion in the city's calendar, for women never normally heard political speeches. *Suppliant Women* enacts the same concerns as this solemn event in the Athenian civic calendar. Its patriotic bent has been a critical commonplace since an ancient scholar baldly stated 'This drama is an encomium of Athens'. It does indeed invite its audience to reflect on the ideals their democracy championed. It is also possible that the play displaces onto the mythical Argives an important sequence of events in very recent Athenian history, for it may be informed by a traumatic defeat suffered by the Athenians at Delium in 424 BCE.

The Thebans had refused to hand over the thousand Athenian dead for burial on the ground that the Athenians had fortified a temple of Apollo. The bodies were eventually recovered, but the Athenians had been severely shaken by the incident: Thucydides' account relates an unpleasant diplomatic exchange which counterposes the 'Hellenic law' forbidding the military occupation of temples and that which enforced the handing back of war dead (4. 89–101). The details of the narrative's possible relationship with *Suppliant Women* are complicated, but some members of the original audience would have been reminded, if not of Delium, then of other confrontations between hostile armies over the treatment of the dead. The mythical Theseus shows, in front of an internal audience including representatives from several Greek city-states, and an equally panhellenic external audience sitting in the Athenian theatre, the 'right' way to talk and act on behalf of the dead in the aftermath of battle. In no Greek tragedy are the Athenians more clearly portrayed as the 'moral policemen' of Greece.

Yet the immediate topicality can be stressed too much. The play is a rare surviving example of a whole sub-genre of Athenian tragedy which enacted important moments in Athenian mythical prehistory. According to Plutarch's *Life of Theseus* (29), Euripides' *Suppliant Women* tragedy dealt with the same episode as Aeschylus' lost *Eleusinians*. For Euripides' contemporary Athenians, Theseus was their most important mythical ancestor. By the late sixth century his myths had been elaborated into a cycle of exploits to rival those of Heracles. As a local hero he was honoured in festivals, poetry, and the visual arts. By the middle of the fifth century he was regarded as the founding father of Athenian democracy (Thucydides 2.15). It is therefore to Theseus that Euripides gives some of his finest poetic monologues, exploring important human concerns in a distinctively philosophical register—an exposition of humanity's rise from the animal level by the acquisition of language, agriculture, shelter, sailing, trade, and augury (201–13), and meditations, informed by political theory, on the virtues of democracy (238–47, 433–56).

Yet the action and the poetry of the play undermine its superficial status as Athenian panegyric. Euripides juxtaposes the 'rational' rhetoric of Theseus the statesman with a series of heartrending laments. Theseus can recover the bodies of the dead, but he can never restore their lives. The play's message is further complicated by visual pictures of wild beasts; the bereaved fear that the bodies of their dead will be mutilated by animals, Adrastus had a dream likening his future sons-in-law to a lion and a boar (140), the chorus compare a suppliant with a wild beast taking refuge in a cave (267), and Evadne sees herself as a bird hovering above a cliff (1046). Such images focus the audience's mind on the inadequacy of those social institutions and conventions—forums of debate, the rights of the suppliant, and international diplomacy—that supposedly distinguish humans from beasts by regulating passions and resolving conflicts.

The intervention of the Theban herald further complicates the play's ethical dimension. However unlikeable, he makes cogent points: sophisticated political oratory can do great harm (412–16); love for one's children should be stronger than respect for one's fatherland or parents; peace, under which children and the arts flourish, must always be the priority (486–91). Moreover, Theseus' own order to the Athenians to go into battle is just a little too enthusiastic (587, 593). The price paid by warring states is expressed by the traumatized messenger—men dragged bouncing in the reins, rivers of red blood, charioteers hurled headlong from their shattered vehicles (689–93). Finally, Evadne's shocking leap to her death not only demonstrates that war ruins lives, but in an inspired piece of writing makes Evadne herself echo the competitive, masculine ethos that started the war in the first place. Like a Homeric hero, she has come 'to claim a glorious victory' and to win eternal renown by dying gloriously (1059–61, 1067). Thucydides' Pericles told the bereaved women of Athens that their greatest glory was to be spoken of as little as possible (2. 46). He would not have approved of Evadne, who ensures that the grief of her widowhood is remembered for all time, nor of the chorus of Argive mothers, who lament insatiably. This tragedy may not contain the intense familial conflict or psychological intimacy of some other Euripidean dramas. But as an exercise in the subtle subversion of a patriotic story it is—intellectually and emotionally—one of his finer achievements.

## *ELECTRA* (DATE UNKNOWN)

Euripides' *Electra* made a less obvious impact than some of his plays on later antiquity, although its domestic tone and rustic setting were formative in the development of New Comedy. Yet one ancient anecdote reveals that *Electra*'s profound tragic force was recognized. When Athens lost the Peloponnesian War in 404 BCE, the story goes that a Theban leader proposed that the city be razed to the ground. But Athens was saved by a man who performed to the allied generals the chorus' entrance song from Euripides' *Electra* (beginning at 167). Electra's pitiable plight seemed similar to that of conquered Athens; as a result they are supposed to have decided against destroying such an illustrious city (Plutarch, *Life of Lysander* 15).

Amongst extant Greek tragedies the only story dramatized by all three playwrights relates Electra and Orestes' conspiracy to murder their mother and usurping uncle Aegisthus. Consequently much scholarly ink has been expended on comparing this play with Aeschylus' *Libation-Bearers* (458 BCE) and Sophocles' *Electra*, and in particular on the relative chronology of the Sophoclean and Euripidean versions. It is fascinating how differently two individuals can read a myth: in Sophocles the matricides' triumphalism is undercut only implicitly, with slippery irony (see below, pp. 309–13). But there is no way to prove the date of either *Electra*, or which was the earlier. More instructive is Euripides' parody of the Aeschylean recognition scene. When Euripides' Electra objects that her foot cannot be the same size as a man's, even if he is her brother (534–7), it is not only an unusual 'intertextual' comment on the Aeschylean prototype (227–8): it is undoubtedly meant to be funny. Consequently the precise emotional register of Euripides' *Electra* has defied specification. The play's detractors have complained that all the preparations for the crimes are marked by levity. At the other extreme it has been regarded as a bleak example of psychosocial realism anticipating Chekhov, a masterpiece, whose 'power of sympathy and analysis' was 'unrivalled in ancient drama'.[10] Another critic has noted the complex shifts of register, especially the pattern by which the choral songs move from pictures of charm and allure to darkness and destruction, a pattern in keeping with the 'questioning mode' and 'irrecoverably dark world' of the tragedy.[11]

Indeed, most admirers have seen its moral position as unambivalent: its humour simply sharpens its exposure of the barbarism inherent in unthinking reciprocal violence.

Does Euripides' Clytemnestra deserve to die at all? The play's ethical tension results from the absence of an answer. The Greek mind was more able than ours simultaneously to contain contradictory dimensions of a situation: the action is presented as both outrageous and delivering a kind of justice. Clytemnestra was a murderess: it was just that she had been executed. But matricide was (equally?) an outrage: her killing by Orestes and Electra was dreadful. As Castor finally announces, the fate Clytemnestra suffered was right, but the children did not act rightly (1244). However comic some of its scenes, the play ends on the bleakest of notes: Orestes begs Electra to sing him a dirge as if at his grave (1325–6), a request so jarring in the context of the 'happy ending' that it shocks even the god in the machine. It is difficult for a modern reader not to conceptualize the incipient pursuit of Orestes by the Erinyes as symbolizing our notion of internal torture by conscience, by a personal sense of 'guilt'. Perhaps this notion is not so modern: Cicero argued that 'the blood of a mother... has a great power; it is a mighty bond, of awful sanction. If any stain be conceived from it, not only can it not be washed out, but it penetrates through to the mind to such an extent that raving madness and insanity results... These are the constant, secret, Furies which... exact punishment on behalf of their parents both by day and by night' (*Pro Sexto Roscio Amerino* 24. 66).

Euripides' Electra incorporates extremes. She participates in the action more than in Sophocles, jointly wielding the matricidal sword (1225). But her commitment to a 'masculine' vengeance code conflicts with her immoderate assertions of the patriarchal view that women are secondary to men. It is shameful, she announces to Aegisthus' corpse, for a woman to be in charge of a household: but it is Electra, not Orestes, who is 'in charge' of the tragic action of the play (931–3). She thus implicitly subverts the gender hierarchy she explicitly endorses. It is left to Clytemnestra to articulate the inequity of marriage: why, she asks, should women be criticized for acquiring a new partner when male adultery is never censured (1036–40)?

Euripides put his inimitably demotic stamp on Electra's story by having Aegisthus marry her off to a peasant. Aegisthus' goal was to prevent her from bearing to an illustrious father a son who might one day punish him. The mythical motif of the cruel parent persecuting a daughter through fear of a possible grandchild has parallels. The audience is introduced to the idea of Electra bearing a child in the prologue (22–42), where they learn that Aegisthus feared that if she married a nobleman she might 'bear a son to avenge Agamemnon'. The folkloric notion that a father-figure might be afraid of his daughter's offspring is instantiated in Greek myth by the story of Danaë, Perseus, and Acrisius (Perseus is depicted on Achilles' shield in the first stasimon of *Electra*, 458–63). Herodotus relates another example in his tale of Astyages, king of the Medes in Asia, Mandane, and her baby Cyrus, who deposed his grandfather to become the first king of a united Medo-Persian Empire (1. 107–8). It was stories such as these which Euripides had in mind when he invented Aegisthus' fear of Electra bearing a child who would one day take vengeance upon his wicked step-grandfather. From there it was a short step to give Electra a fictional baby. Yet it is instructive to see how Euripides discovered in this motif the brilliant ruse of the invented grandchild which fundamentally colours the theatricality and the pathos of his tragedy. This tragedy required its male leading actor to display the female character he was playing at a moment when she was *pretending* to be a newly delivered woman in front of a person intimately acquainted with her physiology and temperament: her own mother. Euripides thus invited his audience to engage in a tragic version of the procedure which also marked the 'escape' scene of the fraudulently pregnant woman in *Lysistrata*: they were to watch his Electra faking a woman close to the time of birth. But equally, the fictional baby lures Clytemnestra to her death, focuses attention on Electra's pitifully childless status, and extraordinarily complicates the distribution of audience sympathy. It is difficult to appreciate the heroic justice of reciprocal blood-letting when the victim thinks she has just become a grandmother.

## *HERACLES* (DATE UNKNOWN)

*Heracles* is a play about survival. Its superlative conclusion portrays the moral courage of a man whose life sentence of emotional pain is unbearable. He knows that the psychological torture awaiting him will be unremitting, like the physical pain suffered by Ixion, chained to a wheel throughout eternity (1298). For Euripides' Heracles, as for many perpetrators and victims of atrocity throughout history, the suicide he rejects would have been incomparably an easier option.

This bloody, inspiring tragedy pushes traditional beliefs about the nature of divine justice to their limits. Heracles suffers the worst imaginable fate for a parent—he kills his own beloved children. As the play presents his story, he has done absolutely nothing to deserve this. Heracles is hated by Hera because he is magnificent and because she is his stepmother, but that is the extent of the explanation offered for her attack on his sanity. The action thus articulates, in the most lucid manner, the problem of unmerited suffering. Euripides has gone out of his way to pose this ethical conundrum unambiguously. In some other tragedies, such as Sophocles' *Women of Trachis*, Heracles is an indifferent, even brutal father. But Euripides' Heracles is a loving and responsible parent.

*Heracles* has always been regarded as a work of an extreme nature. Antiquity recorded a tradition that Euripides was prosecuted by the fifth-century Athenian statesman Cleon for showing Heracles going mad in a play at the Dionysia.[12] The story, although probably untrue, reveals something of antiquity's shocked reaction to the drama. The perceived extremity of *Heracles* has also produced extreme reactions in its more recent reception. Byron acknowledged its masculine potency when he laughed at an earnest bluestocking (*Don Juan* 11.52):

> That prodigy Miss Araminta Smith
> (Who at sixteen translated *Hercules Furens*
> Into as furious English).

Browning introduces his translation of the play in *Aristophanes' Apology* (1875) with explicit panegyric: it is 'the consummate tragedy', the test for 'true godship', even 'the perfect piece'. In 1905 an important Euripidean scholar, A. W. Verrall, announced that 'For power, for truth, for poignancy, for depth of penetration into the nature and history of man, this picture of the Hellenic hero may be matched against anything in art.'[13]

Many aesthetic reactions to *Heracles* have, however, been proportionately negative. Some Euripidean tragedies, such as *Trojan Women*, are 'spilt milk' dramas which begin with the 'reversal' and most if not all of the carnage. Others, such as *Medea*, keep the explosion of violence until near the end. *Heracles* places the turning-point in its hero's fortunes at its precise centre. Since the eighteenth century, complaints have been directed against the play's 'diptychal' or 'broken-backed' structure. There are different ways of addressing this alleged problem. One is to emphasize themes which are central to the whole play—hope, luck, salvation, excellence, reputation, violence, friendship. Another is to point to some of the more disturbing uses of language in the earlier references to Heracles, and argue that his madness is subtly prefigured in the first half. A third line of defence sees the unique structure as a response to the unique nature of Heracles: Euripides designed the bifurcated plot in order to explore his hero's ontological hybridity, his blurring of the margin between human and divine.

Yet discussions of the play's structure have not usually considered the impact of the play in performance. On stage the diction and action completely transcend the alleged dislocation. Only performance can demonstrate the aural impact of the poetry in the 'madness' panel; the remarkable range of verbal ambiguity, etymologies, repetition, punning, and jingles produces a sense of linguistic madness, a tornado of poetic diction through which meaning is revealed.[14] Furthermore, performance reveals that Heracles is omnipresent as a topic of discussion if not actually in person. The tragedy concludes by sending him to Athens to receive a hero cult, but in doing so asks what such a violent, anachronistic firebrand of a hero can offer a fifth-century democracy, in which the glorious exploits of brilliant individuals need to be subordinated to the welfare of the wider community. The play examines almost every aspect of the earlier mythical traditions surrounding Heracles. But ultimately it is only Athens and the Athenian genre of tragedy which can save Heracles from the cultural death and obsolescence which threaten him in the first part of the play, and produce a new, less traditional kind of hero whose powers are more metaphysical than physical, a hero more suited and valuable to the Athenians of the fifth century BCE.

Finally, it is only performance that fully reveals the importance of Amphitryon's role. He is himself a profoundly tragic figure, who loses everything, but must live on alone in Thebes and organize the funerals of his daughter-in-law and grandchildren. Heracles 'adoptive' father is on stage throughout almost the entire action (except only 348–450 and 733–1041), and his role demands a versatile actor. He delivers the prologue, which establishes his claim on the audience's sympathy (cf. Aristotle, *Politics* 7.1336b27–31), and a major rhetorical speech in the 'archery' debate with Lycus (170–235). His voice utters the crucial offstage cries marking the death of the children (886–908); he is the only singing actor in the play, and performs a complex sung dialogue with the chorus (1042–88). To him belongs the terrible task of breaking the news to Heracles (1109–62). Above all, as a man who unswervingly loves another man to whom he is biologically unrelated, Amphitryon is the chief representative of the force of human affective ties— *philia*—and their power to transcend even the very worst that the gods can send.

In myth and cult Heracles was the universal Best Friend, the divine figure with whom the Greeks associated the advanced human capacity for loving non-kin. In *Heracles* (as in *Alcestis*) his relationships with other humans exemplify this principle and prove that it alone can offer some protection against the gods' vindictiveness. Thus of all surviving Greek tragedies *Heracles* most demands the epithet 'humanist' in its truest sense. Although on one level a religious drama providing a mythical explanation for a traditional hero's place in Athenian cult, *Heracles* radically calls traditional religion into question and replaces it with more human-centred ethics. Euripides' contemporary Athenians associated such ideas with Protagoras, an agnostic thinker who denied that human attempts to intercede with the gods could shape events. Significantly, later antiquity believed that it was at Euripides' house that Protagoras read out his famous treatise on the gods, beginning 'Man is the measure of all things' (Diogenes Laertius 9.8.5). Heracles denies that gods can be vindictive and calls myths mere poetic fictions; Amphitryon and Theseus ignore traditional pollution taboos in order to help the traumatised criminal. In *Heracles* Euripides forces his heroes, and thereby his audience, to leave heroic myth behind in the toy box, and to enter the more exacting adult world of moral responsibility, autonomy, and accountability.

## TROJAN WOMEN (415 BCE)

In spite of its brilliant ancient reputation, this play was held in low critical estimation from the Renaissance until the twentieth century. Its lack of an identifiably Aristotelian 'plot' involving error and reversal prompted the judgement of A. W. Schlegel, which was profoundly to influence reactions until well into the twentieth century, that 'the accumulation of helpless suffering, without even an opposition of sentiment, at last wearies us, and exhausts our compassion'. He was offended both by the famous debate between Helen and Hecuba, which he saw as 'an idle altercation, which ends in nothing', and by the protagonist Hecuba, represented throughout 'in sackcloth and ashes, pouring out her lamentations'.[15] It is interesting that Schlegel saw as weaknesses what are now believed to be this remarkable play's great strengths—its uncompromising despair, concerted lyrical lamentation, elaborate rhetoric, and the commanding, central figure of Hecuba.

The corrective to this modern view of *Trojan Women* was not to come until the twentieth century, when the play began to be *performed*. The first performance in a modern-language translation was probably the 1905 production mounted at the Royal Court Theatre in London, in the translation of the Greek scholar and humanitarian Gilbert Murray, in order to protest against the concentration camps in which the British had incarcerated Boer women and children during the terrible war in South Africa. Murray was convinced that Euripides had written the play to protest against the very recent Athenian massacre of many of the male inhabitants of the rebellious island of Melos (see Thucydides 5.116). There are problems with this simplistic interpretation, not least that the Spartan ethnicity of the malign Greek characters in the play is rather insistently stressed. But Murray's 'pacifist' interpretation has been widely embraced, and led to a whole series of performances during and after World War I.[16]

One scholar wrote in 1930 of his 'conversion' to a work he previously seen as 'a most unpleasant play to read' after watching a performance which proved to him that 'the incidents which seemed like disconnected scenes when read appeared to be much more closely knot together, so that there actually seemed to be a plot which advanced steadily to a climax.'[17] For it is only a performance that makes it possible to appreciate the *cumulative* effect of the sequence of scenes revealing the appalling effect of the war on the female inhabitants of Troy: Hecuba's pain at her multiple bereavements and humiliation at her enslavement, Cassandra's psychotic 'celebration' of impending sexual union with her conqueror, Andromache's anguish at the loss of her baby son Astyanax, Helen's desperate—but successful—bid to save her own life, and the climax in which the Greeks set fire to Troy itself and Hecuba attempts to charge headlong into the flames. It is the reactive presence of the widowed old queen which draws into a coherent vision all the other characters' perspectives: she never leaves the stage from the beginning to the end, and her role must have challenged even the greatest of ancient actors. Her part requires not only a powerful singing voice and the ability to deliver complex, pointed rhetoric, but considerable physical stamina. Her body seems to symbolize Troy itself: first seen by Poseidon prostrate with grief, she alternately struggles to her feet and collapses to the ground throughout the entire action. At the close she is trying to raise herself from the earth, which she has been pounding in a formal dirge, in order to stumble off to her fate in slavery (see Fig. 6.5).

*Trojan Women* is unusual in that we know just a little about the other Euripidean plays produced at the same time. The sequence consisted of the lost *Alexander* and *Palamedes*, the surviving *Trojan Women*, and a lost satyr play, *Sisyphus*. It is clear that the three tragedies were to a certain extent interconnected. They were all set at or near Troy and treated episodes from the war in chronological order; some characters (for example Hecuba, Cassandra, and Odysseus) appeared in more than one of them. In *Alexander* the poet dramatized the Trojans' mistake in exposing Paris as a child (obliquely alluded to in *Trojan Women* 597) and his eventual reunion with his family; *Palamedes* enacted the Greeks' wrongful persecution of the innocent Palamedes at Troy after Odysseus (apparently at

FIG. 6.5. Margot dan der Burgh as Hecuba in *The Trojan Women*, The Theatre Royal, London (1964), reproduced courtesy of the APGRD.

least as unpleasant a character as in *Trojan Women*) laid false evidence against him. The tragedies as a group thus contained some kind of unity, and some of the original resonances of *Trojan Women* must be lost on us, who have access only to the third. But it is possible to overstate this problem, since most of antiquity read or watched *Trojan Women* as an independent artwork, just as we do today.

In three of the plays dating from the last decade of Euripides' life Helen appears as a character (*Trojan Women, Helen, Orestes*). In his *Helen* of 412 BCE he was to use the version of her myth which claimed that it was not the heroine herself who went to Troy, but a cloud-carved simulacrum; through this device he was able to use the mythical heroine to explore questions raised by contemporary philosophers in the fields of ontology (what is being?) and epistemology (how do we know things?). But the Greeks had another, even more pressing philosophical question—'how should we live?'—and before Plato, from the *Iliad* onwards, the ethical debates fought in mythical narratives over culpability for the carnage at Troy—debates in which the name of Helen insistently recurred—were the most important forerunners of Greek *moral* philosophy. In *Trojan Women* Euripides makes his characters strain their intellectual and theological muscles as they attempt to find a reason for the catastrophe, an impulse which the pressure of bereavement quickly transforms turns into a quest for a single scapegoat—the Spartan Helen—to shoulder all the blame.

On the superhuman level Hecuba, in her more reflective moments, can see abstract forces such as 'Necessity' and 'Chance' at work (616, 1204), in addition to the particular hatred the gods felt against Troy (612–13, 696, 1241). The chorus are suspicious that Zeus himself, the supreme Olympian, has betrayed the city he once loved well (1060–70); Poseidon himself blames the goddesses Hera and Athena for the destruction of Troy (8–12, 24); others sometimes allege that the war-god, Ares, is individually responsible for the carnage (376, 560). But blaming metaphysical and divine forces does not satisfy the traumatized women of Troy. Nor does acknowledging the culpability of the male players in the drama of the war, whether Odysseus who had the idea of killing the infant Astyanax (1225), Paris who first offended the sons of Atreus (598), or even the collective Greek invaders, denounced by Andromache in a famous paradoxical apostrophe: 'Oh you Greeks, you who have devised atrocities worthy of barbarians!' (764). In a moment of profound psychological insight Hecuba can see that it has been the Greeks' *fear*, fear above all of what Astyanax might one day become, which has made them behave so abominably (1159–65). But not even these male hate figures prove adequate to the Trojan women's need for a focus for their rage. It is Helen above all whom Hecuba blames for the death of Priam and all her personal misery (130–7, 498, 969–1032, etc.), the chorus agree with her (1111–17), and the overwrought Andromache goes even further, denouncing her lovely sister-in-law as the offspring of a series of malign forces— 'The Avenging Spirit . . . Envy and Murder and Death and all the evils that the earth breeds' (768–9).

The issue of blame is most heavily underscored by Helen's astonishing defence speech, in which she exploits to the full the ancient rhetoricians' technique of defence through counter-attack (see above pp. 37–8)—by blaming others for the very crime of which she stands accused. The play thus shows with devastating clarity not only how men in wartime treat women and children, but how women barbarized by men blame other women, and how humans in desperate straits exhaust their emotional energies on attributing blame and exacting punishment rather than on thinking constructively about the future. But for Troy, of course, there is to be no future: as the chorus sing in the closing dirge, 'Like smoke on the wings of the breezes, our land, laid low in war, now vanishes into nothingness' (1297–9).

## *IPHIGENIA AMONG THE TAURIANS* (DATE UNKNOWN)

Euripides was attracted to storylines set in faraway, exotic lands, which turned the theatre of Dionysus into a panoramic window onto the barbarian margins of the known world. He may have been consciously reviving one of the traditions of earlier tragedy, for the earliest extant play, Aeschylus' *Persians*,. had in 472 BCE thrilled its audience with the oriental setting, costumes, and protocols of the Persian court at Susa. Exactly sixty years later Euripides transported his audience to the Ethiopian coast in his lost *Andromeda*, and in *Helen* to the mouth of the Egyptian Nile; in his (possibly earlier) *Iphigenia among the Taurians* his spectators could feast their eyes on a barbarian temple, running with the blood of human victims, on the craggy coast of the Crimean peninsula. This is the most remote setting of any Greek tragedy except the Aeschylean *Prometheus Bound*.

More clearly than any other tragic drama except *Helen*, *Iphigenia among the Taurians* reflects the popularity in Athens of the eastern Greek historian and ethnographer Herodotus. His prose treatise on the Persian Wars, which had become familiar at Athens by the 420s, had included a description of the Taurians of the Crimea (4.99, 103). It is this strange people, whose economy rests on cattle farming, that Euripides brings to life in the theatre. Several details in Herodotus' account reappear in the tragedy, especially the custom of sacrificing shipwrecked sailors and the impalement of victims on stakes (38–41, 1429–30).[18] The people who lived in this remote peninsula did historically worship a 'Maiden goddess', who was associated with wild animals and was perceived as being equivalent to the Greeks' Artemis (Herodotus actually says that they called their maiden goddess 'Iphigenia'). Moreover, of Artemis' Greek titles, Tauropolos ('bull-hunting'), was aurally sufficiently similar to suggest that Artemis was closely connected with the Taurians.

This helps to illuminate the invention of the myth which told of Orestes' Black Sea quest for Artemis' ancient cult image, destined to come from the Taurians to Greece. But it is just as important that in his later career Euripides became increasingly interested in what happened to Orestes after he killed his mother; in *Electra*, in the immediate aftermath of the murder, Orestes suffers feelings of intense self-hatred; in *Orestes*, in the grip of a nervous breakdown, he is condemned to death by the people of Argos, tries to kill Helen, but is rescued from the angry mob by Apollo. In *Iphigenia among the Taurians* the same god diverts him to the Black Sea on a quite different mission, the quest for the image of Artemis. In the land of the Taurians he is nearly sacrificed (see Fig. 6.6), but is reunited in time with his long-lost sister, and through her quick thinking and resourcefulness makes good his escape to Greece.

At times the play's atmosphere is not unlike that of 'Westerns' made before in the 1950s, where white frontiersmen are taken captive by Red Indians, to face barbaric death and mutilation. Superficially, Euripides seems to take every available opportunity to contrast Greek valour with barbarian cowardice, Greek cunning intelligence with barbarian gullibility, and Greek sensibility with barbarian savagery. For some of its spectators it may therefore have offered little more than an escapist romp legitimizing their patriotism and xenophobia. Yet on a deeper level the play presents a greater challenge to unthinking Greek ethnic supremacism than any other text of the fifth century. For the averted catastrophe of the tragedy—the sacrifice of Orestes—is consistently paired in the audience's imaginations with the intended sacrifice of Iphigenia by her Greek father, so long ago at Aulis. The parallelism between the fates of the siblings is repeatedly stressed, forcing the audience to question whether Greek ethics were really so superior. After all, as far as the Taurians were concerned, Orestes was only a shipwrecked sailor: the Greek Agamemnon, on the other hand, had been prepared to authorize the ritual killing of his own beloved daughter.

FIG. 6.6. Benjamin West, *Pylades and Orestes brought as Victims before Iphigenia* (1766), reproduced courtesy of the Trustees of the British Museum.

The most explicit questioning of the 'double standard' underlying conventional Greek thinking about the inferiority of other cultures is, strikingly and appropriately, put into the mouth of the barbarian king Thoas: when told that Orestes had murdered his own mother, he exclaims, in horror, 'By Apollo, no one would have dared to do this even among barbarians!' (1174).

Scholarship has tended to focus on the play's interest in religious ritual and especially in aetiology, the provision of mythical explanations for religious customs still practised in Euripides' day. For example, the play offers an original explanation for the presence of the cult image of Artemis at one of her sanctuaries in Attica. But it also shows how Iphigenia and Orestes, who in today's language are horrifically 'abused' children of a catastrophically dysfunctional family, are enabled by their encounter to come to terms with their psychological trauma, and to avoid re-enacting their family past by transforming it into ritual. Their acquired wisdom allows the substitution of harmless rites for actual atrocity.

This deeply thoughtful, moving, atmospheric, and humane drama has nevertheless caused critics much consternation, especially during the last two hundred years. Its escapist plot, lack of a catastrophic death or suffering, and happy ending have led it to be classified as a tragicomedy, a satyric tragedy owing much to the conventions of satyr play, as a burlesque, or as a 'romantic' tragedy. Its enigmatic status has led it to be neglected even more than *Helen*, which, although not dissimilar, is far more clearly intended to be overtly funny. But the ancients had no such problem with the play; even Aristotle, who preferred unhappy endings, admired the skilfully crafted recognition scene, which involves the fascinating device of Iphigenia's 'letter home'. Aristotle's admiration was deserved: the reunion is not only emotionally touching but in preventing the performance of human sacrifice is integral to the development of the plot. The tragedy was repeatedly performed in later antiquity, becoming familiar enough to inspire a bizarrely parodic mime in which the heroine is stranded among barbarians who speak an ancient dialect of India.[19] At Rome the tragedy's celebration of the friendship between Orestes and Pylades was much admired; Cicero's treatise *On Friendship* records that an audience rose to its feet and applauded spontaneously at the scene in Pacuvius' lost

Latin adaptation of the play when Pylades volunteered to die in his friend's place (7.24).

Yet by far the greatest strength of the play undoubtedly lies in its articulate, expressive, brave, and intelligent heroine, a charming character unique amongst the remains of extant Greek tragedy. Euripides' tragedy, astonishingly, makes it easy for his audience—who were almost entirely male—to relate powerfully to the emotional plight of a childless, lonely, exiled woman in at least early middle age, who has never married and (unlike her sister Electra in other plays) certainly never will. In *Iphigenia among the Taurians* the unlikely figure of a spinsterly older sister has an extraordinary opportunity to confide her innermost thoughts and fears to the assembled citizens of Athens and beyond them to posterity.

## *ION* (DATE UNKNOWN)

Antiquity believed that Euripides was an artist as well as a tragic poet, and that paintings of his were on display in the city of Megara (*Life of Euripides*, 5). This tradition was probably an invention inspired by the frequency of the references in his plays to the visual arts. In no play is this interest more apparent than in *Ion*, from the moment when the entering chorus of Athenian women admiringly describe the mythical scenes sculpted onto the facades of the temple of Apollo, including an awesome image of Athena (184–218). When Ion and Creusa are discussing her grandfather Erichthonios, an important figure in Athenian foundation mythology, Ion comments that the moment when Athena gave Erichthonios as a baby to the daughters of Cecrops was a scene beloved of artists (271). When Ion erects his ceremonial tent, he uses tapestries adorned with a series of mostly patriotic scenes (1141–52); at the tent's entrance Ion positions a statue of Cecrops, the snake-man who had sprung from the Athenian soil to become the original ancestor of the 'autochthonous', earthborn Athenians (1141–66). These passages draw attention to the status of theatre, by making the audience contemplate the visual dimension of the dramatic poem they are experiencing, but the myths chosen for visualization also situate the play's master narrative—the reunion of Ion and his mother Creusa, Queen of Athens—within the tradition of local mythology celebrated in every art form in the Athenians' city. Creusa's determination that the monarchy must be inherited by a true son of the Athenian royal family may result in what strikes the modern audience as a thought-provoking exploration of xenophobia, yet it is consonant with the pleasure Euripides' countrymen felt in believing that their ancestors were not immigrants, but born from the soil of their own city.

Paradoxically, *Ion* is a deeply private, personal drama. The setting is indeed the public shrine of the panhellenic Delphic oracle, where Creusa and her husband have come to enquire about their (apparent) childlessness, and the play concludes with Athena uttering grand prophecies of importance to the whole Greek world (1575–94). But at the play's emotional centre is the evolving relationship between Creusa and her long-lost baby, a son conceived after Apollo had raped her. Most of the play consists of intimate dialogue between Creusa and people related to her by blood or close to her heart; even the chorus are her loyal servants. Much of the action involves sexual secrets, including Xuthus' secret that before marrying Creusa he had once slept with a girl at an all-night festival. Even the happy ending is compromised by the audience's collusion in the dangerous secret that Creusa and Ion are biological mother and son, knowledge that is never to be shared by Xuthus, the other member of their little nuclear family (1601–3).

In *Ion* Euripides experimented with plot devices which were to be of incalculable importance in later European theatre. Mistaken identity, for example, is shown to have both comic and tragic potential. Xuthus' assumption that Ion is his biological son produces a moment of pure farce; Xuthus tries to hug the astonished youth, who understandably enquires whether he has lost his mind (517–30). But when Creusa makes the same mistake, the result is reciprocal attempted murder. Euripides also explores the way random coincidence or chance (*tuchē*) influences events; although the discovery of Ion's true identity, and his return to Athens, are part of a divine plan prepared by Apollo, chance events create dramatic tension, and almost sabotage the divine programme.

This enchanting, atmospheric drama was certainly performed in later antiquity (Demetrius, *On Style* 195), but it exerted a far greater, subterranean influence as one of several Euripidean dramatic precursors of the Greek 'New Comedy' of Menander and his contemporaries, the Roman comedies of Terence and Plautus, and consequently of the ancient romantic prose fiction written by the novelists Heliodorus, Achilles Tatius, and Longus. Chance not only became one of the most important dramaturgical principles of New Comedy; it sometimes even made an appearance in the form of the goddess *Tychē* as prologist. Like *Ion*, New Comedy is driven by a fascination with foundlings, with family psychology, with servants, secrets, recognition, (mistaken) identity, paternity, and maternity; the difference is that these fascinations are explored in the context of contemporary everyday life, rather than a Bronze Age royal family. The theme of the foundling child was of course far more ancient than Euripides: it has an Old Testament parallel in the story of Moses, an Asiatic one in Herodotus' version of the infancy of Cyrus the Great, king of Persia (1.108–22), and a sombre Greek tragic counterpart in Sophocles' account of the life of Oedipus, tyrant of Thebes. But it was Euripides more than any other writer whose fresh spin on this particular story pattern informed the incipient transformation of Greek comedy from the political and social satire of Aristophanes into middle-class domestic fiction.

Euripides' most important innovation was to focus on Creusa's sensibility. Although not as well known as Medea, Phaedra, or Hecuba, in Creusa Euripides painted his most elaborate—and arguably his most sympathetic—portrait of female psychology. Few rape victims in western literature have until recently been offered such a full hearing, and Creusa's reaction to the assault is informed by a realistic, malignant anger against her rapist. Her anguish explodes in a heart-rending scene during which she divulges to the audience suppressed memories of the traumas she suffered as a teenager. While Apollo raped her she called ineffectually for her mother (893); she endured labour alone, without a midwife (948–9); she was in psychological agony as she tried to ignore her infant's arms stretched out towards her (958–61). It is the intimacy of the exploration of Creusa's pain that makes the eventual recognition scene so affecting; its emotional force upstages the public significance of the tokens left in the crib, miniature artworks depicting scenes from Athenian mythology appropriate for Athens' future king.

In *Ion* Euripides shows how the blood of the autochthonous Athenians was infused with the divine blood of Apollo, lord of the Delphic oracle. But the divine paternity of Ion, in the end, seems far less significant than the revelation of how catastrophic an unwanted pregnancy can be for an unmarried girl. Euripides even underlines his unusual angle on Creusa's pregnancy by pointing out that the other (male) poets who have narrated myths involving scandalous sexual unions have routinely blamed the women involved. The angry chorus suggest that it is time for some poetry which tells how women have suffered at the hands of men (1096–8):

> May a song and a raucous Muse with the opposing theme
> Be let loose against men, to sing about *their* sex-life!

## HELEN (412 BCE)

At the close of *Electra* Castor explains *ex machina* that Helen 'has come from the house of Proteus from Egypt—she did not go to Troy'. The explanation for Helen's illusory presence at Troy was an artificial image sent by Zeus to cause strife and death among men (1280–3). This mythical exculpation of Helen had originally been invented by the lyric poet Stesichorus, and had been rationalized by Herodotus in his account of Egyptian antiquities (2.118–20). In his *Helen* of 412 BCE Euripides elaborated on these sources by constructing an entire play around Helen's sojourn in Egypt.

*Helen* has caused even more problems of generic categorization than *Electra*. Of all Greek tragedies, including the not dissimilar *Iphigenia among the Taurians*, it is by far the lightest and funniest. It certainly conforms least with commonplace preconceptions of 'the tragic' ultimately derived from Aristotle. Nobody dies (except some Egyptian sailors the audience has not met), the ending is happy, and there are many laughs along the way to Helen's escape from the libidinous pharaoh Theoclymenus. Criticism has consequently often centred on definitions: is *Helen* light-hearted 'self-parody', 'melodrama', 'tragicomedy', 'romantic comedy', or just plain 'comedy'?

A year after *Helen* and *Andromeda* Aristophanes treated them both to extended parody in his comedy *Women at the Thesmophoria*. He was struck by *Helen*'s 'escape' plot, the comic 'door-knocking' scene with the female porter, and the geographical context of Egypt, which seems never to have been the setting for a tragedy previously. But it had formed the backdrop to both comedies and satyr plays: Euripides himself produced a satyric *Busiris*, featuring a mythical king of Egypt who subjected all foreigners to human sacrifice. Thus Theoclymenus seems to have walked in almost straight from the satyric stage. There are other features reminiscent of satyr drama, especially the motif of Menelaus' shipwreck and the coastal setting. It may therefore be that *Helen*'s genre-transgressive quality has more to do with satyric than comic drama: an appropriate definition of this tragedy, as we noted in the discussion of *Cyclops*, could be the critic Demetrius' description of satyr drama—'tragedy at play' (*On Style* 169).

Whatever challenge it presents to generic classification, *Helen*'s complex tissue of plots and sub-plots has long attracted admirers; it has been supposed to mark the birth of fiction and to represent the first text with recognizably 'novelistic' features to be found in Greek literature. Many readings have drawn on Northrop Frye's study of the lighter plays of Shakespeare to demonstrate that a distinctive feature of *Helen* is its collision of two worlds: a 'real' world of pain and trouble and an 'ideal' world of serenity and simplicity, a duality negotiated in the manner of true 'romance' by a calumniated heroine whose virtue restores her and her beloved to happiness ever after in their kingdom.[20] The play's brilliance lies in its juxtaposition of this romantic dimension with considerable intellectual bravura. Euripides uses the folkloric notion of a human simulacrum to explore the epistemological issue of the impossibility of true belief: the plot as well as the form and the language of the play are all generated by a tension between the real world and actual events, and the fantasies and stories that only 'seem' to be true. Sophists contemporary with Euripides such as Gorgias had questioned whether there is a fully knowable real world, and whether language was adequate to describe it: *Helen* repeatedly explores the gap between reality and repute, speech and truth. Gorgias had written a rhetorical exercise consisting of a defence of the mythical Helen (see above, p. 37) in which he argued that a speech can 'mould the mind in the way it wishes', is able to 'please and persuade a large crowd because written with skill, not moulded with truth', and that philosophical speeches, in particular, show that 'quick-wittedness makes the opinion which is based on belief changeable' (13).

Fittingly for a play so emphatically dealing with the impossibility of cognitive certitude, the visual element of *Helen* is unusually important. The heroine perceives that her beauty—her superficial 'appearance'—has been her undoing, and wishes that it could be washed off her face like the paint off a beautiful statue (262–3); this raises the issue of 'metatheatricality', for 'Helen' herself is but a male actor wearing a sculpted mask painted with beautiful colours. By drawing attention to this false 'face' the actor draws attention to one of the illusory conventions of the theatrical performance in which he is participating. Much additional play is made of illusion and of doubleness. The entrance of Menelaus mirrors the previous appearance of Teucer; the Egyptian twins have a pair of equally spectacular entrances (Theonoe with incense and religious procession at 865–72, Theoclymenus with hunting dogs and nets, 1165–70), and the play concludes with a theophany of twins. Costume possesses significance; besides the comic effect of seeing Menelaus wrapped in salvaged materials from a shipwreck (422), Helen herself completely changes her appearance (probably both robes and mask) in order to 'appear' as a widow (1186–8), when paradoxically she has just regained the status of 'wife' in the true sense again.

*Helen* also confronts ontological paradoxes, especially the problematic notions of subjectivity, the self, and identity: who is the 'true' Helen? If 'Helen of Troy' did not cause the Trojan War, then why is she the subject of a work of literature? In semiotic terms, how can the signifier, the proper name 'Helen', be so widely separated physically, ethically, psychologically, from the woman that it signifies? The trope of mistaken identity serves to emphasize further both the theme of recognition, and its ironic duality in this play: Menelaus' recognition of his wife involves recognizing that he fought a protracted and bloody war for the sake of an illusion. Here lies a clue to the relation between this superficially frothy, whimsical romp and its immediate historical context. Against the 'real' backdrop of the Sicilian carnage (see above, p. 105), Euripides' spectators cannot have failed to draw some connection between their own bereavements and the play's implication that all the losses of the Trojan War had been incurred for no reason at all.

## *PHOENICIAN WOMEN* (411–408 BCE, PROBABLY 409)

This grim tragedy presents its audience with several generations of a famous tragic household. The Thebans in *Phoenician Women* had long been famous stage characters from Aeschylus' 'Theban' tetralogy, which had included the enactment of the death of the brothers Eteocles and Polynices in the extant *Seven against Thebes*. Euripides, however, decided to crowd his version of this myth with numerous members of their profoundly dysfunctional Labdacid family; the incestuous spouses Jocasta and Oedipus are still alive, although Oedipus is now mad as well as blind and has already cursed his sons.

In reality Thebes was a bitter and longstanding enemy of Athens, and in tragedy it is often treated as the Athenian democracy's mirror opposite, a closed-in, suffocating, xenophobic tyranny whose royalty specialized in making both love and war within their immediate family. In this play Euripides has gone out of his way to emphasize the close but confused physical relationships in the royal family (Jocasta, we learn, even suckled her motherless nephew Menoeceus (987)). Euripides concentrates attention on his stifling picture of Thebes by choosing to add the perspective of a chorus of visitors from unusually far away, Phoenician devotees of Apollo from the Levant, who are understandably shocked by the goings-on they discover in this incestuous Greek city.

Brothers in conflict are staples of world mythology (see above, p. 204). The Greek imagination produced other fratricides such as the Phocian twins Phanoteus and Crisus, who were already fighting in their mother's womb. But for Euripides it is the political dimension of the fratricide story which is of particular interest. At the climax of the play the messenger reports that as he died Polynices expressed pity for his brother, 'a kinsman who became my enemy, but remained my own dear brother' (1446). The play places under a theatrical microscope the contradictions in group identity created when nation-states are so sundered that members of the same family take up arms against one another. Euripides' contemporaries had in recent decades acquired experience of these contradictions: Thucydides, describing the effects of civil war in Corfu in 427, bleakly describes the breakdown of familial loyalties while partisan politics tore this city and subsequently the rest of the Greek world apart (3. 81–2):

People went to every extreme and beyond it. There were fathers who killed their sons; men were dragged from the temples or butchered on the very altars... family relations were a weaker tie than political allegiance... revenge was more important than self-preservation.

Although its picture of civil war is firmly rooted in contemporary experience, *Phoenician Women*, like most of late Euripidean drama, is also acutely conscious of the literary legacy which lies beneath it. Besides ironic allusions to its Aeschylean prototype, it examines many of the conventions of Homeric epic war poetry. Antigone excitedly views the heroes marshalled beneath the city walls; this scene (a *teichoscopia*) has a famous prototype in the third book of the *Iliad*, and treats war, in epic mode, as a glorious spectacle. In contrast, the most innovative sequence is the story of Creon's son Menoeceus' self-immolation, an episode whose impact lies in its very brevity and absence of sentiment. Menoeceus takes only a few unemotive lines to state his reasons for dying (997–1012). His dreadful leap from the walls is subsequently reported in a handful of words (1090–2), and Jocasta's response is callously epigrammatic: Creon, she says, has suffered a personal calamity which is nevertheless 'fortunate for the city' (1206–7). The Menoeceus episode not only underlines the tension between familial love and patriotic duty: it stresses that most people who die in war do not have the opportunity to deliver elaborate speeches and are not memorialized in poetry. Very few are publicly lamented like the royal princes Eteocles and Polynices.

Jocasta may not be emotionally overwhelmed by the death of her nephew, but this eloquent, ageing queen certainly provides the central focus of the tragedy. Her physical body is the key symbol of the drama, uniting in one form the maternal body which physically bore the family at war, and symbolizing the very earth of Thebes and its body politic which that family is tearing asunder. As mother/wife to Oedipus and sister to Creon she binds two ancient Theban households—from her womb sprang the two warriors whose fraternal violence tears her city apart. The poetry returns repeatedly to the imagery of childbirth and lactation; it also construes the relationship of a citizen to the country 'which bore him' as that of a child to its mother. Jocasta's prologue draws curious attention to the moment she became pregnant with Oedipus, and the later birth of her four children by him (22, 55–7); she is conspicuously physical with Polynices, embracing and caressing him tenderly (303–9); when she appears, too late, on the battlefield, she remembers suckling the boys long ago (1434–5). In killing herself by a stab wound she tears the flesh of her own body as the war has torn the flesh of the Thebans, and she dies entwined with both sons' mutilated corpses (1458–9). At the play's heartbreaking climax the gory body of this incestuous mother, grandmother, sister, and aunt, this ageing symbol of the once proud kingdom of Thebes, returns to the stage to be displayed alongside those of her fratricidal offspring.

While the 'classic' repertoire of Greek tragedies was being consolidated in the fourth century BCE, its texts were vulnerable to interpolation, especially by actors. *Phoenician Women* has been suspected of including many spurious lines. Although it is unlikely that the text we possess is the exact version composed by Euripides, it is important to remember that the play, more or less as we have it, is a written record of performances enjoyed by thousands of ancient spectators. But the modern reader should be aware that many editors and theatrical directors choose to conclude the play at line 1581 of the Greek text. They omit the final scene transmitted in the manuscripts; in this Oedipus prepares to depart for the exile and death enacted in Sophocles' *Oedipus at Colonus*, while Antigone defies Creon's refusal of burial to Polynices in a sequence reminiscent of Sophocles' *Antigone*. Although it is possible to make a good case for the dramatic coherence of this conclusion, many scholars, from antiquity onwards, have doubted its authenticity and deemed that the play packs a more powerful punch if it concludes with the laments for Jocasta.

The tragedies comprising the group of plays in which *Phoenician Women* was performed were *Hypsipyle*, *Phoenician Women*, and *Antiope*, apparently in that order. The fragments of the two lost plays suggest that all three depicted a relationship between a middle-aged mother and her two adult sons. *Hypsipyle* was popular (it was still being performed in Mauretania (Morocco) in the first century CE (Athenaeus, *Deipnosophists* 8.343e–f)). Since it included references to the story of the *Seven against Thebes*, it is possible that there are aspects of *Phoenician Women* which the loss of its companion tragedies have rendered unrecoverable.[21] But most of antiquity enjoyed the tragedy, much as we do today, in the form of an independent artwork.

## *ORESTES* (408 BCE)

This breathtakingly lively drama, an Argive soap opera, was probably the most famous of all Euripides' tragedies in antiquity: it was certainly more quoted than any play by Aeschylus or Sophocles. Virgil takes from it Aeneas' impulse to kill Helen (*Aeneid* 2.567–76), and the only simile in the whole *Aeneid* using the figure of a theatrical actor likens the raving Dido to 'Orestes, the son of Agamemnon' as he is pursued over the stage by visions of his mother's ghost and avenging Furies (4.471–3). *Orestes* was certainly still read and enjoyed in the Byzantine era—the trial scene informs the trial of Jesus Christ in the *Christus Patiens*, an 'imitation' classical tragedy on the theme of Christ's passion, composed as late as the twelfth century CE. After Euripides' revivification in the Renaissance, however, the play was poorly regarded until the last two decades of the twentieth century, largely because it was considered episodic and marred by inappropriate levity.

Yet the postmodern critical climate of recent times has rehabilitated the play's roller-coaster plot and distinctively self-parodying tone, together with the self-conscious—even arch—awareness of the literary legacy which underlies it. It is probably no accident that *Orestes* was first produced exactly fifty years after Aeschylus' *Oresteia*; in providing an entirely original and outrageous version of the events that transpired after Clytemnestra's death but before

Orestes went to Athens—that is, in 'filling in' the time between the plots of Aeschylus' *Libation-Bearers* and *Eumenides*—it may well be consciously written against its seminal Aeschylean forerunner. Yet despite all the frenetic stage activity, the plot is simple: Orestes is condemned to death by the citizens of Argos for murdering his mother, and retaliates by attempting to kill her sister Helen. Argos descends into anarchic civil conflict, whipped up by Orestes' ambitious uncle Menelaus, and a catastrophic ending (entailing Orestes' murder of his cousin Hermione and the burning down of the royal palace) is only averted in the very nick of time by Apollo.

An ancient scholar commented on *Orestes* that, besides Pylades, everyone in this play is bad. (He apparently had not noticed that the plan to murder Helen is Pylades' idea). Part of the play's distinctive tone indeed results from the poor moral calibre of nearly everyone involved, from the vain and silly Helen, to the duplicitous Menelaus, to the horrifically bloodthirsty Electra. Orestes, in particular, has been transformed from Aeschylus' tortured but dignified Argive prince into an anarchic and cocky youth, whose appalling rudeness to his old grandfather Tyndareus both shocks and amuses. Indeed, the vicious argument between Orestes and Tyndareus sets the scene for one of the most important issues in the play: its emphasis on intergenerational conflict.

The age gap theme is connected with the immediate historical background in 408 BCE, when Athens was blighted by the trials of those suspected of involvement in the short-lived oligarchic coup of 411. Reprisals and a mentality of vendetta dominated both public and private life. One of the most important social developments had been the important role which 'clubs' of upper-class young people, had played in working against the democracy; the 'clubs' swore oaths of undying loyalty and engaged in illicit and violent revolutionary activities (see above pp. 140–1). The unholy alliance of the renegade Orestes, Pylades, and Electra, founded on the murder of Clytemnestra and now taking indiscriminate decisions to commit suicide, arson, and further murders, evokes the dangerous new political phenomenon of upper-class youthful conspirators. It is a paradox, therefore, that the play's most touching moments arise out of the obsessive emotional tie binding these three disaffected adolescents. Their scenes are full of embraces and kisses, affirmations of love, saccharine tenderness, and an informality of diction unheard of elsewhere in tragedy. The colloquialism suggests that the chaos articulated in ethical terms extends to the play's genre orientation. Indeed, two alternative denouements are offered, both belonging more to the realm of comedy than to tragedy: the burning down of the palace (reminiscent of the end of Aristophanes' comedy *Clouds*), or a triple wedding. The superficially happy ending is of exactly the type deemed appropriate to *comedy* by Aristotle, the conclusion of *Orestes* being one in which 'those who are the bitterest enemies in the story...go off at the end, having made friends, and nobody kills anybody' (*Poetics* ch. 13, 1453a 35–9). Even one ancient scholar notes that the denouement is 'more of the comic type'. The play itself is therefore locked in a battle between tragedy and comedy; it not only fragments the Athenian democratic charter-myth enacted in Aeschylus' *Oresteia*; it also threatens to dissolve the very genre, tragedy, which had always been the most important example of Athenian democratic cultural prestige. It seems entirely appropriate that during the original production of *Orestes* the entire theatre cracked up in laughter, because Hegelochus, the actor playing Orestes, mispronounced the noun 'calmness', saying, with horrific bathos, the word for 'weasel' instead (so says the scholiast on line 279).

Numerous Euripidean plays end with the sudden intervention of a divinity, but *Orestes* is the only play where the conflict requiring resolution is patently political. Orestes is in conflict not only with Menelaus, but with the democratic citizens of Argos, who have voted that he must suffer capital punishment for the murder of his mother. Apollo suddenly appears to resolve the situation: he will, he claims, set the situation right as regards the Argive citizenry, and Orestes will rule over them happily henceforward. The play thus offers a fantastic ideological settlement, which enforces harmony between the criminalized young royals and the Argive democracy—a political compromise which the events of the last few years at Athens had shown was, in reality, quite impossible. Real life cannot be controlled like a literary narrative. While social and factional divisions of the type that afflicted Athens in 408 BCE still existed, the class conflicts could never evanesce, as they do in Euripides' mythical Argos, at the wave of an omnipotent authorial wand.

Many great dramas have been born out of moments of political conflict, but thereafter transcend the historical circumstances of their original composition to become 'Classics' in the repertoire. It is possible to enjoy Euripides' Argive soap opera, in the way that most of later antiquity did, as an exceptionally fine piece of theatrical writing and an exceptionally funny tragedy. But the levity of tone and happy outcome never quite manage to obscure its bleak pessimism about human nature, a pessimism directly related to the dark days when it was first written and acted.

## *IPHIGENIA IN AULIS* (405 BCE)

From pious Abraham and his son Isaac to the tale of Jephthah's sacrifice of his only daughter in the *Book of Judges*, the motif of the child sacrificed to please divinity has taken various forms in Judaeo-Hellenic tradition. *Iphigenia in Aulis* offers the most detailed and developed literary version of this archetypal myth, but also the one which most calls into question the motives and integrity of the sacrificing parent. One of the most shocking moments in Greek tragedy occurs at the point in *Iphigenia in Aulis* where Clytemnestra, the heroine's mother, is desperately trying to prevent her husband Agamemnon from carrying out the intended sacrifice. Clytemnestra opens her appeal with the information that Iphigenia is not the first child of hers whom Agamemnon has killed. Clytemnestra says that she married him against her will, after he murdered her first husband, Tantalus, and tore her baby from her breast to dash him to the ground (1151–2).

In no other tragedian does this information appear: the effect of the nasty little secret which proves that Agamemnon has always been capable of slaughtering innocents in his own self-interest is therefore quite devastating. Euripides has turned a tragedy about Agamemnon's famous dilemma over Iphigenia into one incident in the life of a self-serving warlord guilty of previous atrocity. But Clytemnestra, in the past and currently a blameless victim of her husband's callousness, goes on in the same speech to imply that if Agamemnon kills Iphigenia he may himself be killed on his return from Troy—that is, she threatens Agamemnon with the plot of

Aeschylus' *Agamemnon*. Even a virtuous and forgiving woman, it is suggested, can be transformed into a vindictive murderess under sufficient pressure. Indeed, almost all the characters are portrayed as strangely wedded to the past, from which they provide narratives to justify a present attitude or action or decision. Yet they also seem curiously conscious of their futures, or at least of the characters they later became according to the mythical and dramatic tradition—an 'intertextual' feature which lends this tragedy a distinctively 'modern' tone. The inclusion in the drama of the tiny baby Orestes, it could be argued, forces the audience to 'remember the future' even as it recalls these characters' past.

Clytemnestra's future is suggested by her characterization in earlier tragedy, but for the male characters the text against which *Iphigenia in Aulis* works is, above all, the *Iliad*. The youthful and naive Achilles of Euripides, for example, is given a trial run at conceiving a great grudge against Agamemnon, a precursor of the 'wrath' that determines the plot of the *Iliad*, and the Argive king himself is shown vulnerable to the moral weakness and inconsistency which in epic mars his generalship at Troy. The psychological depth with which Euripides treats the familiar story thus makes *Iphigenia at Aulis* one of his most introspective and painful plays.

Euripides was fascinated by the factors which condition the moral choices made by individuals, and in his tragedies repeatedly explored the dangers inherent in precipitate and unconsidered decision-making. In *Hippolytus*, for example, the hero's death is caused by his father's hasty decision to curse and exile him without proper deliberation or due legal process. Athenian history provides several examples of similar decisions, especially in time of war (see above, pp. 67–8): a notorious incident was the Athenian assembly's furious decision in 427 BCE summarily to execute all the male inhabitants of Mytilene, a decision they revoked the very next day after a 'sudden change of heart' (Thucydides 3.36). *Iphigenia in Aulis* uses myth to stage an occasion during a military crisis when several members of the same family took and rescinded hasty decisions about the life of an innocent girl.

Aristotle notoriously complained about the 'inconsistent' characterization of Iphigenia, whose understandable rejection of the plan to sacrifice her is subsequently replaced by a passionate death-wish (*Poetics* ch. 15, 1454a 26). It has occasionally been proposed, in defence of Euripides, that Iphigenia's predicament has virtually driven her mad.[22] But Iphigenia is only imitating the male characters in her own play. Agamemnon has summoned her to be sacrificed, changes his mind at the beginning of the play, but is incapable of sticking to the better moral course when Iphigenia's arrival forces his hand: fear of his own army's reaction prevents him from rescinding the authorization of the sacrifice. Menelaus changes his mind no less dramatically, emotionally rejecting his earlier 'rational' view that Iphigenia's sacrifice was an unfortunate necessity when he sees his brother's distress. Even Achilles, who longs to prove his heroic stature and defend Iphigenia against the army, allows her to persuade him that she really wants to die. Is it so surprising that a young girl should be swayed by the militaristic ideology of the community in which she finds herself, when the strongest warriors in Greece are incapable of real moral reflection or maintaining a consistent moral position?

One school of interpretation used to insist that the tragedy offered an uncomplicated patriotic celebration of a Greek heroine's selfless heroism in offering herself for immolation on the altar of her country. It is of course true that women were regarded as inferior to men in Euripides' day, and that war against the barbarians of Asia would not have been seen in itself as morally problematic. There might well have been a warm glow in the theatre when Iphigenia declares that she is happy to die because 'it is right that the Greeks should rule barbarians, mother, and not barbarians Greeks' (1400–1). Yet the overall impression made by the play is of a community in absolute moral crisis. The prospect of Iphigenia's death is unbearably moving, but it is inseparable from the tragedy's portrayal of the volatile, unreflective Greek mob, manipulated by the sinister, unseen Odysseus, and above all the hypocrisy, self-justification, self-delusion, and cynical duplicity (underscored by the motif of the fraudulent letter) practised by its leaders. Iphigenia's real problem is how to die with honour in an ignoble cause for the sake of unworthy men.

Euripides did not write the whole text of the play as it stands. It may be relevant that it was produced posthumously by his son, who possibly completed or rewrote it. There is a question mark over Agamemnon's 'delayed' prologue, positioned after the opening dialogue; there are also several spurious passages scattered throughout the play, probably interpolated by actors after the fifth century. But by far the most significant interpolation begins with the appearance of the second messenger, or at least at that part of his speech which reports the disappearance of Iphigenia, whisked away by Artemis, and the substitution of a deer. This comforting alternative ending to the tragedy—perhaps inserted by an ancient theatrical company familiar with *Iphigenia among the Taurians*—radically affects both its theological meaning and its emotional impact. Modern directors often prefer, quite legitimately, to conclude performances with Iphigenia's unrelievedly tragic walk to her death at line 1531.

## *BACCHAE* (405 BCE)

Although a popular play in antiquity (it was a favourite of the emperor Nero), the modern admiration for *Bacchae* is a relatively recent development. In the late eighteenth century a critic of Greek tragedy could still hardly contain his revulsion, warning his readers that 'the refined delicacy of modern manners will justly revolt against this inhuman spectacle of dramatick barbarity'.[23] But the great upsurge of interest in Dionysus and the connections between ancient Greek ritual and myth which developed at the end of the nineteenth century drew scholars magnetically to this extraordinary play, and it is now rightly considered one of Euripides' supreme masterpieces.

It has long been debated how far, if at all, the savage rites in *Bacchae* reflect the 'real' maenadism known to have been practised in antiquity. Yet it is certainly legitimate to see the play as staging a narrative symbiotically connected with the rituals performed in honour of Dionysus, as for Christians the narrative of the Last Supper is inextricably bound up with the ritual breaking of bread and drinking of wine, ceremonial substitutes for the flesh and blood of the sacrificed body of Jesus. The *Bacchae* includes many elements suggestive of the experience of those participating in Dionysus' mysterious cult: stories relating the birth of the god, odes describing the altered state of consciousness—the sublime state of *ekstasis* or ecstasy ('standing outside of oneself')—which his cult offers,

FIG. 6.7. Drawing of a sarcophagus relief in Rome showing Pentheus being torn apart by maenads, reproduced courtesy of the Trustees of the British Museum.

messenger speeches recounting the Bacchants' collective worship on the mountain of Cithaeron with their ivy-twined branches and dappled fawnskins, the ritual sacrifice of a man whose flesh is torn apart (see Fig. 6.7), and miracles and epiphanies through which the god manifests himself to mortals.

The cult of Dionysus was regarded by the Greeks as an import from barbarian lands, and the play enacts an ancient myth narrating its problematic arrival at the mainland Greek city of Thebes. The story is one of numerous mythical illustrations of an archaic Greek imperative: those who doubt the power of the gods must be disabused of their disbelief. The royal house of Thebes must be punished because it questioned the divine paternity of Dionysus, its most illustrious offspring. Yet the work is much more than an exemplum of divine prerogative expressed through the consecutive motifs of resistance, punishment, and acceptance. Dionysus is not only the play's protagonist: his drama is a study of his own elusive personality and of his devastating power.

Most Greek tragedy did not treat myths directly involving Dionysus. His connection with the theatre expresses his function as god of altered consciousness, of appearance, and of illusion. In one of the most powerful moments in world theatre Dionysus, himself disguised as a mortal, puts the finishing touches to the Bacchanal disguise of Pentheus, his mortal cousin and adversary, and sends him to the mountains to be dismembered by the women of the city he is supposed to rule. Pentheus is in a Dionysiac trance; he can no longer distinguish between reality and illusion; he is taking on the identity of someone other than himself. This scene self-consciously forces the onlooker into contemplating the experience of watching any performance which entails the impersonation of one being by another. Drama demands that performer and spectator collude in a suspension of the empirically 'real' world, and an involvement in a world that is not really there. Pentheus dresses in a maenad's attire, just as each chorus-member had adopted the costume and mask of a maenad before actuality was forsaken and the drama began; in the original production this also required assuming the identity of the opposite sex, for all the performers would have been male. *Bacchae*, therefore, can be seen as a meditation on the very experience of theatre; a mimetic enactment of the journey into and out of illusion, the journey over which Dionysus presides in the mysterious fictive worlds he conjures up in his theatre.

The Greek mind was trained to think in polarities; to categorize, distinguish, and oppose. If the divine personality of Dionysus can be reduced to any one principle, it is the demonstration that conventional logic is an inadequate tool with which to apprehend the universe as a whole. Dionysus confounds reason, defies categorization, dissolves polarities, and inverts hierarchies. He is a youthful god and yet as an immortal, respected by the elderly Cadmus and Tiresias, cannot be defined as young. He is a male god and yet in his perceived effeminacy and special relationship with women cannot be defined as conventionally masculine. Conceived in Thebes yet worshipped abroad he is neither wholly Greek nor barbarian. He conflates the tragic and comic views of life, as the patron deity of both genres. Similarly, his worship can bring both transcendental serenity and repulsive violence: the slaughter of Pentheus, followed by his mother's invitation to the Bacchants to share in the feast, entails three crimes considered by the ancient Greeks to be among the most abominable: human sacrifice, filicide, and cannibalism. Dionysus may be worshipped illicitly on the wild hillsides of Thebes, but he is also the recipient in Euripides' Athens of a respectable cult at the heart of the city-state: as such, he cannot be defined as the representative of nature in opposition to culture and civilization. And in using illusion to reveal the truth he confounds all conventional distinctions between fiction and fact, madness and sanity, falsehood and reality. In *Bacchae* Dionysus causes the imprisoned to be liberated, the 'rational' to become demented, humans to behave like animals, men to dress as women, women to act like men, and an earthquake physically to force the untamed natural world into the 'safe', controlled, interior world of the household and the city.

Until the last minute, when the deluded Agave appears, Thebes is represented exclusively by males; the beliefs of the 'other', dangerous culture which the disguised Dionysus threatens to introduce have been articulated in the mouths of women. But with the arrival of Agave and her gradual return to 'normal' consciousness, even this binary, gendered opposition is exploded. Here is a Theban woman who once doubted the existence of the god, but who comes to know as she emerges from her Dionysiac mania that in the severed head of her son she bears the physical proof that Dionysus is a living reality in Thebes. The revealed truth is that the denied god, the outsider, the alien, has belonged inside all along.

The transhistorical appeal of *Bacchae* is partly due to its insusceptibility—appropriate for a Dionysiac text—to any single interpretation. Its portrayal of the unrestrained emotionalism which can lead human crowds into inhuman conduct spoke loud to scholars at the time of the rise of fascism;[24] its portrayal of the conflict within Pentheus' psyche has also fascinated psychoanalytical critics. But ultimately the tragedy frustrates all attempts to impose upon it a unitary central 'meaning'. It neither endorses nor repudiates the cult whose arrival in Thebes it narrates. It never did prescribe for its audience a cognitive programme by which to understand an inexplicable universe. It simply enacts one occasion on which the denial, repression, and exclusion of difference—psychological, ethnic, and religious—led to utter catastrophe.

## *RHESUS* (DATE UNKNOWN)

This colourful and unusual tragedy has been direly neglected for the simple reason that it is probably not by Euripides himself, although it has been preserved in the manuscripts of his works, and he did almost certainly write a (lost) play entitled *Rhesus*. But the emotional, intellectual, aesthetic, and theatrical impact made by the play is so unlike that produced even by Euripides' least distinguished tragedies that even in the ancient world some literary critics claimed that it was spurious. The modern reader will be struck in particular by the un-Euripidean lack of interest in women, and absence of the intellectual bravura which marks every one of his surviving plays.

In the 1960s one respectable scholar published a spirited defence of the Euripidean authorship of *Rhesus*, arguing that its distinctive qualities are signs that it dated from early in his career.[25] But most experts now agree that the ancient written record somehow substituted the text we possess for Euripides' tragedy of the same name. There are several possible explanations for such a substitution: Euripides was widely imitated by other tragedians, and others bore his name, including his own youngest son, who was responsible for the posthumous production of *Iphigenia in Aulis* and *Bacchae*. The prevalent scholarly view holds therefore that *Rhesus* is the work of an unknown playwright active in the fourth century BCE (when there was a revival of interest in dramatizing themes from the *Iliad*), and as such it is a unique document, since all the other surviving Greek tragedies date from the century before.

The activities in the military camps of the Trojan war had provided the Greek tragedians with the plots of numerous tragedies, such as Sophocles' *Ajax*, inaugurating a western theatrical tradition still evident in the camp scenes of Shakespeare's *Troilus and Cressida*. *Rhesus* dramatizes the exciting and bloody story of Rhesus and Dolon, familiar to the Athenian audience from the tenth book of the *Iliad* (which just so happens to be the book of that epic whose own authenticity is most suspected). It is the only Greek tragedy whose entire action takes place at night. Its setting is military—the temporary sleeping quarters of the Trojan army, between their city and the camp of the Greeks. The tragic action consists of the arrival of the Trojans' great ally, King Rhesus of Thrace, and his murder by two Greeks, Odysseus and Diomedes, who have been sent on a secret mission into the enemy camp. They also kill Dolon, the

Trojan spy sent to discover the plans being made by the Greeks. The occasion is the night after Hector has nearly succeeded in setting fire to their ships and routing them. Hector seems invincible, and the Greek campaign doomed to failure. But by the end of the play the situation has been reversed: although Hector concludes the piece by resolutely ordering the army to prepare for action, for the dawn brings him confidence that the Trojans can fire the enemy ships, and thus 'herald the day of freedom for the Trojans', his audience, who knew the *Iliad* intimately, will have heard the tragic irony in his totally misguided optimism.

The ethical interest centres on the virtues and vices of military leaders, by providing a gallery of fighting men with different approaches to the war. Hector is a brilliant warrior, but hasty and impetuous, just as he is in Homer. Aeneas' presence in the play is largely to point a contrast with his imprudent leader, to urge caution and to suggest that espionage should precede any major military decision (86–130); further contrasts are drawn between Hector and his sexually obsessed brother Paris, and between Hector and his late-arriving ally Rhesus of Thrace. Rhesus' reputation seems to rest on nothing but a frontier war, and his bombastic boasts and ambitions know no limits: he is a prototype of the *miles gloriosus*, or braggart soldier, of the incipient genre of New Comedy. Rhesus is completely incompetent: he neglects even the most elementary precautions, letting his contingent fall asleep without posting a single sentry to keep watch, or even laying out arms and chariot gear in preparation for combat. It is probably relevant that Athenian history of the late fifth and early fourth centuries includes some extremely hostile relationships with the kings of Thrace, who were believed to be unreliable and disloyal military allies; the figure of Rhesus as portrayed in this tragedy may well have been consonant with the audience's real historical views of his countrymen. The play certainly endorses the notion that Greeks were better warriors: both the Trojan and Thracian fighters are contrasted with the cunning Greek Odysseus and his companion Diomedes, who lay their plans carefully, secure Athena's goodwill, and complete their assignment with ruthless efficiency.

Yet despite the tragedy's emphasis on its aristocratic heroes, it is a curiously democratic rewriting of the epic story. Two of the minor characters—the shepherd and Rhesus' charioteer—are vocal and independent-minded men, whose scenes greatly enliven the effect of the drama. Moreover, tragedy's convention of the chorus allows a much fuller development of the lower-class perspective on the action than the aristocratic focus of epic ever could. The chorus of sentries provide an interesting commentary on the activities of their superiors, and offer an unusual amount of interventionist advice, criticism, and support.

*Rhesus* certainly does not deserve the relegation it has suffered to the margins of literary history. Perhaps more than any play by Euripides, it needs to be read as a theatrical script for enactment by expert actors. It is not particularly great literature (although some passages, particularly in the choral odes, are not inconsiderable poetry). But it is likely to have been highly successful theatre. The nocturnal, masculine, military atmosphere, with its passwords and watch fires, disguises, scouts and reconnaissance, will have enthralled the male spectators for whom it was designed, many of whom will have seen military action themselves. The play also offered them a series of flamboyant visual effects. The play opens on a lively note, with the sleeping Hector being wakened by the noisy entrance of the chorus of Trojan sentries, bursting with the news that the enemy have convened a meeting. Rhesus' arrival, with jangling bells on his shield, golden armour, twin spears, and Thracian entourage, must have provided a splendid spectacle. At the heart of the play the goddess Athena appears on stage to offer help to the Greek spies Odysseus and Diomedes, and then, in a theatrical stunt without equivalent in extant tragedy, pretends to be Aphrodite in order to divert Paris' attention: Dionysus in *Bacchae* also assumes a disguise, but not that of another immortal.

Yet the theatrical climax of the play is postponed until the end, with the surprise appearance of a second female immortal, rising above the all-male plane of the human action. Rhesus' corpse is carried on in the arms of his mother, a Muse borne aloft in the theatrical machine. The Muse, an epic rather than a tragic figure, provides a link with the Homeric archetype, reminding the audience of the poem from which the tragedy takes its inspiration, and also underlining the imminence of the Trojan defeat. In a musical moment without parallel in the other plays, this divine embodiment of song sings a solo lyric lament over her son's body, announces that she will consecrate him at a mysterious oracle of Dionysus in Thrace, and predicts the deaths of both Hector and Achilles. The play, which deftly telescopes within a single night of military subterfuge the story of the whole Trojan War, constitutes a fast-paced, action-packed, theatrical *Iliad* in miniature.

# 7
# Sophoclean Drama

In this book the detailed discussion of Sophocles follows that of Euripides, which is unusual. The conventional arrangement is to place Sophocles between Aeschylus and Euripides. But the reason for this is rather suspect; Sophocles has often been perceived as somehow representing an ideal 'mean' between the grandeur of Aeschylus and the idiomatic directness of Euripides. This idea can be traced back to the opposition established between Aeschylus and Euripides in Aristophanes' *Frogs*. But although Sophocles seems to have been selected as a drama festival competitor at an earlier age than Euripides, perhaps as early as 468 BCE when he was still in his twenties, they were approximate coevals, with Euripides dying just a year or two before his rival. I have chosen, therefore, to place Sophocles last in the discussion, taking my cue from the poet Samuel Taylor Coleridge, who found in his youth that Aeschylus was congenial reading, turned to Euripides in his prime, but preferred Sophocles in his advanced years.[1] It is always possible that altering the traditional order of scrutiny may cast fresh light on the relationship between their works. Sophocles was reacting quite as much to Euripidean advances in tragedy as *vice versa*.

Sophocles, the son of a prosperous arms-factory owner, was unlike the other two famous tragedians in that he had a political career as well as an artistic one. He held at least three significant public offices at Athens, and seems to have been on excellent terms with Pericles. He served as a treasurer in 443/2 BCE, and subsequently as a general in the Samian War which began in 441/0; an ancient tradition recorded that he was elected to this position by the Athenians on account of their high opinion of his *Antigone*.[2] This may be justification for dating the play to around 442/1 BCE, or it may just reveal that in antiquity people drew connections, plausibly enough, between Sophocles' political experience and the political focus of this tragedy. In any case, he was well enough respected to be invited to serve as a magistrate in 413 BCE after the disastrous Athenian expedition to Sicily.

It is fairly certain that Sophocles dedicated a cult of the healing god Asclepius in his own home, but the claims made by the ancient biographical tradition about his personal piety are extravagant. He is supposed to have been specially loved by the gods, to have been a favourite of Heracles, and to have held a priesthood himself. This reputation has resulted in many scholarly attempts to discover evidence of special religious conviction in his plays. But the only generalization that can safely be made applies to all Greek tragedy, even to Euripides' more outrageous plays: divine will is always, eventually, done.

The ancient *Life of Sophocles* contains numerous other pieces of information which it would be delightful to be able to believe. Sophocles is alleged to have led with his lyre the Athenian chorus which celebrated the victory over the Persians at the battle of Salamis, to have acted leading roles in his own plays, and to have died either while reciting a long sentence from *Antigone* without pause for breath, or by choking on a grape (the fruit of Dionysus, the god of drama). These anecdotes say a good deal about how Sophocles was seen in later antiquity, but are otherwise sadly unreliable.

It is certain, however, that he composed about 120 dramas, of which only seven tragedies and a substantial chunk of a satyr drama (discussed below p. 339) survive. Something is known, however, about some of his other productions.[3] In the plays which survive, mythical parallels are often drawn with other stories we know he was sufficiently interested in to dramatize, for example the famous story of Procne, who was turned into a nightingale. He also wrote a *Niobe*, about a tragically bereaved mother, with whose misery both Antigone and Electra identify (*Antigone* 825–6, *Electra* 149–51). He was victorious in the dramatic competitions about twenty times (an unparalleled achievement), for example with *Philoctetes* in 409 BCE, and apparently never came last. He is thought to have won in the year he produced *Antigone*, but the group of plays that included *Oedipus Tyrannus*, astonishingly, won only second place.

The internal order in which Sophocles' plays are presented in this volume is unusual, but driven by my frustration with the traditional conferment on ancient plays of dates for which there is no reliable evidence. The only firmly dated plays by Sophocles are *Philoctetes* (409 BCE) and *Oedipus at Colonus* (401). The reasons why *Ajax* and *Women of Trachis* have been by custom allocated early dates are particularly naïve and unsatisfactory, since they assume that Sophocles could only have written plays with a certain fierce grandeur as a (relatively) young man. By separating *Oedipus Tyrannus* and *Oedipus at Colonus* as widely as the discussion does in this book, the latterday myth of a Theban 'cycle' or even 'trilogy' is exploded. The three surviving plays by Sophocles focusing on the family of Oedipus were not designed to be performed together sequentially. They seem to have been conceived independently, were probably composed over a period spanning decades, and were first produced separately, in groups with other, unknown tragedies. *Oedipus Tyrannus* and *Antigone* are, however, at least basically consistent with one another, whereas *Oedipus at Colonus* contains one important factual difference. *Antigone* assumes that Oedipus died ingloriously at Thebes, whereas *Oedipus at Colonus* brings him to a beatific death at Athens.

Sophocles was extremely popular within his own lifetime, and his place in the gallery of the greatest poets of all time was canonized by the generation immediately succeeding him. Even Plato, who was to banish drama from his ideal Republic, was gentle in his assessment of Sophocles (*Republic* 1.329b–c), and in his *Poetics* Aristotle seems to indicate that his own view was that Sophoclean drama had brought the genre of tragedy to its consummate achievements, especially in *Oedipus Tyrannus*. The general consensus of Sophocles' contemporaries and successors was that he was a man blessed with a virtuous disposition and, unlike his characters, a remarkably trouble-free life. A charming epitaph was heard in a fragmentary comedy entitled *The Muses*, by a dramatist named Phrynichus: 'lucky Sophocles lived a long life, made many beautiful tragedies, and, in the end, died without suffering anything evil' (fr. 32 *PCG*). Sophoclean poetry has been admired by countless literary figures, including John Milton, Percy Shelley (who died with a copy of Sophocles in his pocket), Virginia Woolf, W. B. Yeats, Ezra Pound, and Seamus Heaney.

## *OEDIPUS TYRANNUS* (DATE UNKNOWN)

When the citizens of Athens gathered with guests and allies in their open-air theatre to watch the premiere of Sophocles' *Oedipus* at a drama competition, they knew that its author was a public-minded individual. He won distinction serving the democracy in the offices of both Treasurer and General. They knew that his plays usually drew on his experiences of leadership by exploring how rulers react to civic emergencies. Spectators will not have been surprised that a central theme in *Oedipus* is the tendency of leaders, once in power, to turn into friendless autocrats who throw their weight about. But nobody can have suspected that the play was destined to become one of the most important in cultural history.

Perhaps it made them feel too uncomfortable. In a moment of spine-tingling perspicacity, Oedipus' wife and mother Jocasta tells him that sleeping with one's own mother is 'Many a man's mad dream'. An ancient dream interpreter, Artemidorus, confirms this by recording many variations on the mother–son incest theme in the dreams told to him by his real-life clients (*Interpretation of Dreams* 1.79). Incest across the generations, real rather than mythical, sometimes hits the modern headlines. Usually it is an abusive father asserting sexual power over his daughter. There is little data on mother–son incest in any world culture. But when siblings are separated at birth it is known that they can feel strong sexual desire for each other in later life; is the attraction between Jocasta and Oedipus, separated mother and son, disturbing because it reflects a real possibility?

Yet the psychological discomfort prompted by the play in antiquity was by no means confined to the visceral reaction caused by its depiction of two people breaking a fundamental sexual taboo. Oedipus' killing of his father Laius prompted an equally physical reaction, although this is more difficult for us to understand. Killers, above all kin-killers, were felt to be materially polluted. They could transmit that pollution—the Greek word is *miasma*—through physical contact with others. Most ancient spectators of both *Oedipus* plays would have felt that this parricidal man was dangerous to be near. In Athens, only a roofless court could be used for murder trials, in an open-air space not unlike the theatre. Oedipus' own sense of his pollution goes a long way to explaining why he blinds himself, since the Greeks felt that intimate contact took place between one person and another through the eyes. The Thebans' reaction explains why he ends the play driven into exile. The audience's sense of his pollution will certainly have added tension as well as pathos to his final embrace with his daughters.

*Miasma* is an organic phenomenon unaffected by legal or moral niceties. Oedipus' pollution has infected all Thebes with a contagious disease. Oedipus was polluted regardless of whether or not he had known what he was doing when he broke those taboos. Nobody ever uses the defence in *Oedipus* that he had no *intention* to commit kin-murder or incest. That is not to say that the question of his moral culpability is not raised, however. Oedipus' character is put under the harshest of scrutiny, as his past actions are repeatedly investigated, and the action unfolds in a way that spotlights his reactions to stress in the current crisis.

What emerges is a picture of an unlucky man who is, as Aristotle commented in chapter 13 of his *Poetics*, the perfect material for a tragic hero. This is because he is neither particularly good nor particularly bad, rather like most of the people in any audience, who therefore identify emotionally with him. Just one incident in his past, the confrontation with the strangers at the triple crossroad on the route between Delphi and Thebes, raises a serious question mark over his basic decency. The question asked is this: if insulted and assaulted by someone travelling in the opposite direction from you, is killing him the mark of a feisty Bronze Age hero defending his dignity, or of a dangerously violent, even psychotic individual? Sophocles is careful to make Oedipus' memories of this incident differ from the account given by others—just how many men did he kill? Here the play turns its spectators into something like readers of a detective novel or indeed jurors at a murder trial, comparing evidence and assessing the reliability of witnesses. It also makes them wonder whether Oedipus, beaten around the head with a horse-whip, was using justifiable self-defence.

This question is fundamental to our interpretation of the metaphysics as well as the ethics of the tragedy. Just what is the relationship between a man's fate and his character, and does he actually have any free will at all? Oedipus was doomed *before he was born*. Some interpreters have argued that in this hero Sophocles confronts his audience with the absolute injustice (from the human perspective) of divine predetermination, and with the feebleness of human cognition and agency in the context of the forces that run the universe. Other critics, however, stress the unappealing aspects of his character—his temper, his paranoia, his threatening behaviour towards Tiresias, Creon, and the Theban shepherd, and his supreme arrogance in assuming that his intellect can surmount any obstacles in his, or his people's, path. According to this view, Oedipus is somehow culpable after the event: his destiny is justified by his abrasive personality and his increasingly tyrannical conduct.

Yet neither interpretation does justice to the delicacy of Sophocles' negotiations between responsibility, action, and character. Although the Greeks had only an emergent sense of an autonomous individual will, and did not share the Christian conceptual equipment with which, for example, Renaissance audiences assessed their theatrical heroes, in Sophocles' tragic world it is entirely plausible that a tragic figure only suffers because of the type of person that he or she is. If Oedipus had not been a youth with self-confidence and initiative, he would never have wondered who he really was and left Corinth in the first place. If he had not been proud and courageous, he would not have retaliated against the Thebans on the road to Delphi. If he did not have a penetrating intellect and a sense of collective responsibility, he would not have solved the riddle of the supernatural Sphinx, thus earning election to the throne and the hand of the Queen. It is the same public spirit, combined with his old, relentless curiosity, that drives him on almost obsessively to solve the riddle of the murder of Laius, and thereafter to discover his own identity. The nuances in Sophocles' characterization thus lend credibility even to the most extraordinary coincidences in the story. Oedipus, who had every reason to feel confident in his powers of understanding, has entirely failed to understand that he has been under Apollo's control all along. Their relationship is perfectly expressed at the climax of the action, when the chorus asks how he could bear to blind himself. He replies that it may have been Apollo's will, but it was still entirely the act of his own human hand (1329–32):

> Apollo, my friends—this deed was Apollo's.
> He brought about my cruel, insufferable suffering.
> But no-one else's hand struck out these eyes except for mine.

Oedipus has recognized not only that he has committed parricide and incest, but that he is the trueborn scion of the ancient royal bloodline of Thebes, and therefore the hereditary monarch (in Greek the *basileus*) of that city. Until this moment he has believed, rather, that he is a leader who had been brought to power on a wave of popular support, which is the primary meaning of the Greek *turannos*, although such leaders were believed to be particularly prone to developing 'tyrannical' tendencies in our modern sense of the term. This is the reason why the Latin version of the title in common use, *Oedipus Rex*, is so misleading: *Oedipus Tyrannus* at least retains something of the fine political distinctions drawn in the play.

## *ANTIGONE* (POSSIBLY 442 BCE)

Sophocles probably wrote *Antigone* earlier than his other two plays about the Theban royal family, *Oedipus Tyrannus* and *Oedipus at Colonus*. Yet the action of the play, in which Antigone is now grown to young womanhood, actually occurs several years 'later' in mythical time. The setting in Thebes is highly significant: in reality this city was anti-democratic and hostile to Athens, which was the democratic home of Sophocles, his audience, and most of his performers. The patriotic Athenian dramatists consequently often displaced enactments of political strife, tyranny, and domestic chaos onto legendary Thebes rather than legendary Athens.[4] *Antigone* opens at a moment of political crisis caused directly by internecine warfare: Oedipus and Jocasta, now deceased, had four children. The two sons quarrelled over the kingship of Thebes, and Polynices was driven into exile: Eteocles was left ruling Thebes, apparently with the support of his maternal uncle Creon. Polynices formed an alliance with the king of the important Peloponnesian city of Argos, and raised a force with which to attack his own city under the famous seven warriors who led the alliance. The assault failed, but in the battle Polynices and Eteocles killed one another.

The tragedy begins at dawn after the Theban victory; Creon, as the nearest surviving male relative of the two sons of Oedipus, has (rather hastily) assumed power. The play enacts the catastrophic events which take place on his first day in office. It thus ironically demonstrates the truth of his own inaugural speech, in which he declares that no man's character can be truly known until he has been tested by the experience of government and legislation. For the very first law that Creon passes—that the body of Polynices is to be refused burial—is in direct contravention of the 'unwritten law' (see above pp. 159, 179–80) protecting the rights of the dead. Mortals who in tragedy transgress these immortal edicts invariably come to see the error of their ways. It may be pragmatically expedient for Creon in *Antigone* to take measures to deter possible traitors to the city, but the play reveals that human reasoning faculties are insufficient means for understanding an inexplicable universe. Antigone buries Polynices, is arrested, and sentenced to death by being walled up in a cave. Her fiancé—Creon's son Haemon—pleads with his father to change his mind. But the sentence is not revoked until after a visit by the prophet Tiresias, who assures him that Polynices should be buried and Antigone spared. Creon changes his mind, but just too late. Antigone hangs herself, Haemon stabs himself, and so does his mother Eurydice. Creon loses everyone that matters to him and ends the play howling in despair.

It has sometimes been argued that Creon's law was defensible given the divisive nature of the civil war which had disturbed Thebes, and the urgency of the need for a decisive hand on the rudder of government. Funerals, as politicians everywhere know, are dangerous occasions. It is also possible to see Creon's failure to achieve the heroic stature achieved by Antigone as a result of his unsteadiness in the face of opposition. For he is, above all, erratic: having decided that Ismene is as guilty as Antigone, he then changes his mind about her. He vacillates wildly about Antigone's fate: the original edict decreed death by stoning, but at one point he is going to have her executed publicly; finally he opts for entombing her alive, but eventually revokes even this decision. He is the consummate example of the type of tragic character Aristotle described as 'consistently inconsistent' (*Poetics*, ch. 15, 1454a 27–8). Despite his recognition of his own error and his contrition, beside the unrelenting Antigone and Haemon—let alone Oedipus—he looks like a moral invertebrate.

Thinkers contemporary with Sophocles were involved in the development of a new political theory to match the needs of the new Athenian democracy, and thought hard about the mechanisms that allow humans to live together, achieve a consensus (*homonoia*), and cooperate. Protagoras, for example, argued that the ability to live together in a community required the virtues of self-control and sense of justice (Plato, *Protagoras* 322e) in which Creon is so palpably lacking. His edict was passed autocratically, without listening to others or achieving *homonoia*, and his increasingly domineering attitude towards the views of others renders the outcome of his reign, and of the play, inevitable. What makes *Antigone* so astonishing, especially when it is remembered that it was written by a male in an ancient patriarchy, is that Creon is tested by the initiative of a young female relative. This completely incenses him. Her goal is not political influence: she is only obeying the divine law which laid on the senior surviving member of all families the solemn duty of performing funeral rites for their kin. Antigone is mysterious, arrogant, deliberately inflammatory, and inflexible as Creon is erratic. But she is nonetheless shown by the play to have been absolutely right.

There is something airless and oppressive about the provincial town portrayed in Sophocles' *Antigone*. It is also the only Greek tragedy (except for Aeschylus' historical *Persians*) in which the entire cast and chorus were all born and have always lived side-by-side in the same inland community. It is as if the incest which created Antigone, Ismene, and their two dead brothers, Eteocles and Polynices—the sexual union of Oedipus with his mother—has psychologically infected the entire population. Everybody knows everyone else, and every detail of their domestic lives; there is no more escape from the public gaze than from the anger of the gods, outraged by Creon's profane refusal to give the corpse of the 'traitor' Polynices burial. Their fury is expressed in the disgusting stench of the putrefying fragments of his flesh which birds of prey have now left scattered on the hearths and altars of the city. Thebes is an inward-looking place where the boundaries of simple moral decency—Antigone's 'unwritten laws'—are repeatedly transgressed, just as its city walls have been breached by military invasion.

Against this stifling background, the imagery of *Antigone* implies other, more hopeful, possibilities. Creon's mercantile and technological metaphors are opposed to the beauty of untamed nature associated with his young opponent. Antigone is likened to a fresh northern wind, and Haemon speaks of wild storms, sea waves, and trees in flooding rivers. The young people in this play, given a chance, could have allowed fresh air to blow through the streets, hearts, and minds of their long-suffering city and its people. What prevents them is not just their new overlord's intolerance of disagreement, but the oppressive legacy of their own family history. Creon will not listen to Antigone partly because she is young and female, but partly because she is his niece, engaged to his son, and he has long regarded her as troublesome. But even more significant is the fact that she is the daughter of his brother-in-law (and nephew) Oedipus, a hard act to follow as ruler. It is Creon's misfortune that she happens to be not only his son's fiancée but his niece. The play thus calls into profound question the distinction between Creon's performance as a public figure and as a family man. Creon fails to keep his two worlds separate, and the drama shows that they are as intertwined as the corpses of Antigone and Haemon, locked in a bizarre travesty of a nuptial embrace. It is, above all, the social complexity of the play's plea for both politicians *and* parents to *listen* to dissenting voices which lends this heartbreaking tragedy such perennial importance and power. *Antigone* is by far the most explicitly political of Sophocles' tragedies. It confronts the problems involved in ruling a community with verve and vigour—and in the unusually direct, everyday 'plain words' for which Sophocles' dialogue was so admired in antiquity.[5] The ancient Greeks already recognized the political immediacy and force of the drama. In more modern times the political element has inspired many overtly topical versions and imitations: Antigone has made historically significant protests not only against Nazism (especially in Brecht's version of 1948), but against South African apartheid, Polish martial law (see Fig. 7.1), and British imperialism in Ireland.[6]

FIG. 7.1. The programme for Andrzej Wajda's production of *Antigone* in Krakow (1984), reproduced courtesy of the APGRD.

## *ELECTRA* (DATE UNKNOWN)

This is the only surviving play by Sophocles centred on the family of Agamemnon and set at his palace at Mycenae (here somewhat inaccurately conflated with nearby Argos) in the Peloponnese. The action of the tragedy takes place on the day, perhaps fifteen years after Agamemnon returned, to be axed to death (according to Sophocles' version) by Clytemnestra and Aegisthus together. In Aeschylus' play on the same episode, *Libation-Bearers*, it was emphasized that Orestes was putting a stop to a tyranny. But the crisis awaiting resolution, in Sophocles' version, is very much more domestic than political. The intimate, family atmosphere is elaborated by the introduction of the important figure of Clytemnestra's conciliatory third daughter Chrysothemis, who was neither killed by her father nor wishes to kill her mother; her presence in the play seems designed to stress that even within the most abnormal families, some children are determined to live a 'normal' life. Yet the strongest emotion in the play is undoubtedly Electra's hatred of her mother and stepfather; the first half of the play is saturated with her sense of the dead, who lurk just beyond the sightline of the living, and of the rawness of the outrages that have been committed against them (see Fig. 7.2). It is with her full participation and

FIG. 7.2. Zoe Wanamaker as Electra at the Chichester Festival Theatre (1997), reproduced courtesy of the APGRD.

collusion that the revenge killings of Clytemnestra and Aegisthus, in that order, are in this version executed.

Significant props in Sophocles are symbols often culturally freighted with death. Ajax's shield and Philoctetes' bow are weapons for defending against and inflicting death; Electra's urn, brought to her by her disguised brother at about line 1113, contains, she believes, the ashes of her dead brother—the man the audience can see, physically alive, beside her. This scene has inspired numerous painters and produced one of the most remarkable theatrical performances in antiquity, when Polus the great fourth-century tragic actor moved his audiences to tears in the role of Electra as he caressed the urn containing his own, real-life son's ashes (Aulus Gellius, *Noctes Atticae* 6.4). But by a brilliantly economical dramatic device, the urn links the presumed death of Orestes with the all too real death of Clytemnestra, thus becoming a potent symbol of the bond linking a child to its mother. Sophocles makes Orestes execute his mother at the moment that she is decking out his alleged burial urn for the funerary ritual. At the climax of the play there is an ironic inversion of this scene in a second visual tableau of great influence, both ancient and modern, involving mistaken identity of the remains of the dead, indeed the mistaken assumption that the physical remains are those of Orestes.[7] When Aegisthus pulls back the cloth covering the face of the corpse he believes belongs to his arch-enemy Orestes, again, like Electra with the urn, in the physical presence of the character the audience knows is Orestes, he discovers with horror that it is the face of his murdered wife Clytemnestra. This is a rare instance in extant Greek tragedy of a person who has throughout retained full possession of their wits 'identifying' another individual's corpse on stage.

The central question in the other two playwright's versions of the story of Orestes' revenge is the justice of his actions. In Aeschylus' *Oresteia* he needs to be absolved both ritually and legally of his mother's blood, and then only after considerable suffering. In the more torrid psychological world of Euripides, on the other hand, he and Electra decline into guilt, remorse, and misery. Yet Sophocles appears, on a superficial reading, to have put his individual stamp on the story by completely exonerating the matricide. There is no explicit prediction in the text that Orestes is to be hounded by the Erinyes, put on trial, or that he or Electra will suffer any consequences at all.

The play has therefore often been seen as a morally uncomplicated vindication of the divine law that a death within the family must be punished by another death, and a fulfilment of the matricidal injunction given to Orestes by Apollo at Delphi. This view asserts that the play's focus is, rather, on the psychological disturbances undergone by Electra. Sophocles certainly found an effective dramatic vehicle in this remarkable figure, driven by deprivation and cruelty into near-psychotic extremes of behaviour; no other character in his extant dramas dominates the stage to such an extent. In contrast, Orestes seems two-dimensional, a simple 'killing machine' as one French critic famously put it.[8] Sophocles seduces his audience into a quasi-voyeuristic enjoyment of Electra's obsession with her past, her despair, her anger, her embarrassingly demonstrative recognition of her brother and her correspondingly bloodthirsty exultation at the deaths of her persecutors. It is the directness and bitter emotional clout of her calls for revenge that made lines from a Roman adaptation of the play by the poet Atilius be sung at Julius Caesar's funeral games, in order 'to rouse pity and indignation at his death' (Suetonius, *Life of Caesar* 1.84.2).

This line of interpretation fails, however, to do justice to the irony and ambivalence of the play's comment on the ancient story. Electra's speech in her great debate with her mother, for example (the vigour and vitriol of which was intensely admired by Virginia Woolf[9]), throws up several hints that the play's ethics are not quite as simple as they seem. She is quite shockingly dismissive of her mother's claim that her murder of Agamemnon was an act of retribution for his sacrifice of their daughter Iphigenia, which raises the question of whether she can see beyond the single murder that obsesses her to the tragic family history that anticipated it. She also, like an Erinys, articulates to her mother the principle of retributive killing, blood in return for blood, a life for a life (579–83). But an attentive audience, which will have known the *Oresteia*, must have realized that intra-familial murder, by this law, is bound to result in an endless cycle of violence down the generations. If Clytemnestra is killed, her blood too must ultimately be avenged. Sophocles even obliquely suggests candidates to take on this responsibility, by attributing children to her by Aegisthus. According to Electra's own principle, they must sooner or later avenge their parents' death.

Even more sinister are the words of Aegisthus (who is in this play, unusually, credited with prophetic powers), which reverberate around the theatre at the end of the play. Just before he enters the palace to his death, he enigmatically laments that it must 'behold death upon death, those now and those to come' (1497–8). The play provides no solution to the contradictions inherent in the archaic system of reciprocal murder. It neither condemns nor condones the killing of Clytemnestra and Aegisthus. But it does ironically undermine the apparently complacent closure of this outstandingly familiar myth. Surely Nabokov was correct in commenting that the 'effect of a play cannot be final when it ends with a murder'.[10]

## *AJAX* (DATE UNKNOWN)

In a play full of striking visual tableaux, one scene crystallizes the complexity of its leading character, who elicits awe, respect, pity, and revulsion simultaneously. Sophocles was held to have introduced the use of the third actor into tragedy, and the skill with which he uses triangular scenes suggests how the tradition came into being. The enquiry into suffering undertaken in this fascinating play begins from the opening scene—unique in Greek tragedy—where a vindictive god toys sadistically with her human victim in front of a third character, a human spectator who is utterly powerless to prevent the outrage. Athena has sent Ajax mad, and goads him, in the presence of Odysseus, to assault domestic animals which he thinks are his deadly enemies, the Atridae. As a result, the play, long regarded as structurally flawed and almost unperformable, has now been rehabilitated as one of the most 'metatheatrical' and 'generically self-reflexive' of all tragedies—that is, one that exploits most vividly the understanding of what is at stake for the spectators in the experience of participation in a production of tragic theatre. But 'metatheatre', always inexplicit in Greek tragedy, is only a helpful concept if we see the points underlying its use that are more serious than simply reminding the audience that they are in a theatre.

What the audience of *Ajax* actually watch is the failure of a society to cope with one of the 'losers' in the zero-sum game of public competition. Ajax, one of the most successful and respected of the Greeks at Troy, ends up dead and disgraced, and very nearly unburied as well. He is furious because he was not awarded the arms of Achilles, which, according to a vote taken by the Greeks, had been given, instead, to Odysseus. Ajax believes that the Atridae are particularly at fault in this decision (97–8, 445–6), and his half-brother Telamon, indeed, claims that Menelaus had tampered with the votes (1135). But this allegation is never proven. Both Menelaus and Agamemnon insist that Ajax and his supporters are unable to accept that the decision was taken by majority vote of the judges (1136, 1243). Two problems faced in any democracy—the risk of corruption, and the disgruntlement of minorities—are thus implicated as causes of Ajax's suffering.

The second half of the play revolves entirely around the question of whether Ajax, who is held by the Atridae to be a traitor since he intended to harm them, is to be allowed funeral rites. The pleas from his family, eloquently voiced by his half-brother Teucer, fail to move the outraged Spartans, but eventually they relent under pressure from Ajax's great rival Odysseus. The play therefore inquires into the viciousness with which people officially on the same 'side' in a war can treat each other, and into the importance of physical ownership of a loved one's corpse to the bereaved. It asks whether a person who has earned respect all his life deserves to lose the most basic claims on decent treatment because of a single mistake. Since Ajax is ultimately being punished for disrespecting Athena, it also underlines, as all Sophoclean drama does, that however rational the basis for a man's confidence in his own abilities, he cannot afford to alienate the gods by setting himself up, alone, against them. And indeed, Ajax is the loneliest figure in Greek tragedy. He begins the play, isolated in his psychotic delusion, while Athena, Odysseus, and the audience inspect his ravings under the theatrical microscope. The spectacular tableau which rolls out from the tent, revealing him surrounded by blood-streaked livestock, emphasizes how far he has departed from the shared sensibility of his human community. Defeated in the matter of the shield, he is effectively insulted by his own comrades-in-arms. His own men, in the chorus, stand in

FIG. 7.3. The suicide of Ajax, on an Etrurian red-figure wine-bowl (400–350 BCE), reproduced courtesy of the Trustees of the British Museum.

absolute awe of him: the relationship is one of total dependence rather than mutual support. The way he speaks to Tecmessa reveals how little psychological intimacy this couple shares; his treatment of his little son scarcely implies a paternal tenderness. In his suicidal despair he is unable to confide even in his wife or half-brother. The fact that he is the only man to kill himself on stage in Greek tragedy seems to underline his special isolation (see Fig. 7.3).

Ajax's problematic personality results from Sophocles' meditation on the question of the type of soldier you want fighting on your side in desperate straits. In the *Iliad* Ajax is a massive man, slow of thought and speech, but quick in battle and reliably courageous. He is the key defensive fighter on the Greek side, and is therefore called the 'bulwark' of the Greeks (3.229, 6.5, 7.211). In the *Odyssey* he keeps up his hatred against Odysseus, from whom he turns without a word into the darkness of Erebos. With Ajax there can never be any compromise, and although intransigence is a problem in a member of a community on an everyday basis, it is exactly what is required in a hero summoned from time to time to defend the borders of his fatherland.

The play is set in and near the Greek camp at Troy, with an unusual shift of location to the seashore implied by the text when Ajax enters to commit suicide. But the choral perspective in this play, and that of several of its characters, lend it an Athenian resonance. Ajax's last days, death, and burial mattered intensely to the Athenian audience because he was a local hero, one of the ten official 'heroes of Attica' whose statue was displayed in the agora. His home was the island of Salamis, controlled by the Athenians and crucial in their history as the site of the sea-battle of 472 BCE when they had emphatically defeated the Persians. Some Athenians saw him appear to help in the fighting, and after the battle a captured enemy ship was dedicated to him (Herodotus 8.64, 121). Little wonder that his story was a popular theme in the theatre, treated in whole trilogy by Aeschylus. Sophocles wrote two other plays about his close family, a *Teucer* and a *Eurysaces*. Yet there is no evidence that allows us to date the premiere of this fascinating play. Many scholars have simply acquiesced in a modern tradition that it is relatively early work, perhaps dating from the 440s. The irrational basis of this theory is that the elemental hero Ajax himself 'feels' less 'advanced' than some other characters in Greek tragedy. But just as good a case can be made for dating the play to the era of the Peloponnesian War, perhaps around 428. Ajax's dying curse on the Atridae, who are depicted as vindictive and power-hungry Spartans, can be seen as manipulation of a myth which serves as an aetiological explanation for the enmity between Athens and Sparta.

## *WOMEN OF TRACHIS* (DATE UNKNOWN)

This atmospheric play takes its name from its chorus, the local women of an ancient town nestling at the foot of Oeta, the high mountain in the Pindus range. Its peak was traditionally the place where Heracles had met his death. The whole tragedy in one sense is a preparation for its closing moment, where Heracles' son Hyllus commands his attendants to begin the arduous ascent, carrying his mortally ill father on a stretcher, to the 7,000-foot summit. The semi-divine Heracles was without doubt the most important ancient Greek hero, and the one whose cult was most widespread (see above pp. 166–71). At Athens he was celebrated in an annual men-only festival held in the high summer in a gymnasium attached to his sanctuary outside the city walls. These ritual features—the exclusion of women, the physical prowess that comes through arduous training, and the crossing of the boundary marked by the city walls—were associations of the hero and his cult that inform the play on every level.

A set of oracular pronouncements concerning Heracles' life and death underpin this tragedy on the divine plane, on which his father Zeus is prominent. The play asks its audience to accept an unusually strange and supernatural antecedent to its plot, the attempt of the horse-bodied centaur Nessus to rape Deianira, which resulted in Nessus' death at Heracles' hands. On the human level, however, the raw and sexualized tragic action springs from the problems created in the marriage of Heracles and Deianira by his prolonged absences and emotional crassness. Heracles has sacked the city of Oechalia because he has fallen for its princess, Iole, and now sends her ahead of him to his wife's current residence in Trachis. Unable to tolerate the presence of a sexual rival in the marital home, Deianira sends him the gift of a robe smeared with an ointment she thinks is an aphrodisiac, but it turns out to have been given her by Nessus (the foiled rapist) in his dying moments; it has lethal corrosive properties. She kills herself before Heracles arrives in his final agonies, bellowing and cursing; he orders their son to marry Iole since he cannot, and is then carried off to die.

The fierce subject-matter of *Women of Trachis*—what was done by and to its awesome hero during the last, violent episode of his life on earth—has been consistently confused with Sophocles' purpose and methods in writing it. This has led to the play being judged a 'raw' and 'primal' artwork and indeed to it receiving an early date relative to Sophocles' other extant dramas. Many have felt not only that it depicts a far distant heroic age somehow more irrational, savage, and closer to nature than the Argos of Sophocles'

*Electra* or the Thebes of his plays about Oedipus and Antigone, but that the play itself 'is' somehow more crude, irrational, elemental, and savage than they are. This view is derived from the influential set of lectures on drama published by A. W. Schlegel between 1809 and 1811, who dismissed the play in a single paragraph, claiming that it was unlikely that Sophocles wrote it at all.[11] It was perhaps Ezra Pound's idiosyncratic 1956 version which put the play on the literary map. Since this culminated in the announcement of the dying superhero, once he recognized the fulfilment of the oracles, and has put all the available information together, 'What splendour, it all coheres',[12] it subsequently began to be fashionable to emphasize the themes of knowledge and 'late learning' in the play. Its sophistication was demonstrated in Pat Easterling's magnificent commentary, published in 1982; there have also been several fine productions and adaptations in the professional theatre and other media.[13]

In the course of the drama the audience learns how Heracles has on separate occasions hurled two innocent men to their deaths from lofty precipices. His own screams resounded amongst the mountains until he 'hurled himself often to the ground' (787–90). A male body crashing at great velocity to earth is an ominous picture, emblematic of the atmosphere of primeval violence that suffuses the whole play but is different from the atmosphere in anything else that survives by Sophocles. Charles Segal influentially pointed out that the elemental landscapes in *Women of Trachis*, with their torrential rivers and high mountain peaks, serve to 'throw into relief the question of man's place in a world whose violence he both shares and subdues'.[14]

One of the central issues in the play is the importance of deliberation before action: everyone in Heracles' family acts before thinking through the consequences. Since the characters of Deianira and Heracles are likely to have been played by the same actor, some critics have argued that there is a sharp contrast created by the meek, un-authoritative wife and her masterful, controlling husband. But in one crucial respect—their incompetence at deliberation and tendency to take precipitate decisions—they are remarkably similar. Sophocles' Deianira is not guilty of premeditated murder, but nor is she an entirely passive victim of delusion or of supernatural machinations or envy. Having seen Iole, she *decides on her own initiative* to send the robe, and also decides on her own initiative to deliberate and take advice on whether her policy is prudent. But she decides too, on a sudden impulse when Lichas enters, to rescind the impulse towards deliberation and take risk-laden action anyway. Sophocles here displays an unparalleled degree of precision and delicacy in his calibration of tragic characters' performance as moral agents.

In a final twist to the tale, however, the philosophical depth of *Women of Trachis* is surely one of the reasons why it proved popular far *beyond* democratic Athens in antiquity. Besides quotations in ancient authors, its continuing presence in the cultural imagination is proved beyond all doubt by the fact that it was adapted into the imperial tragedy *Hercules Oetaeus* attributed to Seneca. Deianira's grave was pointed out in Pausanias' time (2.23.5); the encounter between Hercules, Nessus, and Deianira was beautifully painted as a mural at Pompeii; the story told in *Women of Trachis* seems to have been incorporated in the images on the reliefs at the North African theatre of Sabratha. Deianira's tale was danced in the imperial medium of pantomime (Libanius, *Orations* 64.67). This play could be exported without difficulty far beyond the immediate cultural context of Athenian democratic deliberation, and this versatility and staying power owed more to its metaphysics than to its ethics. To any ancient spectator sensitive to the idea of Heracles' divinity, *Women of Trachis* will always have suggested that the cosmic imperative of the establishment of his cult partly resulted from the ineptitude of deliberating brains on the human level. The tragic paradox—that the inevitability of the divine order of things is inseparable from the contingency of incompetence in the mortal sphere—is surely lent, by the play's compromised deliberations, one of its most weighty expressions.

## *PHILOCTETES* (409 BCE)

Seventeen Greek males (a chorus and five speaking parts) encounter one another on a deserted island. There are no cities, institutions, lawgivers, judges, priests, prophets, or other authority figures to provide a moral framework for the action. Distinctions between right and wrong have to be made up as they go along. The starkness, even minimalism of this scenario throws the action and words into the sharpest possible focus, and the implications are grim: isolated from civilization, these men fail completely to resolve conflict without supernatural help. The ethical crisis is further highlighted by the simplicity of the plot.

Odysseus and Neoptolemus arrive at the island of Lemnos. Their aim is to capture its sole human inhabitant, the exiled Philoctetes. Without the help of his special bow (given him by his deceased comrade Heracles) and his skill with it (the audience are kept in suspense as to whether the bow or his skill is the more important), the Greeks will not win the Trojan War. The problem is that Philoctetes hates the Greek leaders at Troy, because they abandoned him on the island when they could not tolerate the odour given off by his festering leg wound. Only guile, violence, or (as it turns out) Heracles appearing *ex machina* can get him to board Odysseus' ship. This demi-god tells Philoctetes to go to Troy and use the bow to kill Paris; Philoctetes and the young Neoptolemus, the son of the dead Achilles, are destined at last to take Priam's city, 'like two lions in a pride' (1436). On returning to Greece Philoctetes is then to dedicate spoils to Heracles on a pyre on Mount Oeta (where Heracles is taken to die at the end of *Women of Trachis*). This is, says Heracles, the will of Zeus.

*Philoctetes* is the original 'desert island' play, its central role that of a castaway. Philoctetes' cultural descendants include the hero of Defoe's *Robinson Crusoe* (1719) and Chuck Noland (Tom Hanks) in Robert Zemeckis' movie *Cast Away* (2000). The story of a man who had to use Neolithic survival techniques allowed Sophocles to explore recent advances in political theory, associated above all with the sophist Protagoras, who had discussed man's progress through different modes of production, from nomad to agriculturalist and eventually international trader and city-dweller (see above, pp. 178–81). But the core of the play is the celebration of the transmission of patriarchal virtue and power, through myth and cult, from Zeus to his actual son Heracles, and from Heracles to his friend Philoctetes, through the talismanic, all-powerful bow. Philoctetes then hands the qualities of integrity and heroic masculinity, by sheer force of example, down to the next generation in the form of his son-surrogate, Neoptolemus. This process awakens in Neoptolemus an urge to live up to his own father Achilles' reputation.

The preparation Neoptolemus receives for entrance into the adult world of war and politics has been plausibly read as a mythical reflection of the structure of the *ephēbeia*, the Athenian equivalent of military service, by which youths (ephebes) were initiated into manhood.[15] But it is also explores, on an intellectual level, how men shape other men in an unceasing process of moral and social education as well as biological reproduction. Unusually amongst Greek tragedies, there is neither a death nor even any reported combat. Uniquely amongst Greek tragedies, there are no females at all. Also uniquely among Greek tragedies, no character is related by blood to any other. Yet surrogate father–son relationships are central, since Odysseus and Philoctetes are rivals for the fatherless Neoptolemus' filial attachment. By removing the biological element, indeed, the social and moral aspects of fatherhood appear starkly defined.

Odysseus is a corrupt individual, for whom ends can always justify means: the requirement to win the war overrides any qualms about the morality of the measures taken. Disguise, lies, and treachery are weapons in this politician's armoury. He behaves appallingly in any human, moral sense, and yet there is a level on which he is right: getting the war over has become a priority for the entire Greek community, and it would be irrational to allow Philoctetes' personal pride to jeopardize the greater good. In this play Sophocles uses Odysseus to examine both the Utilitarian argument that society needs to aim at achieving the greatest happiness for the greatest number (which inevitably means the unhappiness of dissenting minorities), and the ethical conundrum of whether moral Ends can ever justify immoral Means. Philoctetes, on the other hand, lives by the code of integrity and honour that characterized Neoptolemus' father, according to which true heroes remain loyal to their friends through thick and thin, and avoid all subterfuge. Before the action of the play is over, he manages to persuade Neoptolemus to reject Odysseus' cynical strategy, shun the Greek army, and accompany him back to Greece where he can live out his old age.

The play is a tour-de-force in performance. In the psychological background there seethes away the great volcano of Lemnos, into the fires of which Philoctetes, in his onslaughts of pain, wants to hurl himself. The entire action—however intellectual its ramifications—revolves in a lucid, almost symbolist manner around the contest for possession of the single prop of the great bow, and the physical body of Philoctetes. The roles of Odysseus and Neoptolemus demand tight control, since both require the actor to portray the very process of acting—dissembling and role-playing—in a concrete situation. But it is the role of Philoctetes, who never says anything not straight from the heart, that provides the greatest challenge. From his desperate attempt, despite his disability, to kneel as a suppliant, he presents the most pitiful picture in ancient theatre of a man locked in struggle with pain. Before he temporarily loses consciousness, he begs Neoptolemus to cut off his agonized foot (742–50):

> I am annihilated, child. I can't hide
> This agony I'm in from you any longer.
> Aaaah! Aaaah! It sears right through me, right through!
> It's unbearable, excruciating! I'm destroyed, child!
> I'm devoured, child!
> Aaaah! Aaaah! Aaaah!
> By the gods, boy, if you have a sword,
> Strike my foot at the heel! Cut it off now! You cannot save me!
> Do it, boy.

He endures assault by Odysseus' men, and the heartbreaking loss of his bow; when the chastened Neoptolemus returns it to him, he has to be forcibly restrained from launching an arrow at Odysseus. He experiences a range of emotions—elation, despair, wrath, disappointment, suicidal impulses—and his speeches express by turns cynical scorn, defiant intransigence, and lyrical reminiscence. But he never shifts from his moral certainty, and it is this quality which ultimately wins the respect and cooperation of the naïve Neoptolemus. Philoctetes is also the ultimate example of the tragic hero because his suffering is constant, 'in-your-face', and yet is never given any acceptable justification.[16] Perhaps the sheer extent of his agony is what attracted the other two tragedians to this hero, who appeared in Aeschylean and Euripidean plays famous enough in later antiquity to have been discussed by Dio Chrysostom (*Orations* 52 and 59). Philoctetes' suffering is what makes this struggle over a young man's soul not only Sophocles' most experimental tragedy from a theatrical perspective, but also the one with the most intellectual clout.

## *OEDIPUS AT COLONUS* (401 BCE)

This remarkable play was produced after Sophocles' death by his grandson, who was also named Sophocles. Since its hero Oedipus dies in the course of the play at Sophocles' own home deme of Colonus, it is tempting to read autobiographical elements into the drama. But although Sophocles is interested in the religious history of his local cults, and in the art of dying with dignity, the figure of Oedipus in this play transcends all parochial concerns. Sophocles had been thinking about this brilliant, irascible hero for decades, and in *Oedipus at Colonus* brings together all the strands in the winding story of his miserable life. But now he begins the final stage in the process of becoming a hero, dying a peaceful death as a welcome guest, surrounded by friends, in a beautiful location. The play as a whole, more than any other Greek tragedy, extols the humane virtues of kindness and reasonableness, tolerance and mutual assistance.

In a seminal article, Peter Burian showed that it follows the fundamental pattern of a 'suppliant drama'. Oedipus begins the play as a suppliant, fleeing his enemy, Creon. He needs to find someone to rescue him, and makes his case to Theseus, king of Athens. There is a confrontation between Oedipus and his persecutor, which ends in violence when Creon abducts both Oedipus' daughters. This is followed by a further confrontation between Creon and Theseus, which ends in the expulsion of the persecutor and an offstage battle. The suppliant is saved. But this suppliant drama develops into something unique and fascinating: the helpless, blind old man himself turns into a saviour who can protect the Athenians who protected him. The play is a celebration of important aspects of the self-image of the Athenian city-state as a whole, instantiated both in the chorus and especially in Theseus their king: this community is portrayed as humane, charitable to strangers, law-abiding, quick-witted, resourceful, valorous, favoured by the gods, and devout in the practice of religion.[17]

The theological upshot is that Oedipus, in death, transfers his allegiance and the supernatural powers of protection it confers from his natal city of Thebes to his adoptive city of Athens. Moreover, he passes on a sacred secret to the king of Athens, which Theseus is only ever to transmit to his successor. This bond of friendship between two heroes who have never previously met, a bond created by an act of human kindness and respect for the divinities of Colonus, is formally elevated over the kinship bond. This also entails Oedipus 'officially' severing his relationship with his sons, by rejecting Polynices' pleas and uttering a curse. This was an exceptional measure for any Greek father, and underlines the magnitude of the dishonour his sons have paid him. But the tragic atmosphere of the play, despite its uplifting conclusion, is partly generated by its emphasis on the true cost in emotional terms of family break-up. This emphasis is ensured by the presence of Antigone, who although the loyal constant companion to her father, is devastated by the loss of her brother.

That Oedipus has a special relationship with Colonus becomes clear as soon as he hears that the ground onto which he and Antigone have stumbled is sacred to the Eumenides (42). From this point onwards, Oedipus' physical body is to be the object of all the conflict in the play (this emphasis on who controls the leading actor's body is something that the play emphatically shares with both *Ajax* and *Philoctetes*): the blind, defiled, pathetic old body suddenly assumes an inestimable value. It is to protect Oedipus against his exploitative family and compatriots that Theseus, in the name of Athens, bestows his crucial humanitarian promise of protection and asylum. At this moment, the previously wary chorus perform a lyric welcoming the polluted outcast to their city and their deme. The first antistrophe sings of flowers, water, the Muses, and Aphrodite. The second strophe describes the protective influence of the olive, Zeus, and Athena. The second antistrophe praises the region's horses, skill at seafaring, and Poseidon. But the opening strophe had invoked another god with a special place in the Athenian pantheon (668–80):

> Stranger, the land you have reached, with its fine horses,
> Offers the best shelter in the country—shining Colonus.
> Here the clear-voiced nightingale warbles with particular frequency
> Within the green dells, dwelling amid the wine-dark ivy
> And the divinity's inviolate foliage, with its abundant fruit,
> Neither scorched by the sun nor battered by any winter wind.
> Here the reveller Dionysus treads the ground perpetually,
> Accompanied by his divine nurses.

Dionysus, of course, is the divine patron of the tragic theatre. The *Oedipus at Colonus*, performed at the festival of Dionysus, enacts the transformation of the quintessential tragic hero upon his acceptance into the grove of the Eumenides. But amongst the divine personnel at Colonus are the Muses, goddesses of poetry and song, and Dionysus the reveller, the theatre god, in whose presence the very tragedy was being performed. Even the nightingales have a special significance, since the mournful laments of this tuneful bird had in tragic poetry always symbolized the laments of heroines from Aeschylus' Danaids and Cassandra through to Sophocles' own Electra and Euripides' Antigone in *Phoenician Women*.[18]

No other Greek tragic protagonist is blind from beginning to end of his play, and Sophocles seems to have risen to the challenge this presented, heightening the whole aural experience by writing some of the most outstanding poetry in ancient Greek, much of which is delivered by the old man himself. Beginning as an exhausted, homeless vagrant (see Fig. 7.4), Oedipus acquires authority and confidence when he realizes that he has arrived at the place where he is destined to die. He also harbours deep anger, and has to deliver both a terrible attack on his own sons' characters, and a terrifying curse. In the last few minutes before his departure from the stage, the audience is given a transformed Oedipus, and a sense of the awesome, supernatural power at work in preparing him for his heroic status after death. He can powerfully sense the presence of divinity—of Hermes, the god who escorted the dying to the Underworld, and Persephone, its Queen. The feeble, blind old man, who has leant physically on others throughout the play, can suddenly now walk

FIG. 7.4. The blind Oedipus being led through the wilderness by his daughter Antigone. Mezzotint by Johann Gerhard Huck (1802), after a painting by Charles Thévenin, reproduced courtesy of the Trustees of the British Museum.

without difficulty, alone, certain of the route he must take to his destination (1540–8):

> for the presence of the god hurries me on;
> Let us delay no longer. Children, follow me this way,
> Since I am newly revealed as guide to the pair of you,
> As you have been to me. Keep moving, but do not touch me.
> Allow me discover myself the sacrosanct tomb
> Where it is fated that this man here shall be concealed in this very earth.
> Over here, this way, come this way. For this is the direction in which
> Hermes the Escort is leading me, and the goddess below.

Yet in order to reach this mystical preliminary stage of his apotheosis, it has been crucial for Oedipus' tale to be told, and for him to be accepted by the Athenians. Theseus in a sense represents the model audience-member, interested in Oedipus and feeling pity for his plight; he comes to meet the reviled old man in a spirit of non-judgmental humanity. Indeed, his very entrance speech describes perfectly the philosophical attitude that the spectators at the Dionysia would ideally have adopted before listening to Oedipus themselves. Having previously endured exile and threats to his life himself, Theseus will never fail to help a suffering stranger (566–8),

> Since I know well that I am just a man, and that
> I have no more claim on what tomorrow brings than you do.

Oedipus, as long-time sufferer who is about to become a blessing to the community as he dies, can be seen as the symbol of all the heroes in Greek tragedy. We long, like Theseus, to hear from his own lips about what suffering has befallen him; we still honour him, as Theseus promises to do, long after he has expired. On learning of the Thebans' desire to gain possession of his talismanic corpse, Oedipus asks a rhetorical question that might be asked by almost any of the tragic heroes and heroines discussed in this book—suffering, enslaved, spurned, insulted, exiled, and humiliated as they are in their lifetimes (393): 'Is it then only when I cease to be that my value as a man begins?'

# 8

# Greek Tragedy and Tragic Fragments Today

> It's quite legitimate to take a play and treat it in a context which is closer to our experience. After all, that's exactly what Sophocles was doing. He was using an old legend anyway, and making it modern.[1]
>
> (Derek Walcott)

The plays of the Greek tragedians were first printed in the early years of the sixteenth century, and by its last decades had begun to be performed, if only in relatively radical adaptation. In the English-speaking world the story really begins with the 1566 production at Gray's Inn in London of *Jocasta*, a version by George Gascoigne and Francis Kinwelmershe of Lodovico Dolce's Italian adaptation (1549) of Euripides' *Phoenician Women*. The seventeenth and eighteenth centuries produced many neoclassical adaptations, operas and subsequently ballets on Greek tragic themes, including some that achieved canonical status themselves, such as Racine's *Phèdre* (1677) and Goethe's *Iphigenie auf Tauris* (1787). The first great revival of the ancient plays themselves in performance can be dated to the Philhellenism of the 1880s (see Fig. 8.1), and by World War I, performances in both modern languages and ancient Greek had become a recognized cultural phenomenon, at least in western Europe and North America. A few tragedies—especially *Oedipus Tyrannus*, *Antigone*, *Medea*, and *Trojan Women*—had become especially familiar, and some of these were performed and adapted intermittently during the interwar years and the first two postwar decades; by this time, ancient

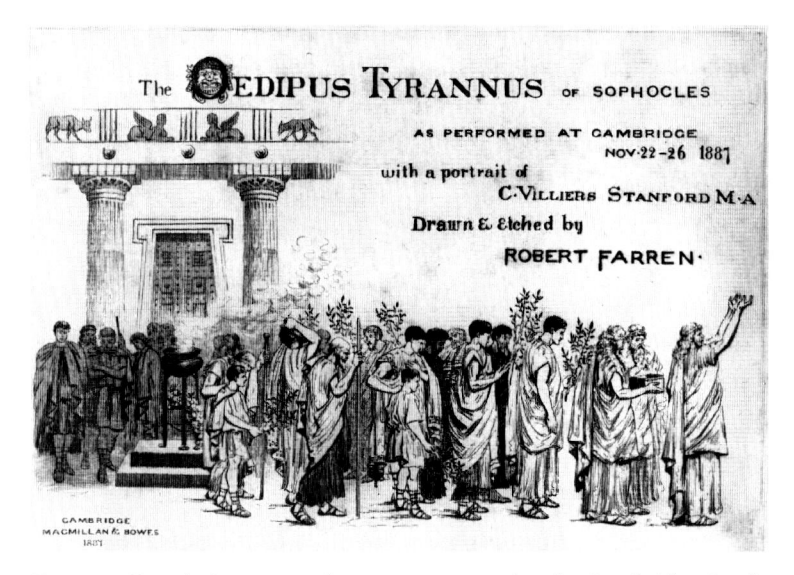

FIG. 8.1. Frontispiece to a volume commemorating the Cambridge Greek play (1887), reproduced courtesy of the APGRD.

Greek tragedy was a standing feature of the established theatre in Greece itself. But over the last three or four decades there has been a revival of interest in Greek tragedy, internationally, that has been completely unprecedented in scope and scale. All the plays have been performed, in every continent of the world, and dozens of new translations and adaptations are commissioned for productions every year.

There are several causes of this latest revival and increasing globalization. The most obvious reason has been the rise in the 1970s and continuing impact of the feminist movement. Yet the story of feminism's rediscovery of ancient drama needs to be set in the context of the slightly earlier 'hippie' movement, and in particular the so-called sexual revolution. Such social developments created a need for a theatre which talked frankly about sexual relationships. In Britain the theatrical censorship which had been in place for over two centuries was abolished in 1968. There was however a particular need for plays which were frank about *female* sexuality. Aristophanes and Plato had long ago established a precedent for criticizing the tragedians, especially Euripides, for writing plays with a sexually motivated woman or one who spoke up for herself against her husband at their centre. But they were responding to plays which still—or again—make a remarkably uninhibited impact. In the tragedies of the Greeks, where erotic love is much discussed, deeply respected, but also portrayed as one of the most dangerous forces in the family and society, late twentieth-century directors quickly discovered ways of exploring the repercussions of the sexual revolution.

Greek tragedy was rediscovered by women in the 1970s and 1980s because it gave an appearance of honesty concerning the opportunities life offered their ancient counterparts, and especially concerning the relatively greater importance of affective ties with children, siblings, and parents compared to those with lovers and husbands. Greek tragic narratives are strong on marital breakdown and stepfamilies, but weak on what we call 'romantic' liaisons. Over the last three and a half decades, Greek tragedies have been rewritten to upgrade the importance of female experience, and challenge the gender roles and stereotyped sexualities canonized in the history of western theatre. Greek heroines such as Medea, Jocasta, Hecuba, Electra, and Clytemnestra have exerted a magnetic force over actors of both sexes, including cross-dressed actors, and writers seeking to reconfigure the gender relations of the plays altogether. A crucial factor has been the growing frustration of women theatre professionals with the standard repertoire. Female actors in search of interesting roles have discovered in the texts of ancient Greek drama far more interesting parts than in almost any period of later theatre.

The critique of conventional gender roles has led to a spotlight being cast on the role of men, and indeed on the unpalatable truth that society's view of ideal masculinity—indomitable, self-sufficient, physically powerful, decisive, emotionally controlled—has been complicit in the oppression of both women and children. The figure of Heracles in Greek tragedy has proved especially suggestive for exploring these issues. The Greeks had already asked whether this monster-slayer is a liberator of the civilized world or some kind of global terrorist, and both Sophocles' *Women of Trachis* and Euripides' *Heracles* have recently proved excellent arenas for updating the frame of that question, and confronting the audience with the trained killer whose insensitivity and disregard for his responsibilities as husband and father must turn his homecoming into a tragedy.

Greek theatre was itself born in a moment of revolutionary change and late twentieth-century directors were galvanized by its political potential. The heroine of Sophocles' *Antigone* is a hardy perennial who has protested against South African apartheid, the abuse of human rights in several countries in Latin America, and (in Anouilh's version) patriarchy in Jakarta. In Euripides' war plays, too, there has been discovered painful resonance. *Trojan Women* has revealed the terrible consequences of war for people all over the world; *Hecuba* has been revived as a regular performance text since the fall of the Berlin Wall. It portrays atrocities committed by no fewer than three neighbouring ethnic groups, and their nauseating attempts at self-justification. It is set in the southern Balkans; in the early 1990s the parallels with the genocidal violence in the war that broke out in agonizing stages during 1991-2, in what had so recently been Yugoslavia, seemed almost unbearable. With the deepening of the third-millennium war between the USA and Islam, Greek tragedy once again became a medium for the exploration of East–West tension, and Aeschylus' *Persians* and Euripides' *Iphigenia in Aulis* have both enjoyed marked revivals.

As we saw in Chapter 3, Greek plays offer great potential for the exploration of ethnic difference, and some of them, especially *Medea*, have as a result had long and complicated relationships with European colonialism and imperialism. Greek tragedy was discovered on the stages of Europe at exactly the moment of the discovery of the New World, and by the eighteenth century the connection between some of the myths enacted in Greek tragedy and the European experience of far-flung colonies became explicit: the popularity in the eighteenth century of Euripides' *Iphigenia among the Taurians*, for example, was a response to that play's portrayal of the experience of Greek adventurers on the wild northern shore of the Black Sea. What is more surprising is that in the period that has seen the finals stages in the slow, painful process of decolonization, especially in Africa, writers searching for new forms of identity have found fertile material in the texts which could be said to epitomize imperial Europe: the dramas of classical antiquity. Yet the fact that the ancient Greek language is so 'incontrovertibly dead' (in the poet Louis MacNeice's memorable phrase) has itself proved liberating; its deadness has inspired creative writers, and helped dramatists from colonized countries to explore the part of their own heritage that is undeniably European. Greek drama has often felt like a root which it can be pleasurable and legitimate to dig towards, bypassing some of the pain connected with literature in the actual language of the colonial power—English, French, or Afrikaans. Interculturalism and internationalism thrive on the process of interpreting these plays, composed before the religious, political, and cultural barriers that now divide the world were fully erected, let alone set seemingly in stone.

Poets, translators, and composers have been keen to experiment with the effect of elevated verse drama and an aural form that shifted between speech and song, and entailed some instrumental accompaniment. Theatre directors, designers, actors, and drama theorists have been attracted by the aesthetic potential of these ancient plays, especially those engaging in postmodern experiments in the electronic age. Some of ancient theatre's formal devices find unexpected modern analogues in the machines we have designed for the electronic recording and retrieval of experience, such as the audiotape recorder or the split screen. Peter Sellars, for example, the director of several acclaimed productions of Greek tragedy, has said that the ancient Greek mask offered both a strong sense of formal public address and of a private interior monologue, a combination which is profoundly suggestive to him of cameras, shooting from multiple angles, and the different levels of address that can be created with a microphone. Indeed, adaptations of Greek tragedy have reflected every trend in contemporary western theatre, including one important example of the confrontational 'In-yer-face' theatre of the 1990s, Sarah Kane's *Phaedra's Love*.

The recent prominence of Greek tragedy is also connected with the so-called Performative Turn, the moment when physical theatre, especially in Central Europe, began to challenge the theatre of the spoken word. Above all this process entailed an assault on the proscenium arch, with its constraining separation of the worlds of the audience and of the stage, an assault fuelled by encounters with other, non-western theatrical traditions. There developed a powerful urge to explore new types of performance space (whether converted factories, roofed thrust stages, or out-of-doors in city parks), new configurations between audience and performers (for which the Greek chorus has proved useful) and the observation of performances from different angles and levels in a constantly shifting perception of the action.

The return to the Greeks was also related to the emergence of television. It is not that television has proved particularly successful as a medium for Greek tragedy. It is difficult to convert the ancient theatrical texts, with their formal conventions, into visual entertainment for the small screen. What television does brilliantly, however, is contemporary social realist drama. Television's preeminence in this genre, it has been argued, has compromised its potential in live theatre, which has, as a result, been left more open to experimental stage styles and forms. But a more important factor may be the popularity of soap opera, which shares some defining features with Greek tragedy. The central topic and source of narrative energy in both genres is a threat to the family. Both enact conflicted relationships between parent and child, husband and wife, and sibling against sibling. In both genres the fundamental plots revolve around sexual fidelity, familial bereavement, and domestic violence.

Another factor in the revival of Greek tragedy has been the popularity of the plays by Brecht and Beckett, whose creative aesthetics were shaped in direct response to the drama of the Greeks. Brecht's *Antigone* (an adaptation of Hölderlin's translation), like Anouilh's, has always been one of the more important avenues by which audiences have approached Greek tragedy. His experience of Greek tragedy certainly affected his own plays in that he admired the towering, powerful female figures created by the ancient playwrights, women whose distant descendants therefore include Mother Courage. But the presence of Greek theatre in Beckett's plays is all-pervasive. Beckett is the inheritor of a tradition of pared-down, relationship-centred, philosophical drama which originated in classical Athens. This is partly a result of the enormous impact made in the early 1960s by Jean-Paul Sartre's existentialism, the intellectual school with which Beckett was associated, on several directors who have been crucial to the revival of Greek tragedy, including Ariane Mnouchkine (Sartre's own intellectual version of *Trojan Women*, *Les Troyennes*, was first performed at the Théâtre National Populaire, Paris, in 1965). But the formal aspects of Beckett's theatrical aesthetic have been just as significant. One reason why the Greeks have been back on the world stage is that Beckett's plays, now standards of the repertoire, fostered an appetite for them. The experiments of the Theatre of the Absurd (and of Beckett above all) made audiences more receptive to Greek tragedy, and the productions of Greek tragedies which they saw became, in response, more stylized and minimalist.

The directions taken by the late twentieth- and early twenty-first-century mind have also contributed to the popularity of Greek tragedy. The increasingly widespread use of psychotherapy has certainly helped to keep Greek tragedy on the public mind. Several influential psychoanalysts have used Greek tragedy, especially its fascination with children, to develop models of the human psyche going far beyond Freud's interest in Sophocles' *Oedipus Tyrannus* or Jung's in his *Electra*. The ancient plays also provide an ideal site for investigating the human subject. Does it have an unchanging core—is it in some respects the same today as in classical Athens? Or do cultural changes mean that there is no permanent, essential, or lasting commonality of human experience? Producing Greek drama entails unceasing shifts between these two contrasting ways of relating to the past. Any audience of a Greek tragedy drifts between awareness of the dimension of the performance that is determined by the attitudes and tastes of our own era, and a (usually) pleasurable sense that certain dimensions of human experience transcend time. At an emotional level of apprehension there is nothing like hearing live theatrical delivery of speeches first formulated thousands of years ago, even in a quite different language, to bring this tension home.

Greek tragic ethics have offered our era opportunities for exploring modern problems of crime and punishment. Many of the plays, especially the conclusion of *Children of Heracles*, ask whether the emotional need for revenge on the part of victims of serious crime and their families should be a factor in the way that decisions about punishment are made and implemented. *Hecuba* asks to what sort of trial, in front of what sort of tribunal, should political and military leaders accused of war crimes be subject. Medea, who does plan her murders but only under enormous pressure of time, challenges the distinction between premeditated murder and suddenly provoked manslaughter (see above, pp. 189–91). She and other tragic criminals certainly allow exploration of the topical relationship between crime and physiological factors—hormones, genes, mental disturbance, or neurological breakdown. Euripides' Medea could argue today in court that Pre-Menstrual Tension or her dysfunctional limbic amygdale made her do it.

Yet it is the gods on whom the suffering of many tragic characters is blamed, and it is the gods who provide a further possible answer to the question of Greek tragedy's relevance today. The opportunity to create charged, spiritual atmospheres through the performance of prayer and ritual have proved attractive. Moreover, an increasingly secular society has found in the Olympian religion portrayed in the plays, their interrogatory, intellectual quality, and their interest in the workings of the human psyche, rich material through which to explore the big, unanswerable questions about metaphysics and the human condition—the problem of suffering, the limits of human agency—in a multicultural way.

The topic of the performance history and performative presence of Greek tragedy is a vast one, which has become an important academic field in its own right, and on which several substantial published studies are now available. The topic is also constantly renewed and changing, as each new season brings new productions that reflect the shifting cultural agenda. In June 2008, as this book was being written, a massive Brechtian *Persians*, with a chorus consisting of hundreds of ordinary local people, was directed in Braunschweig, Lower Saxony, by Claudia Bosse (see Fig. 8.2). This process had an extraordinary resonance in the city that originally gave the Austrian Adolf Hitler his German citizenship. In Sydney and Melbourne, an adaptation of Euripides' *Trojan Women* that was described as 'hallucinogenic' and 'intimate' in its exploration of violence was staged by Barrie Kosky and Tom Wright. In the autumn, a minor scandal developed over the funding of Jonathan Kent's production *Oedipus*, with its portrayal of a land afflicted by pollution, at the National Theatre in London by the international oil company Shell, which has experienced some serious

Fig. 8.2. The Queen's Dream, from the programme to the Braunschweig production of *Persians* (2008), reproduced courtesy of the APGRD.

problems over the last twenty years with its public relations. In November, the Taiwanese director Wu Hsing-kuo began rehearsals for a transformation of his famous 1993 production of *Medea*, which used the performance techniques of Beijing Opera, in order to take it on tour to Shanghai and Hong Kong. Some of the current trends in the performance of Greek tragedy are obviously political, but others are more difficult to interpret, for example the pronounced trend towards versions of Greek tragedy that turn it into ironic musical comedy, often with transvestism used to comment on issues of sexual identity.[2]

One trend that has been less well documented in other studies than the performance of entire ancient plays, but which warrants particular interest because it offers space for creative writers to extend their field of engagement with Greek tragedy, is the creation of new drama from the fragments of lost plays. The very idea of the fragment has had particular resonance in the postmodern cultural era, with its resistance to grand narratives and love of cutting-and-pasting, multiplicity, and splintered representations of human experience.[3] A Greek tragic fragment has a curious status; it is a tiny textual window on a multimedial ancient event; a few words hacked out of both their performance environment and their literary context, to speak—sometimes eloquently—over the centuries. The strange journey across time taken by the physical fragments of tragedy—their *survival*—also resonates with the idea of the survivor of trauma that is central both to Greek tragedy and to our contemporary sense of historical identity.

Almost all the fragments of Aeschylus and Sophocles, and a good number of those by Euripides, can now be read in reliable English translation, sometimes with excellent commentaries. This new accessibility of the fragments is proving a stimulus to contemporary theatre. The tragedians composed as many as ten times more plays than those which have actually survived from the ancient world as complete texts; even some of the dramas that are generally treated as complete surviving works and have been discussed in this volume, such as *Bacchae* and *Children of Heracles*, arrived in the Renaissance on manuscripts with missing sections, and are therefore short of some important lines and speeches. Unfortunately, we have lost the texts of several of the plays that were actually the most popular and famous over the thousand-year performance reception of Greek tragedy in antiquity. These included, for example, Aeschylus' *Niobe*, Sophocles' *Tereus*, and Euripides' *Telephus* and *Andromeda*.

But a substantial quantity of information about the lost ancient tragedies, and actual fragments, sometimes of considerable length, have survived in two main ways. One is as excerpts preserved in ancient anthologies, or in quotations of varying length. These were preserved until the invention of printing as parts of medieval manuscripts that contained other kinds of literature with a fondness for quoting tragedy or satyr play, including moral and philosophical treatises and biographies. The other fragments have been preserved on very much older pieces of paper or *papyrus*, often in tiny scraps, found free from rot in the dry sands of Egypt where Greek-speaking communities, especially the people of Oxyrhynchus, still read Greek plays under the Roman Empire. Numerous papyrus texts have been deciphered over the last hundred and thirty years. Occasionally papyrus fragments are large enough to allow us to understand a great deal about the lost play. This can be specially significant when the play was performed in the same group as one which has survived, for example Euripides' *Hypsipyle*, which was performed in the same group as his *Phoenician Women*. The lost play, like the surviving one, featured a mature mother of two grown-up sons (see above, pp. 282–5).

Fragments and fragmentary plays are important to specialist scholars because they supplement our understanding not only of the individual dramatists, but of classical Athenian theatre and society more widely defined. But they can also be important to even the elementary understanding of a particular play. We know, for example, that sexual love was praised by the goddess Aphrodite herself in the final play of the group by Aeschylus to which the surviving *Suppliants* belongs (see above, p. 209). This means that the Danaids' case against erotic relationships with men was at least balanced by a counter-argument. Even where the plays performed together were less tightly bound into a sequential trilogy, information about a lost play in the group can still illuminate the one that survives: a good example here is Euripides' lost *Alexander*, which belonged to the same group as his surviving *Trojan Women*. This play allowed the audience of *Trojan Women* to meet several of the men who are dead in the surviving play: not only Paris/Alexander but Priam and Hector themselves. Moreover, Hecuba's role in the action of *Alexander* was already important. The play described how Alexander had been exposed as a baby, and how Hecuba was urged to kill him: this cannot but throw light on the accusation Helen lodges against Hecuba in *Trojan Women* that as mother of the man who had started the Trojan War she should take some of the blame herself (see above, p. 37–8).

Yet the place in which fragmentary Greek tragedy has recently become most important is in the contemporary theatre. The revival of interest in performing Greek tragedy over the last few decades has led directors and translators beyond the surviving scripts to investigate even the more obscure byways of tragic scholarship, and to attempt to stage reconstructions of the fragments, both those contained in the manuscript tradition and those that have been discovered on papyrus. Quite often a particular play will be preserved in fragments of both kinds.

In 1988 Tony Harrison created a new play out of the portion of Sophocles' *Trackers* (a satyr play) that had been found on a papyrus. The original play had dramatized the theft of the cattle of Apollo by the newborn Hermes, and the search for the cattle on Apollo's behalf by the satyrs. The new work, entitled *The Trackers of Oxyrhynchus*, embedded Harrison's version of the ancient Greek text within an otherwise completely original drama. This begins with the classical scholars, Bernard Grenfell and Arthur Hunt, rummaging in the archaeological finds at Oxyrhynchus, where they come across the papyrus. Grenfell turns into Apollo and Silenus, the father and leader of the satyrs, while the Egyptian peasants working on the dig become the satyrs. The play then develops into an exploration of the social conflicts reflected in art by the scorn that elites hold for popular culture, and symbolized by the relationship between elevated tragedy, with its traumatized aristocrats, and satyr drama, with its comic, semi-bestial satyrs. The class politics of the play became even more explicit in the new ending that Harrison wrote for the National Theatre production that opened in London in the Olivier auditorium in March 1990. Here the satyrs underwent a transformation into the homeless who sleep rough on the South Bank of the Thames, near the National Theatre. Since they are freezing, they shred the papyrus of the *Trackers*, from which they sprang as satyrs, to use as bedding, and Silenus distributes small bits to use as toilet paper. Harrison's play not only breathed life into the fragments of Sophocles' satyr drama, but created a telling new piece of theatrical commentary on society. No amount of great art matters at all if people are freezing cold and lack even the most basic physical necessities of life, symbolized in the papyrus-bedding and papyrus-toilet-roll.[4]

At about the same moment in the late 1980s when Harrison was inspired by Sophocles' *Trackers*, Timberlake Wertenbaker was using the fragments of the same Greek playwright's lost tragedy *Tereus* as a springboard for her new play about rape, *The Love of the Nightingale* (1989). Sophocles' *Tereus* was one of his most important and influential plays, and sufficient fragments and other testimony survive to allow us to reconstruct its outlines. It dealt with the story of Procne, an Athenian princess, who was married off to Tereus, a barbarian monarch from Thrace north of mainland

Greece. He raped her sister Philomela, and in order to prevent her from talking about the crime, compounded it by cutting out her tongue. But she managed to communicate to her sister what had happened by weaving into a robe either words, or pictures, or both. Procne's revenge on her husband was terrible; she killed their little son Itys and served him up for his father to eat. She, Tereus, and Philomela were then transformed into birds.

Wertenbaker prints two important fragments from the Sophoclean play as the epigraph to her own (one of which is the protest against women's plight quoted and discussed above p. 153) and makes much use of other materials, including Ovid's famous retelling of the tragic story in *Metamorphoses 6*. By including a performance of Euripides' *Hippolytus* within the play, however, she invites intimate reflection on the medium of Greek tragedy in her own audience, through reference to an extant Greek play about the lethal violence that sexual desire can cause. There is an important sense in which the antique formal expectations that an audience brings to Greek tragic material affect the way in which she makes them read the very issues it explores—rape, violence against women, militarism, child-killing—as absolutely contemporary. The male chorus says, 'What is a myth? The oblique image of an unwanted truth, reverberating through time.'[5]

Sophocles is not the only poet whose lost plays have proved suggestive over the last two decades. In 1996–7, the Romanian director Silviu Purcarete toured internationally with *Les Danaides*, a performance of Aeschylus' *Suppliants*, extended to include a reconstruction of the three lost plays in its tetralogy. The surviving play, through light touches, implied the situation of Islamic refugees in Bosnia (a reality during the war of the early 1990s); when their brutal cousins arrived to force them into marriage, Purcarete's work moved from adaptation of an ancient Greek tragedy into reconstruction, enacting the Danaids' mass murder of their husbands on the wedding night. The reconstructed plays produced the effect of a dazzlingly choreographed, violent, and protracted sex war. Purcarete's Hypermnestra-figure was a Danaid who spared her husband from death on their wedding night, an event which constituted the basis of the other tragedies in the Aeschylean tetralogy; the ancient satyr play, which we know was called *Amymone* and dealt with

Poseidon's rape of another Danaid, Amymone, was represented by the dream of the Hypermnestra-figure involving satyrs as well as the sea-god. Throughout *Les Danaides*, the Olympian gods represented decadent and cynical political leaders.

Purcarete was inspired by the idea of an ancient tetralogy to compose a unified performance encompassing one surviving tragedy and three fragmentary plays. Another group of tragedies performed at the same time, although not a unified 'tetralogy', gave rise to Colin Teevan's *Alcmaeon in Corinth*, an original play inspired by and incorporating what we know about the lost play of the same title by Euripides. This was first performed under the title *Cock o' the North* at the Live Theatre, Newcastle Upon Tyne, in 2004 (see Fig. 8.3). The loss of this Euripidean tragedy is particularly painful because it was first performed in a prize-winning group of three, the jam in the sandwich between two extant plays acclaimed as masterpieces, *Iphigeneia in Aulis* and *Bacchae*. Teevan had previously translated both of these for performance.[6] In *Iphigenia*, Agamemnon has his adolescent daughter sacrificed; in *Bacchae* a mother, Agave, slaughters her son, who has barely reached adulthood. In Euripides' original but now missing middle play a father, Alcmaeon, unwittingly acquired his long-lost teenage daughter as a slave. Relationships between parents and children on the verge of adulthood clearly formed a thread running though the group of plays.

The text of *Alcmaeon in Corinth* did not survive the millennia separating us from classical Athens. Nor would it have been possible actually to 'reconstruct' the original play, since neither a single scene, nor even a list of characters has survived. The barest outlines of the story were recorded in a Greek mythological handbook, written under the Roman Empire in the first or second centuries CE. Apollodorus' *Library* (3.7.7) says that Alcmaeon's relationship with Manto produced two children, Amphilochus and Tisiphone, whom he left in Corinth for King Creon to bring up. Creon's wife sold the girl into slavery, because she was afraid that her own husband would marry her; Alcmaeon bought his daughter without realizing who she was; at Corinth he retrieved his son Amphilochus as well, who founded Amphilochian Argos.

Teevan's tragedy follows this skeletal outline. Approximately twenty-three Euripidean fragments that may be from the original

FIG. 8.3. The programme for *Cock o' the North*, inspired by Euripides' fragmentary *Alcmaeon in Corinth* (2004), reproduced courtesy of the APGRD.

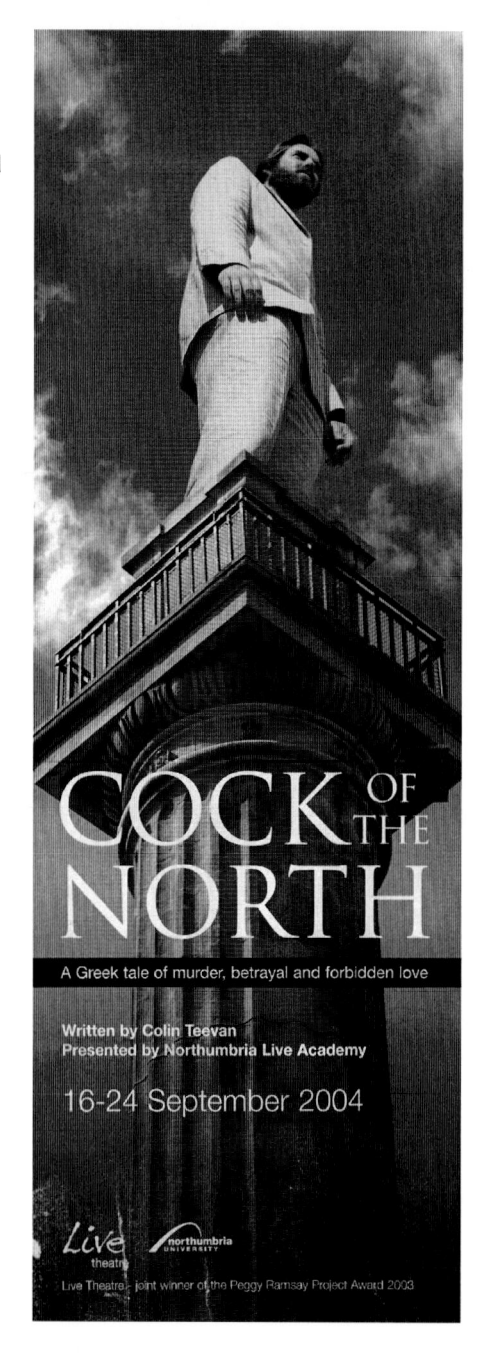

tragedy—perhaps forty lines—have been incorporated into *Alcmaeon in Corinth*. One seemed particularly comic in its 'take' on kin-murder: it may have been Alcmaeon himself who said in a dialogue that he had 'killed his mother, to put it in a nutshell'; his interlocutor responded, 'Was this a consensual act, or were you both reluctant?'[7] The obvious humour of this interchange suggested, early in the writing process, that the drama would be predominantly comic—surely more so than its Greek original. Reimagining a lost ancient artwork opens up questions about the tone and contemporary 'relevance' of plays conceived long ago. As Marx first argued was the case with the French revolutionaries' sense of affinity with the Roman republicans in *The Eighteenth Brumaire of Louis Napoleon* (1852), and Borges elaborated in his famous story 'Pierre Menard, Author of the Quixote',[8] recovering a text or idea produced in an earlier period of culture inevitably entails the ideology of the reading or spectating subject *outweighing* the outdated ideology inherent in the ancient material. When we watch any Greek tragedy, above all a reconstituted one, we watch it with irredeemably twenty-first century eyes. We can never know how the original audiences of Sophocles' *Trackers* or *Tereus*, Aeschylus' *Danaids*, or Euripides' *Alcmaeon in Corinth* would have reacted to Apollo's insulting treatment of the satyrs, the rape and mutilation of Philomela, the murder of the sons of Aegyptus, or Alcmaeon's abandonment of his children.

These plays, then, are less exercises in piecing something together, than in plunging into fresh, contemporary dramatic waters from an identifiably ancient Greek diving board. As part of the Greek 'national' cultural heritage, the fragmentary plays have attracted particular interest amongst Greek poets and dramatists writing in Greek and other languages today. A reconstruction of the fragments of Euripides' *Hypsipyle* into contemporary Greek by Tassos Roussos premiered at Epidauros on 12 July 2002, where it was directed by Spyros Evangelatos.[9] But the most awe-inspiring performance inspired by tragic fragments in very recent times must surely have been *Phaeton*, a musical and dramatic tour-de-force directed by Nikos Charalambous which premiered in Ephesus on 3 July 2008 during the İzmir International Festival. Part of this festival is always dedicated to providing a platform for collaboration between Greek and Turkish artists in the beautiful Library of Celsus (117 CE). This context perfectly suited the inherently international theme of Euripides' *Phaethon*, which portrayed the son of the Sun travelling across the sky in his father's chariot, and a triangular geography encompassing the entire Mediterranean area.

In Euripides' play, Phaethon's mother Clymene, who is married to the king of the Ethiopians, tells him when he has grown to adulthood that his real father is Helios. He visits Helios, partly in connection with contracting a marriage himself, and takes up a right he apparently possesses to demand a single favour from Helios in proof of his paternity. Phaethon foolishly asks to drive his father's chariot, and will not be dissuaded. The chariot goes out of control, Zeus strikes Phaethon with his thunderbolt, and the rash young hero crashes to earth. His body, still smoking, is hidden by his mother, but the truth comes out. A great deal of the play is missing, and for the Ephesus performance the remains were supplemented with material from other ancient sources, especially the tradition that Phaethon's sisters the Heliades grieved so much for him that that they were turned into trees that weep golden amber. The performance also featured a musical collage of hymns to Apollo and Helios, inspired by authentic specimens of ancient music, sung by Mario Frangoulis, the celebrated Greek tenor.

By a coincidence it was only a few months later that Alistair Elliot (the translator of the highly regarded version of *Medea* used in Jonathan Kent's production, starring Diana Rigg) published his more literary, English-language reconstruction of *Phaethon* for performance. This play explores the notions, to be found everywhere in Greek tragedy, that the Sun is both the universal witness of suffering, and a unifying focal point shared by the whole human race who live and have always lived beneath him. But it fuses these ideas poetically with the distinctive feature of this play's use of the Sun as prime instigator of the untimely death of a beloved child (see Fig. 8.4). In Elliot's version, Clymene's penultimate speech is a sorrowful dirge for her son's untimely and terrible death:[10]

> O Phaethon! Whenever I look up
> And see the sun, as long as I endure,
> I shall remember how you fell today —

FIG. 8.4. Helios driving his chariot, on an Athenian red-figure wine-bowl of the 5th century BCE, reproduced courtesy of the Trustees of the British Museum.

> Alone and terrified and burned to death.
> Many will tell me that you chose, yourself,
> To drive the chariot that belongs to Helios.
> But it's not right for one so young to die.

Yet the appalling death of Euripides' Phaethon's in the Sun-god's chariot was the climax of a play whose chorus entered singing a dulcet ode, partly preserved, in praise of the joys of the early dawn. The violence of Greek tragedy is inseparable from its pleasures. Terry Eagleton, indeed, entitled his recent study of tragedy *Sweet Violence*, a phrase he borrowed from Philip Sidney's discussion of theatre in the first substantial example of literary criticism in the English language, his *Defence of Poetry* (1581).[11] Sidney's use of the phrase comes in his paraphrase of a story from ancient Greece he had found in Plutarch, which illustrated tragedy's emotive power. Sidney was struck that a wicked tyrant in ancient Greece had wept so hard at a performance of Euripides' *Trojan Women*, unable to resist its 'sweet violence', that he had been forced to leave the theatre for fear it might soften his hardened heart.

Eagleton has said that he was unaware that his title positions his book, through Plutarch to Euripides' tragedy, in a millennia-old process whereby tragedy has been constantly refreshed and redefined through engagement with specific examples of its earliest manifestations in fifth-century Athens. Yet Eagleton's own discussion of the 'tragic' is a rich one for those seeking to understand the enduring power of the medium in general, and its original Greek texts in particular. Eagleton proposes that this ancient and troublesome art-form still has the potential to offer a significant living presence in the theatres of the third millennium, but only if it combines three essential elements: the ethically honest representation of hardcore suffering, open-ended metaphysics, and aesthetic beauty. If my book has helped any reader to appreciate that the horrible suffering undergone by characters in Greek tragedy stimulates aesthetic pleasure as well as serious ethical and metaphysical enquiry in its spectators, then its main aim has been achieved.

# NOTES

INTRODUCTION

1. Friedrich Nietzsche, *The Birth of Tragedy* (original German edn published in 1872), section 8.
2. See Fiona Macintosh's excellent study, *Dying Acts: Death in Ancient Greek and Irish Tragic Drama* (Cork, 1994).
3. See Adrian Poole's elegant and succinct *Tragedy: A Very Short Introduction* (Oxford, 2005).
4. Arthur Miller, *Death of a Salesman* (Harmondsworth, 1961 [1949]), 16.
5. Aldous Huxley, 'Tragedy and the whole truth', in *Music at Night: and Other Essays* (London, 1949), 3–18, pp. 3–4.
6. Terry Eagleton, *Sweet Violence: An Essay on the Tragic* (Oxford, 2003).
7. See Donald J. Mastronarde, 'Actors on high: the skene roof, the crane, and the gods in Attic drama', *Classical Antiquity* 9 (1990), 247–94.
8. N. J. Lowe, 'Tragic and Homeric ironies: response to Rosenmeyer', in Michael Silk (ed.), *Tragedy and the Tragic: Greek Theatre and Beyond*, 520–33, pp. 526–7 (Oxford, 1996).
9. See e.g. the versions by Seamus Heaney, Tony Harrison, Ted Hughes, and Anne Carson.
10. *Frogs* 912–13. See Pat Easterling, 'Sophocles: the first thousand years', in J. Davidson, F. Muecke, and P. Wilson (eds.), *Greek Drama III: Essays in Honour of Kevin Lee* (= BICS Supplement 87) (London, 2006) 1–15, pp. 11–15.
11. Studying the ancient vase-paintings relating to the tragedies has become much easier and more enjoyable since the publication of Oliver Taplin's lavishly illustrated *Pots and Plays* (Oxford, 2007).
12. C.-L. Leong Seow (ed.), *Ecclesiastes* (New Haven and London, 1997), esp. 12–21 and 643–66, argues for a date in the early fourth or even late fifth century BCE.

1. PLAY MAKERS

1. See Edith Hall, 'Greek tragedy and the politics of subjectivity in recent fiction', *Classical Receptions Journal* 1 (2009).
2. The play entitled *Rhesus* and attributed to Euripides; see below, pp. 294–8.

3. See Dana Ferrin Sutton, 'The theatrical families of Athens', *American Journal of Philology* 108 (1987), 9–26; Sarah B. Pomeroy, *Families and Classical and Hellenistic Greece* (Oxford, 1978), 147–8.
4. The ancient *Life of Sophocles*, 4. The ancient biographies of all three tragedians are translated into English in Mary R. Lefkowitz, *The Lives of the Greek Poets* (London, 1981), 157–69.
5. Horace, *Ars Poetica*, 276; Diogenes Laertius 3.56.
6. On the controversy over the presence of women in theatrical audiences, see Simon Goldhill, 'Representing democracy: women at the Great Dionysia', in Robin Osborne and Simon Hornblower (eds.), *Ritual, Finance, Politics: Athenian Democratic Accounts Presented to David Lewis* (Oxford, 1994), 347–69.
7. See Oliver Taplin, 'Spreading the word through performance', in Simon Goldhill and Robin Osborne (eds.), *Performance Culture and Athenian Democracy* (Cambridge, 1999), 33–57; Eric Csapo, 'Some social and economic conditions behind the rise of the acting profession in the fifth and fourth centuries BC', in C. Hugoniot, F. Hurlet, and S. Milanezi (eds.), *Le statut de l'acteur dans l'Antiquité grecque et romaine* (Tours, 2004), 53–76; Edith Hall, 'Greek tragedy 430–380 BC', in R. Osborne (ed.), *Debating the Athenian Cultural Revolution* (Cambridge, 2007), 264–87.
8. For English translations of the sources, a papyrus (*The Oxyrhynchus Papyri* 2737, fr. 1, col. ii), and a fragment of a comedy by Cratinus (*PCG* F 17), see Csapo & Slater, 135 no. 71, and 108, no. 1.
9. Antiphanes fr. 201 PCG, translated in Csapo & Slater, 148 no. 91.
10. The sources for this information, Aeschines *Against Ctesiphon* 66–7, scholia (ancient scholars' comments), and Plato, *Symposium* 194, are translated in Csapo & Slater, 109–10, nos. 4–7.
11. The ancient *Life of Euripides*, 11.
12. The source for this information, an ancient scholar's comment on Aristophanes' *Acharnians* 243, is translated in Csapo & Slater, 110 no. 9.
13. See the sources as translated in Csapo & Slater, 111–12, nos. 10–14.
14. Csapo & Slater, 112–13, nos. 15–16.
15. For translations of the sources see Csapo & and Slater, 113–15, nos. 19–29.
16. The information derives from the scholion on Aristophanes' *Clouds* 1266, and *Wasps* 579–80.
17. Xenophon, *Symposium* 6.3; Zenobius 1.42.
18. Eric Csapo, 'Kallipides on the floor-sweepings: the limits of realism in classical acting and performance styles', in Pat Easterling and Edith Hall (eds.), *Greek and Roman Actors* (Cambridge, 2002), 127–47.

19. Theophrastus, *On Delivery* fr. 713 in W. W. Fortenbaugh and D. Gutas (eds.), *Theophrastus: His Psychological, Doxographical, and Scientific Writings* (New Brunswick and London, 1992).
20. See e.g. the disparaging remarks of the music theorist Damon, translated in W. D. Anderson, *Ethos and Education in Greek Music* (Cambridge, Mass., 1966), 147–9.
21. There is a photograph of Demetrios, with full discussion, in E. Hall, 'Demetrios' rolls and Dionysos' other woman: the Pronomos Vase and tragic theatre', in Oliver Taplin and Rosie Wyles (eds.), *The Pronomos Vase* (Oxford, 2010).
22. See C. W. Marshall, '*Alcestis* and the ancient rehearsal process (*P.Oxy.* 4546)', *Arion* 11 (2004), 27–45.
23. Most of the surviving Greek musical papyri, including those relating to tragedy, are transcribed, with the words they accompanied, into modern musical annotation by M. L. West in his *Ancient Greek Music* (Oxford, 1992), ch. 10.
24. John Gould, 'Dramatic character and "human intelligibility" in Greek tragedy', *Proceedings of the Cambridge Philosophical Society* 24 (1978), 43–67, esp. 54–8.
25. See further Hall (2006), ch. 10.
26. The great orator Aeschines, an ex-actor with a legendarily beautiful voice who became the political rival of Demosthenes, had once played the role of Polymestor (Dem. 18.267, 19.337).
27. F. W. Riemer (ed.), *Briefwechsel zwischen Goethe und Zelter* (Berlin, 1833), pt. 1, 69 (letter 29),
28. See further the essays in Fiona Macintosh (ed.), *The Ancient Dancer in the Modern World* (Oxford, 2010).
29. Steven H. Lonsdale, *Dance and Ritual Play in Greek Religion* (Baltimore, Md., and London, 1993), 2.
30. Csapo & Slater, 103.
31. For discussion see E. Hall, 'Tragedy personified', in C. Kraus, S. Goldhill, H. P. Foley, and J. Elsner (eds.), *Visualizing the Tragic: Drama, Myth and Ritual in Greek Art and Literature* (Essays in Honour of Froma Zeitlin, Oxford, 2007), 221–56.
32. Albert Henrichs, 'Drama and *dromena*: bloodshed, violence, and sacrificial metaphor in Euripides', *Harvard Studies in Classical Philology* 100 (2000), 173–88.
33. The exception is the highly comic *Orestes* 128–9, where Electra asks a question in the second person plural, although the only person on stage, Orestes, is fast asleep.
34. The fundamental work is Anne Righter, *Shakespeare and the Idea of the Play* (London, 1962), although the term 'metatheatre' seems to

have been coined by Lionel Abel, *Metatheatre: A New View of Dramatic Form* (New York, 1963).
35. See Richard Hornby, *Drama, Metadrama, and Perception* (London and Toronto, 1986), 32–5.
36. Oliver Taplin, 'Fifth-century tragedy and comedy: a synkrisis', *Journal of Hellenic Studies* 106 (1986), 163–74.
37. Pat Easterling, 'Anachronism in Greek tragedy', *Journal of Hellenic Studies* 105 (1985), 1–10, p. 6.
38. See Mireille Lee, '"Evil wealth of raiment": deadly *peploi* in Greek tragedy', *Classical Journal* 99 (2004), 253–79.

## 2. COMMUNITY IDENTITIES

1. E. Hall, *The Return of Ulysses: A Cultural History of Homer's Odyssey* (London, 2008), 35–7.
2. See further Hall (2006), ch. 12.
3. See P. J. Rhodes, *The Athenian Boule*, (2nd edn, Oxford, 1985), 1 and n. 3.
4. Thucydides 8.69–70.1; [Aristotle] *Athenian Constitution* 32.3; see the fascinating remarks in Julia Shear, 'Cultural change, space, and the politics of commemoration in Athens', in R. Osborne (ed.), *Debating the Athenian Cultural Revolution: Art, Literature, Philosophy, and Politics 430–380 B.C.* (Cambridge, 2007), 91–115, pp. 102–3.
5. Rhodes, *The Athenian Boule*, 4, 6–7.
6. Rhodes, *The Athenian Boule*, 4. One scholiast on Aeschines 3.4 described the Council, indeed, as a 'mini-polis' (*mikra polis*).
7. There is some evidence that originally only the top three property classes could serve, to the exclusion of the thetes, but this qualification for eligibility seems to have been dropped in the later fifth century, or not rigidly enforced. See Rhodes, *The Athenian Boule*, 2–3.
8. See Simon Goldhill, 'Character and action, representation and reading: Greek tragedy and its critics', in C. B. R. Pelling (ed.), *Characterisation and Individuality in Greek Literature* Oxford, 1990), 100–27.
9. Ros Ballaster, 'The first female dramatists', in Helen Wilcox (ed.), *Women and Literature in Britain 1500–1700* (Cambridge, 1996), 267–90, p. 280 and n.28.
10. Pat Easterling, 'Constructing the heroic', in C. Pelling (ed.), *Greek Tragedy and the Historian* (Oxford, 1997), 21–37, p. 25.
11. See Hall (2006), 187–8.
12. See Euripides, *Children of Heracles* 994, Menander *Epitrepontes* 252 and E. Hall, 'Deianeira deliberates', in Simon Goldhill and Edith Hall (eds.), *Sophocles and the Greek Tragic Tradition* (Cambridge, 2009), 64–96.
13. See Donald Lateiner, 'Heralds and corpses in Thucydides', *Classical World* 71 (1977), 97–106.

14. See Helene Foley. 'The politics of tragic lamentation', in *Female Acts in Greek Tragedy* (Princeton, 2001), ch. 1.
15. Isaeus 4.19–20; Dinarchus 2.18.
16. See esp. Mark Toher, 'Euripides' "Supplices" and the social function of funeral ritual', *Hermes* 129 (2001), 332–43.
17. See also 1084–5, 1312–13, and the excellent article by M. Dyson and K. H. Lee, 'The funeral of Astyanax in Euripides' *Troades*', *Journal of Hellenic Studies* 120 (2000), 17–33.
18. See Kerri J. Hame, 'All in the family: funeral rites and the health of the oikos in Aischylos' *Oresteia*', *American Journal of Philology* 125 (2004), 513–38.
19. See Richard Seaford, *Reciprocity and Ritual: Homer and Tragedy in the Developing City-State* (Oxford, 1994); Melissa Mueller, 'The language of reciprocity in Euripides' *Medea*', *American Journal of Philology* 122 (2001), 471–504.
20. Edgar Allan Poe (1846), 'The philosophy of composition', *Graham's Magazine*, April, repr. in James A. Harrison (ed.), *The Complete Works of Edgar Allan Poe*, vol. 14 (New York, 1965), 193–208, p. 201.
21. R. Drew Griffith, 'Corporality in the ancient Greek theatre', *Phoenix* 52 (1998), 230–56, p. 232.
22. Gisela Richter, *Perspective in Greek and Roman Art* (London 1970).
23. On the rivers see esp. Harry Brewster, *The River Gods of Greece* (London, 1997).
24. Hall (2006), 104.
25. Froma Zeitlin, 'The artful eye: vision, ecphrasis and spectacle in Euripidean theatre', in Simon Goldhill and Robin Osborne (eds.), *Art and Text in Ancient Greek Culture* (Cambridge, 1994), 138–96.
26. Democritus, 68 A 33 *DK*; Hippias, 86 A 2 *DK*.
27. See the scholion on Aelius Aristides 3, p. 535 in W. Dindorf (ed.), *Aristides ex recensione G. Dindorfii* (Leipzig, 1829).
28. Donald J. Mastronarde, 'Actors on high: the skene roof, the crane, and the gods in Attic drama', *Classical Antiquity* 9 (1990), 247–94, p. 253.
29. Lillian B. Lawler, 'Cosmic dance and dithyramb', in Lillian B. Lawler, Dorothy M. Robathan, and William C. Korfmacher (eds.), *Studies in Honour of B. L. Ullman* (St Louis, 1960); A. Laks, 'Legislation and demiurgy: on the relationship between Plato's *Republic* and *Laws*', *Classical Antiquity* 9 (1990), 226–9.
30. A. C. Bradley, *Shakespearean Tragedy* (London and New York, 1904), 37–8.
31. See further Hall (2006), ch. 8.
32. See E. Hall, 'Is there a polis in Aristotle's *Poetics*?', in M. Silk (ed.), *Tragedy and the Tragic: Greek Theatre and Beyond* (Oxford), 295–309, p. 300.

## 3. CONFRONTATIONS

1. *Inscriptiones Graecae* I³ 1147.
2. For the different types of military service at Athens, and their relationship with the social class of the citizen, see the 'Constitution of Athens' attributed to Xenophon, 1.2, and Hans van Wees, 'Politics and the battlefield: ideology in Greek warfare', in Anton Powell (ed.), *The Greek World* (London and New York, 1995), 153–78.
3. V. Hanson, *The Western Way of War* (New York 1989), 220.
4. John Keegan, 'Introduction' to Hanson, *The Western Way of War*, xii–xiii.
5. Paul Fussell, *The Great War and Modern Memory* (London, 1975), 169–70.
6. See John Lazenby, 'The killing zone', in V. Hanson (ed.), *The Classical Greek Battle Experience* (London, 1991), 87–109.
7. Hall (1989), 148–54.
8. *Inscriptiones Graecae* I³ 421.
9. Hall (2006), 196–206.
10. Sian Lewis, 'Slaves as users and viewers of Athenian pottery', *Hephaistos* 16–17 (1998–9), 71–90.
11. See Thucydides 2.29.
12. N. Frye, *A Natural Perspective: The Development of Shakespearean Comedy and Romance* (New York and London, 1965), 146.
13. W. Donlan, *The Aristocratic Ideal in Ancient Greece* (Lawrence, Kan., 1980), 139; see esp. P. W. Rose, *Sons of the Gods, Children of Earth* (Ithaca, NY, and London, 1992), 266–30.
14. Antiphon, *Tetralogies* 1.3.5. See P. DuBois, *Torture and Truth* (New York and London, 1991), 35–8; Virginia Hunter, *Policing Athens: Social Control in the Attic Lawsuits* (Princeton, 1994), 70–95.
15. A. Cameron, *The Identity of Oedipus the King* (New York and London, 1968), 22.
16. W. S. Barrett (ed.), *Euripides. Hippolytus* (Oxford, 1964), 313–14. In the Sophoclean version Theseus was in Hades, believed dead.
17. See Froma Zeitlin's incomparable study *Playing the Other: Gender and Society in Classical Greek Literature* (Chicago, 1996).
18. See Alan Boegehold, 'Perikles' citizenship law of 451/0 BC', in A. Boegehold and A. Scafuro (eds.), *Athenian Identity and Civic Ideology* (Baltimore and London, 1994), 57–66.
19. A. E. Hanson, 'The medical writers' woman', in J. Halperin, J. Winkler, and F. I. Zeitlin (eds.), *Nothing to do with Dionysos?* (Princeton, 1990), 309–37, p. 320.
20. James Boswell and Samuel Johnson, *The Journal of a Tour to the Hebrides* (6th edn, London, 1813), 206–7.

21. See p. 164 and ch. 4 n. 5 below.
22. N. B. Crowther, 'Male "beauty" contests. The Euandria and Euaxia,' *L'Antiquité Classique* 54 (1985), 285–91.
23. Barry S. Strauss, *Fathers and Sons in Classical Athens: Ideology and Society in the Era of the Peloponnesian War* (Princeton, 1993), 22.
24. R. Fowler, 'Genealogical thinking, Hesiod's *Catalogue*, and the creation of the Hellenes', *Proceedings of the Cambridge Philological Society* 44 (1998), 1–20, p. 5.
25. Strauss, *Fathers and Sons in Classical Athens*, 22.
26. E. Hall, 'Subjects, selves and survivors', *Helios* 34 (2007), 125–59.
27. *How Young men Should Listen to Poetry* 28a; *Contra Celsum* 7.36.34.
28. See Peter Wilson, 'Euripides' tragic muse', in Martin Cropp, Kevin Lee, and David Sansone (eds.), *Euripides and Tragic Theatre in the Late Fifth Century*, *Illinois Classical Studies* [Special Issue] 24–5 (1999–2000), 427–49.

4. MINDS

1. Jon D. Mikalson, 'Unanswered prayers in Greek tragedy', *Journal of Hellenic Studies* 109 (1989), 81–98.
2. Jon D. Mikalson *Honor thy Gods: Popular Religion in Greek Tragedy* (Chapel Hill, NC, and London, 1991), 81–4. See Judith Fletcher, 'Women and oaths in Euripides', *Theatre Journal* 55 (2003), 29–44
3. Elizabeth Belfiore, 'Xenia in Sophocles' *Philoctetes*', *Classical Journal* 89 (1993–4), 113–29.
4. David Kovacs, 'Zeus in Euripides' *Medea*', *American Journal of Philology* 114 (1993), 45–70.
5. Jens David Baumbach, *The Significance of Votive Offerings in Selected Hera Sanctuaries in the Peloponnese, Ionia and Western Greece* (Oxford, 2004); Sarah Iles Johnston, 'Corinthian Medea and the cult of Hera Akraia', in James J. Clauss and Sarah Iles Johnston (eds.), *Medea* (Princeton, 1997), 44–70.
6. See the speech *Against Aristogeiton*, attributed to Demosthenes (25.79–80), and Derek Collins, 'Theoris of Lemnos and the criminalization of magic in fourth-century Athens', *Classical Quarterly* 51 (2001), 477–93.
7. Euripides fragments. 1018, 330.3–5, and 941 *TrGF*.
8. See T. C. W. Stinton, '"*Si credere dignum est*": some expressions of disbelief in Euripides and others', *Proceedings of the Cambridge Philological Society* 22 (1976), 60–8.
9. Rush Rehm, *Marriage to Death. The Conflation of Wedding and Funeral Rituals in Greek tragedy* (Princeton, 1994).

10. Froma Zeitlin, 'The motif of the corrupted sacrifice in Aeschylus' *Oresteia*', *Transactions of the American Philological Association* (1965), 463–508.
11. For a translation of the inscription see Hall (2006), 55 and n. 139. The boxer may have been an Arcadian named Apollogenes.
12. Fr. 19 *TrGF*. On this play (which has a relationship, through Ovid's *Heroides*, with John Ford's '*Tis Pity She's a Whore* of 1633), see further Hall (2006), 74–5.
13. Serenus in Stobaeus, *Florilegium* 5, 82; see also Plutarch, *de Audiendis Poetis* 12.33C, Athenaeus 13.582D.
14. F. Hölderlin, *Essays and Letters on Theory*, ed. Thomas Pfau (Albany, NY, 1988), 83.
15. Albert Camus, 'L'Avenir de la tragédie' (1955), translated as 'On the future of tragedy' in Philip Thody (ed.), *Lyrical and Critical Essays* (New York, 1969), 301.
16. A. Ferrain, 'On the philosophy of Prometheus in Protagoras', *Review of Metaphysics* 54.2 (2000) 289–319.
17. David Sansone, *Aeschylean Metaphors for Intellectual Activity* (= *Hermes* Einzelschr. 35, Wiesbaden, 1975), 27, 33.
18. There is, however, no reason to suppose that this must put the play's date subsequent to the terrible real-life epidemic of plague that afflicted Athens from 430 BCE, since ancient myth featured numerous plagues, including the one sent by Apollo which opens the *Iliad*.
19. See further Hall (2006), 385–6.
20. William Manchester, *Goodbye, Darkness: A Memoir of the Pacific* (New York, 1979), 83.

5. AESCHYLEAN DRAMA

1. See e.g. 3, 36, 824–8, 891–4, 1258–9, 1473, 1115, 1492, 1125–6, 1050, 1063, 1093, 1141–2, 1298, 1445–6.
2. Gregory Nagy, '"Dream of a shade": refractions of epic vision in Pindar's *Pythian* 8 and Aeschylus' *Seven against Thebes*', *Harvard Studies in Classical Philology* 100 (2000), 97–118.
3. Walter Burkert, *The Orientalizing Revolution: Near Eastern Influence on Greek Culture in the Early Archaic Age* (Cambridge, Mass., and London, 1992), 106–14.
4. See Phiroze Vasunia, *The Gift of the Nile: Hellenizing Egypt from Aeschylus to Alexander* (Berkeley, Los Angeles, and London, 2001).
5. See further below pp. 227–30 and Fig. 5.3.
6. *Oxyrhynchus Papyri* no. 2256, fr. 3.

7. See esp. Euripides' *Children of Heracles* and *Suppliant Women*; this plot type is also reflected in some episodes in his *Heracles*, *Helen*, and *Ion*, and in Sophocles' *Oedipus at Colonus*.
8. For a sensible review of the different theories see J. K. MacKinnon, 'The reason for the Danaids' flight', *Classical Quarterly* 28 (1978), 74–82.
9. See Hall (1989), 206.
10. 75, 81, 277, 327–8, 385–6, 394, 479, 1163, 1606. See further E. Hall, 'Eating children is bad for you: the offspring of the past in Aeschylus' *Agamemnon*', in D. Stuttard and T. Shasha (eds.), *Essays on Agamemnon* (Brighton, 2002), 11–26.
11. Christopher Faraone, 'Aeschylus' *humnos desmios* (*Eum.* 306) and Attic judicial curse tablets', *Journal of Hellenic Studies* 105 (1985), 150–4.
12. Anaxagoras 107 A 59 *DK*, although other evidence suggests that Anaxagoras said that both mother and father contributed semen to the process of embryo creation.

## 6. EURIPIDEAN DRAMA

1. Thaddeus Zielinski, *Tragodoumenon Libri Tres* (Krakow, 1925), 133–240.
2. Philemon fr. 118 *PCG*.
3. *Poetics* ch. 18, 1456a 25–7; ch. 15, 1454 b1; ch. 25, 1461 b21; ch. 13, 1453 a30.
4. Axionicus fr. 3 *PCG*.
5. See Hall (2006), ch. 5.
6. D. W. Lucas, *The Medea of Euripides. Translated into English Prose* (London, 1949), 3.
7. See above, pp. 159–60.
8. See Hall (1989), 175–6.
9. See Hall (1989), 181–2 and nn. 70, 74.
10. G. M. A. Grube, *The Drama of Euripides* (London, 1941), 314.
11. James Morwood, 'The pattern of the Euripides *Electra*', *American Jornal of Philology* 102 (1981), 362–70.
12. *The Oxyrhynchus Papyri* no. 2400 (vol. 24. 107–9), lines 101–4.
13. In *Essays on Four Plays of Euripides* (Cambridge, 1905), 134–5.
14. See the dazzling article by Christina Kraus, 'Dangerous supplements: etymology and genealogy in Euripides' *Heracles*', *Proceedings of the Cambridge Philological Society* 44 (1998), 137–57.
15. A. W. Schlegel, *A Course of Lectures on Dramatic Art and Literature*. Eng. trans. John Black (new edn. London, 1846), 179–80.
16. See Edith Hall and Fiona Macintosh, *Greek Tragedy and the British Theatre 1660–1914* (New York and Oxford, 2005), 508–11.

17. William N. Bates, *Euripides: A Student of Human Nature* (Philadelphia and London, 1930), 199–200.
18. Hall (1989), 110–12.
19. See E. Hall, *Adventures with Iphigeneia* (forthcoming, New York, 2011) ch. 5.
20. Northrop Frye, *A Natural Perspective: The Development of Shakespearean Comedy and Romance* (New York, 1965); C. P. Segal, 'The two worlds of Euripides' *Helen*', in *Interpreting Greek Tragedy* (Ithaca, NY, 1986), 222–67.
21. See G. W. Bond (ed.), *Euripides' Hypsipyle* (Oxford, 1963), 87–90, 144.
22. e.g. H. Siegel, 'Self-delusion and the *volte-face* of Iphigenia in Euripides' *Iphigenia at Aulis*', *Hermes* 108 (1980), 300–21.
23. Richard Paul Jodrell, *Illustrations of Euripides on the Ion and the Bacchae* (London 1781), vol. ii, 550.
24. R. P. Winnington-Ingram, *Euripides and Dionysos: An Interpretation of the Bacchae* (first published 1946, 2nd edn with foreword by P. E. Easterling, Bristol, 1997).
25. William Ritchie, *The Authenticity of the Rhesus of Euripides* (Cambridge, 1964).

## 7. SOPHOCLEAN DRAMA

1. *Coleridge's Miscellaneous Criticism*, ed. Thomas Middleton Raysor (London, 1936), 421.
2. The information is recorded in the ancient hypothesis to the play, attributed to Aristophanes of Byzantium (Hyp. *Ant* 1).
3. See pp. 339–40.
4. Froma Zeitlin, 'Thebes: theater of self and society in Athenian drama,' in. J. P. Euben (ed.), *Greek Tragedy and Political Theory* (Berkeley, Los Angeles, and London, 1986), 101–41.
5. Pat Easterling, 'Plain words in Sophocles', in Jasper Griffin (ed.), *Sophocles Revisited: Essays Presented to Sir Hugh Lloyd-Jones* (Oxford, 1999), 95–107.
6. See the forthcoming collection of essays on *Antigone* in performance, edited by Helene Foley and Erin Mee, to be published by Oxford University Press.
7. Charles Segal 'Tragedy, corporeality, and the texture of language: matricide in the three Electra plays', *Classical World* 79 (1985), 7–23, p. 19.
8. G. Ronnet, *Sophocle, poète tragique* (Paris, 1961), 208–9.
9. 'On not knowing Greek' (1925), in Virginia Woolf, *The Common Reader* (12th impression, London, 1975), 41, 43–4.

10. Quoted in Richard Reid (ed.), *Elektra: A Play by Ezra Pound and Rudd Fleming* (Princeton, 1989), xiii.
11. A. W. Schlegel, *A Course of Lectures on Dramatic Art and Literature*, trans. John Black (new edn, London, 1846), 109.
12. Ezra Pound, *Women of Trachis: A Version* (London, 1969), 66.
13. Just two examples from the United Kingdom alone: Timberlake Wertenbaker's, performed on radio in 1999 and published in her *Plays Two* (London, 2002), and Martin Crimp's stage play *Cruel and Tender*, first performed in 2004 by the Young Vic and published by Faber and Faber (London, 2004).
14. Charles Segal, *Sophocles' Tragic World: Divinity, Nature, Society* (Cambridge, Mass., 1995), 29.
15. See J. P. Vernant and P. Vidal-Naquet, *Myth and Tragedy in Ancient Greece*, trans. J. Lloyd (New York, 1988), ch. 7.
16. All we are told is that Philoctetes, apparently unwittingly, had intruded into the shrine of Chryse, the nymph who lived on an island named after her, and been bitten by the poisonous snake who guarded it (so says Neoptolemus at 1327–8).
17. Pat Easterling, 'The language of the polis in *Oedipus at Colonus*', in J.-Th. A. Papademetriou (ed.), *Praktika* (Athens, 1997), 273–83. On Athenian 'reasonableness' see G. Kirkwood, 'From Melos to Colonus', *Transactions of the American Philological Association* 116 (1986), 99–117.
18. See Aara Suksi, 'The poet at Colonus: nightingales in Sophocles', *Mnemosyne* 54 (2001), 646–58. According to an old legend, the nightingale had originally been an Athenian princess named Procne, but she had been transformed into the bird because of her unceasing laments for her son Itys. This story had earlier been dramatized by Sophocles himself in one of his most famous lost dramas: see p. 340.

## 8. GREEK TRAGEDY AND GREEK TRAGIC FRAGMENTS TODAY

1. Quoted from James Campbell, 'You promised me poems', interview with Derek Walcott, *The Guardian*, 'Books', Saturday 4 October 2008).
2. See above all Helene Foley, 'Generic ambiguity in modern productions and new versions of Greek tragedy', in E. Hall and S. Harrop (eds.), *Theorising Performance: Greek Drama, Cultural History, and Critical Practice* (London, 2010).
3. See the remarks of Josephine Balmer in her introduction to *Classical Women Poets* (Newcastle upon Tyne, 1996), 9. These ideas were explored with particular intensity in Kelly Copper's play about the effect of going to war in contemporary New York in *Fragment*, directed

by Pavol Liska (which premiered on 22 March 2006 at the off-Broadway Classic Stage Company). This included more than 5,000 fragments of Sophocles and Euripides.
4. See E. Hall 'Classics, class and Cloacina: Tony Harrison's human coprology', *Arion* 15 (2007), 83–108.
5. Timberlake Wertenbaker, *The Love of the Nightingale* and *The Grace of Mary Traverse* (London and Boston, 1989), 19.
6. *Iph . . . Euripides, a new Version of Iphigeneia in Aulis* (London, 2002); *Bacchai, Euripides, a new translation* (London, 2002).
7. The attribution of this sardonic fragment, which is certainly the work of Euripides, to his character Alcmaeon was a guess made by a 19th-century scholar called F. W. Wagner; in the latest edition of the fragments of Euripides it has been assigned, however, to his *Bellerophon* (fr. 304a *TrGF*).
8. First published in May 1939, it was included in his collection *Ficciones* (Buenos Aires, 1944).
9. Roussos' play has itself been translated into English by Athan Anagnostopoulos, and has been performed in Boston. For a play 'inspired by' the fragments of Euripides' *Alope* see Demetrios Georgides, *Euripides' Alope: Reconstructed with Liberal Doses of Poetic License* (rev. edn, 2006).
10. Alistair Elliot, *Phaethon by Euripides: A Reconstruction* (London, 2008), 58.
11. *Miscellaneous Prose of Sir Philip* Sidney, ed. Katharine Duncan-Jones and Jan van Dorsten (Oxford, 1973 [1581]), 96–7.

# FURTHER READING

These necessarily selective lists are intended to help users of this book identify reasonably recent and accessible bibliography that will take them further into the issues raised by each section of each chapter, and almost all of which is written in English. The items specified here are intended to supplement the often very significant publications that have already been identified in the footnotes.

## *Introduction*

Terry Eagleton, *Sweet Violence: A Study of the Tragic* (Oxford, 2002).
P. E. Easterling (ed.), *The Cambridge Companion to Greek Tragedy* (Cambridge, 1997).
Simon Goldhill, *Reading Greek Tragedy* (Cambridge, 1992).
John Gould, *Myth, Ritual, Memory, and Exchange* (Oxford, 2001).
Richard Green, *Theater in Ancient Greek Society* (London, 1994).
—— and Eric Handley, *Images of the Greek Theatre* (Austin, Tex., 1995).
Justina Gregory (ed.), *A Companion to Greek Tragedy* (Oxford, 2005).
John Kerrigan, *Revenge Tragedy: Aeschylus to Armageddon* (Oxford, 1996).
B. M. W. Knox, *Word and Action* (Baltimore, Md., 1979).
Jan Kott, *The Eating of the Gods: An Interpretation of Greek Tragedy* (Eng. trans., New York, 1973).
Nancy Sorkin Rabinowitz, *Greek Tragedy* (Malden, Mass., 2008).
Rush Rehm, *Greek Tragic Theatre* (London, 1992).
Charles Segal, *Interpreting Greek Tragedy: Myth, Poetry, Text* (Ithaca, NY, and London, 1986).
Adrian Poole, *Tragedy: A Very Short Introduction* (Oxford, 2005).
Oliver Taplin, 'Fifth-century tragedy and comedy: a synkrisis', *Journal of Hellenic Studies* 106 (1986), 163–74.
—— *Greek Tragedy in Action* (rev. edn, London, 1985).
J. P. Vernant and P. Vidal-Naquet, *Tragedy and Myth in Ancient Greece* (Eng. trans., Brighton, 1981).
John J. Winkler and F. I. Zeitlin (eds.), *Nothing to do with Dionysos? Athenian Drama in its Social Context* (Princeton, 1990).

Bernhard Zimmermann, *Greek Tragedy* (Eng. trans., Baltimore, Md., and London, 1991).

## 1. *Play Makers*

PERSONNEL

D. Boedeker and K. Raaflaub (eds.), *Democracy, Empire, and the Arts in Fifth-Century Athens* (Cambridge, Mass., 1999).
P. Cartledge (ed.), *The Cambridge Illustrated History of Ancient Greece* (Cambridge, 1998).
—— *The Greeks: A Portrait of Selves and Others* (2nd edn, New York, 2002).
J. K. Davies, *Wealth and the Power of Wealth in Classical Athens* (New York, 1981).
Pat Easterling and Edith Hall (eds.), *Greek and Roman Actors* (Cambridge, 2002).
Joint Association of Classical Teachers, *The World of Athens* (2nd edn, 2008).
Nicholas F. Jones, *Rural Athens under the Democracy* (Philadelphia, 2004).
E. Krummen, 'Athens and Attica: *polis* and countryside in tragedy', in A. Sommerstein et al. (eds.), *Tragedy, Comedy and the Polis* (Bari, 1993), 191–217.
Robin Osborne, *Demos: The Discovery of Classical Attika* (Cambridge, 1985).
—— *Classical Greece* (Oxford, 2000).
Martin Revermann, 'The competence of audiences in fifth- and fourth-century Athens', *Journal of Hellenic Studies* 126 (2006), 99–124.
Ruth Scodel (ed.), *Theater and Society in the Classical World* (Ann Arbor, 1993).
David Whitehead, *The Demes of Attica* (Princeton, 1986).
Peter Wilson, *The Athenian Institution of the Khoregia: The Chorus, the City and the Stage* (Cambridge, 2004).

WRITING ROLES

Shirley Barlow, 'The language of Euripides' monodies', in J. H. Betts, J. T. Hooker, and J. R. Green (eds.), *Studies in Honour of T. B. L. Webster*, vol. 1 (Bristol, 1986), 10–22.
James Barrett, *Staged Narrative: Poetics and the Messenger in Greek Tragedy* (Berkeley, Calif., 2002).
V. Bers, 'Tragedy and rhetoric', in I. Worthington (ed.), *Greek Rhetoric in Action* (London and New York, 1994), 176–95.
Richard Buxton, *Persuasion in Greek Tragedy* (Cambridge, 1982).
Terence Cave, *Recognitions: A Study in Poetics* (Oxford, 1988).

Mark Damen, 'Actor and character in Greek tragedy', *Theatre Journal* 41 (1989), 316–40.
Barbara Goward, *Telling Tragedy: Narrative Technique in Aeschylus, Sophocles and Euripides* (London, 1999).
Albert Henrichs, 'Why should I dance? Choral self-referentiality in tragedy', *Arion* 3 (1994–5), 56–111.
John Herington, *Poetry into Drama: Early Tragedy and the Greek Poetic Tradition* (Berkeley, Los Angeles, and London, 1985).
H. Friis Johansen, *General Reflection in Tragic Rhesis: A Study of Form* (Copenhagen, 1959).
Maarit Kaimio, *Physical Contact in Greek Tragedy* (Helsinki, 1988).
Richmond Lattimore, *The Poetry of Greek Tragedy* (Baltimore, Md., 1958).
—— *Story Patterns in Greek Tragedy* (London, 1964).
Penelope Murray and Peter Wilson (eds.), *Music and the Muses: The Culture of 'Mousikē' in the Classical Athenian City* (Oxford, 2004).

CELEBRATING DIONYSUS

I. Brooke, *Costume in Greek Classical Drama* (London, 1962).
W. Burkert, 'Greek tragedy and sacrificial ritual', *Greek, Roman, and Byzantine Studies* 7 (1966), 87–121.
Thomas H. Carpenter, *Dionysian Imagery in Archaic Greek Art* (Oxford, 1986).
C. Calame, 'Facing otherness: the tragic mask in ancient Greece', *History of Religions* 26 (1986), 125–42.
Sue-Ellen Case, 'Classic drag: the Greek creation of female parts', *Theatre Journal* 37 (1985), 317–27.
Eric Csapo, 'Riding the phallus for Dionysus: iconology, ritual, and gender-role de/construction', *Phoenix* 51 (1997), 253–95.
C. Faraone and Thomas Carpenter (eds.), *Masks of Dionysus* (Ithaca, NY, 1993).
Helene Foley, 'Choral identity in Greek tragedy', *Classical Philology* 98 (2003). 1–30.
B. Gredley, 'Greek tragedy and the "discovery" of the actor', in *Themes in Drama 6: Drama and the Actor* (Cambridge, 1984), 1–14.
S. Halliwell, 'The function and aesthetics of the Greek tragic mask', *Drama* 2 (1993), 195–211.
Jeffrey Henderson, 'Women and the Athenian dramatic festivals', *Transactions of the American Philological Society* 121 (1991), 133–47.
Sarah Iles Johnston, *Restless Dead: Encounters Between the Living and the Dead in Ancient Greece* (Berkeley, Calif., and London, 1999).

C. W. Marshall, (1994), 'The rule of three actors in practice', *Text and Presentation* 15, 53–61
—— 'Some fifth-century masking conventions', *Greece and Rome* 46 (1999), 188–202.
Zoja Pavloskis, 'The voice of the actor in Greek tragedy', *Classical World* 71 (1977–8), 113–23.
T. A. Tarkow, 'Thematic implications of costuming in the *Oresteia*,' *Maia* 32 (1980), 153–65.
David Wiles, *Mask and Performance in Greek Tragedy* (Cambridge, 2007).
Peter Wilson (ed.), *The Greek Theatre and Festivals: Documentary Studies* (Oxford, 2007).
Yana Zarifi, 'Chorus and dance in the ancient world', in Marianne McDonald and J. Michael Walton (eds.), *The Cambridge Companion to Greek and Roman Theatre* (Cambridge, 2007), 227–46.

## 2. *Community Identities*

### GATHERINGS

D. M Carter, *The Politics of Greek Tragedy* (Bristol, 2007).
Paul Cartledge, *The Greeks* (Oxford, 1996).
—— (ed.), *The Cambridge Illustrated History of Ancient Greece* (Cambridge, 1998).
J. K. Davies, *Democracy and Classical Greece* (Glasgow, 1978).
—— 'Athenian citizenship: the descent group and the alternatives', *CJ* 73 (1977–8). 105–21
Mark Golden, *Sport and Society in Ancient Greece* (Cambridge, 1998).
M. H. Hansen, *The Athenian Democracy in the Age of Demosthenes* (Oxford, 1991).
Jon Hesk, *Deception and Democracy in Classical Athens* (Cambridge, 2002).
Christian Meier, *The Political Art of Greek Tragedy* (Eng. trans., Cambridge, 1993).
Stephen G. Miller, *Ancient Greek Athletics* (New Haven, and London, 2004).
J. Ober, *Mass and Elite in Democratic Athens: Rhetoric, Ideology and the Power of the People* (Princeton, 1989).
Christopher Pelling (ed.), *Greek Tragedy and the Historian* (Oxford, 1997).
Anton Powell, *Athens and Sparta: Constructing Greek Political and Social History from 478 BC (London, 1988).*
P. J. Rhodes, 'Nothing to do with democracy: Athenian drama and the polis', *Journal of Hellenic Studies* 123 (2003), 104–19
R. K. Sinclair, *Democracy and Participation in Athens* (Cambridge, 1988).
S. Usher, *Greek Oratory: Tradition and Originality* (Oxford, 1999).

## DEALING WITH DEATH

Meg Alexiou, *The Ritual Lament in Greek Tradition* (2nd edn, Lanham, Md., 2002).
Elizabeth Belfiore, *Murder among Friends: Violations of Philia in Greek Tragedy* (New York and Oxford, 2000).
Casey Dué, *The Captive Woman's Lament in Greek Tragedy* (Austin, Tex., 2006).
Robert Garland, *The Greek Way of Death* (2nd edn, London and Bristol, 2001).
Elise P. Garrison, *Groaning Tears: Ethical and Dramatic Aspects of Suicide in Greek Tragedy* (Leiden, 1995).
Gail Holst-Warhaft, *Dangerous Voices: Women's Laments and Greek Literature* (London and New York, 1992).
Nicole Loraux, *The Invention of Athens: The Funeral Oration in The Classical City* (Eng. trans., Cambridge, Mass., 1986).
—— *Tragic Ways of Killing a Woman* (Eng. trans. Cambridge, Mass., and London, 1987).
Christiane Sourvinou-Inwood, *'Reading' Greek Death* (Oxford, 1995).
Rachel Hall Sternberg, *Tragedy Offstage: Suffering and Sympathy in Ancient Athens* (Austin, Tex., 2006).

## CONTEXTS

André Bernand, *La carte du tragique: la géographie dans la tragédie grecque* (Paris, 1985).
Pat Easterling, 'Women in tragic space', *Bulletin of the Institute of Classical Studies* 34 (1988), 15-26.
Mary Kuntz, *Narrative Setting and Dramatic Poetry* (Leiden, 1993).
Jennifer Neils (ed.), *The Parthenon: From Antiquity to the Present* (Cambridge, 2005).
N. Sultan, *Exile and the Poetics of Loss in Greek Tradition* (Lanham, Md., 1999).
Jeffrey M. Hurwit, *The Acropolis in the Age of Pericles* (Cambridge, 2004).
Rush Rehm, *The Play of Space: Spatial Transformation in Greek Tragedy* (Princeton, 2002).
Robin Francis Rhodes, *Architecture and Meaning on the Athenian Acropolis* (Cambridge, 1995).
Jacqueline de Romilly, *Time in Greek Tragedy* (Ithaca, NY, 1968).
David Wiles, *Tragedy in Athens: Performance Space and Theatrical Meaning* (Cambridge, 1997).

## MYTHS AND THE CITY

J. Davie, 'Theseus the king in fifth-century Athens', *Greece and Rome* 29 (1982). 25-34.

Page duBois, *Centaurs and Amazons: Women and the Prehistory of the Great Chain of Being* (Ann Arbor, Mich., 1982).

Emily Kearns, *The Heroes of Attica* (Bulletin of the Institute of Classical Studies suppl. 57, London, 1989).

E. Natanblut, *The Seven against Thebes Myth in Greek Tragedy* (Montreal, 2005).

Nicole Loraux, *The Children of Athena* (Eng. trans. C. Levine, Princeton, 1993).

Sophie Mills, *Theseus, Tragedy and the Athenian Empire* (Oxford, 1997).

W. Blake Tyrrell and Frieda S. Brown (eds.), *Athenians Myths and Institutions* (New York and Oxford, 1991).

J. P. Vernant and P. Vidal-Naquet, *Myth and Tragedy in Ancient Greece* (Eng. trans. J. Lloyd, New York, 1988).

M. Visser, 'Worship your enemy: aspects of the cult of heroes in ancient Greece', *Harvard Theological Review* 75 (1982), 403–28.

H. J. Walker, *Theseus and Athens* (New York, 1995).

S. Woodford, 'Cults of Heracles in Attica', in D. G. Mitten et al. (eds.), *Studies Presented to George M. A. Hanfmann* (Mainz, 1971), 211–25.

## 3. Confrontations

### WAR

Emma Bridges, Edith Hall, and P. J. Rhodes (eds.), *Cultural Responses to the Persian Wars* (Oxford, 2007).

T. Everson, *Warfare in Ancient Greece: Arms and Armour from the Heroes of Homer to Alexander the Great* (Stroud, 2004).

Peter Hunt, *Slaves, Warfare, and Ideology in the Greek Historians* (Cambridge, 1998).

Russell Meiggs, *The Athenian Empire* (Oxford, 1972).

Anton Powell, *Athens and Sparta* (London, 1988).

Richard Sewell, *In the Theatre of Dionysos: Democracy and Tragedy in Ancient Athens* (Jefferson, NC, 2007).

### ETHNICITY AND CLASS

David Bain, *Masters, Servants, and Orders in Greek Tragedy* (Manchester, 1981).

Helen Bacon, *Barbarians in Greek Tragedy* (New Haven, 1961).

Page duBois, *Slaves and Other Objects* (London and Chicago, 2002).

Edith Hall, *Inventing the Barbarian: Greek Self-Definition through Tragedy* (Oxford, 1989).

Jonathan Hall, *Hellenicity: Between Ethnicity and Culture* (Chicago and London, 1999).

M. Miller (1997), *Athenians and Persians in the Fifth Century BC: A Study in Cultural Receptivity* (Cambridge, 1997).

Suzanne Saïd, 'Grecs et barbares dans les tragédies d'Euripide: le fin des différences', *Ktema* 9 (1984). 27–53. Eng. trans. in T. Harrison (ed.), *Greeks and Barbarians* (Cambridge, 2002), 62–100.

Ruth Scodel, 'The captive's dilemma: sexual acquiescence in Euripides' *Hecuba* and *Troades*,' *Harvard Studies in Classical Philology* 98 (1998), 137–54.

D. P. Stanley-Porter, 'Mute actors in the tragedies of Euripides', *Bulletin of the Institute of Classical Studies* 20 (1973), 68–93.

Katerina Synodinou, *On the Concept of Slavery in Euripides* (Ioannina, 1979).

WOMEN AND MEN

Karen Bassi, *Acting Like Men: Gender, Drama and Nostalgia in Ancient Greece* (Ann Arbor, Mich., 1998).

J. Blok and H. Mason (eds.), *Sexual Asymmetry: Studies in Ancient Society* (Amsterdam, 1987), 1–57.

Sue Blundell, *Women in Ancient Greece* (Cambridge, 1995).

D. Cohen, *Law, Sexuality, and Society: The Enforcement of Morals in Classical Athens* (Cambridge, 1991).

Elaine Fantham et al. (eds.), *Women in the Classical World* (New York and Oxford, 1994).

Helene Foley, *Female Acts in Greek Tragedy* (Princeton and Oxford, 2001).

Virginia Hunter, *Policing Athens* (Princeton, 1994).

R. Just, *Women in Athenian Law and Life* (London and New York, 1989).

Deborah Lyons, *Gender and Immortality: Heroines in Ancient Greek Myth and Cult* (Princeton, 1997).

Nancy Sorkin Rabinowitz, *Anxiety Veiled: Euripides and the Traffic in Women* (Ithaca, NY, and London, 1993).

A. Sommerstein, 'The language of Athenian women,' in F. de Martino and A. Sommerstein (eds.), *Lo spettacolo delle voci* (Bari, 1995), vol. 2, 61–85.

Victoria Wohl, *Intimate Commerce: Exchange, Gender and Subjectivity in Greek Tragedy* (Austin, Tex., 1998).

Froma Zeitlin, *Playing the Other: Gender and Society in Classical Greek Literature* (Chicago and London, 1996).

AGE GROUPS

Thomas M. Falkner, *The Poetics of Old Age* (Norman, Okla., and London, 1995).

—— and J. de Luce (eds.), *Old Age in Greek and Latin Literature* (Albany, NY, 1989).

Mark Golden, *Children and Childhood in Classical Athens* (2nd edn, Baltimore, Md., and London, 1993).

J. Neils and J. H. Oakley, *Coming of Age in Ancient Greece: Images of Childhood from the Classical Past* (New Haven and London, 2003).

G. M. Sifakis, 'Children in Greek tragedy,' *Bulletin of the Institute of Classical Studies* 26 (1979)., 67–80.

Emily R. Wilson, *Mocked with Death: Tragic Overliving from Sophocles to Milton* (Baltimore, Md., and London, 2004).

F. I. Zeitlin, 'Intimate relations: children, childbearing, and parentage on the Euripidean stage', in M. Revermann and Peter Wilson (eds.), *Performance, Iconography, Reception: Studies in Honour of Oliver Taplin* (Oxford, 2008), 318–32.

## 4. Minds

### THEOLOGY, CULT, AND RITUAL

H. Bowden, *Classical Athens and the Delphic Oracle: Divination and Democracy* (Cambridge, 2005).

Francis M. Dunn, 'Euripides and the rites of Hera Akraia', *Greek, Roman, and Byzantine Studies* 35 (1994), 103–15.

Pat Easterling, 'Tragedy and ritual: "Cry woe, woe, but let the good prevail"', *Mētis* 3 (1988), 87–109.

—— 'Gods on stage in Greek Tragedy', in J. Dalfen, G. Petersmann, and F. F. Schwarz (eds.), *Religio Graeco-Romana: Festschrift für Walter Pötscher* (= *Grazer Beiträge* Suppl. 5, Graz, 1993), 77–8.

Barbara Goff, *Citizen Bacchae: Women's Ritual Practice in Ancient Greece* (Berkeley, Calif., 2004).

Jon D. Mikalson, *Athenian Popular Religion* (Chapel Hill, NC, 1983).

—— 'Unanswered prayers in Greek tragedy', *Journal of Hellenic Studies* 109 (1989), 81–98.

—— *Honor thy Gods: Popular Religion in Greek Tragedy* (Chapel Hill, NC, and London, 1991).

Robert Parker, *Athenian Religion: A History* (Oxford, 1996).

P. Roth, 'The theme of corrupted *xenia* in Aeschylus' *Oresteia*', *Mnemosyne* 46 (1993), 1–17.

Christiane Sourvinou-Inwood, *Tragedy and Athenian Religion* (Lanham, Md., and Oxford, 2003).

Harvey Yunis, *A New Creed: Fundamental Religious Beliefs in the Athenian Polis and Euripidean Drama* (= *Hypomnemata* 91, Göttingen, 1988).

## PHILOSOPHY

D. J. Conacher, *Euripides and the Sophists: Some Dramatic Treatments of Philosophical Ideas* (London, 1998).
W. K. C. Guthrie, *The Sophists* (Cambridge, 1971).
Edward Hussey, *The Pre-Socratics* (London, 1972).
S. Jarratt, *Rereading the Sophists: Classical Rhetoric Refigured* (Carbondale, Ill., and Edwardsville, Ill. 1991).
G. B. Kerferd, *The Sophistic Movement* (Cambridge, 1981).
Martha C. Nussbaum, *The Fragility of Goodness: Luck and Ethics in Greek Tragedy and Philosophy* (Cambridge, 1986).
J. de Romilly, *The Great Sophists in Periclean Athens* (Eng. trans., Oxford, 1992).
F. Solmsen, *Intellectual Experiments of the Greek Enlightenment* (Princeton, 1975).
A. J. Podlecki, *Perikles and his Circle* (London, 1988).

## PSYCHES, MADNESS, AND MEDICINE

J. M. Bremer, *Hamartia: Tragic Error in the Poetics of Aristotle and in Greek* (Amsterdam, 1969).
Lesly Ann Dean-Jones, *Women's Bodies in Classical Greek Science* (Oxford, 1994).
Nancy Demand, *Birth, Death and Motherhood in Classical Greece* (Baltimore, Md., and London, 1994).
N. Fisher, *Hybris* (Warminster, 1992).
J. Gibert, *Change of Mind in Greek Tragedy* (= Hypomnemata 108, Göttingen, 1995).
Christopher Gill, *Personality in Greek Epic, Tragedy, and Philosophy* (Oxford, 1996).
Helen King, *Hippocrates' Woman: Reading the Female Body in Ancient Greece* (London and New York, 1998).
Robin Mitchell-Boyask, *Plague and the Athenian Imagination* (Cambridge, 2008).
Ruth Padel, 'Women: model for possession by Greek daemons', in Averil Cameron and Amelie Kuhrt (eds.), *Images of Women in Antiquity* (Detroit, 1983), 3–19.
—— *In and Out of the Mind: Greek Images of the Tragic Self* (Princeton, 1992).
—— *Whom Gods Destroy: Elements of Greek and Tragic Madness* (Princeton, 1995).
W. B. Stanford, *Greek Tragedy and the Emotions* (London, 1983).
T. C. W. Stinton, '*Hamartia* in Aristotle and Greek tragedy', *Classical Quarterly* 25 (1975), 21–254.

William G. Thalmann, 'Aeschylus's physiology of the emotions', *American Journal of Philology* 107 (1986), 489–511.

## 5. Aeschylean Drama

D. J. Conacher, *Aeschylus: The Earlier Plays and Related Studies* (Toronto, Buffalo, and London, 1996).
Pat Easterling, 'Presentation of character in Aeschylus', *Greece and Rome* 20 (1973), 3–19.
M. Gagarin, *Aeschylean Drama* (Berkeley, Los Angeles, and London, 1976).
T. Gantz 'Inherited guilt in Aeschylus' *CJ* 78 (1982), 1–23.
John Herington, *Aeschylus* (New Haven, 1986).
S. Ireland, *Aeschylus* (Oxford, 1986).
M. Lloyd (ed.), *Oxford Readings in Classical Studies: Aeschylus* (Oxford, 2007).
Marsh McCall (ed.), *Aeschylus: A Collection of Critical Essays* (Englewood Cliffs, NJ, 1972).
A. J. Podlecki, *The Political Background of Aeschylean Tragedy* (2nd edn, London, 1999).
—— 'Aeschylus' women,' *Helios* 10 (1983), 23–47.
Thomas G. Rosenmeyer, *The Art of Aeschylus* (Berkeley, Calif., 1982).
Oliver Taplin, 'Aeschylean silences and silences in Aeschylus', *Harvard Studies in Classical Philology* 76 (1972), 57–97.
—— *The Stagecraft of Aeschylus* (Oxford, 1977).
R. P. Winnington-Ingram, *Studies in Aeschylus* (Cambridge, 1983).

PERSIANS: COMMENTARIES

H. D. Broadhead (ed.), *The Persae of Aeschylus* (Cambridge, 1960).
Edith Hall (ed.), *Aeschylus' Persians* (Warminster, 1996; includes translation).

INTERPRETATIONS

Michael Anderson, 'The imagery of "The Persians"', *Greece and Rome* 19 (1972), 166–74.
Attilio Favorini, 'History, collective memory, and Aeschylus' *The Persians*', *Theatre Journal* 55 (2003), 1 [= *Special Issue on Ancient Theatre*], 99–111.
Edith Hall, 'Asia unmanned; images of victory in classical Athens', in J. Rich and G. Shipley (eds.), *War and Society in the Greek World* (London, 1993), 107–33.
Tom Harrison, *The Emptiness of Asia* (London, 2000).

I. Kantzios, 'The Politics of Fear in Aeschylus' "Persians"', *Classical World* 98 (2004), 3–19.

A. N. Michelini, *Tradition and Dramatic Form in the Persians of Aeschylus* (Leiden, 1982).

David Rosenbloom, *Aeschylus' Persians* (London, 2005).

William G. Thalmann, 'Xerxes' rags: some problems in Aeschylus' *Persians*', *American Journal of Philology* 101 (1980), 260–82.

*SEVEN AGAINST THEBES*: COMMENTARIES

G. O. Hutchinson (ed.), *Seven against Thebes* (Oxford, 1985).

INTERPRETATIONS

Daniel Berman, *Myth and Culture in Aeschylus' Seven against Thebes* (Rome, 2007).

L. Byrne, 'Fear in the *Seven against Thebes*', in S. Deacy and K. F. Pierce (eds.), *Rape in Antiquity* (London, 1997), 143–62.

H. D. Cameron, *Studies on the 'Seven against Thebes' of Aeschylus* (The Hague and Paris, 1971).

Gregory Nagy, '"Dream of a Shade": refractions of epic vision in Pindar's *Pythian* 8 and Aeschylus' *Seven against Thebes*', *Harvard Studies in Classical Philology* 100 (2000), 97–118.

Eva Stehle, 'Prayer and curse in Aeschylus' "Seven against Thebes"', *Classical Philology* 100 (2005), 101–22.

W. G. Thalman, *Dramatic Art in Aeschylus' Seven Against Thebes* (New Haven, 1978).

Froma Zeitlin, *Under the Sign of the Shield: Semiotics and Aeschylus' Seven against Thebes* (Rome, 1982).

*SUPPLIANTS*: COMMENTARIES

H. Friis Johansen and Edward W. Whittle (eds.), *The Suppliants*, 3 vols. (Copenhagen, 1980).

INTERPRETATIONS

Timothy Gantz, 'Love and death in the "Suppliants" of Aischylos', *Phoenix* 32 (1978). 279–287.

J. K. MacKinnon, 'The reason for the Danaids' flight', *Classical Quarterly* 28 (1978), 74–82.

Lynette G. Mitchell, 'Greeks, Barbarians and Aeschylus' "Suppliants"', *Greece and Rome* 53 (2006), 205–23.

Robert Duff Murray, *The Motif of Io in Aeschylus' Suppliants* (Princeton, 1958).

J. N. Rash, *Meter and Language in the Lyrics of the Suppliants of Aeschylus* (New York, 1981).

Chad Turner, 'Perverted supplication and other inversions in Aeschylus' Danaid trilogy', *CJ* 97 (2001), 27–50.

R. P. Winnington-Ingram, 'The Danaid trilogy of Aeschylus', *Journal of Hellenic Studies* 81 (1961), 141–52.

## ORESTEIA

A. M. Bowie, 'Religion and politics in Aeschylus' *Oresteia*', *Classical Quarterly* 43 (1993), 10–31.

A. L. Brown, 'The Erinyes in the *Oresteia*: real Life, the Supernatural, and the Stage', *Journal of Hellenic Studies* 93 (1983), 13–34.

D. Cohen 'The theodicy of Aeschylus: justice and tyranny in the *Oresteia*', *Greece and Rome* 33 (1986), 129–41.

C. Collard (ed.), *The Oresteia* (trans. with introd. and notes, Oxford, 2003).

D. J. Conacher, *Aeschylus' Oresteia: A Literary Commentary* (Toronto and London, 1987).

E. R. Dodds 'Morals and politics in the *Oresteia*', *Proceedings of the Cambridge Philological Society* 6 (1960), 19–31, repr. in *The Ancient Concept of Progress* (Oxford, 1973), ch. 4.

Simon Goldhill, *Language, Sexuality, Narrative: The Oresteia* (Cambridge, 1984).

—— *Aeschylus. The Oresteia* (2nd edn, Cambridge, 2004).

Mark Griffith, 'Brilliant dynasts: power and politics in the *Oresteia*', *Classical Antiquity* 14 (1995), 62–129.

J. Heath, 'Disentangling the beast: humans and other animals in Aeschylus' *Oresteia*', *Journal of Hellenic Studies* 119 (1999), 17–47.

A. Lebeck, *The Oresteia: A Study in Language and Structure* (Cambridge, Mass., 1971).

C. W. Macleod, 'Politics and the *Oresteia*', *Journal of Hellenic Studies* 102 (1982), 124–44, repr. in his *Collected Essays* (Oxford, 1983), ch. 3.

L. McClure, '*Logos Gunaikos*: speech and gender in Aechylus' *Oresteia*', in L. McClure, *Spoken Like a Woman: Speech and Gender in Athenian Drama* (Princeton, 1999), 70–111.

J. J. Peradotto, 'Some patterns of nature imagery in the *Oresteia*' *American Journal of Philology* 85 (1964), 378–93.

A. J. N. W. Prag, *The Oresteia: Iconographic and Narrative Tradition* (Warminster, 1985).

N. S. Rabinowitz, 'From force to persuasion: Aeschylus' *Oresteia* as cosmogonic myth', *Ramus* 10 (1981), 159–91.

Deborah Roberts, *Apollo and his Oracle in the Oresteia* (Göttingen, 1984).
W. Whallon, *Problem and Spectacle: Studies in the Oresteia* (Heidelberg, 1980).
Oliver Taplin and Peter Wilson, 'The "aetiology" of tragedy in the *Oresteia*', *Proceedings of the Cambridge Philological Society* 39 (1993), 169–80.
R. P. Winnington-Ingram, 'Clytemnestra and the vote of Athena', *Journal of Hellenic Studies* 68 (1948), 130–47, repr. in E. Segal (ed.), *Oxford Readings in Greek Tragedy* (Oxford 1983), 84–103.
Froma Zeitlin, 'The dynamics of misogyny: myth and mythmaking in the *Oresteia*', *Arethusa* 11 (1978), 149–84.

AGAMEMEMNON: COMMENTARIES

Philip de May, *Aeschylus' Agamemnon. A New Translation and Commentary* (Cambridge, 2003).
J. D. Denniston and D. L. Page (eds.), *Aeschylus' Agamemnon* (Oxford, 1957).
H. Lloyd-Jones, *Agamemnon, a Translation with Commentary* (Englewood Cliffs, NJ, 1970).

INTERPRETATIONS

G. Ferrari, 'Figures in the text: metaphors and riddles in the *Agamemnon*', *Classical Philology* 92 (1997), 1–45.
Barbara Goward, *Aeschylus. Agamemnon* (London, 2005).
L. McNeil, 'Bridal cloths, cover-ups, and kharis: the "carpet scene" in Aeschylus' *Agamemnon*', *Greece and Rome* 52 (2005), 1–16.
R. Mitchell-Boyask, 'The marriage of Cassandra and the *Oresteia*: text, image, performance', *Transactions of the American Philological Society* 136 (2006), 269–97.
Seth Schein, 'The Cassandra scene in Aeschylus' *Agamemnon*', *Greece and Rome* 29 (1982), 11–16.
R. Seaford, 'The last bath of Agamemnon', *Classical Quarterly* 34 (1984), 247–54.
Peter M. Smith, *On the Hymn to Zeus in Aeschylus' Agamemnon* (Cico, Calif., 1980).
S. V. Tracy, 'Darkness from light: the beacon fire in the *Agamemnon*', *Classical Quarterly* 36 (1986), 257–60.
W. Blake Tyrrell, 'Zeus and Agamemnon at Aulis', *CJ* 71 (1976), 328–34.
W. Whallon, 'Why is Artemis Angry?', *American Journal of Philology* 82 (1961), 78–88.

## LIBATION-BEARERS: COMMENTARIES

A. Garvie (ed.), *Aeschylus: Choephori* (2nd edn, Oxford, 2006).

### INTERPRETATIONS

A. F. Garvie, 'The opening of the *Choephori*', *Bulletin of the Institute of Classical Studies* 17 (1970), 79–91.

P. A. Hansen, 'The robe episode of the *Choephori*', *Classical Quarterly* 28 (1978), 239–40.

W. E. Higgins, 'Double-dealing Ares in the *Oresteia*', *Classical Philology* 73 (1978), 24–35.

Anne Lebeck, 'The first stasimon of Aeschylus' *Choephori*: myth and mirror image', *Classical Philology* 62 (1967), 182–5.

K. O'Neill, 'Aeschylus, Homer, and the serpent at the breast', *Phoenix* 52 (1998), 216–29.

A. R. Rose, 'The significance of the nurse's speech in Aeschylus' *Choephoroi*', *Classical Bulletin* 58 (1982), 49–50.

F. Solmsen, *Electra and Orestes: Three Recognitions in Greek Tragedy* (Amsterdam, 1967).

T. C. W. Stinton, 'The first stasimon of Aeschylus' *Choephori*', *Classical Quarterly* 29 (1989). 252–62.

D. C. Young, 'Readings in Aeschylus' *Choephoroe*', *Greek, Roman, and Byzantine Studies* 12 (1971). 303–30.

## EUMENIDES: COMMENTARIES

A. J. Podlecki (ed.), *Aeschylus' Eumenides* (Warminster, 1989; includes translation).

Sommerstein, A. H. (ed.), *Aeschylus. Eumenides* (Cambridge, 1989).

### INTERPRETATIONS

H. Bacon, 'The Furies' homecoming', *Classical Philology* 96 (2001), 48–59.

K. J. Dover, 'The political aspect of the *Eumenides*', *Journal of Hellenic Studies* 77 (1957), 230–7; repr. in his *Greek and the Greeks* (Oxford, 1987), 161–75.

J. Peter Euben, *The Tragedy of Political Theory* (Princeton, 1990), 67–95.

John H. Finley, *Pindar and Aeschylus* (Cambridge, Mass., and London, 1955), 246–88.

Yopie Prins, 'The power of the speech act: Aeschylus' Furies and their binding song', *Arethusa* 24 (1991), 177–95.

Keith Sidwell, 'Purification and pollution in Aeschylus' *Eumenides*', *Classical Quarterly* 46 (1996), 44–57.

*PROMETHEUS BOUND*: COMMENTARIES

A. Griffith (ed.), *Aeschylus: Prometheus Bound* (Cambridge, 1983).
A. J. Podlecki (ed.), *Aeschylus: Prometheus Bound* (Warminster, 2005; includes translation).

INTERPRETATIONS

John Davidson, '"Prometheus Vinctus" on the Athenian stage', *Greece and Rome* 41 (1994), 33–40.
Barbara Hughes Fowler, 'The imagery of the *Prometheus Bound*', *American Journal of Philology* 78 (1957), 173–84.
Mark Griffiths, *The Authenticity of the Prometheus Bound* (Cambridge, 1977).
David Konstan, 'The Ocean episode in the "Prometheus Bound"', *History of Religions*, 17 (1977), 61–72.
Judith Mossman, 'Chains of imagery in *Prometheus Bound*', *Classical Quarterly* 46 (1996), 58–67.
William C. Scott, 'The development of the chorus in *Prometheus Bound*', *Transactions of the American Philological Society* 117 (1987), 85–96.
Stephen White, 'Io's world: intimations of theodicy in *Prometheus bound*', *JHS* 121 (2001), 107–40.

## 6. Euripidean Tragedy

Shirley Barlow, *The Imagery of Euripides* (London, 1971).
Peter Burian (ed.), *Directions in Euripidean Criticism* (Durham, NC, 1985).
A. P. Burnett, *Catastrophe Survived: Euripides' Plays of Mixed Reversal* (Oxford, 1971).
C. Collard, 'Formal debates in Euripidean drama', *Greece and Rome* 22 (1975), 58–71.
D. J. Conacher, 'Rhetoric and relevance in Euripidean drama', *American Journal of Philology* 102 (1981), 3–25.
Francis M. Dunn, *Tragedy's End: Closure and Innovation in Euripidean Drama* (New York and Oxford, 1996).
Robert Eisner, 'Euripides' use of myth', *Arethusa* 12 (1979), 153–74.
J. H. Finley, 'Euripides and Thucydides', in *Three Essays on Thucydides* (Cambridge, Mass., 1967), 1–24.
Justina Gregory, *Euripides and the Instruction of the Athenians* (Ann Arbor, Mich., 1991).
Michael R. Halleran, *Stagecraft in Euripides* (Totowa, NJ, 1985).

Richard Hamilton, 'Prologue, prophecy and plot in four plays of Euripides', *American Journal of Philology* 99 (1978), 277–302.

—— 'Euripidean priests', *Harvard Studies in Classical Philology* 89 (1985), 53–73.

Nicolaos C. Hourmouziades, *Production and Imagination in Euripides: Form and Function of the Scenic Space* (Athens, 1965).

M. Huys, *The Tale of the Hero who was Exposed at Birth in Euripidean Tragedy: A Study of Motifs* (Leuven, 1995).

I. J. F. de Jong, *Narrative in Drama: The Art of the Euripidean Messenger-Speech* (Leiden, 1991).

M. Lloyd, *The Agon in Euripides* (Oxford, 1992).

Gary S. Meltzer, *Euripides and the Poetics of Nostalgia* (Cambridge, 2006).

Daniel Mendelsohn, *Gender and the City in Euripides' Political Plays* (Oxford, 2002).

A. N. Michelini, *Euripides and the Tragic Tradition* (Madison, Wis., 1987).

Judith Mossman (ed.), *Oxford Readings in Euripides* (Oxford, 2003).

E. O'Connor-Visser, *Aspects of Human Sacrifice in the Tragedies of Euripides* (Amsterdam, 1987).

Martin Revermann, 'Euripides, tragedy and Macedon: some conditions of reception', *Illinois Classical Studies* 24–5 (1999–2000), 451–67.

Charles Segal, *Euripides and the Poetics of Sorrow* (Durham, NC, and London, 1993).

H. P. Stahl, 'On extra-dramatic communication of characters in Euripides', *Yale Classical Studies* 25 (1977), 159–76.

Sophie Trenkner, *The Greek Novella in the Classical Period* (Cambridge 1958), 31–78.

CYCLOPS: COMMENTARIES

Richard Seaford (ed.), *Euripides' Cyclops* (Oxford, 1984).
Robert Ussher (ed.), *Euripides' Cyclops* (Rome, 1978).

INTERPRETATIONS

W. G. Arnott, 'Parody and ambiguity in Euripides' *Cyclops*', in Rudolf Hanslik, Albin Lesky, H. Schwabl (eds.), *Antidosis: Festschrift für Walther Kraus zum 70. Geburtstag* (Vienna, 1972), 21–30.

N. E. Collinge, 'Some reflections on satyr plays', *Proceedings of the Cambridge Philological Society* 185 (1958–9), 28–35.

R. Hamilton, 'Euripides' Cyclopean symposium', *Phoenix* 33 (1979), 287–92.

Boris Nikolsky, 'Slavery and freedom in Euripides' *Cyclops*', in R. Alston, E. Hall, and L. Proffitt (eds.), *Reading Ancient Slavery* (London, 2010).

P. O'Sullivan, 'Of sophists, tyrants and Polyphemos: the nature of the beast in Euripides' *Cyclops*', in G. Harrison (ed.), *Satyr Drama: Tragedy at Play*, (Swansea, 2005), 119–59.

D. F. Sutton, *The Greek Satyr Play* (Meisenheim am Glan, 1980).

R. G. Ussher, 'The *Cyclops* of Euripides', *Greece and Rome* 18 (1971), 166–79.

Nancy Worman, 'Euripides, ingestive rhetoric, and Euripides' *Cyclops*', *Helios* 29 (2002), 101–25.

*ALCESTIS*: COMMENTARIES

D. J. Conacher (ed.), *Euripides' Alcestis* (Warminster, 1988; includes translation).

L. P. E. Parker (ed.), *Euripides' Alcestis* (Oxford, 2007).

INTERPRETATIONS

C. R. Beye, 'Alcestis and her critics', *Greek, Roman, and Byzantine Studies* 2 (1959), 109–27.

E. M. Bradley, 'Admetus and the triumph of failure in Euripides' *Alcestis*', *Ramus* 9 (1980), 112–27.

A. P. Burnett, 'The virtues of Admetus', *Classical Philology* 60 (1965), 240–55.

R. G. A. Buxton, 'Euripides' *Alkestis*: five aspects of an interpretation', *Papers Given at a Colloquium in Honour of R. P. Winnington-Ingram* (London, 1987), 18–27.

J. J. Dellner, 'Alcestis' double life', *CJ* 96 (2000–1), 1–25.

Helene P. Foley, '*Anodos* drama: Euripides' *Alcestis* and *Helen*', in Ralph Hexter and Daniel Selden (eds.), *Innovations of Antiquity* (New York and London, 1992), 133–60.

R. Garner, 'Death and victory in Euripides' *Alcestis*', *Classical Antiquity* 7 (1988), 58–71.

J. Gregory, 'Euripides' *Alcestis*', *Hermes* 107 (1979), 259–70.

M. Halleran, 'Text and ceremony at the close of Euripides' *Alkestis*', *Eranos* 86 (1988), 123–9.

M. Lloyd, 'Euripides' *Alcestis*', *Greece and Rome* 32 (1985), 119–31.

R. M. Nielsen, '*Alcestis*: a paradox in dying', *Ramus* 5 (1976), 92–102.

N. W. Slater, 'Dead again: (en)gendering praise in Euripides' *Alcestis*', *Helios* 27 (2000), 105–21.

G. Smith, 'The *Alcestis* of Euripides: An interpretation', *Rivista di Filologia e di Istruzione Classica* 111 (1983), 129–45.

W. D. Smith, 'The ironic structure in *Alcestis*', *Phoenix* 14 (1960), 127–45.

J. R. Wilson (ed.), *Twentieth-Century Interpretations of Euripides' Alcestis* (Englewood Cliffs, NJ, 1968).

## MEDEA: COMMENTARIES

Alan Elliott, *Euripides' Medea* (Oxford, 1969).
Denys Page (ed.), *Euripides, Medea* (Oxford, 1938).
D. J. Mastronarde (ed.). *Euripides. Medea* (Cambridge, 2002).
J. Mossman, *Euripides' Medea* (Warminster, forthcoming; includes translation).

## INTERPRETATIONS

Pat Easterling, 'The infanticide in Euripides' *Medea*', *Yale Classical Studies* 25 (1977), 177–91.
Helene Foley, 'Medea's divided self,' *Classical Antiquity* 8/1 (1989), 61–85.
Michelle Gellrich, 'Medea hypokrites', *Arethusa* 35 (2002), 315–37.
Leon Golden, 'Children in the *Medea*,' *Classical Bulletin* 48 (1971), 10–15.
Bernard Gredley, 'The place and time of victory: Euripides' *Medea*', *Bulletin of the Institute of Classical Studies* 34 (1987), 27–39.
David Kovacs, 'Zeus in Euripides' *Medea*', *American Journal of Philology* 114 (1993), 45–70.
C. A. E. Luschnig, *Grand-daughter of the Sun: A Study of Euripides' Medea* (Leiden, 2007).
E. A. McDermott, *Euripides' Medea: The Incarnation of Disorder* (University Park, Pa., 1989).
Pietro Pucci, *The Violence of Pity in Euripides' Medea* (Ithaca, NY, 1980).
Charles Segal, 'Euripides' *Medea*: vengeance, reversal, and closure,' *Pallas* 45 (1996), 15–44.
S. D. Syropoulos, 'The invention and the use of the infanticide motif in Euripides' *Medea*', *Platon* 52 (2001–2), 126–38).
Margaret Williamson, 'A woman's place in Euripides' *Medea*', in A. Powell (ed.), *Euripides, Women, and Sexuality* (London and New York, 1990), 16–31.

## CHILDREN OF HERACLES: COMMENTARIES

William Allan, *Euripides: The Children of Heracles* (Warminster, 2001; includes translation).
John Wilkins, *Euripides' Heraclidae* (Oxford, 1993).

## INTERPRETATIONS

H. C. Avery, 'Euripides' *Heraclidai*', *American Journal of Philology* 92 (1971), 539–65.
P. Burian, 'Euripides' *Heraclidae*: an interpretation', *Classical Philology* 72 (1977), 1–21.
A. P. Burnett, 'Tribe and city, custom and decree in *Children of Heracles*', *Classical Philology* 71 (1976), 4–26.

J. Davidson, 'Two notes on Euripides' *Heraclidae*', *Athenaeum* 84 (1996), 243–7.
J. W. Fitton, 'The *Suppliant Women* and the *Heraklidai* of Euripides', *Hermes* 89 (1961), 30–61.
A. Lesky, 'On the *Heraclidae* of Euripides', *Yale Classical Studies* 25 (1977), 2272–38.
J. McLean, 'The *Heraclidae* of Euripides', *American Journal of Philology* 55 (1934), 197–224.
Rush Rehm, 'The staging of suppliant plays', *Greek, Roman, and Byzantine Studies* 29 (1988), 263–307.
J. A. Spranger, 'The political element in the *Heraclidae* of Euripides', *Classical Quarterly* 19 (1925), 117–29.
J. Wilkins, 'The young of Athens: religion and society in the *Herakleidai* of Euripides', *Classical Quarterly* 40 (1990), 329–39.
G. Zuntz, 'Is the *Heraclidae* mutilated?', *Classical Quarterly* 41 (1947), 46–52.
—— *The Political Plays of Euripides* (2nd edn, Manchester, 1963).

HIPPOLYTUS: COMMENTARIES

W. S. Barrett (ed.), *Euripides' Hippolytus* (Oxford, 1964).
Michael Halleran (ed.), *Euripides: Hippolytus* (corr. edn, Oxford, 2004; includes translation).
Gilbert and Sarah Lawall, *Euripides: Hippolytus. A Companion with Translation* (Bristol, 1986).

INTERPRETATIONS

George E. Dimock, 'Euripides' *Hippolytus* or virtue rewarded', *Yale Classical Studies* 25 (1977), 239–58.
Barbara Goff, *The Noose of Words: Readings of Desire, Violence and Language in Euripides' Hippolytus* (Cambridge, 1990).
Michael R. Halleran, 'Gamos and destruction in Euripides' *Hippolytus*', *Transactions of the American Philological Society* 121 (1991), 9–121.
Bernard Knox, '*Hippolytus*: a study in causation', in *Euripide, Entretiens Hardt* 6 (Geneva, 1960), 171–91.
C. A. E. Luschnig, *Time Holds the Mirror: A Study of Knowledge in Euripides'* Hippolytus (Leiden, 1988).
Sophie Mills, *Euripides' Hippolytus* (London, 2002).
Robin N. Mitchell, 'Miasma, mimesis, and scapegoating in Euripides' "Hippolytus"', *Classical Antiquity* 10 (1991), 97–122.
Kenneth Reckford, 'Phaedra and Pasiphaë: the pull backward', *Transactions of the American Philological Society* 104 (1974), 307–28.

Charles Segal, 'The tragedy of the *Hippolytus*: the waters of ocean and the untouched meadow', *Harvard Studies in Classical Philology* 70 (1965), 117–69.
—— 'Pentheus and Hippolytus on the couch and on the grid: psychoanalytical and structural readings of Greek tragedy', *Classical World* 72 (1978), 129–48.
Wesley D. Smith, 'Staging in the central scene of the *Hippolytus*', *Transactions of the American Philological Society* 91 (1960), 62–77.

ANDROMACHE: COMMENTARIES

Michael Lloyd (ed.), *Euripides. Andromache* (Warminster, 1995; includes translation).
P. T. Stevens (ed.), *Euripides' Andromache* (Oxford, 1971).

INTERPRETATIONS

Keith M. Aldrich, *The* Andromache *of Euripides (Lincoln, Neb., 1961)*.
W. Allan, *The* Andromache *and Euripidean Tragedy* (Oxford, 2000).
H. Erbse, 'Euripides' *Andromache*', *Hermes* 94 (1966), 276–97.
P. Kyriakou, 'All in the family: present and past in Euripides' "Andromache"', *Mnemosyne* 50 (1997), 7–26.
Judith Mossman, 'Waiting for Neoptolemus: the unity of Euripides' Andromache', *Greece and Rome* 43 (1996), 143–56.
D. L. Page, 'The elegiacs in Euripides' *Andromache*', in *Greek Poetry and Life* (Studies for Gilbert Murray, Oxford 1936), 206–30.
D. S. Robertson, 'Euripides and Tharyps', *CR* 37 (1923), 58–60.
I. C. Storey, 'Domestic disharmony in Euripides' *Andromache*', in I. McAuslan and P. Walcot (eds.), *Greek Tragedy* (Oxford, 1993), 180–92.

HECUBA: COMMENTARIES

Christopher Collard (ed.), *Euripides' Hecuba* (Warminster, 1991; includes translation).
Justina Gregory (ed.), *Euripides, Hecuba* (Atlanta, Ga., 1999).
John Harrison (trans. and comm.), *Euripides' Hecuba*, with an introduction to the Greek theatre by P. E. Easterling (Cambridge, 2008).

INTERPRETATIONS

Stephen Daitz, 'Concepts of freedom and slavery in Euripides' *Hecuba*', *Hermes* 99 (1971), 217–26.
George Gellie, '*Hecuba* and tragedy', *Antichthon* 14 (1980), 30–44.
M. Heath, 'Iure principium locum tenet: Euripides' *Hecuba*', *Bulletin of the Institute of Classical Studies* 34 (1987), 40–68.

Katherine King, 'The politics of imitation: Euripides' *Hekabe* and the Homeric Achilles', *Arethusa* 18 (1985), 47–66.
D. Kovacs, *The Heroic Muse: Studies in the Hippolytus and Hecuba of Euripides* (Baltimore, Md., and London, 1987).
C. A. E. Luschnig, 'Euripides' *Hecabe*: the time is out of joint', *CJ* 71 (1976), 227–341.
C. W. Marshall, 'The costume of Hecuba's attendants', *L'antiquité classique* 44 (2001), 185–97.
R. Meridor, 'The function of Polymestor's crime in the *Hecuba* of Euripides', *Eranos* 81 (1983), 13–20.
—— 'Plot and myth in Euripides' *Heracles* and *Troades*', *Phoenix* 38 (1984), 205–15.
Judith Mossman, *Wild Justice: A Study of Euripides' Hecuba* (Oxford, 1995).
C. Segal, 'Violence and the other: Greek, female and barbarian in Euripides' *Hecuba*', *Transactions of the American Philological Society* 120 (1990), 109–31.
Theodore Tarkow, 'Tragedy and transformation: parent and child in Euripides' *Hecuba*', *Maia* 36 (1984), 123–36.
F. I. Zeitlin, 'Euripides' Hekabe and the somatics of Dionysiac drama', *Ramus* 20 (1991), 53–94.

SUPPLIANT WOMEN: COMMENTARIES

C. Collard (ed.), *Euripides' Supplices* (Groningen, 1975).
James Morwood, *Euripides. Suppliant Women* (Oxford, 2007; includes translation).

INTERPRETATIONS

C. Collard, 'The funeral oration in Euripides' *Supplices*', *Bulletin of the Institute of Classical Studies* 19 (1972), 39–53.
D. J. Conacher, 'Religious and ethical attitudes in Euripides' *Suppliants*', *Transactions of the American Philological Society* 87 (1956), 8–26.
W. R. Connor, 'Theseus in classical Athens', in A. G. Ward (ed.), *The Quest for Theseus* (London, 1970), 143–74.
R. B. Gamble, 'Euripides' *Suppliant Women*: decision and ambivalence', *Hermes* 98 (1970), 385–405.
A. Michelini, 'The maze of the *logos*: Euripides, *Suppliants* 163–249', *Ramus* 20 (1991), 16–36.
—— 'Political themes in Euripides' *Suppliants*', *American Journal of Philology* 115 (1994), 219–52.

A. Michelini, 'Alcibiades and Theseus in Euripides' *Suppliants*', *Colby Quarterly* 33 (1997), 177–84.
M. H. Shaw, 'The *ethos* of Theseus in the "Suppliant Women"', *Hermes* 109 (1982), 3–19.
W. D. Smith, 'Expressive form in Euripides' "Suppliants"', *Harvard Studies in Classical Philology* 71 (1966), 151–70.
John E. G. Whitehouse, 'The dead as spectacle in Euripides' "Bacchae" and "Suppliant Women"', *Hermes* 114 (1986), 59–72.
S. Scully, 'Orchestra and stage and Euripides' *Suppliant Women*', *Arion* 4 (1996), 61–85.

*ELECTRA*: COMMENTARIES

M. J. Cropp (ed.), *Euripides' Electra* (Warminster, 1988; includes translation).
J. D. Denniston (ed.), *Euripides' Electra* (Oxford, 1954).

INTERPRETATIONS

W. G. Arnott, 'Double the vision: a reading of Euripides' *Electra*', *Greece and Rome* 28 (1981), 179–92.
George Gellie, 'Tragedy and Euripides' *Electra*', *Bulletin of the Institute of Classical Studies* 28 (1981), 1–12.
N. G. L. Hammond, 'Spectacle and parody in Euripides' *Electra*,' *Greek, Roman, and Byzantine Studies* 25 (1984), 373–87.
K. C. King, 'The force of tradition: the Achilles ode in Euripides' *Electra*', *Transactions of the American Philological Society* 110 (1980), 195–21.
M. Kubo, 'The norm of myth: Euripides' Electra', *Harvard Studies in Classical Philology* 71 (1966), 15–31.
Michael Lloyd, 'Realism and character in Euripides' "Electra"', *Phoenix* 40 (1986), 1–19.
James Morwood, 'The pattern of the Euripides *Electra*', *American Journal of Philology* 102 (1981), 326–70.
Judith Mossman, 'Women's speech in Greek tragedy: the case of Electra and Clytemnestra in Euripides' "Electra"', *Classical Quarterly* 51 (2001), 374–84.
Michael J. O'Brien, 'Orestes and the Gorgon: Euripides' *Electra*', *American Journal of Philology* 85 (1964), 13–39.
D. Raeburn, 'The significance of stage properties in Euripides' *Electra*,' *Greece and Rome* 47 (2000), 149–68.
Vincent J. Rosivach, 'The "Golden Lamb" ode in Euripides' *Electra*', *Classical Philology* 73 (1978), 189–99.
F. I. Zeitlin, 'The Argive festival of Hera and Euripides' *Electra*', *Transactions of the American Philological Society* 101 (1970), 645–69.

*HERACLES*: COMMENTARIES

Shirley Barlow, *Euripides' Herakles* (Warminster, 1996; includes translation).

Godfrey Bond, *Euripides' Heracles* (Oxford, 1981).

INTERPRETATIONS

Shirley Barlow, 'Structure and dramatic realism in Euripides' *Herakles*', *Greece and Rome* 29 (1982), 115–25.

Martin Cropp, '*Heracles*, *Electra* and the *Odyssey*', in Martin Cropp et al. (eds.), *Greek Tragedy and its Legacy* (1986), 187–99.

Francis Dunnis, 'Ends and means in Euripides' *Heracles*', in D. H. Roberts, Francis M. Dunn, and Don Fowler (eds.), *Classical Closure: Reading the End in Greek and Latin Literature* (Princeton, 1997), 83–111.

G. Karl Galinsky, *The Herakles Theme* (Oxford 1972), 40–80.

J. C. Gibert, 'Euripides *Heracles* 1351 and the hero's encounter with death', *Classical Philology* 92 (1997), 247–58.

J. Gregory, 'Euripides' *Heracles*', *Yale Classical Studies* 25 (1977), 259–75.

E. M. Griffiths, 'Euripides' *Heracles* and the pursuit of immortality', *Mnemosyne* 55 (2002), 641–56.

M. R. Halleran, 'Rhetoric, irony, and the ending of Euripides' *Herakles*', *Classical Antiquity* 5 (1986), 171–81.

R. Hamilton, 'Slings and arrows. The debate with Lycos in the *Heracles*', *Transactions of the American Philological Society* 115 (1985), 19–25.

J. C. Kamerbeek, 'Unity and meaning of Euripides' *Heracles*', *Mnemosyne* 19 (1966), 1–16.

K. H. Lee, 'The Iris-Lyssa scene in Euripides' *Heracles*', *Antichthon* 16 (1982), 44–53.

J. D. Mikalson, 'Zeus the father and Heracles the son in tragedy', *Transactions of the American Philological Society* 116 (1986), 89–98.

Thalia Papadopoulou, *Heracles and Euripidean Tragedy* (Cambridge, 2005).

H. Parry, 'The second stasimon of Euripides' *Herakles*', *American Journal of Philology* 86 (1965), 363–74.

D. H. Porter, 'Only connect: Euripides' *Heracles*', in *Only Connect: Three Studies in Greek Tragedy* (Laxham, 1987), 85–112.

Kathleen Riley, *The Reception and Performance of Euripides'* Herakles (Oxford, 2008).

C. Ruck, 'Duality and the madness of Herakles', *Arethusa* 9 (1976), 53–75.

M. S. Silk, 'Heracles and Greek tragedy', *Greece and Rome* 32 (1985), 1–22.

C. Willink, 'Sleep after labour in Euripides' *Heracles*', *Classical Quarterly* 38 (1988), 86–97.

## TROJAN WOMEN: COMMENTARIES

S. A. Barlow (ed.), *Euripides. Trojan Women* (Warminster, 1986).
K. H. Lee (ed.), *Troades. Euripides* (London, 1997).

## INTERPRETATIONS

A. P. Burnett, '"*Trojan Women*" and the Ganymede ode', *Yale Classical Studies* 25 (1977), 291–316.
N. Croally, *Euripidean Polemic: The Trojan Women and the Function of Tragedy* (Cambridge, 1994).
F. M. Dunn, 'Beginning at the end in Euripides' *Trojan Women*', *Rheinisches Museum* 136 (1993), 22–35.
P. Green, 'War and morality in fifth-century Athens: the case of Euripides' *Trojan Women*', *Ancient History Bulletin* 13 (1999), 97–110.
Michael Lloyd, 'The Helen scene in Euripides' *Troades*', *Classical Quarterly* 34 (!984), 303–13.
C. A. Luschnig, 'Euripides' *Trojan Women*: all is vanity', *Classical World* 65 (1971), 8–12.
Ranana Meridor, 'Some observations on the structure of Euripides' *Troades*', *Scripta Classica Israelica* 11 (1991/2), 1–21.
—— 'Creative rhetoric in Euripides' "Troades": some notes on Hecuba's speech', *Classical Quarterly* 50 (2000), 16–29.
A. Poole, 'Total disaster: Euripides' *Trojan Women*', *Arion* 3 (1976), 257–87.
P. Pucci, 'Euripides: the monument and the sacrifice', *Arethusa* 10 (1977), 165–95.
J. Roisman, 'Contemporary allusions in Euripides' *Trojan Women*', *Studi italiani di filologia classica* 15 (1997), 38–47.
R. Scodel, *The Trojan Trilogy of Euripides* (= *Hypomnemata* 60, Göttingen 1980).
T. J. Sienkewicz, 'Euripides' *Trojan Women*: an interpretation', *Helios* 6 (1978), 81–95.
T. C. W. Stinton, *Euripides and the Judgement of Paris* (London, 1965).

## IPHIGENIA AMONG THE TAURIANS: COMMENTARIES

M. J. Cropp (ed.), *Euripides. Iphigenia in Tauris* (Warminster, 2000; includes translation).
Poulheria Kyriakou (ed.), *A Commentary on Euripides' Iphigenia in Tauris* (Berlin, 2006).

## INTERPRETATIONS

R. Caldwell, 'Tragedy romanticized: the *Iphigenia Taurica*', *CJ* 70 (1974/5), 23–40.

G. Ekroth, 'Inventing Iphigenia? On Euripides and the cultic construction of Brauron', *Kernos* 16 (2003), 59–118.
Barbara Goff, 'The violence of community: ritual in the *Iphigenia in Tauris*', in M. W. Padilla (ed.), *Rites of Passage in Ancient Greece* (*Bucknell Review* 43/1, London, 1999). 109–25
Edith Hall, 'The geography of Euripides' *IT*', *American Journal of Philology* 108 (1987), 427–33.
—— *Adventures with Iphigenia: From the Black Sea to the Global Village* (New York and Oxford, forthcoming).
K. Hartigan, 'Salvation via deceit: a new look at *Iphigeneia at Tauris*', *Eranos* 84 (1986), 119–25.
M. J. O'Brien, 'Pelopid history and the plot of *Iphigenia in Tauris*', *Classical Quarterly* 38 (1988), 98–115.
S. O. O'Bryhim, 'The ritual of human sacrifice in Euripides', *Classical Bulletin* 76 (2000), 29–37.
S. Said, 'Exotic space in *Iphigenia in Tauris*', *Dionis* 1 (2002), 48–61.
D. Sansone, 'The sacrifice-motif in Euripides' *IT*', *Transactions of the American Philological Society* 105 (1975), 283–95.
S. Stern-Gillet, 'Exile, displacement and barbarity in Euripides' *Iphigenia among the Taurians*', *Scholia* 10 (2001), 4–21.
J. C. G. Strachan, 'Iphigenia and human sacrifice in Euripides' *Iphigenia Taurica*', *Classical Philology* 71 (1976), 131–40.
D. F. Sutton, 'Satyric qualities in Euripides' *Iphigeneia at Tauris* and *Helen*', *Rivista di Studi Classici* 3 (1972), 321–30.
C. Wolff, 'Euripides' *Iphigenia among the Taurians*: aetiology, ritual, and myth', *Classical Antiquity* 11 (1992). 308–34
Matthew Wright, *Euripides' Escape-Tragedies: A Study of Helen, Andromeda, and Iphigenia Among the Taurians* (Oxford, 2005).

*ION*: COMMENTARIES

K. H. Lee (ed.), *Euripides, Ion* (Warminster, 1997; includes translation).
A. S. Owen (ed.), *Euripides' Ion* (Oxford, 1939).

INTERPRETATIONS

A. P. Burnett, 'Human resistance and divine persuasion in Euripides' *Ion*', *Classical Philology* 57 (1962), 89–103.
G. Gellie, 'Apollo in the *Ion*', *Ramus* 13 (1985), 93–101.
Barbara Goff, 'Euripides' *Ion* 1132–1165: the tent', *Proceedings of the Cambridge Philological Society* 34 (1988), 42–54.
Vasiliki Giannopoulou, 'Divine agency and tyche in Euripides' *Ion*: ambiguity and shifting perspectives', *Illinois Classical Studies* 24–25 (1999–2000), 257–71.

K. Hartigan, *Ambiguity and Self-Deception: The Apollo and Artemis Plays of Euripides* (Frankfurt, 1991).

K. Lee, 'Shifts of mood and concepts of time in Euripides' *Ion*', in Michael Silk (ed.), *Greek Tragedy and the Tragic* (Oxford, 1996), 85–109.

Michael Lloyd, 'Divine and human action in Euripides' *Ion*', *Antike und Abendland* 32 (1986), 33–45.

D. J. Mastronarde, 'Iconography and imagery in Euripides' *Ion*', *California Studies in Classical Antiquity* 8 (1975), 163–76.

V. J. Rosivach, 'Earthborns and Olympians: the parodos of the *Ion*', *Classical Quarterly* 27 (1977), 284–94.

A Saxonhouse, 'Myths and the origins of cities: reflections on the autochthony theme in Euripides' *Ion*', in J. P. Euben (ed.), *Greek Tragedy and Political Theory* (Berkeley, Calif., 1986), 252–73.

Laura Swift, *Euripides. Ion* (London, 2010).

J. E. Thornburn, 'Apollo's comedy and the ending of Euripides' *Ion*', *L'antiquité classique* 44 (2001), 221–36.

G. B. Walsh, 'Rhetoric of birthright and race in Euripides' *Ion*', *Hermes* 106 (1978), 301–15.

C. Wolff, 'The design and myth in Euripides' *Ion*', *Harvard Studies in Classical Philology* 69 (1965), 169–9.

K. Zacharia, *Converging Truths. Euripides' Ion and the Athenian Quest for Self-Definition* (Leiden, 2003).

F. I. Zeitlin, 'Mysteries of identity and designs of the self in Euripides' *Ion*', *Proceedings of the Cambridge Philological Society* 35 (1989), 144–97.

### *HELEN*: COMMENTARIES

William Allan (ed.), *Euripides' Helen* (Cambridge, 2008).
A. M. Dale (ed.), *Euripides' Helen* (Oxford, 1967).

### INTERPRETATIONS

W. G. Arnott, 'Euripides' newfangled *Helen*', *Antichthon* 24 (1990), 1–18.

Norman Austin, *Helen of Troy and her Shameless Phantom* (Ithaca, NY, and London, 1994).

John Griffith, 'Some thoughts on the *Helen* of Euripides', *Journal of Hellenic Studies* 73 (1953), 36–41.

K. V. Hartigan, 'Myth and the *Helen*', *Eranos* 79 (1981), 32–51.

I. E. Holmbnerg, 'Euripides' Helen: most noble and most chaste', *American Journal of Philology* 116 (1995), 19–42.

D. M. Juffras, 'Helen and other victims in Euripides' *Helen*', *Hermes* 121 (1993), 45–57.

Bernard Knox, 'Euripidean comedy', in *Word and Action: Essays on the Ancient Theater* (Baltimore, Md., and London, 1979), 250–74.
G. S. Meltzer, 'Where is the glory of Troy? *Kleos* in Euripides' *Helen*', *Classical Antiquity* 13 (1994), 234–55.
A. J. Podlecki, 'The basic seriousness of Euripides' *Helen*', *Transactions of the American Philological Society* 102 (1971), 553–614.
D. B. Robinson, 'Helen and Persephone, Sparta and Demeter. The Demeter ode in Euripides' *Helen*', in G. W. Bowersock, W. Burkert, and C. J. Putnam (eds.), *Arktouros: Hellenic Studies Presented to Bernard Knox* (Berlin, 1979), 162–72.
D. Sansone, 'Theonoe and Theoclymenus', *Symbolae Osloenses* 60 (1985), 17–36.
Friedrich Solmsen, '*Onoma* and *pragma* in Euripides' *Helen*', CR 48 (1934), 119–21.

*PHOENICIAN WOMEN*: COMMENTARIES

E. Craik (ed.), *Euripides' Phoenician Women* (Warminster, 1988; includes translation).
D. J. Mastronarde (ed.), *Euripides' Phoenissae* (Cambridge, 1994).

INTERPRETATIONS

M. B. Arthur, 'The curse of civilization: the choral odes of the *Phoenissae*', *Harvard Studies in Classical Philology* 81 (1977), 163–85.
J. M. Bremer, 'The popularity of Euripides' *Phoenissae* in late antiquity', *Actes du VIIe Congrès de la FIEC*, vol. 1 (Budapest, 1985), 281–8.
P. Burian, 'Introduction', in P. Burian and B. Swann (trans.), *Euripides, The Phoenician Women* (New York, 1971), 3–17.
D. J. Conacher, 'Themes in the exodos of Euripides' *Phoenissae*', *Phoenix* 21 (1967), 92–101.
R. Cribiore, 'The grammarian's choice: the popularity of Euripides' *Phoenissae* in Hellenistic and Roman education', in Yun Lee Too (ed.), *Education in Greek and Roman Antiquity* (Leiden, Boston, and Cologne, 2001), 241–60.
Barbara Goff, 'The shields of the *Phoenissae*', *Greek, Roman, and Byzantine Studies* 29 (1988), 135–52.
D. Mastronarde, 'The optimistic rationalist in Euripides: Theseus, Jocasta, Teiresias', in M. Cropp, E. Fantham, and S. Scully (eds.), *Greek Tragedy and its Legacy: Essays Presented to D. J. Conacher* (Calgary, 1987), 201–11.
A. J. Podlecki, 'Some themes in Euripides' *Phoenissae*', *Transactions of the American Philological Society* 93 (1962), 355–73.
E. Rawson, 'Family and fatherland in Euripides' *Phoenissae*', *Greek, Roman, and Byzantine Studies* 11 (1970), 109–27.

J. de Romilly, '*Phoenician Women* of Euripides: topicality in Greek tragedy', *Bucknell Review* 15 (1967), 108–32.

ORESTES: COMMENTARIES

Martin West (ed.), *Euripides' Orestes* (Warminster, 1987; includes translation).
C. W. Willink (ed.), *Euripides' Orestes* (Oxford, 1986).

INTERPRETATIONS

W. G. Arnott, 'Euripides and the unexpected', *Greece and Rome* 20 (1973), 49–64.
P. N. B. Boulter, 'The theme of *agria* in Euripides' *Orestes*', *Phoenix* 16 (1962), 102–6.
T. M. Falkner, 'Coming of age in Argos: *physis* and *paideia* in Euripides' *Orestes*', *CJ* 78 (1983), 289–300.
C. Fuqua, 'Studies in the use of myth in Sophocles' *Philoctetes* and Euripides' *Orestes*', *Traditio* 32 (1976), 29–95.
—— 'The world of myth in Euripides' *Orestes*', *Traditio* 34 (1978), 1–28.
N. Greenberg, 'Euripides' *Orestes*: an interpretation', *Harvard Studies in Classical Philology* 66 (1962), 157–92.
Edith Hall, 'Political and cosmic turbulence in Euripides' *Orestes*', in Alan Sommerstein et al. (eds.), *Tragedy, Comedy and the Polis* (Bari, 1993), 263–85.
M. R. Lefkowitz, 'Apollo in the *Orestes*', *Studi italiani di filologia classica* 20 (2002), 46–54.
H. Parry, 'Euripides' *Orestes*: the quest for salvation', *Transactions of the American Philological Society* 100 (1969), 337–53.
Z. Pavlovskis, 'Electra's monody and the role of the chorus in Euripides' *Orestes* 960–1012', *Transactions of the American Philological Society* 120 (1990), 133–45.
John R. Porter, *Studies in Euripides' Orestes* (Leiden, 1994).
Elizabeth Rawson, 'Aspects of Euripides' *Orestes*', *Arethusa* 5 (1972), 155–67.
Seth Schein, 'Mythical allusion and historical reality in Euripides' *Orestes*', *Wiener Studien* 88 (1975), 49–66.
W. D. Smith, 'Disease in Euripides' *Orestes*', *Hermes* 95 (1967), 291–307.
F. Will, 'Tyndareus in the *Orestes*', *Symbolae Osloenses* 37 (1961), 96–9.
C. Wolff, '*Orestes*', in E. Segal (ed.), *Oxford Readings in Greek Tragedy* (Oxford, 1983), 340–56.
Froma Zeitlin, 'The closet of masks: role-playing and myth-making in the *Orestes* of Euripides', *Ramus* 9 (1980), 51–77.

## *IPHIGENIA IN AULIS*: COMMENTARIES

Christopher Collard (ed.), *Euripides' Iphigenia in Aulis* (forthcoming, Warminster; includes translation).

E. B. England (ed.), *The Iphigenia at Aulis of Euripides* (New York, 1979).

Theodore A. Tarkow and Sally MacEwen (eds.), *Iphigeneia at Aulis* (Bryn Mawr, Pa., 1988-9).

## INTERPRETATIONS

David Bain, 'The prologues of Euripides' *Iphigenia in Aulis*', *Classical Quarterly* 27 (1977), 10-26.

V. Castellani, 'Warlords and women in Euripides' *Iphigenia at Aulis*, in J. Redmond (ed.), *Drama, Sex and Politics* (= *Themes in Drama*, 7) (Cambridge, 1985), 1-10.

Dale Chant, 'Role inversion and its function in the *Iphigenia at Aulis*,' *Ramus* 15 (1986), 83-92.

H. Foley, 'Marriage and sacrifice in Euripides' *Iphigenia in Aulis*', *Arethusa* 15 (1982), 159-80.

John Gibert, 'Clytemnestra's First Marriage: Euripides' *Iphigenia in Aulis*', in V. Pedrick and S. Oberhelman (eds.), *The Soul of Tragedy: Essays on Athenian Drama* (Chicago, 2005), 227-48.

Edith Hall, 'Iphigenia and her mother at Aulis', in John Dillon and S. E. Wilmer (eds.), *Rebel Women: Staging Ancient Greek Drama Today* (London, 2005), 3-41.

S. E. Lawrence, '*Iphigenia at Aulis*. Characterization and psychology in Euripides', *Ramus* 17 (1988), 91-109.

C. A. E. Luschnig, 'Time and memory in Euripides' *Iphigenia at Aulis*', *Ramus* 11 (1982), 99-104.

—— *Tragic Aporia: A Study of Euripides' Iphigenia at Aulis* (Ramus Monographs 3. Berwick, Victoria, 1988).

M. McDonald, 'Iphigenia's *philia*: motivation in Euripides' *Iphigenia at Aulis*', *Quaderni Urbinati di Cultura Classica* 63 (1990), 69-84.

P. Michelakis, *Achilles in Greek Tragedy* (Cambridge, 2002).

—— *Euripides' Iphigenia at Aulis* (London, 2006).

Herbert Siegel, 'Self-delusion and the *volte-face* of Iphigenia in Euripides' "Iphigenia at Aulis"', *Hermes* 108 (1980), 300-21.

Christina Elliot Sorum, 'Myth, choice, and meaning in Euripides' *Iphigenia at Aulis*', *American Journal of Philology* 113 (1992), 527-42.

F. I. Zeitlin, 'Art, memory and *kleos* in Euripides' *Iphigenia in Aulis*', in B. Goff (ed.), *History, Tragedy, Theory: Dialogues on Athenian Drama* (Austin, Tex., 1995), 174-201.

## BACCHAE: COMMENTARIES

E. R. Dodds, *Euripides. Bacchae* (2nd edn, Oxford, 1974).

Richard Seaford (ed.), *Euripides' Bacchae* (Warminster, 1996; includes translation).

## INTERPRETATIONS

M. Arthur, 'The choral odes of the *Bacchae* of Euripides', *Yale Classical Studies* 22 (1972), 145–79.

Richard Buxton, 'News from Cithaeron: narrators and narratives in the *Bacchae*', *Pallas* 37 (1991), 39–48.

S. Esposito, 'Teaching Euripides' *Bacchae*', in R. Mitchell-Boyask (ed.), *Approaches to Teaching the Drama of Euripides* (New York, 2002), 188–201.

Helene Foley, 'The masque of Dionysus', *Transactions of the American Philological Society* 110 (1980), 107–33.

R. Friedrich, 'City and mountain: dramatic spaces in Euripides' *Bacchae*', in R. Bauer et al. (eds.), *Space and Boundaries in Literature* (Proceedings of the 12th Congress of the International Comp. Lit. Assoc. 2) (Munich, 199), 538–45.

S. Goldhill, 'Doubling and recognition in the *Bacchae*', *Metis* 3 (1988) 137–56.

J. Gregory, 'Some aspects of seeing in Euripides' *Bacchae*', *Greece and Rome* 32 91985), 23–31.

Valdis Leinieks, *The City of Dionysos: A Study of Euripides' Bakchai* (Stuttgart, 1996).

J. R. March, 'Euripides' BAKCHAI: A reconsideration in the light of vase-paintings', *Bulletin of the Institute of Classical Studies* 36 (1989), 33–65.

Sophie Mills, *Euripides' Bacchae* (London, 2006).

S. D. Olson, 'Traditional forms and the Euripidean adaptation: the hero pattern in *Bacchae*', *Classical World* 83 (1989–1990), 25–8.

H. Oranje, *Euripides'* Bacchae: *The Play and its Audience* (Leiden, 1984).

M. Parker, 'The choruses of Euripides' *Bacchae*', in M. Joyal (ed.), *In Altum: Seventy-Five Years of Classical Studies in Newfoundland* (St John's, 2001), 243–71.

C. Segal, *Dionysiac Poetics and Euripides' Bacchae* (Princeton, 1982).

B. Seidensticker, 'Comic elements in Euripides' *Bacchae*' *American Journal of Philology* 99 (1978), 303–20.

## RHESUS: COMMENTARIES

Arne Feickert (ed.), *Euripidis Rhesus* (Frankfurt and Oxford, 2005; includes German translation).

E. C. Kennedy and A. R. Davis (eds.), *Scenes from Rhesus and Helen* (repr., Bristol, 1998).
J. Morwood, *Euripides' Bacchae and Other Plays* (Oxford, 1999; includes annotated translation of *Rhesus*).
W. H. Porter (ed.), *The Rhesus of Euripides* (2nd edn, London, 1929).

INTERPRETATIONS

L. Battezzato, 'The Thracian camp and the fourth actor at *Rhesus* 565–91', *Classical Quarterly* 50 (2000), 367–73.
R. S. Bond, 'Homeric echoes in *Rhesus*', *American Journal of Philology* 117 (1996), 255–73.
Anne Burnett, '*Rhesus*: are smiles allowed?', in Peter Burian (ed.), *Directions in Euripidean Criticism* (Durham, NC, 1985), 13–52.
Bernard Fenik, *Iliad X and the Rhesus: The Myth* (= *Latomus* 73, Brussels, 1964).
H. D. F. Kitto, 'The *Rhesus* and related matters', *Yale Classical Studies* 25 (1977), 317–50.
Grace Macurdy, 'The dawn songs in *Rhesus* (525–556) and in the parodos of *Phaethon*', *American Journal of Philology* 64 (1943), 408–16.
Hugh Parry, 'The approach of dawn in the *Rhesus*', *Phoenix* 18 (1964), 283–93.
J. P. Poe, 'Unconventional procedures in *Rhesus*', *Philologus* 148 (2004), 21–33.
W. Ritchie, *The Authenticity of the Rhesus of Euripides* (Cambridge, 1964).
V. Rosivach, 'Hector in the *Rhesus*', *Hermes* 104 (1978), 54–73.
J. M. Walton, 'Playing in the dark: masks and Euripides' *Rhesus*', *Helios* 27 (2000), 137–47.

## 7. Sophoclean Tragedy

Josh Beer, *Sophocles and the Tragedy of Athenian Democracy* (Westport, Conn., 2004).
M. W. Blundell, *Helping Friends and Harming Enemies* (Cambridge, 1989).
C. M. Bowra, *Sophoclean Tragedy* (Oxford, 1944).
Felix Budelmann, *The Language of Sophocles: Communality, Communication and Involvement* (Cambridge, 2000).
R. W. B. Burton, *The Chorus in Sophocles' Tragedies* (Oxford, 1980).
C. P. Gardiner (1987). *The Sophoclean Chorus: A Study of Character and Function* (Iowa City, 1987).
Simon Goldhill and Edith Hall (eds.), *Sophocles and the Greek Tragic Tradition* (Cambridge, 2009).

Rachel Kitzinger, *The Choruses of Sophokles' Antigone and Philoktetes: A Dance of Words* (Leiden, 2008).
B. M. W. Knox, *The Heroic Temper: Studies in Sophoclean Tragedy* (Berkeley, Calif., 1964).
A. A. Long, *Language and Thought in Sophocles* (London, 1968).
Kirk Ormand, *Exchange and the Maiden: Marriage in Sophoclean Tragedy* (Austin, Tex., 1999).
K. Reinhardt, *Sophocles* (Oxford, 1979).
Mark Ringer, *Electra and the Empty Urn: Metatheater and Role Playing in Sophocles* (Chapel Hill, NC, and London, 1998).
D. Seale, *Vision and Stagecraft in Sophocles* (London, 1982).
Charles Segal, *Tragedy and Civilization: An Interpretation of Sophocles* (Cambridge, Mass., 1981).
—— *Sophocles' Tragic World: Divinity, Nature, Society* (Cambridge, Mass., 1995).
R. P. Winnington-Ingram, *Sophocles: An Interpretation* (Cambridge, 1980).
Leonard Woodbury, 'Sophocles among the Generals', *Phoenix* 24 (1970), 209–24.

## *OEDIPUS TYRANNUS*: COMMENTARIES

R. D. Dawe (ed.), *Oedipus Rex. Sophocles* (2nd edn, Cambridge, 2006).
J. Rusten, *Sophocles. Oidipous Tyrannos* (2nd edn, Bryn Mawr, Pa., 1990).

## INTERPRETATIONS

F. Ahl, *Sophocles' Oedipus: Evidence and Self-Conviction* (Ithaca, NY, 1991).
C. Carey, 'The second stasimon of Sophocles' *Oedipus Tyrannus*', *Journal of Hellenic Studies* (106), 175–9.
E. R. Dodds, 'On misunderstanding the Oedipus Rex', *Greece and Rome* 13 (1966), 37–49.
M. Dyson, 'Oracle, edict and curse in *Oedipus Tyrannus*,' *Classical Quarterly* 23 (1973), 202–12.
L. Edmunds, *Oedipus: The Ancient Legend and its Later Analogues* (Baltimore, Md., 1996).
Helene Foley, 'Oedipus as Pharmakos', in R. Rosen and J. Farrell (eds.), *Nomodeiktes: Essays in Honor of Martin Ostwald* (Ann Arbor, Mich., 1993), 525–38.
R. Drew Griffith, 'Oedipus Pharmakos? Alleged scapegoating in Sophocles' "Oedipus the King"', *Phoenix* 47 (1993), 95–114.
B. M. W. Knox, *Oedipus at Thebes* (New Haven, 1957).

Fiona Macintosh, *Sophocles: Oedipus Tyrannus* (Cambridge, 2009).
Michael J. O'Brien (ed.), *Twentieth-Century Interpretations of* Oedipus Rex: *A Collection of Critical Essays* (Englewood Cliffs, NJ, 1968).
Rick M. Newton, 'Oedipus' Wife and Mother', *CJ* 87 (1991), 35–45.
Maurice Pope, 'Addressing Oedipus', *Greece and Rome* 38 (1991), 156–70.
P. Pucci, *Oedipus and the Fabrication of the Father* (Baltimore, Md., 1992).
Stelios Ramphos, *Fate and Ambiguity in Oedipus the King* (Eng. trans., Boston, Mass., 2005).
Jeffrey Rusten, 'Oedipus and Triviality', *Classical Philology* 91 (1996), 97–112.
David Sansone, 'The third stasimon of the *Oedipus Tyrannos*', *Classical Philology* 70 (1975), 110–17.
C. P. Segal, 'The chorus and the gods in *Oedipus Tyrannus*,' *Arion* 4 (1996), 20–32.
—— *Oedipus Tyrannus: Tragic Heroism and the Limits of Knowledge* (2nd edn, New York and Oxford, 1996).

*ANTIGONE*: COMMENTARIES

Andrew Brown (ed.), *Sophocles' Antigone* (Warminster, 1987; includes translation).
Mark Griffith (ed.), *Sophocles. Antigone* (Cambridge, 1999).

INTERPRETATIONS

Martin Cropp, 'Antigone's final speech (Sophocles, "Antigone" 891–928)', *Greece and Rome* 44 (1997), 137–60.
Pat Easterling, 'The second stasimon of *Antigone*', in R. D. Dawe, J. Diggle, and P. E. Easterling (eds.), *Dionysiaca: nine studies in Greek poetry presented to Sir Denys Page* (Cambridge, 1978).
R. F. Goheen, *The Imagery of Sophocles' Antigone* (Princeton, 1991).
Philip Holt, 'Polis and tragedy in the "Antigone"', *Mnemosyne* 52 (1999), 658–90.
P. J. Johnson, 'Woman's third face: a psycho-social reconsideration of Sophocles' *Antigone*', *Arethusa* 30 (1997), 369–98.
S. Murnaghan, '*Antigone* 904–920 and the institution of marriage', *American Journal of Philology* 107 (1986), 192–207.
M. Neuburg, 'How like a woman: Antigone's "inconsistency"', *Classical Quarterly* 40 (1990), 54–76.
C. W. Oudemans and A. Lardinois, *Tragic Ambiguity. Anthropology, Philology and Sophocles' Antigone* (Leiden, 1987).
V. J. Rosivach, 'On Creon, Antigone, and not burying the dead', *Rheinisches Museum für Philologie* 126 (1983), 193–211.

Scott Scullion, 'Dionysos and katharsis in "Antigone"', *Classical Antiquity* 17 (1998), 96–122.

C. Sourvinou-Inwood, 'Assumptions and the creation of meaning: reading Sophocles' *Antigone*', *Journal of Hellenic Studies* 109 (1989), 134–48.

W. Blake Tyrrell and Larry J. Bennett, *Recapturing Sophocles' Antigone* (Lanham, Md., 1998).

S. F. Wiltshire, 'Antigone's disobedience,' *Arethusa* 9 (1976), 29–36.

### ELECTRA: COMMENTARIES

P. J. Finglass (ed.), *Sophocles. Electra* (Cambridge, 2007).

Jennifer March (ed.), *Sophocles. Electra* (Warminster, 2001; includes translation).

### INTERPRETATIONS

A. Batchelder, *The Seal of Orestes: Self-Reference and Authority in Sophocles' Electra* (Lanham, Md., and London, 1995).

P. J. Finglass, 'Is there a polis in Sophocles' "Electra?"', *Phoenix* 59 (2005), 199–209.

Rachel Kitzinger, 'Why mourning becomes *Electra*,' *Classical Antiquity* 10 (1991), 298–327.

I. M. Linforth, 'Electra's day in the tragedy of Sophocles', *University of California Publications in Classical Philology* 19 (1963), 89–125.

Michael Lloyd, *Sophocles' Electra* (London, 2005).

Leona MacLeod, *Dolos and Dike in Sophocles'* Elektra (*Mnemosyne* suppl. 219, Leiden, 2001).

R. W. Minadeo, 'Plot, theme and meaning in Sophocles' *Electra*', *Classica et Mediaevalia* 28 (1967), 114–42.

Mark Ringer, *Electra and the Empty Urn: Metatheater and Role Playing in Sophocles* (Chapel Hill, NC, and London, 1998).

Richard Seaford, 'The destruction of limits in Sophocles' *Elektra*', *Classical Quarterly* 35 (1985), 315–23.

C. E. Sorum, 'The Family in Sophocles' *Antigone* and *Electra*,' *Classical World* 75 (1982), 201–11.

P. T. Stevens, 'Sophocles: "Electra," Doom or Triumph?', *Greece and Rome* 25 (1978), 111–20.

T. Woodard, 'The *Electra* of Sophocles', in T. Woodard (ed.), *Sophocles* (Englewood Cliffs, NJ, 1966), 125–45.

### AJAX: COMMENTARIES

A. Garvie (ed.), *Sophocles' Ajax* (Warminster, 1998; includes translation).

W. B. Stanford, *Ajax. Sophocles* (Bristol, 1981).

INTERPRETATIONS

P. Burian, 'Supplication and hero-cult in Sophocles' *Ajax*', *Greek, Roman, and Byzantine Studies* 13 (1972), 151–6.
M. S. Farmer, 'Sophocles' Ajax and Homer's Hector: two soliloquies', *Illinois Classical Studies* 23 (1998), 19–45.
A. Henrichs, 'The tomb of Aias and the prospect of hero cult in Sophokles', *Classical Antiquity* 12 (1993), 165–80.
Jon Hesk, *Sophocles: Ajax* (London, 2003).
P. Holt, 'The debate scenes in the *Ajax*', *American Journal of Philology* 102 (1981), 275–88.
T. K. Hubbard, 'The architecture of Sophocles' "Ajax"', *Hermes* 131 (2003), 158–71.
G. M. Kirkwood, 'Homer and Sophocles' *Ajax*', in M. J. Anderson (ed.), *Classical Drama and its Influence* (London, 1965), 51–70.
Stuart Lawrence, 'Ancient ethics, the heroic code, and the morality of Sophocles' *Ajax*', *Greece and Rome* 52 (2005), 18–33.
J. R. March 'Sophocles' *Ajax*: the death and burial of a hero', *Bulletin of the Institute of Classical Studies* 38 (1991–3), 1–36.
Joe Park Poe, *Genre and Meaning in Sophocles' Ajax* (Frankfurt am Main, 1987).
Vincent J. Rosivach, 'Sophocles' *Ajax*', *CJ* 72 (1976), 47–61.
M. Simpson, 'Sophocles' Ajax: his madness and transformation', *Arethusa* 2 (1969), 88–103.
Christina Elliot Sorum, 'Sophocles' "Ajax" in context', *Classical World* 79 (1986), 361–77.
J. Tyler, 'Sophocles' *Ajax* and Sophoclean plot construction', *American Journal of Philology* 95 (1974), 24–42.
G. Zanker, 'Sophocles' *Ajax* and the heroic values of the *Iliad*', *Classical Quarterly* 42 (1992), 20–5.

*WOMEN OF TRACHIS*: COMMENTARIES

P. E. Easterling (ed.), *Trachiniae* (Cambridge, 1982).

INTERPRETATIONS

E. R. Carawan, 'Tragic heroines and their models: Deianira's guilt', *Transactions of the American Philological Society* 130 (2000), 189–237.
D. J. Conacher, 'Sophocles' *Trachiniae*: some observations', *American Journal of Philology* 118 (1997), 21–34.
John Davidson, 'Sophocles' *Trachiniae* and the *Odyssey*', *Athenaeum* 91 (2003), 517–23.
Bruce Heiden, *Tragic Rhetoric: An Interpretation of Sophocles' Trachiniae* (New York and Bern, 1989).

Thomas F. Hoey, 'Causality and the *Trachiniae*', *CJ* 68 (1973), 306–9.
Robert L. Kane, 'The structure of Sophocles' *Trachiniae*: "diptych" or "trilogy"?', *Phoenix* 42 (1988), 198–211.
G. M. Kirkwood, 'The dramatic unity of Sophocles' *Trachiniae*', *Transactions of the American Philological Society* 72 (1941), 203–11.
S. Lawrence, 'The dramatic epistemology of Sophocles' *Trachiniae*', *Phoenix* 32 (1978), 288–304.
D. Wender, 'The will of the beast: sexual imagery in the *Trachiniae*', *Ramus* 3 (1974), 1–17.

PHILOCTETES: COMMENTARIES

R. G. Ussher (ed.), *Sophocles' Philoctetes* (Warminster, 1990; includes translation).
T. B. L. Webster (ed.), *Philoctetes. Sophocles* (Cambridge, 1991).

INTERPRETATIONS

Elizabeth Belfiore, 'Xenia in Sophocles' *Philoctetes*', *CJ* 89 (1993–4), 113–29.
Pat Easterling, '*Philoctetes* and modern criticism', *Illinois Classical Studies* 2 (1978), 27–39.
Thomas M. Falkner, 'Containing tragedy: rhetoric and self-representation in Sophocles' *Philoctetes*', *Classical Antiquity* 17 (1998), 25–58.
Anne Hunsaker Hawkins, 'Ethical tragedy and Sophocles' "Philoctetes"', *Classical World* 92 (1999), 337–57.
I. Lada-Richards, 'Neoptolemus and the bow: ritual *thea* and theatrical vision in Sophocles' *Philoctetes*', *Journal of Hellenic Studies* 117 (1997), 179–83.
—— 'Staging the *ephebeia*: theatrical role-playing and ritual transition in Sophocles' *Philoctetes*', *Ramus* 27 (1998), 1–26.
Martha Nussbaum, 'Consequences and character in Sophocles' *Philoctetes*', *Philosophy and Literature* 1 (1976–7) 25–53.
D. Roberts, 'Different stories: Sophoclean narrative(s) in the *Philoctetes*', *Transactions of the American Philological Society* 119 (1989), 161–76.
S. Schein, 'Heracles and the ending of Sophocles *Philoctetes*', *Studi italiani di filologia classica* 19 (2001), 38–52.
Aristide Tessitore, 'Justice, politics, and piety in Sophocles' "Philoctetes"', *The Review of Politics* 65 (2003), 61–88.

OEDIPUS AT COLONUS: COMMENTARIES

Mary Whitlock Blundell, *Sophocles' Oedipus at Colonus. Translated with Introduction, Notes and Interpretive Essay* (Newburyport, Mass., 1990).

Pat Easterling, *Sophocles. Oedipus at Colonus* (Cambridge, forthcoming).
R. C. Jebb, *Oedipus Coloneus* (new edn, with an Introduction by Rush Rehm, London, 2004).

INTERPRETATIONS

Darice Birge, 'The grove of the Eumenides: refuge and hero shrine in *Oedipus at Colonus*', *CJ* 80 (1984), 11–17.
Peter Burian, 'Suppliant and saviour: *Oedipus at Colonus*', *Phoenix* 28 (1974). 408–29.
E. B. Ceadel, 'The division of parts among the actors in Sophocles' *Oedipus Coloneus*', *Classical Quarterly* 35 (1941), 139–47.
Pat Easterling, 'Oedipe à Colone: personnages et réception', in A. Machin and L. Pernée (eds.), *Sophocle* (Aix-en-Provence, 1993), 191–200.
—— 'The language of the polis in *Oedipus at Colonus*', in J.-Th. A. Papademetriou (ed.), *Praktika* (= Acts of the First Panhellenic and International Conference on Ancient Greek Literature) (Athens, 1997), 273–83.
—— 'The death of Oedipus and what happened next', in D. Cairns and V. Liapis (eds.), *Dionysalexandros: Essays on Aeschylus and His Fellow Tragedians in Honour of Alexander F. Garvie* (Swansea, 2006), 133–50.
L. Edmunds, *Theatrical Space and Historical Place in Sophocles' Oedipus at Colonus* (Lanham, Md., 1996).
B. Johnston, 'The metamorphoses of Theseus in *Oedipus at Colonus*', *Comparative Drama* 27 B (1993), 271–85.
A. S. McDevitt, 'The nightingale and the olive: remarks on the first stasimon of *Oedipus Coloneus*', in R. Hanslik, A. Lesky, and H. Schwabl (eds.), *Antidosis* (Festschrift for W. Kraus, Vienna, 1972), 227–37.
Umit Singh Dhuga, 'Choral identity in Sophocles' *Oedipus Coloneus*', *American Journal of Philology* 126 (2005), 333–62.
R. Travis, *Allegory and the Tragic Chorus in Sophocles' Oedipus at Colonus* (Lanham, Md., Boulder, Colo., New York, and London, 1999).

## 8. *Greek Tragedy and Tragic Fragments Today*

PERFORMANCE

Pat Easterling, 'Gilbert Murray's readings of Euripides', *Colby Quarterly* 33 (1997), 113–27.
John Dillon and S. E. Wilmer (eds.), *Rebel Women: Staging Ancient Greek Drama Today* (London, 2005).
Stuart Gillespie, *The Poets on the Classics* (London and New York, 1988).
Barbara Goff and Michael Simpson, *Crossroads in the Black Aegean: Oedipus, Antigone, and Dramas of the African Diaspora* (Oxford, 2007).

Simon Goldhill, *How to Stage Greek Tragedy Today* (Chicago, 2007).
Edith Hall and Fiona Macintosh, *Greek Tragedy and the British Theatre 1660–1914* (Oxford, 2005).
Edith Hall, Fiona Macintosh, and Oliver Taplin (eds.), *Medea in Performance 1500–2000* (Oxford, 2000).
Edith Hall, Fiona Macintosh, and A. Wrigley (eds.), *Dionysus since 69: Greek Tragedy at the Dawn of the Third Millennium* (Oxford, 2004).
K. Hartigan, *Greek Tragedy on the American Stage* (Westport, Conn., 1995).
Fiona Macintosh, P. Michelakis, E. Hall, and O. Taplin (eds.), *Agamemnon in Performance* (Oxford, 2005).
K. Mackinnon, *Greek Tragedy into Film* (London and Sydney, 1986).
Marianne McDonald, *Euripides in Cinema: The Heart Made Visible* (Philadelphia, 1983).
—— *Ancient Sun, Modern Light: Greek Drama on the Modern Stage* (New York and Oxford, 1992).
—— *Sing Sorrow: Classics, History, and Heroines in Opera* (Westport, Conn., and London, 2001).
—— and J. Michael Walton (eds.), *Amid Our Troubles: Irish Versions of Greek Tragedy* (London, 2002).
Martin Mueller, *The Children of Oedipus and other Essays on the Imitation of Greek Tragedy 1550–1800* (Toronto, 1980).
Ruth Padel, 'Ion: lost and found', *Arion* 4 (1996), 216–24.
Rush Rehm, *Radical Theatre: Greek Tragedy and the Modern World* (London, 2003).
J. Michael Walton, *The Greek Sense of Theatre* (2nd edn, Amsterdam, 1996).
Kevin Wetmore, *The Athenian Sun in an African Sky: Modern African Adaptations of Classical Greek Tragedy* (Jefferson, NC, 2002).
—— *Black Dionysus: Greek Tragedy and African American Theatre* (Jefferson, NC and London, 2003).

FRAGMENTS

C. Collard, M. Cropp, and K. H. Lee (eds.), *Euripides: Selected Fragmentary Plays*, vol. 1 (Warminster, Wilts., 1995; includes translation).
C. Collard, M. J. Cropp and J. Gibert (eds.), *Euripides: Selected Fragmentary Plays*, vol. 2 (Warminster, Wilts., 2004; includes translation).
James Diggle (ed.), *Phaethon; Edited with Prolegomena and Commentary* (London and Cambridge, 1970).
Demetrios Georgides, *Euripides' Alope: Reconstructed with Liberal Doses of Poetic License* (revised edn, 2006).

Akiko Kiso, *The Lost Sophocles* (New York, 1984).
Hugh Lloyd-Jones (ed.), *Sophocles: Fragments* (Loeb edn of Sophocles, vol. 3, Cambridge, Mass., and London, 1994; includes translation).
—— text and translation of fragments of Aeschylus in Herbert Weir Smyth (ed.), *Aeschylus*, vol. 2 (Loeb edn, London and Cambridge, Mass., 1971).
Fiona McHardy, James Robson, and David Harvey (eds.), *Lost Dramas of Classical Athens* (Exeter, 2005).
Dana Ferrin Sutton, *The Lost Sophocles* (Lanham, Md., 1984).
Alan H. Sommerstein, David Fitzpatrick, and Thomas Talboy (eds.), *Sophocles: Selected Fragmentary plays, with Introductions, Translations and Commentaries* (Oxford, 2006).

# INDEX

Academy (Athenian olive-grove
    sacred to Athena) 22
actors, acting
    experience of 50–1, 148
    families 16–17
    female 330
    impact 2, 19, 18 fig. 1.1, 285,
        287
    'interpolations' 27, 192, 205,
        284, 291
    itinerant 92, 169
    relationship with Dionysus
    selection of 21
    styles and techniques 25–7, 34,
        39–40, 47, 52, 91, 182,
        215–16, 242, 264, 267,
        269, 311, 313, 349 n.26
    terms for 54, 62
    vocality 10, 16, 26, 27,
        39–43
Aeschylus
    life and reputation 15, 19, 28,
        47, 92, 108, 198–9, 172,
        199–201, 230
    fragments
        *Amymone* 340–1
        *Bassarids* 148
        *Danaids* tetralogy 62, 340–1,
            343
        *Eleusinians* 260
        *Niobe* 10, 26, 195, 337
        *Prometheus Unbound* 230
        *Proteus* 21, 55
        *Thamyris* 148
        *Women of Etna* 92
    plays
        *Agamemnon* 3, 21, 26, 28,
            29, 30, 33, 35, 40–1, 43,
            46, 55, 58, 68, 78, 84, 89,
            91, 93–4, 97, 106, 107,
            111, 112, 117, 119, 126,
            128, 131–2, 137, 144–5,
            154, 156, 158, 161, 176,
            183, 188, 196, 211–17 and
            fig. 5.1, 288–9, 325
        *Eumenides* 2, 3, 21, 25, 30,
            38, 52, 55, 61–2, 81, 87,
            90, 100–1, 137, 144, 156,
            161–2 and fig. 4.2, 173,
            184, 220–7 and fig. 5.2
        *Libation-Bearers* 7, 21, 30,
            33, 52, 55, 58, 79, 84, 94,
            97, 117, 121, 128, 139,
            150–1, 192–4, 217–20,
            262, 309
        *Oresteia* 21, 40–1, 55, 75,
            78, 91, 96, 96, 104, 167,
            198–201, 210–27, 186,
            230, 285–7, 311–12
        *Persians* 2, 7, 33, 34, 40,
            48, 52, 54, 57, 65, 69–70
            and fig. 2.1, 73, 87, 90,
            92, 98, 105, 108, 111, 128,
            139, 145, 167, 187–8,
            198–200, 201–4, 272, 331,
            335–6
            and fig. 8.2
        *Prometheus* 12, 26, 87, 97,
            156–7 and fig. 4.1, 181, 195,
            198, 227–30 and fig. 5.3

*Seven against Thebes* 33, 35, 73, 97, 104, 108, 109, 126, 198–9, 204–7, 282, 285
*Suppliants* 33, 63, 64, 83, 86, 96, 105, 111, 115, 126, 160, 173, 183, 198–200, 207–10, 325, 340–1
techniques 33, 41, 57, 65, 192, ch. 5 *passim*
aetiology 98, 101, 103, 161, 210, 224–7, 247, 267, 275, 316
Agathon (tragedian) 52, 116
age, age groups 29, 57, 64, 101, 133, 137–47, 148, 184, 245–8, 286–7, 293
*agōn*, *see* debates, debate scenes
Agora (market-place) 15, 89, 101
*aition* (mythical precedent), *see* aetiology
Amazons 90, 124, 249
*anagnōrisis*, *see* recognition
Anaxagoras (pre-Socratic philosopher) 93, 232, 355 n.12
Anaximander (pre-Socratic philosopher) 80
Anouilh, Jean (dramatist, 1910–1987) 331, 333
Aphrodite 37, 68, 81, 86, 123–5, 156, 163, 165–6, 209, 250–1, 297, 324
Apollo
in tragedy 10, 89, 156, 158, 166, 168, 188, 216, 219, 220–7, 239, 240, 251, 273, 275, 279, 282, 286–7, 304–5, 312, 339
cults of 17, 260
hymns to 144, 344
*See also* Delphi
archery 10, 170, 187, 267, 320

*Archōn eponymos* (senior magistrate at Athens) 21, 147
Areopagus ('Hill of Ares' in Athens where trials were held) 30, 81, 87, 100–1, 210, 224–7
Ares 44, 82, 158–9, 161, 206, 210, 212–13, 271
Argos 87, 99–100, 103, 161, 207–10, 286, 309, 318
aristocrats, aristocracy 23, 49, 59, 75, 113, 116–18, 121, 140, 150, 198–9, 286, 296–7
Aristophanes
evidence for tragedy 231, 330
plays
*Acharnians* 67, 348 n.12
*Birds* 169
*Clouds* 108, 115, 116, 232, 287, 348 n.16
*Ecclesiazusae* 116
*Frogs* 33, 42–3, 52, 59, 155, 169, 171, 196, 200, 206, 231, 234, 299
*Lysistrata* 264
*Peace* 53, 116
*Wasps* 10, 26, 348 n.16
*Women at the Thesmophoria* 95, 178, 279–80
Aristotle
*Athenian Constitution* 64, 147, 350 n.4
*Nicomachean Ethics* 80
*Poetics* 3, 4, 5–7, 12, 27, 49, 52, 64, 99, 102, 103, 116, 182, 187, 202, 233, 256, 268, 275, 287, 289–90, 301, 303, 306
*Politics* 27, 28, 112, 126, 129, 134, 267
*Problems* 41
*Rhetoric* 34, 102, 135, 234

## INDEX

Aristoxenus (musical theorist) 40
arms, armour 2, 12, 24–5, 72, 76–7, 90, 104, 106, 108, 169–70, 311, 314, 320
Artemis 10, 30, 90, 112, 137, 156, 158, 165–6, 209, 250, 272–5, 291
Asclepius 194–5, 300
Assembly (*Ekklēsia*) 15, 23, 36, 63, 67, 96, 129, 139, 225
asylum 62–3, 96–7, 207–10, 242, 246–8, 340
*Atē* ('Ruin') 187–8
atheism 165–6, 171, 178–9
Athena 55, 60–1, 88, 90, 98–9, 144, 156, 158, 161–2 and fig. 4.2, 186, 220–7, 225–6, 271, 276, 296–7, 313, 323–4
Athenaeus 28, 234
Athens, Athenian
    Acropolis 18, 90–1, 99, 224
    building programme 64, 89–91, 99, 199
    citizenship 20, 59–69, 89–91, 94–103, 128–31
    countryside 15, 16, 17, 23
    cults and festivals 20–5, 59–61, 64, 90–1, 260
    demes 15, 92, 96, 102, 108, 114, 323
    Empire 24, 25, 67, 80, 85, 90, 106, 149, 202, 211
    foundation myths 90, 94–103, 149, 276–9
    foundation of democracy 15, 17, 96, 198, 211, 226, 260, 287
    identity of citizens 15, 96, 99–103, 196, 220, 323
    political culture 21, 59–60
    praise of 98, 149, 259–60, 290, 324
    social constitution 20, 23, 97–8
    territory 22, 87
    competitions 24, 36, 40, 60, 61, 62, 63, 169–70, 234, 237
    athletics 61–2, 169, 317
Attica (territory belonging to city-state of Athens), *see* Athens
audiences 14, 20, 24, 25, 33, 40, 47, 53, 57, 62, 71, 85, 86, 88, 94–103, 105, 140, 148, 195, 216, 225–6, 230, 247, 297, 303, 334
*auloi* (musical pipes) 39, 41, 45, 47, 115
autochthony 99, 145, 276–7, 279

bacchant, *see* maenad
barbarian, barbarians 33, 33, 87, 93, 95, 110–16, 148–50, 201–4, 271, 272–3, 280–2, 290, 292, 339–40
Beckett, Samuel 333–4
Bible 10–11, 68, 248–9, 278, 288
Black Sea 86, 96–7, 98–9, 110, 168, 172–4, 331
blindness 8, 33, 41, 258, 325–7
body, bodily 4, 6, 26, 77, 107, 134–5, 144–6, 169–70, 183–5, 194–5, 207, 253–4, 269, 283–4, 322, 324, 335, 344
Bosse, Claudia (theatre director) 335 and 336 fig. 8.2
*Boulē see* Council
Brecht, Bertolt 308, 333, 335
burial 2, 71, 73–6, 306–7, 314
    *See also* funeral

censorship 103, 329
Chance (*Tuchē*) 177, 277–8
character, characterization 28, 64, 65, 140, 151, 182, 251, 289, 296, 302–4, 306, 315

# INDEX

chariot, chariots 57, 61, 72, 93, 143, 149, 156, 163, 211, 214, 344–5 with fig. 8.4
child, children
  in Athens 63, 113, 114, 126, 130
  representation of, in tragedy 29, 71, 75–8, 120–2, 127, 138, 141–5, 147, 149, 151, 157, 163–4, 176, 184–5, 189–92, 195, 213, 216–17, 224, 240–1, 244, 245–8, 259, 261, 265, 269, 271, 276, 289, 310, 315, 330, 340
childbirth and pregnancy 59, 122, 134–5, 143–6, 153, 158, 164, 166, 171, 193, 222–7, 241, 249, 253, 263–4, 278, 283–4, 338
*chorēgos* (financial sponsor of tragic choruses) 21–2, 23, 47
*chorodidaskalos* (chorus trainer) 27, 46–7
chorus, choruses, choral dancing
  competitions in 23, 63
  assumed identity 29–30, 76, 111, 145–7, 205, 297
  gender of 17, 19, 126, 145
  in cult 17, 23, 59–60
  in tragedy 21–2, 27, 28, 32–3, 39–40, 43–50, 55, 57, 71, 78, 87, 91, 219, 230, 333
  military 104
  performers of 14, 22, 29, 55, 140
  perspective 316
  ritual actions 69
  secondary 30–1
  social importance of 14, 62, 92–3, 195
chronology 198–9, 232–4, 262, 299, 301, 316–18, 354 n.18

chthonic gods (resident beneath the earth) 220
cithara, *see* lyre
Cleisthenes (politician) 96, 198
Cleon (fifth-century Athenian statesman) 36, 63, 67, 265
comedy 16, 17, 24, 49, 51–5, 91, 96, 115, 116, 149, 169–70, 195, 232, 240, 248, 253, 262, 277–9, 287, 293, 296, 336, 343
Corinth 30, 102, 163–4, 194, 242, 304, 341–2
corpse, corpses 2, 5–6, 10, 12, 70–9, 83–4, 94, 104, 129, 143, 147, 212, 263, 284, 306, 307–8, 311, 327
cosmology 80, 92–3, 124, 232
costumes, costuming conventions 10, 11, 21–3, 27–8, 31, 47, 51, 57–8, 69, 75–6, 78, 86, 105, 130, 169, 171, 201, 203, 207, 214, 223, 224, 237, 244, 268, 272, 281, 292
Council, the Athenian (*Boulē*) 53, 63–9, 96, 129, 139, 225
crane 7–8, 26, 29, 92, 157, 178, 233, 263, 287–8, 297, 320
Crete 249
curse, curses 6, 82, 130, 176, 204, 213–14, 217, 251, 282, 316, 324–5

dance 11, 23, 47–50, 54, 71, 91, 137–8, 146, 170, 223, 227
death
  character in *Alcestis* 72, 156, 239–41
  in tragedy 1, 2, 3, 45, 52, 69–79, 94–5, 101, 126, 143, 245, 271, 310, 323, 344

debates, debate scenes 32, 35–7, 267, 268, 312
decisions, decision-making 63–9, 94–5, 134, 139–40, 183, 189–93, 289–90, 306, 318–19
deliberation, *see* decisions
Delphi, Delphic Oracle 30, 47, 55, 61–2, 87, 88, 102, 118, 120, 123, 128, 132, 136–7, 166, 211, 220, 252, 276–7, 303–4
Demeter 15, 31, 61, 90, 158, 207, 259
demi-gods 167–71, 234, 266, 317
democracy 15, 17, 20–1, 59–69, 96, 99–100, 106–7, 116–17, 149, 153–5, 160, 215, 237, 259, 266, 282, 286, 305, 314
Democritus (Pre-Socratic philosopher) 89, 172
*dēmos* 'people' (democratic citizenry) 63, 140, 155, 173
Demosthenes (Athenian statesman) 63, 135, 154, 196, 252
*deus ex machina* (god in the machine), *see* crane
dialogue 33, 34, 38–9, 46, 65, 230, 234, 242, 247, 277
Dikē (Justice personified) 159, 163, 166, 218
Dionysus
  in tragedy 12, 88, 127 fig. 3.2, 133, 137–8, 156, 161, 165–6, 185–6, 291–4
  'City' or 'Great' Dionysia 20–7, 47, 49, 58, 60, 85, 91, 94, 110, 112, 114, 237, 265, 327
  God of theatre 17, 20, 39, 47, 60, 63, 127, 171, 198, 234, 300, 325
  Lenaea 20, 112
  sanctuary 22–3, 87, 90–1
  worship of 22, 32, 44, 49–51 with fig. 1.5, 56 fig. 1.6, 92, 112, 113, 127, 143–4, 236–7, 291–2, 298, 325
Dioscuri 156, 279, 281
dithyramb (hymn to Dionysus) 17, 45, 49–50
drama competitions 17, 20–2, 24, 47, 49, 60, 62, 91, 102, 111, 112, 198, 225–6, 232, 299, 300
dream, dreams 46, 65, 134, 193–5, 198, 201, 210, 217, 261, 302

Eagleton, Terry 7, 345–6
Earth (divinity) 93, 94, 163
Ecclesiastes 10–11
ecphrasis 88
Egypt, Egyptian 86, 95, 110–12, 199, 207–10, 215–16, 229, 272, 279–82, 339
*Eisagōgē* ('Introduction' of statue of Dionysus to theatre) 22, 25
*ekkuklēma* 83–4, 210, 218
*ekphora* ('carrying-out' of body at funerals) 76
Eleusis, Eleusinian Mysteries 15, 31, 60, 61, 171, 259–60
Elliot, Alistair (poet and translator) 344
Empedocles (Pre-Socratic philosopher) 124
emotion, emotions 1–11, 12, 65–6, 68, 76–7, 80–2, 89, 93, 135–6, 142–3, 147, 182–3,

203–4, 218, 233, 240–1,
  252–3, 256–7, 262, 271,
  294, 310, 312, 322
ephebes (young men of age for
  military training) 23, 24,
  29, 321
Ephialtes (Athenian politician) 225
epic cycle 128, 205
epistemology 176–8, 232, 270,
  280, 294
Erechtheion (Athenian temple) 90,
  99
Erinys, Erinyes (Earth-dwelling
  spirits of vengeance,
  'Furies') 3, 30, 55, 57, 102,
  164, 184, 186–7, 199, 215,
  218, 220–7, 263, 285,
  312
error *see* Hamartia
ethics 5, 159–61, 170–6, 177–8,
  182–3, 187–93, 210,
  212–14, 218, 231–2, 242,
  248, 256, 261, 263, 265,
  267–8, 270–2, 273, 286,
  289–90, 296, 302, 306–7,
  312–13, 318–19, 320,
  334–5, 346
ethnic, ethnicity 25, 29, 42–3,
  99–100, 110–16, 57,
  110–26, 172–3, 204,
  207–10, 244, 254,
  273–5, 291–4, 331–2
Eumenides ('Kindly Ones',
  goddesses also known as
  *Semnai*) 16, 25, 88, 167,
  224
  *See also* Erinys, Erinyes
Euripides
  ancient reputation 15–16, 95,
    231–4, 276
  fragments
    *Aeolus* 173

*Alcmaeon in Corinth* 193,
  341–3
*Alcmena* 171
*Alexander* 269, 338
*Andromeda* 95, 233–4, 272,
  279, 337
*Antigone* 171
*Antiope* 36, 119, 149, 285
*Auge* 171
*Bellerophon* 249
*Busiris* 280
*Erechtheus* 99
*Hypsipyle* 148, 285, 338,
  343
*Palamedes* 269–70
*Peliades* 243
*Phaethon* 343–5
*Telephus* 118, 337
plays
  *Alcestis* 1, 2, 28, 72 and fig.
    2.2, 140, 142, 161, 169–71,
    232, **238–41 and fig. 6.2**,
    245, 267
  *Andromache* 83, 92, 97, 104,
    109, 111, 117–19, 128,
    131–3, 143, 148, 151,
    154, 196, **251–5**,
  *Bacchae* 3, 12, 16, 19, 30, 34,
    41, 45, 49–50, 54, 55, 71,
    104, 112, 121, 126–7 with
    fig. 3.2, 128, 133, 137–8
    and fig. 3.4, 143–4, 147,
    151, 156, 161, 165–6, 176,
    184–6, 189, 195, 232–3,
    244, 247, **291–94 and fig.
    6.7**, 295, 297, 337, 341
  *Children of Heracles* 87, 96,
    99, 105, 117, 119, 131,
    143, 149, 159, 174, 232,
    **245–8**, 334, 337, 350 n.12
  *Cyclops* 97, 104, 231–3,
    **234–8 and fig. 6.1**, 280

Euripides (*cont.*)
  plays (*cont.*)
    *Electra* 16, 45, 57, 96, 119, 121, 134, 139, 161, 232, 253, **262–4**, 273, 311
    *Hecuba* 2, 5, 26, 27, 29, 35, 36, 38, 41–2 and fig. 1.3, 44, 54, 81, 87, 97, 104, 110, 115, 117–18, 160, 183, 232, **255–9 and fig. 6.4**, 331, 334–5, 349 n.26
    *Helen* 52, 54, 95, 96, 104, 111, 118, 150–1, 166, 177, 232, 270, 272, 275, **279–82**
    *Heracles* 38, 45, 57, 71, 85, 92, 101, 113, 128, 130, 133, 141, 143, 145, 147, 156, 162, 169–71, 176, 184–5, 189, 232, **264–8**, 330–1
    *Hippolytus* 30, 32, 44, 68, 72–3 and fig. 2.3, 81, 83–4, 86, 88, 102, 104, 123–5 and fig. 3.1, 128, 132, 134, 140, 144, 158, 165–6, 174, 176, 183–4, 232, **248–51**, 253, 340
    *Ion* 52, 54, 61–2, 66, 88, 90, 96, 102, 105, 118, 121–4, 130, 144–5, 160, 162, 176, 189, 193, 232, **276–9**
    *Iphigenia in Aulis* 6, 7, 8, 9, 16, 34, 39, 41, 42, 45, 64, 65, 66, 87, 104, 110, 113, 131–2, 143, 158, 160, 165–6, 176–7, 189, 232, **288–91**, 295, 331, 341
    *Iphigenia among the Taurians* 25, 34, 43, 44, 45, 52, 58, 59, 87, 93, 96–7, 98–9, 104, 112, 115, 137, 144, 158, 160, 162, 165–6, 186–7, 193–4, 232, **272–6 and fig. 6.6**, 291, 331
    *Medea* 3, 7, 8, 9–10, 13, 27, 28, 30, 35, 38, 44, 58, 61, 72, 80, 93, 96, 102, 104, 111, 115, 121, 126, 128, 130–2, 141–4, 151–3 and fig. 3.5, 158–60, 162–4, 168, 176, 183, 189–93 and fig. 4.5, 232, 234, **242–5 and fig. 6.3**, 248, 328, 335, 336, 344
    *Orestes* 16, 27, 38, 39, 52 n.33, 62, 63, 91, 93, 96, 104, 112, 126, 128, 140–1, 157, 169, 178, 183, 195, 232–3, 270, 273, **285–8**, 349
    *Phoenician Women* 38, 82, 83, 84 fig. 2.5, 86, 89, 91, 99, 104, 135, 140, 160, 232, **282–5**, 325, 328
    *Rhesus* 104, 109, 110, 194, 231, 232, 235, **294–8**
    *Suppliant Women* 30–1, 61, 65, 73–4, 75, 83, 91, 99–100, 103, 104, 137, 143, 145, 162, 180–1, 188–9, 232, **259–61**
    *Trojan Women* 12, 13, 27, 37–8, 47, 52, 76–8 and fig. 2.4, 83, 88, 90, 97, 98, 104, 110, 117–18, 126, 130, 132, 143, 147, 150, 158, 162, 165–6, 177–9, 184, 232, 266, **268–72 and fig. 6.5**, 328, 331, 334, 335, 338, 346
  techniques 33, 41–3, 52, 53, 65, ch. 6 *passim*
exile 96–7, 102, 130, 284, 303, 305, 320

family, families 3, 30, 78–9, 120–1, 146, 275, 277–8, 282–4, 308, 309–10, 324, 333
filicide (murder of children by their own parents) 243–4, 293
fragments, fragmentary plays 285, 336–45
friendship 101, 133, 140–1, 169–71, 245, 255, 266–7, 275–6, 287, 320–1, 324
Frye, Northrop 117, 280
funeral, funerals
  oration 74–5
  presentation of, in tragedy 2, 30–1, 40, 41, 45, 67, 69–79, 100, 104, 126, 146, 151, 167, 187, 205, 213, 240, 252, 259–61, 267, 306–7, 311
  rituals 33, 130, 159, 217–18
  See also Lamentation
Fury, Furies, see Erinys, Erinyes

gangs 140–1
gender 14, 19, 26, 48, 81–3, 126–7, 172, 190, 192, 205–6, 215, 223, 227, 237, 244, 253, 263, 293–4, 319–20, 329–31
geography 14, 25, 86, 215, 229–30, 280
ghosts 1, 2, 3, 29, 49, 55, 69–71, 167, 199, 201, 206, 215, 216, 220–1 and fig. 5.2, 223, 255, 285
gifts, gift-giving, see reciprocity
Gilgamesh 10–11
god, gods 1, 7–8, 23, 25, 47, 61, 90, 92, 101, 124, 156–71, 173, 177, 187, 214, 220, 227, 229, 239, 267, 271, 335
  See also under individual gods' names

Goethe, J.W. (poet and dramatist, 1749–1832) 43, 328
Gorgias (fifth-century sophist) 36–8, 181–2, 280–1
Greek identity 110–16

Hades see Underworld
*hamartia* ('Error') 187, 202, 268
Harrison, Tony 236, 339, 347 n.9
Heaney, Seamus 301, 347 n.9
Hebe 245
Hecate 163–4
Helen of Troy 36–8, 132, 168, 177–8, 184, 215, 251, 253, 268–72, 273, 279–82, 286
Helios, see Sun-god
Hephaestus 101, 156, 158, 227, 229
Hera 61, 158, 161, 163–4, 184, 265, 271
Heracles 38, 44, 86, 100–1, 105, 118, 133, 145, 149, 154, 156, 158, 164, 166–71, 184–5, 215, 223, 228, 234, 239–40, 245, 264–8, 300, 316–19, 320, 330–1
Heraclitus (philosopher) 105, 172
herald, heralds 14, 43, 55, 61, 64, 73–4, 116, 208, 211, 247, 256, 261
Hermes 33, 55, 113, 144, 156–7 and fig. 4.1, 159, 218, 229, 325, 327, 339
hero, heroes, heroines 2, 38, 100, 103, 147, 158, 218, 223, 265, 303–4, 315–16, 322–3, 325–8
hero cult 45, 49, 89, 101, 108, 162, 168–71, 247, 266–7, 298, 316, 319, 320

Herodotus 48, 106, 107, 110, 173, 199, 207, 264, 272–3, 278, 279, 316
Hippocrates 134, 194, 253
Hölderlin, Friedrich 174, 333
homecoming (*nostos*), homecoming theme in tragedy 118–35, 202, 251–2, 331
Homer, Homeric
  epic 3, 17, 28, 40, 50, 60–1, 69, 83, 165, 283
  *Hymn to Dionysus* 50
  *Iliad* 3, 61, 70–1, 108, 144, 173, 206, 235, 249, 270, 283, 289, 295–8, 315
  *Odyssey* 3, 61, 86, 128, 135, 210, 234–5, 251, 315
hoplite, hoplites (heavy-armed infantry) 106–8, 153, 170
  *See also* war
hospitality, *see xenia*
house, household 29, 30, 79, 97, 120–6, 129–34, 146–7, 153, 159, 176, 210–220, 216, 227, 282
*hubris* 187–8, 202, 214, 217
hymn, hymns 22, 23, 30, 44–5, 49, 144, 161, 250
  *See also dithyramb* and *paian*

imagery 34, 68, 86, 88–9, 113, 167, 172, 183, 188, 195, 200, 215, 217, 223, 229–30, 233, 257, 261, 284, 285, 308, 320
imperialism 308, 331–2
incest 99, 147, 159, 173–4, 222, 234, 249, 282, 284, 302–4, 307

justice, *see dikē*

Kent, Jonathan (theatre director) 335, 344
kin-killing 3, 38, 127, 159, 176, 212, 220, 222, 242–4, 302–3
  *See also* family
*kommos* (sung interchange between actors and chorus) 39, 79, 267
*kurios* (senior male householder) 121, 134, 135–6
Koun, Karolos (theatre director) 43–4

lamentation 2–3, 74, 78–9, 130, 188, 202–3, 205–6, 218–19, 268, 269, 284
language, languages 92, 97, 110–11, 114, 177, 179–80, 232, 234, 250, 260, 266, 332, 343
law, legal
  affinities with theatre 35–8, 62–3, 94, 302
  processes 23, 80–1, 96, 98, 117, 119–120, 129, 135–6, 149, 154, 164–5, 177, 189–93, 220–1, 236, 246, 249, 252, 265, 286, 306, 334–5
  trials in tragedy 100–1, 140–1, 209, 210, 220–7, 258–9
libation, libations 24, 25, 57, 167–8 and fig. 4.3, 217–18
lyre 40, 41
Lysias 191–2

Macedon, Macedonian 17, 20, 169, 231
madness 40, 41, 81, 92, 133–4, 156, 158, 169–70, 184–7,

244, 263, 266, 269, 273, 282, 290, 294, 313–14
maenad, maenads 49, 50–1 with fig. 1.5, 57, 127, 250, 291–3 with fig. 6.7
magic 164–5, 220–1
marriage 38, 126–36, 166, 207–10, 222–7, 238–41, 242–5, 249, 251–5, 263, 269, 317, 330, 340–1, 344
masculinity 261, 293, 330–1
masks, masking convention 10, 11, 18–20 with fig. 1.1, 21, 31, 41, 47, 51, 54, 55–7, 86, 89, 205, 223, 281, 293, 332
medicine, medical 45, 134, 144–5, 158, 179–81, 194–5, 229, 232, 253–4, 300, 302
Melos 117, 268
memory, theme in tragedy 29, 46, 71, 203, 303
messenger, messenger speeches 26, 61, 70, 71, 72, 82, 116, 119, 120, 121, 201–3, 205, 261, 282, 291
metamorphosis 50, 157, 178, 228, 246–7, 340, 344
metaphysics 69, 80, 94, 156–71, 177–8, 200, 202, 216, 266, 271, 303–4, 319, 335
metatheatre 53–5, 256–7, 281, 313
metics (foreign residents) 20, 23, 25, 95, 112, 114, 115
metre, *see* poetry
*miasma*, *see* pollution
militia, military 35, 59–60, 104, 107–10, 145, 296–7, 321, 352 n.2
mind, mental 66, 156–97
  *See also* madness

misogyny 83, 125, 219, 231, 250, 279
*monody* (actor's solo song), *see* singing
monologue 32, 53, 68, 192–3, 229, 244–5, 332
Muse, Muses 9–11, 39–41, 148, 279, 297, 324–5
music, musical 11, 26, 27, 39–42, 53, 55, 60, 111, 115, 332, 336, 343, 344, 349 nn. 20, 23
Mysteries, mystery religion 170–1
Mytilene, debate over 67–8, 289

nature, natural 308
  *See also* Nomos and Phusis
Nero 169–70, 291
*nomos* and *phusis* (conventions *versus* nature) 97, 111, 173–6, 179–80, 293–4
*nostos*, *see* homecoming
novel, ancient 126, 278, 280
nurse, nurses 55, 115, 119, 121–6, 150–1, 219, 250, 252–4

oaths 93, 124–5, 135, 137, 140–1, 159–61, 163, 286
Ocean 156, 228–9
offstage cries 8, 142–3, 216, 244, 267
*oikos*, *see* household, family
oligarchic coup (411 BCE) 64, 140–1, 286–7
Olympia, Olympic 24, 37, 40, 61
Olympus, Olympians 52, 90, 156–71, 220, 335, 341
  *See also under names of individual gods*
ontology 177–8, 232
oracles 49, 61, 204, 317–18
*orchēstra* (dancing floor) 54, 91

orators, oratory, *see* rhetoric
Oxyrhynchus Papyri 337–9

*Paidagōgoi* ('tutors') 113, 114, 115, 121–6, 242
*Paian* (hymn to Apollo) 45
painting, paintings 6, 53, 87–90, 216, 257, 260, 276–7
Pan 90
Panathenaea (festival for Athena) 60–1
Panhellenic, Panhellenism 20, 61, 158, 260, 277
Parthenon 90
Pericles 63, 75, 90, 129, 131, 201, 244, 261, 299
*peripeteia*, *see* reversal
Persephone 61, 158, 207, 240, 246, 325, 327
Persia, Persian 34, 57, 86–7, 89–90, 105, 110, 199, 201–4, 214, 264, 272, 278
philosophy 46, 65–6, 93, 124, 148, 171–82, 194–5, 236, 270, 281, 333
Phrynichus (early Athenian tragedian) 19
Pisistratus, Pisistratids (tyrants of Athens) 17, 48–9, 60–1, 67, 92, 198–9
plague 144, 158, 194, 248, 354 n.18
Plato (Athenian philosopher) 3, 11, 270
  *Gorgias* 114, 236
  *Laches* 92
  *Laws* 60, 103, 106, 114
  *Lysis* 112–13
  *Phaedo* 86
  *Protagoras* 307
  *Republic* 5, 27, 60, 87, 92, 114, 148, 301, 329–30

  *Symposium* 24, 348 n.10
  *Timaeus* 93
plot 12, 28, 64, 97, 128, 149, 182, 202, 227, 234, 237, 252, 268–9, 279–80, 286, 320
Plutarch 143, 148, 233, 260, 262, 346
poetry 9, 12–13, 26, 32–3, 38–40, 53, 182, 199–200, 250, 260, 266, 283, 297, 325, 332 32–3, 38–40, 332
poets 148–9, 158, 241, 279, 332
political theory 129, 174, 179–81, 211, 226, 235–6, 260–1, 304, 307, 320
politics 99–100, 103, 116–17, 140–1, 154–5, 224–7, 278, 287, 299–300, 302, 304, 306, 308, 321, 331, 336, 339, 341
pollution 25, 30, 76, 101, 102, 167, 171, 220, 223, 226, 267, 302–3, 307, 324–5, 335–6
*pompē* (procession inaugurating festivals of Dionysus) 22–3
Poseidon 72, 90, 99, 162, 269, 271, 324, 341
Postcolonial, Postcolonialism 331–2
Postmodern, Postmodernist 332, 336–7
Pound, Ezra 301, 318
prayer 159, 177, 224, 335
Pre-Socratic philosophers 80, 89, 93, 172, 178, 222
priestesses, priests 20, 25, 55, 61–2, 136–7, 300
*proagōn* (pre-performance event) 22

# INDEX

procession, processions 22–3, 24, 25, 30, 40, 51, 74, 76, 90, 201, 224, 281
*See also* Pompē
prologue 27, 33–4, 53, 267, 290–1
*prothesis* ('laying out' of body for a wake) 76, 84
Pronomos Vase 28 and 349 n.21
prophecy, prophets 28, 29, 40–1, 61–2, 120, 136–7, 149, 158, 164, 177, 188, 211, 216–17, 246, 306, 313
Protagoras 178–81, 229, 230, 267, 307, 320
provocation (in criminal law) 189–93, 335
Purcarete, Silviu (theatre director) 340
Pythagoreans 172

Racine, Jean (dramatist, 1639–1699) 328
rape 108, 116, 122, 126, 147, 152–3, 193, 200, 207, 235, 237, 277–8, 317, 339–40, 341, 343
reciprocity 79–82, 161, 167, 218, 255, 263, 277
recognition (*anagnōrisis*), recognition scenes 39, 52, 120, 186, 262, 275, 277–8, 281–2, 311
relativism 172–4, 179, 181
religion 59–60, 110, 156–71
Renaissance 4, 43, 147, 238, 256–7, 285, 304, 328, 337
revenge 33, 79–82, 94, 121, 160, 186, 218, 219–20, 242–3, 246, 255–9, 263–4, 283, 286, 288–9, 311–13, 334, 340

reversal 117–18, 172, 187, 266, 268
rhetoric, rhetoricians, rhetorical 34–9, 41, 46, 62–4, 65, 74, 77, 97, 99, 102, 109–111, 114, 130, 152–3, 181–2, 206, 223, 232, 242, 252–4, 261, 267, 268–9, 280–1, 334
ritual 1, 23–5, 156–71, 209, 275, 291, 335
*See also* funeral, sacrifice, libation, marriage, women
Roussos, Tassos 343

sacrifice, sacrificial
 animal 1, 22, 23, 24, 25, 50, 59, 122, 126, 167, 177
 human 5, 83, 89, 112, 131, 137, 149, 165, 168, 173, 189, 193–4, 212, 234, 246–8, 255–7, 272–6 with fig. 6.6, 280, 283, 288–92, 341
sanctuary, sanctuaries 23, 61, 87, 89–91, 99, 101, 149, 160, 163–4, 167, 208, 220, 223–4, 227, 245, 247, 259, 272, 324–5
satyrs, satyr drama 21, 49, 54, 55, 91, 97, 144, 170, 210, 230, 234–8 and fig. 6.1, 240, 275, 280, 337, 339, 340–1, 343
scenery 26, 27, 87–8, 91
sculpture 55–6 and fig. 1.6, 88–90, 169, 208, 220, 224, 241, 257, 273, 276, 281, 316
sea 85, 86, 93
Sellars, Peter (theatre director, 1957– ) 248, 332

sex, sexuality 46, 51, 123–5, 128, 131, 134, 153–4, 170, 183–4, 191–2, 209–10, 214, 234, 237, 243, 248–9, 252–3, 279, 296, 302, 317, 329–30, 340
Shakespeare, William 4, 6, 7, 12, 32, 39, 94, 218, 280, 295
Shelley, Percy Bysshe 9, 239, 301
Sicily, Sicilian 17, 20, 86, 92, 105, 198, 233, 234, 281–2, 300
silent characters 55, 83, 100–1, 119
singing, song 2, 39–53, 118, 142, 148, 158, 203, 233, 242, 267, 269, 297–8, 332
*skēnē* (stage) 54, 91
slaves, slavery
 Classical Greek 12, 71, 90, 95, 105, 112–16, 191, 196, 236
 representation of, in drama 30, 31, 55, 76–7, 93–4, 98, 108, 126, 148–55, 218, 219, 223, 234, 246, 248, 251, 269, 341
social class 4, 23–26, 29–30, 52, 57, 66, 109, 110–26, 140–1, 150l, 172, 225, 263, 287, 296–7, 339, 350 n.7, 352 n.2
Socrates 60, 114, 148, 172, 174, 232
Sophists, sophistic 36–8, 172–6, 178–82, 232, 240, 280
Sophocles
 ancient reputation 16, 21, 63, 65, 195, 299–302, 308
 fragments
  *Niobe* 300
  *Tereus* 115–16, 153, 244, 300, 337, 339–40, 343
  *Thamyris* 148
  *Trackers* 97, 236–7, 339, 343

plays
 *Ajax* 2, 12, 25, 35, 49, 65, 67, 75, 81–2, 84, 89, 109–110, 117, 141, 156, 158–9, 161–2, 184, 186, **313–6 and fig. 7.3**, 324
 *Antigone* 2, 3, 12, 33, 35, 46, 52, 65, 66, 67, 68, 73, 82–3, 97, 99, 104, 116, 126, 131, 134, 135–7, 139, 147, 151, 159, 174, 179–80, 187, 195–6, 284, 299–301, **305–9 and fig. 7.1**, 328, 331
 *Electra* 33, 61, 81, 84 and 85 fig. 2.6, 96, 104, 115, 118, 121, 126, 128, 134–6 and fig. 3.3, 139, 262, 300, **309–13 and fig. 7.2**, 318, 325, 334
 *Oedipus Tyrannus* 3, 6, 13, 28, 30, 31, 34, 39, 41, 45, 65, 66, 83, 86, 96, 99, 104, 118, 119–21, 123, 142, 144, 147, 158, 176, 178–9, 194, 251, 278, 300, 301, 302–5, 328, 329 fig. 8.1, 334, 335–6
 *Oedipus at Colonus* 9, 11, 16, 25, 33, 52, 63, 87–8, 96, 98, 99, 101–2, 104, 167, 184, 284, 301, 305, **323–7 and fig. 7.4**
 *Philoctetes* 6, 26, 30, 31 fig. 1.2, 52, 66, 87, 96, 104, 110, 126, 140, 156, 161, 169, 174–5 and fig. 4.4, 180, 300, 301, **319–23**, 324
 *Women of Trachis* 33, 45, 58, 61, 66, 68, 71–2, 75, 83, 96, 105, 117–19, 120, 126, 128, 132, 134, 140, 154, 160, 169, 176, 194, 265, 301, **316–19**, 320, 330–1
techniques 33, 65, ch. 7 *passim*

space, theatrical 25, 26, 29, 87, 229, 333
Sparta, Spartans 59, 105, 247, 252, 268, 271
*stratēgos, stratēgoi* ('generals', senior officers of state) 24, 129
statues, *see* sculpture
subject, subjectivity 42, 122, 192–5, 276, 278, 281
suffering 2–4, 6–7, 27, 42, 66, 72–3, 81, 93–4, 107–9, 121, 147, 166, 174, 177, 181, 187–8, 195–6, 200, 211, 216, 220, 230, 241, 248, 257, 264–5, 268, 301, 304, 311, 313–14, 322, 335, 346
suicide 34, 68, 71, 81–4, 101, 125, 141, 147, 188–9, 207–8, 248, 253, 261, 265, 269, 283, 286, 306, 315–16 and fig. 7.5, 317
sun, Sun-god, sunlight, sunrise
  as performance context of ancient drama 1, 23, 27, 87, 155
  in Euripides' *Medea* 143, 149, 162–3, 168, 242
  in tragedy 1–3, 13, 45, 48, 58, 86, 93–4, 184, 185, 187, 218, 344–5 with fig. 8.4
  'single revolution' of 28–9, 68–9
suppliant, supplication 30–1, 32, 63, 100, 102, 145, 149, 159–60, 207–10, 245–8, 252, 259, 261, 322, 323
symposium, symposia (drinking parties) 24, 40, 50 and 51 fig. 1.5, 115, 234–5, 240

technology 179–81, 229, 308
Teevan, Colin 341–3 and fig. 8.3
television 62, 333

tetralogy (group of three tragedies and a satyr drama) 21, 24, 25, 47, 91, 199, 201, 208–9, 210, 230, 237, 240, 269, 282, 338, 340–1
theatre, theatrical
  'backstage' operatives 27, 88
  buildings 7, 20, 26, 29, 54, 90–2, 169
  deme 15, 20, 90, 92
  open-air 1, 62–3, 87, 302
  props and equipment 7–8, 26, 27, 54, 58, 70, 90–2, 104, 311, 322. *See also* crane, *ekkuklēma*
  seating 24, 26, 53, 54, 63–4, 91
  setting 52, 66, 87, 99–100
  shape of Athenian 7, 26, 91
Thebes, Theban 19, 30–2, 38, 45, 87, 99–102, 133, 161, 204–7, 262, 282–5, 292, 301, 318, 324
Themis 159, 163
Themistocles 91
theodicy 170
  *See also dikē*
theology 156–71, 177, 220, 271, 324
Theophrastus 114, 125–6, 349 n.19
Theseus 90, 100–3, 123–5, 133, 137, 166–7, 224, 248–51, 260, 267, 323–7
Thespis, traditional founder of tragedy 17, 19
Thetis 156
Thirty Tyrants 140
Thorikos 91
Thrace, Thracian 99, 110, 114, 255, 296–8, 339–40

Thucydides 15, 36, 48, 66, 67–8, 75, 80, 99, 100, 107, 110, 117, 131, 141, 166, 255–6, 260–1, 289, 350 n.4
time 8–9, 12–13, 28–9, 44, 68–9, 203, 229, 334
Timotheus (poet and composer) 41, 43
tragedy, tragic
  aesthetics of 1, 8, 9, 10–11, 46, 51, 54–5, 83, 110–11, 121, 199, 237, 256–7, 346
  definition of 1–11, 180, 233
  historical themes in 2, 103, 202
  ideological complexity 148
  multivocal form 109, 148–55
  personification of 50–1 with fig. 1.5, 169
  origins 48–51
  postclassical performance 4, 39, 147, 328–46
  reception by Romans 28, 31, 169–71, 200, 233–4, 275–6, 278, 285, 312, 319, 337, 341
  ancient revivals 20, 27
  settings 2, 29–30, 86–8, 95, 97
tragicomedy 275, 279
translation, translations 12, 13, 32, 40, 200, 268, 328–46
transvestism, transvestite 19, 27, 50, 127, 215, 253, 264, 292–4, 330, 336
trumpets 24–5, 199
tyranny 99, 145, 151, 173, 198–9, 211, 214–15, 218, 229, 282, 304–5, 309, 346

Underworld 7, 17, 69–70, 72–3, 82, 101, 123, 145, 159, 170–1, 201, 239, 240, 315, 325

'unities' 28–30, 68–9
'unwritten laws' 128, 159, 179–80, 260, 306, 308

vases, vase-painting, Greek 8, 10, 28, 48, 57, 87, 91, 92, 115, 119
violence 10, 34, 50, 71, 104, 218, 247, 256, 261–3, 266, 286, 292–3, 312, 318, 320, 323, 333, 335, 340, 345–6
Vitruvius 97, 237

Walcott, Derek (poet and dramatist, 1930– ) 328
war
  at Athens 14, 25, 90, 97
  attitudes to 25, 158–9, 196–7, 321, 331
  Boer 268
  civil 98, 99, 104, 176, 204–7, 225, 283, 286, 305–6
  crimes 38, 268, 331, 334–5
  dead 74–5, 85–6, 104, 105, 143, 200, 202, 205–6, 212–13, 260, 283
  First World 107, 268, 328
  Iraq War (2003– ) 331
  Third Balkan (1991–2001) 331, 340
  Peloponnesian 15, 59, 75, 81, 105, 107, 140, 259–60, 262, 281, 316
  Persian 23, 34, 89–90, 91, 105, 107, 110, 149, 199–204, 225, 300, 316
  Second World 197, 328
  Theban 30, 35, 104, 176, 204–7, 282–5
  theme of, in tragedy 25, 45, 73, 104–110, 172

Trojan 61, 100, 104, 251, 255, 268–71, 281–2, 295–8, 315–16, 320–1
wealth 21–2, 24, 90, 116
weapons, *see* armour, arms
weaving 55–6, 57–8, 88, 122, 276, 340
weddings 40, 45, 47, 57, 58, 59, 80, 167, 187, 209, 287, 308
Wertenbaker, Timberlake 339–40
witchcraft, *see* magic
women, women's
   and ritual 23, 25, 30, 59, 74–6, 126–7, 158, 161, 166, 207, 224, 249, 261
   movement 329–31
   status in classical Greece 5–78, 74–5, 95, 113, 117, 131, 226, 253
   presence at theatre 20, 114
   representation of, in drama 9–10, 26, 30, 41, 43, 45, 52, 66–7, 81–3, 95, 97, 122–37, 148–55, 225–7, 295, 329–31
Woolf, Virginia 301, 312

*xenia* (correct treatment of hosts and guests) 100–1, 159–61, 163, 239
Xenophon 59, 64, 107, 108, 115, 348 n.17, 352 n.2

Zeitlin, Froma 89
Zeus 13, 44, 61, 87, 90, 93, 144–5, 149, 159–61, 163–5, 168–9, 173, 207, 225, 227–30, 235, 245, 271, 279, 317, 320, 324, 344
Zielinski, Thaddeus (Euripidean scholar) 232–3